I0441802

# AMERICA IN THE 21st CENTURY

## For Better Or Worse

## Book I

## Kathleen Babbitt, D.Sc.

AMERICA IN THE 21st CENTURY, Book I, For Better Or Worse
Copyright 2016 by Kathleen Babbitt, D.Sc.

Other books by Kathleen Babbitt, D.Sc.
HOW TO BE HEALTHIER, WEALTHIER, HAPPY AND WISE: What You Need To Know To Be Healthy, published in 1996 and 2000
AMERICA IN THE 21st CENTURY, Book II: A Political, Historical, Sociological Perspective, published in 2016
LOOKING FOR AMERICA (A non-fiction novel of things that mostly happened), published in 2017

## A DEDICATION

My first book, published in 1996, was "HOW TO BE HEALTHIER, WEALTHIER, HAPPY AND WISE", with a subtitle "What You Need To Know To Be Healthy", that probably would have been better as the title. The title was a play on Benjamin Franklin's "Early to bed, early to rise makes a man healthy, wealthy, and wise." Probably the subtitle would have been better as the title. A president of a natural foods company wrote a brilliant comment about my book that I put on the front cover. It was a perfect description and summary of the book, much better than I could have written. He said "Babbitt......shines the light of truth and knowledge into the darkness of ignorance, destruction, and greed."

A week or two later he tragically disappeared while he was on a skiing trip in the Shasta Mountains, in California. It seemed impossible to have happened. It was hard to believe. They found his parked plane, not crashed, but he was never found.

That same statement, his statement, is a perfect description and summary of this book. So I'm using it again, in memory of him, in appreciation. Because he can't give me permission to do that I'm not revealing his name. This book is dedicated to all people, living and dead, who have tried to make the World a better place to live in.

"Babbitt......shines the light of truth and knowledge into the darkness of ignorance, destruction, and greed."

# TABLE OF CONTENTS

# CHAPTER ONE

## Looking For America

This is a sociological, political, and cultural study of America. It's about living in America in the 21st century. It's about social injustices. There's no defamation of character, it's just the truth. It is not "anti-American". How ridiculous. How Republican. Losing faith in and finding fault with the American Government and legal system and financial systems, and in American people in general, does not mean a person, anyone, is anti-American. Only a paranoid government, and narrow-minded and paranoid politicians and people, would think that was so. Or think that documentaries or what is written are "national security risks".

Thomas Jefferson, a genius, said "A successful government is based on patriotic suspicion, not blind patriotic trust, and any patriot with integrity will criticize their government." The only democracy and free country, out of 24 in the World, that doesn't follow that concept is the United States, since 2001. September 11, 2001 was used as a reason, an excuse, a justification for limiting freedoms and freedom of speech, essential parts of the foundation of America for more than 235 years, since the beginning of America.

Since 2001 public criticism of the United States Government, and of governments in some states, has resulted in loss of jobs, public ridicule, or imprisonment without probable cause or charges, without legal representation or trial. This is all because of the influence of the Neo Cons in power starting in 2001. Democrats in power did nothing to stop it. The Neo Cons destroyed part of what it meant to be an American that is allowed and encouraged in all other 23 Democracies in the World, and that was guaranteed for more than 235 years by The Constitution and The Bill of Rights. Times change, but that wasn't supposed to change.

In order to raise the consciousness of Americans they have to know what their Federal Government and state governments are really doing, and what the United States military is really doing in other countries, to the people in those countries. Misinformation and disinformation are both all-American and anti-American. Twisting and distorting the truth is all-American, a part of daily life. For many years the United States Government has operated on the principle that Americans don't need to know the truth. This is especially true since 9/11, 2001.

Since the elections of 2000 America has become something different than a democracy. Controversial issues that have vested interests, especially government interests and involvement, can be dangerous to publically question or criticize in what used to be "the land of the free." It is not uncommon for people to be mean, unjust and unfair, in any working capacity and environment. Especially in those states and cities where there has been no Resolutions Against The Patriot Act that was passed in 2001, and then renewed indefinitely by President Obama in 2011. It's part of the new America, in the 21st century. It doesn't much matter if the President is Democrat or Republican.

Most American movies have little or no redeeming value or significance other than for entertainment. However, movies help people learn about life. The once popular so-called Westerns, about living in the American Wild West, began what has become the usual depictions and portrayals of right and wrong, good and bad, and redemptions and rewards found in most American movies since then. They are done in an entertaining, colorful, and often noisy way, making hundreds of millions of dollars in profit for each movie, making it a very profitable and productive industry.

On the other hand, many American-made documentaries are very well produced, very well written and filmed, very informative, and entertaining too, but rarely, if ever, make hundreds of millions of dollars in profit. They are usually the only movies with genuine significance or redeeming value, while informing about realities in life. They are the only movies made with intelligence beyond the norm, and therefore don't appeal to the masses. I used more than 50 documentaries for information for this book. I used no information that was controlled, regulated, or monitored. No books. Fair and balanced TV news, especially on CNN and FOX News, and also on FOX Radio news, and fair and balanced newspaper coverage, is a thing of the past, relegated to the 20th century. After the year 2000 the infamous Right Wing abolished and destroyed the Fairness doctrine for the media empire for the entire United States. Fairness in journalism was no longer required.

It was old-fashioned and outdated, a thing of the past. This lowering of standards, so common to the Right Wing since 2000, was done to make room for the bigotry and distortion and the twisting of the truth, and the lies, the endless dishonesty and manipulation of the truth so common on Fox TV News and Fox Radio and on Rush Limbaugh's radio show, all of them followed religiously day and night, anytime 24/7, by many millions of viewers who love every minute of it. The targeted audience gets what they want, what they are looking for. Giving people what they want has always been a formula for success everywhere in the World, but especially in the consumer-driven American culture.

Bush "W" was the first President to give almost a billion dollars every year to news and media sources as payoffs to control the news. This is not what is supposed to be done in a democracy but it is what would be done in a dictatorship, or a government of tyranny and control. Dan Rather, the anchorman for "60 Minutes" for more than 15 years, was fired because he tried to tell the truth, to expose the truth, about Bush "W" and his manipulation of the law, etc. in order to erase and distort his past records of crimes and past actions that would have made him unable to qualify to be a President of the United States, or to run for any election.

Like the obstructive and controlled election that made him the Governor of Texas, that then subsequently made him "qualified" to be the President, as had been planned since the 1970's by the Republican Neo Cons in power at that time. It was planned to be an obstructive and dishonestly controlled Presidential election years before the election actually happened in 2000. As President, Bush "W" was easily able to have Dan Rather fired for exposing the truth about him, especially because of his billion dollar yearly payoffs to the news and to the media in order to control the news. Their cover done for damage control was that the signatures on the documents shown on "60 Minutes" were fraudulent. Rather apologized and then was fired, for what looked like nearly identical signatures done by the same man, not done by different people as the Republican authorities insisted.

The following documentaries are highly recommended. In each case the producers and other people took very real risks to make their films, some more than others. Freedom of expression and freedom of speech are limited in America after 2001. Because of the subject matter it is possible you will not be able to find them at your local libraries if you live in a predominantly Republican region, area, or city. If you do not live in one of the 11 states that has passed Resolutions Against The Patriot Act for their entire state, or you do not live in one of those more than 400 cities.

They are very informative and worth looking for and watching. They are "War Made Easy", "I Know What I Saw", "The End of America", "Taxi to the Dark Side", "Terror Storm" (and the "Extras" part at the end, which is as informative as the movie), "Fuel", the History Channel's "Area 51", "Healing Cancer", "Uncovered", "The Best Government Money Can Buy", "Zeitgeist", "The Inside Job", "No End In Sight", Michael Moore's "Fahrenheit 911" and "Bowling For Columbine" and "Sicko", and the special features part (actual photos) at the end of "Redacted", that is not a documentary but instead a fictionalized drama. Also "Why We Fight", "Fast-walkers", "Iraq For Sale", and Oliver Stone's informative and well-done "Looking For Fidel" and "South of the Border" and "The Untold History of the United States". "Platoon", Stone's very popular movie about the United States war in Viet Nam, is unquestionably the best movie ever made about that subject, besides a great soundtrack.

I used about 30 other documentaries that were not as good as these for information, but I didn't keep a record of their names and their titles for just a sentence or two, or for just a few words, of pertinent information. Look to see what DVDs *your* local libraries have, maybe more, maybe less, and well worth your time to find and to watch. Become informed with the truth, with photos of things that really happened, as they were happening. Last but not least, I could not have written this Book I, or Book II, without the help of the internet from beginning to end. I used *no* books for research.

In the same effort of seeking the truth the only radio station that provides unbiased and truthful information about the United States and the rest of the World is the BBC, the British Broadcasting Corporation, and sometimes NPR, National Public Radio. After keeping records of BBC broadcast information for five years, after listening to it for five years every day for five days a week, I can only say they are remarkably better and much more informative, and truthful, unbiased, and unlimited, than American newscasts, including NPR. Both of these radio companies are exceptional, and are the lone beacons of truth and information everyone needs to know but a lot of people in America do not want to know. You can lead a horse to water but you cannot make him drink.

Since the passing of The Patriot Act in 2001 all library records and all computer use at libraries, and *all* computer use of *everyone* in the United States, all phone records and phone tapping for *all* Americans, all of their bank records, medical records, and library records, and any records of any sort, can be taken by the United States Government to manufacture evidence against that person. This includes any person, anywhere in America. Honesty and truth does not have to be a part of the equation. Personal and private information can be, and is, easily manipulated by Homeland Security, and other Government entities. This can be extremely dangerous for all Americans, especially the expendable masses, and is a cause for major insecurity and major justified concern, especially for those who are caught up in it, who are the victims.

I experienced this myself as I was writing a different book, a novel based on actual experiences, as I was typing it onto a flash drive at local libraries in Evansville, Indiana. Three of the library employees were often rude and difficult to deal with. Apparently they read what I had been typing for two hours on library computers every day for months, available to them to read for twelve hours before being deleted, erased from the system forever, and they didn't like whatever I had written. Or maybe it was because of the name of my book, on my manuscript on the flash drive, which I had never told anyone. Originally I had named it "Looking for America", then changed it to "American Sins, American Glory". After several sarcastic remarks made to me by those same library employees about that title, which I had never told anyone about, I decided to change it to "American Expose".

If it's possible people should *use* adversity. Make adversity your friend. So I tried to benefit from problems, making problems my friend, and deriving something useful from them when it's possible.

At least that sounds good in theory, but it doesn't always work. A library patron had said to me, "God forbid what happens to us when our Government takes away our books, and controls what we read."

I commented to a library employee, as I was requesting a DVD by phone, that another library employee had been lazy because they wouldn't get up to get a reference book to verify information I had just read there 30 minutes earlier. Five days later I got a certified letter, the kind you have to sign for, from the administrator of the library saying she had been informed about that word "lazy" that I had said in a conversation, which had just been in an off-handed observation. She wrote "You will never be able to use the Evansville library system again if you ever again criticize any library employee." Such vehemence and meanness was unique to Far Right Republican areas of the United States I had observed, while I had lived in 55 places in 15 different states. It was, after all, a *public* library, for everyone to use. Her reaction of tyranny was not to find out why I had said that.

Her reaction was both un-American and anti-American. What happened to freedom of speech, freedom of expression, and freedom of opinion? Gone. They're gone, or have been drastically altered, as a result of the Neo Con's "Patriot Act" passed in 2001 and the Neo Con "Project for a New America in the 21st Century", collaborated on and written in 1997 to 1999, before the turn of the century in 2000. Conformity and fitting in, and being silent about your criticisms, especially of the government, were supposed to be the norm in the new century, according to these publications.

Then, one day, my more than 57,800 e-mails sent to me over more than three years and accumulated over more than three years, that were 99.9% advertising and junk mail, disappeared. It seemed they had been frozen. Then, all e-mails that I had sent in those three years were re-sent, then disappeared, except for the ones I had sent to friends and my daughter, and apparently questionable contacts of possible interest to I didn't know who. Those e-mails were saved to somebody else's accounts. Yahoo notified me my account had been "hacked into". I did a lot of research on library computers, one thing leading to another, with some connections blocked, until I discovered who was doing these things to my account. They were named "Newman", and "Roger", and "Turkey". After that I couldn't access my account at all. What was left on it was blocked. My entire yahoo e-mail account was frozen, so I created a new one.

But I couldn't make any sense out of all of it, one thing after another, government forces working against me in completely unnecessary and ridiculous ways. This time I couldn't make adversity my friend. I couldn't figure out a way to benefit from these problems. The government computer spying networks were indeed a reality. And I had just experienced it.

The Patriot Act said librarians were not to tell patrons if Homeland Security accessed their library records. But an employee at the Central Library in downtown Evansville did tell me. When I was almost done typing it onto the flash drive, so I could send it to book agents and publishers that had asked to see it when it was done, it disappeared completely. Something odd flashed onto the screen as I was typing the last three pages, a long grey-colored message of hundreds of numbers and letters unrecognizable to me. Then, two seconds later, my entire manuscript on the flash drive was gone, 200 pages disappearing in only two seconds.

More than three years of concentrated work, writing, re-writing, editing, and then re-editing it, perfecting my book, and it was gone in three seconds, disappearing into thin air. No one at the library tech room could do anything to retrieve it. It had vanished into thin air, like it had been vaporized by some invisible force. Satellites moving endlessly in the endless sky can do amazing things. Neo Cons in power can easily justify anything they do to anyone in America.

Nothing I did would make it reappear. Nothing I could do would make it come back. I asked people who worked with computers as their business, who were computer specialists, to try to retrieve it. Nobody could find it. This 21st century Government advancement was not really for the benefit of the expendable masses, but instead for greater control of the expendable masses. So my book, after writing, re-writing, editing, and re-editing, and then typing it onto a flash drive, all taking more than three years, was gone forever because I had typed it at libraries in Evansville, Indiana, instead of almost any other library anywhere else in America.

Thousands of hours of work had been stolen by my own Government. If I had done these same things at libraries in Minneapolis, Minnesota, where I had lived for 25 years, none of this, none of the problems I had encountered every day in Vanderburgh County and Evansville, Indiana, would have ever happened. Minneapolis and Minnesota have people that are more enlightened, more intelligent, more kind, less mean, not vicious, more civilized. They had passed Resolutions Against The Patriot Act sometime after 2001, making it a much safer and truly American place to live, and to write books.

As I had typed the pages I had thrown them away, thinking I would make a back-up copy only when I was done with the entire book. All I had left of my perfected book was the last two pages I hadn't yet typed onto the flash drive, because the rest was stolen by Homeland Security, or some other Government entity. This would never have happened before 9/11 in 2001, before the Patriot Act, before Bush "W"/Cheney, and the rest of his Neo Con crew from 2001 to 2009. There wasn't a thing I could do about it. Now I had to worry whether any of my writing in that book would be manipulated in any way to incriminate me falsely, as had been done to an unknown number of journalists and authors in the United States since 2001 because of what they had written. It is what it is, and it's a slippery slope to greater loss of freedoms in America in the future.

The Fair Use Clause of 1976 says "Material can be used for criticism and education." The Freedom of Information Act allows everything in this book and any other book I have written or will write to be written about. (This is the first book in a series of three.) A week later a librarian at one of the neighborhood libraries gave me a strange flash drive, saying "We thought this was yours." I had never seen it before but I took it without saying anything, and then plugged it into a library computer. Unbelievably, there was the cover of my book, my stolen book, on this stranger flash drive that looked completely different than the flash drive I had had it on originally. There was nothing else on it.

As it happened, the cover for that book had been designed by someone other than me and mistakenly said on it "A *novel* by Kathleen Babbitt, DSc.". Otherwise, it was a beautiful cover, perfect, exactly as I had wanted and asked her to do. Despite the fact I had asked her repeatedly to e-mail a corrected book cover, as it was non-fiction, she never did. A novel couldn't be potentially "dangerous" in the mind of a controlling government so that must have been why the manuscript thieves left that cover on my flash drive. It was the only part they didn't want, even though it was just a fictionalized account of things that had happened in my life. That cover was all that remained after thousands of hours of my efforts, and my attempts to write a book that was at least very good.

Since 9/11 if anyone writes a book with the word "America" in the title, or in the content of the book, apparently they are a potential "terrorist" according to the United States Government, and probably according to some Republican state governments too. It's insanity. It's a Government out control as it attempts to control everything. So, since 9/11 in 2001 it's a *terrible* thing to write about

America, a red-flag word since after The Patriot Act in 2001, along with *thousands* of other red-flag words that red-flag on Government computers spying on and monitoring all Americans 24/7, billions of entries every day. It's a constant Government menace in a so-called democracy. What happened to me could happen, and undoubtedly has happened, to anyone anywhere in America.

Sometime during his Presidency Kennedy said "Let us welcome controversial authors and controversial books, for they are the defenders of our liberties and freedoms." Since 2001 Republican leaders, the Far Right, and Neo Cons in America would disagree with him. Unless the books are pro-Republican, pro-Far Right, and pro-Neo Cons, no matter how dishonest they may be.

In 2003 I had given myself five years to find peace, truth, and beauty in one place in America. I was looking for the best place to live in America. Besides that, a road trip is for when you want more freedom, when you need to break away, and when you want the adventure of being on the road.

So I traveled throughout America for five years, living for one to six months in 45 different places in 15 states to learn about the local governments and the local people in those places. I was searching for the best quality of living in America. But it doesn't exist unless you're at least upper middle-class financially, and working at something you want to be doing every day, and living where you want to be living. I made a concentrated effort to learn about the indigenous people and the style of living indigenous to each place, each area. And yes, there are very different and distinct differences, north, south, east, and west, and everywhere in between. Then I wrote a book about my experiences and what I had learned along the way.

Unfortunately my journey had ended in a place, Vanderburgh County, Indiana, that had no peace or intellectual beauty. There was some physical beauty, natural beauty indigenous to the area, like most places in the United States. But the truth was that it was an ugly and deplorable place to live because of the people that I encountered on a daily basis. Because of their mean and uncivilized attitudes and personalities. Unmitigated selfishness and meanness was the norm. It was everywhere, at all levels of financial standing, from rich to poor. It stood out as being the worst place I had stayed at. The difference here was that I couldn't leave, I couldn't escape, because of circumstances beyond my control, because of things I couldn't change no matter how hard I tried or what I did. No matter how many times I asked for any kind of help from those people who got paid to do what I asked them to do, always, without fail, I would encounter resistance and meanness, incompetence and selfishness, or just rudeness. It all stood out as being very different than the rest of the United States.

As an example, the Sheriff's deputies were paid to "serve and protect" but never, not once, did that happen, as they always protected and served the criminal drug element that was rampant in Vanderburgh County. Specifically, they served the drug dealers and the users of illegal drugs, making it officially one of the top ten worst counties for illegal drug problems in the entire United States. The Sheriff was the same as his deputies. This was not surprising, as problem behavior in the workplace commonly starts at the top and filters down to the bottom.

Deputies would always tell the drug dealers, who were perpetrators of vandalism often requiring expensive repairs, harassment 24/7, and the breakers of County noise and nuisance ordinances thousands of times, "You aren't doing anything wrong". Usually deputies would then smile and make jokes with them, while making fun of whoever had called in complaints about them, especially if it was a woman who had called 911 about the drug dealers and the problem tenants in the park.

With the support of the deputies they were invincible, and would continue and always repeat their vandalism and harassment, their endless threatening actions and words, their endless anytime 24/7 problem behaviors, knowing the deputies would protect them. Drug dealers were safe if they lived in Vanderburgh County. It was a safe-haven for drug dealers, for drug buyers and users, for drug suppliers, and for the secretive drug bosses, the crime bosses.

It was common knowledge that this deputy behavior was connected to pay-offs, free drugs from the drug dealers, benefits on the side, favors, or just keeping their jobs. Or maybe the welfare of their families was threatened if they didn't go along with the system. Fear is always the most powerful motivator. When a deputy stepped out of line and told the victim that he, or she, would make a report about what they had learned that report would be erased, eliminated, or never appear on official records. The endless system of making victims appear as the problem, and the actual perpetrators always responsible for nothing, meaning they never did anything wrong but were allegedly always falsely accused, made the system extremely corrupt and unable to be fixed or proven wrong. Corruption was so firmly entrenched, undoubtedly also involving politicians, the very wealthy, and local authorities, that living there was dangerous and very stressful if a citizen wasn't able to ignore what was happening and avoid contact with the system of law enforcement, the deputies and Sergeants from the Sheriff Department, and the police and Captains from the Police Department.

There is always strength in numbers, especially when those numbers are deputies with guns and the ability to make false allegations, false charges, and false arrests. When they would tell the perpetrators what I had complained about retaliation was always the result, and of course the deputies knew that would happen. They were clearly set-ups to result in retaliation against me, or anyone else who dared to call in a complaint, often happening within minutes of the deputies leaving. If deputies said they didn't see anything or hear anything then calling 911 again could lead to charges of making false complaints. It was a catch-22 situation, a no-win situation.

Understandably people were afraid of the entire Sheriff Department because the deputies represented the whole Sheriff Department. People would not call in problems because deputies would cause more problems than they ever solved. During the six years I ended up living there lying, deception, and deceit were the status quo for the deputies for the Vanderburgh Sheriff Department. The pattern was to lie for drug dealers, for perpetrators, for criminals, and to make excuses for them, and to lie to protect themselves. It was so common, so very much a pattern, that two nice deputies, helpful and honest deputies, stood out as being very strange. Add being mean and revengeful and all of those behaviors were their m.o., their status quo, their constant and vigilant modus operandi.

In democracies people rely on systems designed to make life fair and right. When the systems don't work right the democracy breaks down, slowly but definitely. The democracy doesn't work the way it's supposed to, and freedoms begin to disappear. That started to happen nationally in 2000, with the dishonest and manipulated Republican Presidential campaign of 2000. Lying, deception, and dishonesty became the status quo in the United States.

What or where is the superiority of America, of the United States? It's superior to third-World countries, but what are first-World and second-World countries anyway? In 2003 I gave myself five years to find the best place to live in America. The best quality of living, the best quality of life, with peace, truth, and beauty all in one place. I found out it doesn't exist in one place unless you're at least upper-middle-class financially. Money makes the difference. After traveling to everywhere that seemed a likely prospect, north, south, east, and west, after traveling more than 10,000 miles in search of my goal for those five years, I knew that I couldn't find the best place to live in America.

After living in 45 places for one to six months each, and after investigating each one thoroughly, their governments, their social structures, their local people, their businesses, their law enforcement, their local economics, their newspapers and libraries, and their real estate market, including rentals, I knew I was qualified to reach objective conclusions. After using the internet to find the best real estate prices I found great buys in New York because people were moving away because there was no work in their towns. Their factories were shutting down and their businesses were closing because of the economy. Another place with great real estate prices was Vanderburgh County, in southern Indiana, that didn't seem to be having a job crisis.

I had never even traveled to Indiana as I had had a foreboding feeling about it, and never even included it as a possibility, as I felt like I should avoid it. Life is about making choice. Right choices, wrong choices. But the real estate market internet photos looked good and the prices were lower than anywhere in the United States except Detroit, so I decided to travel there and check the situation out. Maybe I had been wrong, maybe Indiana was an alright place to live in. I knew for sure it was not going to be the best place to live in America. The best real estate prices were in Detroit, but that had a higher crime rate statistically than anywhere in Indiana, and the yearly real estate taxes were outrageous, being taxed at the highest value from years before regardless of the selling price.

At that time I was in Texas so I decided to first see my daughter in Baton Rouge, Louisiana, where I had lived for about a year before leaving on my journey to find the best place to live in America. I called a friend of mine and asked him if I could stay with him for a week or two. He was not going to be at home for about a week, he said, because he was in Oregon on tour with his band, but I could stay at his home if I wanted to as a friend of his was already staying there. He had been a friend of mine for about 10 years while I had lived in Port Allen, Louisiana and in Baton Rouge. He was a black musician, nine years younger than me, who was devoted to his music, first and foremost. He had always been the funniest man I had ever known, of all colors. He could be hilarious.

After a few weeks staying at his house I left for Indiana and New York to try and find a good buy, even a great buy, in a house to live in for the rest of my life as I had given up on finding the best location in America. It just did not exist unless you were at least upper-middle-class, or rich and wealthy and able to afford the good life.

When I got to Vanderburgh County, Indiana I planned to look at those possible good real estate buys the next day and then continue on to New York to find a great real estate buy in that state and live there, at least for a while. I had been trying to avoid cold winters for five years but maybe I had been wrong and that is where the hidden and mysterious "best place to live" was going to be found.

Before I got a motel for the night I went to get something at a Target store I had driven by. I used the phone book and the phone at the service desk there to call motels to see if they allowed pets, as I had three cats. When I turned to leave a Target employee had put a long and low wooden cart two inches behind me that I had no choice but to fall onto. Immediately I was in a lot of pain. So after sitting in my car for a while to try and stop the pain, to wait until it got better, I went back into the store to talk to the manager about making a complaint.

But 24 hours later I was in more pain everywhere. My neck, back, shoulder, hands. I had a lot of difficulty lifting the pet carriers back into the car so I could leave the motel the next morning. The air conditioning at the Motel 6 hadn't worked all night so I went to the front desk to tell them. The manager said she wouldn't give me a refund of any kind because I had had a cat in the room. I told her I had called from Target about their pet policy and had been told they were allowed, as they were in all other Motel 6 locations everywhere in the United States. She didn't say anything, and just glared at me. Then a maintenance man came in and said to her "You were right! She had a dog in her room. She was hiding it when I walked in and caught her!" The manager said to him "I'll tell her she can't stay again tonight because of the dog." I decided I wasn't going to look at the real estate after all. I just wanted to leave Indiana. This probably represented most of Vanderburgh County.

After driving a few miles I knew I couldn't possibly drive to New York, and I wouldn't be able to lift the pet carriers in and out of the car each night to spend the night at motels before I found a place to live at. The pain was excruciating. So I decided I had to improvise and find an inexpensive place to buy in Vanderburgh County and then leave, sell it, when I recuperated from the injury I got at Target. That's how I ended up in Vanderburgh County, Indiana.

After five years of looking for the best place to live in America I had ended up in one of the worst places to live in America. If truth is beauty and beauty is truth then I was about to find both. But being forced to live with that truth was going to be ugly. Maybe it was karma, something I was destined to work on because of past mistakes, things I had done wrong in a past life. Or maybe it was just destiny. Whatever it was the reality was going to be that living in Vanderburgh County, Indiana was going to be like a nightmare that never ended for the next six years. Order and justice, fairness and kindness, honesty and truth, were mostly missing there. I was a prisoner of circumstances there. Of course there were worse cities, towns, areas, and regions in America but I had avoided them, never staying in any of them even for one night. I had tried to avoid the worst places and concentrate on the best places. But now I was forced to concentrate on and live with the worst for an indefinite period of time. Maybe the best was yet to come, but I doubted it.

I looked at the ads in the newspaper, found a mobile home for $2900, went to look at it, and bought it for $2000. It was in wretched shape inside and out, including the large deck that had never been painted in at least 25 years. But the large white yard barn was in good shape. It was the worst looking home in the mobile home park, but it had the biggest and the best yard barn. When I had less pain I could paint the home inside and out, including the deck, and hire someone to do the repairs. But when the utilities were turned on nothing worked right. There was no stove, no refrigerator, no furniture. But it had a new mattress in a bedroom, a Sealy Posture Pedic, that seemed to be waiting for me to lay on it. I was in a lot of pain. And I wouldn't have to find a bed. It was already partly there.

So for the next week or so I spent a lot of time laying down on that new mattress, planning what to do when the pain would get better, when the incapacitating migraine headache from the cervical injury would end. Meanwhile my three cats were absolutely happy and relieved to be able to do whatever they wanted to do, inside and outside, once again. They especially liked the deck.

Little by little I painted the deck, the railings, and the steps. Then I painted the entire inside of the home, an hour a day unless I was debilitated from painting an hour the day before. An hour a day was the most I could do, as I would often be unable to paint for another day because of the intense pain in my shoulders and my arms. I just couldn't stand doing nothing to improve the place, it was so awful. But the mattress was in a bedroom with beautiful wallpaper and borders so it was my haven, my refuge from the pain, to lay down on the bed while listening to the radio, and looking at the woods, the many trees behind my home, while waiting for the pain to get better.

If I had been living in any of the other 23 Democracies that have free Universal Healthcare I would have gotten a diagnosis, help, and a prescription for a strong pain killer immediately and for free. I called thirty physicians in Evansville but none would see me because I had no health insurance and couldn't pay at least $200 immediately after seeing them. I was one of the at least 33 *million* Americans who couldn't afford to pay cash for hugely over-priced medical services and who didn't have medical insurance to cover it because the insurance was too expensive, or because they had preconditions that excluded them. I hadn't gone to a hospital emergency room, where by law they have to provide care regardless of insurance or ability to pay, because it wasn't an emergency. All hospitals charge everyone hugely inflated prices for what they do, that health insurance then pays for, that then justifies their extremely high insurance premiums as a big part of the medical/sickness industry in America. It's all like a big game, a greedy industry that touches every one's life.

After three weeks of unrelenting intense pain in my shoulder, back, neck, arm, and hand, all on the right side, and the pain of the migraine headache that would not go away, indicating a cervical injury, I had called 25 lawyers in Evansville about suing Target. No lawyer would represent me because Indiana law says the injured person has to see a physician within three days, otherwise there is no case. I was told this 30 times so I assumed it was the ugly truth. Some lawyers said they wouldn't want to be suing Target anyway as Target, the corporation, had a reputation for lying in court (under oath of course), of having phony witnesses, and of purposely losing the videotapes. In the end, while eventually in court before a Judge, this is exactly what happened.

So I had to do a small claims court lawsuit on my own. The limit was for $6000. I found a sports doctor who agreed to have his nurse write a record of my experiences and my subsequent problems so I could present it as evidence in court, charging me $200 for that, to be paid later after the small claims court appearance. I was determined to win what was rightfully mine even if it was just a fraction of what a lawyer could have gotten me in compensation. He didn't even give me a prescription for pain pills because he said in order to do that I had to have a diagnosis for $200 dollars more, and also $400 dollars of x-rays done at another medical facility to enable that diagnosis. All services were to be paid at the time of delivery. I didn't have that money up-front, having put what money I had into my home, so I had a place to live, and my cats had a place to live.

At that time Indiana was the only state where people getting SSI did not get Medicaid or government-supplied health insurance. To get Medicaid people had to be "completely and totally disabled, unable to do anything." That included lifting a phone. Fortunately not many people fit that description. Like all other states people who got Disability in Indiana automatically got Medicare, even if they were getting Disability dishonestly, which is very common in Indiana. No government-supplied health care or health insurance supplied by the state was part of the reason the state of Indiana, their government, always had yearly budget surpluses of hundreds of millions of dollars, and even a billion dollars. But the purpose of tax money is to use it, not to hoard it or hide it, or use it dishonestly. It's not for politicians and officials to steal for their personal use, or to give to friends and relatives, or to businesses, like they have been doing in Indiana for many years.

Within a few days of moving there it was obvious the park of about 500 mobile homes was a haven for white-trash and criminal drug activity anytime 24 hours a day, even though the very lengthy lease had prohibited the activities that were happening every day and night.

My next door neighbor had been evicted because he had asked the managers to do something about the harassment and problems his eight year old daughter encountered daily from the drug dealer's kids, because she was half American Indian and half white, so she had darker skin, and was a little plump. Every day they harassed her and threatened her about it as she would walk home from the school bus stop. Her father said she was terrified of these teenage boys, sons of the drug dealers who never had to follow park rules or County laws, who would follow her from the school bus stop to her home every afternoon after they got off the school bus, always shouting obscenities and threats at her, copying the behavior of their drug dealer white-trash parents. The father said every day when he got home from work she would be crying, asking him to help her.

The park owner's response was the same as it always was for any good rule-abiding tenant who complained about anything in the park and the drug dealers. They said to him "You're a trouble-maker. We don't want people like you living in this park. You're evicted." People said this had been going on for many years, a pattern repeated endlessly by the owners and managers of the park.

So he had 30 days to sell his mobile home because no other parks take homes older than 10 or 15 years, so he couldn't move it. Fortunately for him he was one of the fortunate-few who actually had gotten a title from the man he bought it from, who had moved it into the park as a new mobile home 30 years earlier. I talked to other tenants and found out usually owners would be unable to sell their home in 30 days if they had a title, but usually they didn't have a title. Either way the owners of the park would get another one for free, often with the furniture still in it because the evicted tenants had nowhere to put it, and they were unable to buy or rent another home because they had an eviction notice on their record and no money from their investment, their home. That explained why the sales ads for homes in the park, ads running continually for years in the local newspaper, always said "Many already furnished!". It was the furniture evicted people would have to leave behind because they hadn't found a place to live yet.

As days passed when I would call 911 about any crime or lesser problem day or night nothing would be stopped or dealt with. Deputies always took one to one and a half hours to get there. Drunk drivers wouldn't be stopped even though I would give the license plate numbers at some risk to myself. Drunk drivers would always drive back more drunk than when they left. There was public drunkenness and fights. There was blasting noise "Boom! Boom!", "Thud! Thud!" from cars, pickup trucks, SUVs, and from homes, the bass on CDs and radios turned up too loud, anytime day and night, 24/7. There was vandalism of cars and homes. Most people used the word "fuck" in every other sentence, especially men, like in popular movies and rap music, only worse.

They were like the English punks, the white-trash criminals and demented men in movies made in England about the England of the 21st century. How did it spread 8000 miles over the ocean to America? It was the 21st century version of immigration from England to America. But maybe it started in America and spread to England. It's a small world because of videos, DVDs, TV news, and movies, and because most humans seem to like to copy the worst wherever they find it.

I didn't live in a trailer, but I lived in a mobile home. Or at least it would become a home after I made a lot of improvements. And it hadn't been "mobile" for at least 25 years. But these problem people lived in trailers, as they are commonly referred to. They had no class, but were low-class people. They were uncivilized and they were mean. Their trailers and yards were a mess. They were disgusting human beings. If they weren't drunk or drinking they were high, or both, often with loud disorderly conduct. They were white people, no black people. All were white trailer-trash, and very offensive, selfish and loud lawbreakers who were never apprehended by deputies.

The deputies usually told them "You didn't do anything wrong", and usually told them who had complained about them, who had called 911, even though they weren't supposed to. It was their standard response, their standard deputy procedure. They would always say "If we didn't see it or hear it then it didn't happen." But they would always believe the lies of the drug dealers.

Drug dealing, drug using, drug buying and selling was never stopped as 20 to 30 cars, pickups, motorcycles, and SUVs would stop at the illegal drug store, the "trailer" across the street from me, anytime 24/7, many blasting "Boom! Boom!", "Thud! Thud!", announcing their arrival anytime day or night. It was not uncommon for these many drug customers to talk very loudly, even if it was 2:00 or 3:00 or 4:00 in the morning, at which time they would often be drunk or high. They obviously did not think they had to hide what they were doing. And they were right. Driving while drunk was common and was never stopped when I called 911 with their license plate numbers. I knew this was so because they would be driving drunk again, the next time they visited the illegal "drug store" across the street.

When I first moved there I had talked to twelve neighbors, asking them "Why didn't you report the drug dealing, all that loud noise, the meth labs, the crimes, the 10 to 20 vehicles at their homes every day and night?" All twelve neighbors said the same thing. "Because I was (we were) afraid of who lived there and I was (we were) afraid of the Sheriff Department and the deputies." Or "We were afraid of the retaliation." All of them had stories to tell as long as I didn't ask them their names. The deputies had a reputation for years of telling the perpetrators who had called about them, who had called 911 about them. Retaliation was a certainty. It was a deputy game of set-ups and retaliation.

People who lived in the park had said to me at the beginning "I see you moved into the drug end of the park." And "Stay away from the deputies. They'll make a lot of trouble for you if you complain about the drug dealers." And "Don't be complaining about the park or the drug dealers to the management or to the owners, or you'll be evicted."

I had told each one "Don't worry. I'll take care of it." I figured I was already on their radar. The radar of the deputies, the Sheriff department, the managers and owners of the park, who were good friends of the Sheriff and Police Chief, and the radar of the drug criminals and problem people in the park (mostly men) who lived across the street from me, next to me, and a few hundred feet from me. So I had nothing to lose to try and fix these problems, this ungodly mess where I was going to be stuck for a while against my will. Hopefully I could, because it was only me, myself, and I against all of it. What bad luck I had had. After looking for the best place to live I was stuck indefinitely in the worst place I had been to during those five years of searching in America for the best place to live.

The Sheriff, a Democrat, had a reputation for being inaccessible to everyone except the media. His Sergeants were belligerent and accusatory, protecting "their officers", standing up for "their men". One of these times, after difficulty with a drug-crazed man in his twenties, I had called 911 and requested a

Sergeant. I told him other people in the park had been having the same problems for years as I was having. He said "Then they should move to the city." The two deputies had laughed. I said to them "Do you think this is funny?" The Sergeant said "No they don't." Then, when I walked slowly down the steps on my deck to my yard both the deputies had quickly reached for their guns. I stopped and looked at them. I said "What are you going to do? Shoot me?"

I had talked to an Editor at the Evansville newspaper about these many ongoing problems, asking him to do an investigative article about it. He said the Sheriff was a friend of his and he would talk to him about it. A few days later he told me the Sheriff had said he knew all about me, that I was always calling there because I thought everyone was out to get me. He said "She thinks everyone is out to get her. She's always calling here with lies about the drug dealers." The Sheriff had never returned my phone calls to him. Always I had only left my phone number and no message. He was lying about me. I had never been able to talk to him about anything. And I had never thought, or said to his deputies, that anyone was "out to get me." I always presented things as they happened, truthfully.

I wrote a letter to Indiana Governor Daniels about the problems with the Sheriff department. His response was that it was the jurisdiction of the Sheriff, and that he, as Governor, had no jurisdiction over what the Vanderburgh County Sheriff Department and the deputies did, or didn't, do.

When what is illegal is made legal, when what is wrong is ignored and therefore given approval, when laws or rules are selectively enforced or ignored, disorder is the result. Order is necessary in a civilized society. Kindness and fairness, and truth and honesty, combine with order and justice to make a social structure civilized, and to make a society that's good to live in. When disorder and lies are the norm is what I experienced, at all levels of society, for six years in Vanderburgh County.

Not to mention the criminal activity, the vandalism, that cost me more than $1000 for repairs, that deputies did nothing about apprehending or punishing the perpetrator, even though I always told them who had done it. The criminals, the drug dealers, would always tell me, shouting at me what they had done. They wanted recognition for their crimes. Many other people in the park also experienced vandalism to their cars and homes, besides the theft of their computer and flat screen TV stolen from their homes when they weren't there. In those six years the American dream of home ownership was instead an American nightmare of home ownership.

Politicians have established a reputation for themselves of using manipulation and deception as tools of their too highly paid trade, some areas of the United States more than others. Louisiana had long been maybe the worst, but Indiana was maybe the second or third worst. It is, after all, subjective. People living in each state reflect and are a reflection of their elected politicians. But, in general, people in Indiana took first place for being manipulative and deceptive, for being mean and lying and rude. It attracts people from other states who are like that. Indiana suits them, and they like living there. Of course, this is the way it is for all states. Certain types of people are attracted to certain types of states. Everybody likes to fit in.

Everything that happened in Vanderburgh County that was wrong could feasibly also become the norm for everywhere else in America. It could spread to other states that were superior places to live in. People talk about a better America. Politicians often talk about making America a better place to live in. But if that happened it would make America an unpleasant and unsafe place to live.

Being two-faced used to be a Southern thing. But no more. It has spread to other states like

Indiana. Since 2001 being selfish and lying has become more common for anyone, not just politicians.

The corruption in government, and the lies at all levels of government, is mimicked in personal corruption and personal attitudes everywhere in America. Personal corruption and business corruption and lies are all-pervasive. They can be easily found throughout America in the 21$^{st}$ century. It's the new American norm. Strangely, being truthful is scorned, ridiculed, not believed.

On a personal basis, my phone lines were cut three times, a federal crime, and my car was repeatedly vandalized, so I didn't dare to get a better and newer car, and the handle and electronics on my electric lawn mower were broken off necessitating a $125 repair cost that, strangely, took six weeks to get repaired. My home was broken into 40 times when I would leave, drive away, not when I was there, but the deputies were never interested because nothing was ever stolen. Breaking and entering was inconsequential in Vanderburgh County, and it was so common it was boring to the deputies. Then, in the third year, my storm door was torn off the hinges and the inside handle was broken off. Replacement for that meant the entire door unit, that included the inside front door that was just a plain metal door, would cost a ridiculous $650 for parts and labor. The only mobile home parts center in the area had a monopoly, thus the outrageous prices. But I didn't get it replaced because I knew the same criminal would do it again, to a new storm door, and the deputies would be indifferent, as they always were about all vandalism. I had to make the best of a bad situation.

In the fourth year the next door drug dealer from Hell, the Satan incarnate, slashed my tires, broke the valve stems on my new tires, pounded new nails into my tires, let the air out of my tires, loosened the radiator days after I had a new one installed, and let the hot water out of the hot water heater in my home, thus burning the heating element in three seconds, the plumber told me, necessitating a $800 replacement and repair. Each time deputies would say "We didn't see him do it, so he didn't do it." And "If we didn't see it happen then it didn't happen." And "If we didn't hear him say it then he didn't say it." On the day that he had slashed my tire, unbeknownst to me, as I drove away he shouted at me "I don't think you're gonna' get where you're going." The drug dealer from Hell always needed recognition for his crimes. His drug partner, standing next to him in his driveway, had then laughed. They were truly white-trash lowest level human beings, who were never held accountable for whatever they did, even when they told deputies what they had done wrong.

Deputies would always say the same things for all of those six years of living in a nightmare environment. It was their scripted responses about drug dealers. So no report was ever made for any of the more than 150 calls I made to 911 about problems in six years. Then no pattern was established, and It never happened. No report means no proof of any problem. The person who called them then is the problem, having made so-called "false reports" to the deputies. Deputies didn't believe the truth when they heard it from whoever had called 911. Instead they believed the drug dealers who had been complained about, who always lied to protect themselves, who knew the deputies were on their side and would always believe their lies. It was a system, a part of the whole entrenched drug system.

Or the deputies acted like they believed their lies, saying to the 911 caller "We think you're making it up. We think you're lying. We believe him. We don't believe you." Meaning the 911 caller was the liar, not the perpetrators that always lied to the deputies and always got away with it, as the drug dealer lying was music to their ears. The deputies would smile and laugh, patting them on the shoulder or their back. Or just be very courteous and listening to their every word, and then be belligerent, antagonistic, rude, and sarcastic to the 911 caller, but only if that was a woman over 25 and alone.

They were always enchanted and enraptured with the drug dealer lies. They consistently loved the drug dealers, in a strange deputy way. It was consistently peculiar. All of it was a pattern. They'd always say "We don't believe you. We think you're making it up." And "We believe him, we don't believe you."

All of these responses happened when I called 911 about drug dealers living in the park, about the problems they caused, more than 135 times in those six years. It was a script repeated eventually at least 75 times. Deputies seemed to have programmed responses about the drug dealers, except for two deputies, one black and one white. Except for those two, it was always a losing proposition and very stressful to call 911, and to deal with the responding deputies, the do-nothing deputies.

If drug dealers had been standing in front of them with five pounds of any illegal drugs the deputies would not have seen it. They would have ignored it. Just like no deputies ever smelled the meth labs in the park when I called 911 about them four times in the first month after I moved there, the nauseating all-pervasive meth smell that people told me had permeated the park for years. But the FBI did respond to that problem within days of receiving my letter to them, and the meth labs disappeared. The State Police had told me to not call them anymore about it, saying "We only do Bonnie and Clyde type of things." But the State Police were supposed to have been shutting down meth labs and hadn't for years. Apparently it wasn't enough like Bonnie and Clyde.

Thus retaliation was set-up against me from the first month that I was living there. Doing the right thing in America, doing something good in America, can have bad consequences or be dangerous.

It was the same for other people in the park. Deputies always discredited who had complained, who had called 911 for help, replacing the truth with disinformation, misinformation, and lies, twisting and distorting the truth. But all of this was nothing new. The same things had been happening to people for as long as 15 or 20 years, as twelve neighbors had told me when I had asked them about this strange deputy behavior and drug dealer behavior in the weeks after I had moved into the park.

For years deputies took one to one and a half hours to respond to my 911 calls. In about four years I made about 25 calls to 911. That's six a year. If I would have called every time something went wrong, or about a crime, I would have called at least 200 times. There were *many* more problems that I had never called about because I knew the deputies would do nothing about them, and would take at least an hour to get there. And when they'd finally get there they'd be belligerent, antagonistic, sarcastic, and rude, or obnoxious and threatening to me and very nice, polite, and courteous to the perpetrators of the problems and the crimes, the drug dealers, the drug users, buyers, sellers, and to the drunk men and women who were causing a disturbance or who had been driving while drunk.

Sometimes they would touch their guns in their holsters repeatedly as I talked to them. What did they want to do? Shoot me? They seemed to be restraining themselves while they were not restraining themselves. Eventually, for six years, it was obvious the deputies were controlled by the drug dealers, not the other way around, not deputies controlling the drug dealers. It was a part of the drug system.

All of this, and other things while living in Vanderburgh County, Indiana for six years was like living in the "Twilight Zone", that strange and weird TV show from the 1950's and 1960's. Or like living in some strange parallel universe where reality doesn't seem real.

A few hundred feet down the street from the park manager's building a meth lab flourished, often covering the park with the nauseating and sickening smell of cooking meth. The managers and park owners *must* have smelled it. It was unavoidable. There were seven meth labs in the park, home-based businesses, entrepreneurs, that the park owners and park managers did nothing about stopping. But deputies had to know about it because I reported it, and they couldn't miss the awful smell. But they always said they didn't smell it. "If we don't see it or hear it (or smell it) then it didn't happen." It was a common belief that the Sergeants and the deputies got meth or crack or heroin, or some other drugs, in exchange for giving them a free place to live and a "we don't see it or smell it" attitude.

A nearby chemical plant called DSM covered the park with a different sickening and nauseating smell of poisons and toxins for about half of every month, day and night, but usually was begun under the cover of night. Whenever it rained more than an inch at night, after 12:00, the dry or nearly dry creek bed would rise about 20 feet in about an hour, always stopping a few inches from the top of the embankment, just before it would be flooding the park. It was obviously being monitored. Obviously some company was illegally dumping its dark brown wastewater, its pollutants, into the creek, the dead creek. One of these times I called a TV station and asked them to investigate who was doing this. They announced on the TV news the next day that the creek had flooded and the park had needed to be evacuated. However, it had not flooded. Soon after I had called that TV station there were deputies knocking on people's doors, telling them that the park was flooding and they had to leave. Once again, they were wrong. But they were doing what they had been told to do.

Of course my neighbors next door would see and hear the illegal drug dealer across the street shouting obscenities at me as he stood in the street, describing whatever vandalism he had just done to my property, screaming like a woman at my home while I was inside or sitting on my deck. So the woman next door, in her early fifties, would copy him, shouting obscenities at me from her porch and shouting what vandalism *she* was going to do, always at 2:00 or 3:00 or 4:00 in the morning, when she was usually very drunk. Sometimes she would be staggeringly drunk, leaning against her porch railings and barely able to get back into her home, barely able to walk back through the door, as her dog barked at her incessantly, distressed and confused about why she was acting the way she was acting.

Often the drug dealer across the street would get into somebody else's car when he was drunk, often with a bottle in his hand, and he would drive away, both day and night. He had a DWI and therefore didn't have a car of his own. When I would call in the license plate number and say he was driving drunk he would always return later driving even more drunk. This happened many times in the nearly two years he lived there. It seemed the deputies never stopped him, or if they did they let him go. Later, when he eventually moved to his girlfriend's mobile home, he totaled *her* car. Hopefully he didn't hurt anyone. That had always been the reason I had called 911 to report drunk drivers. To help prevent injuries, pain, and suffering, to help prevent car accidents hurting other innocent people.

Eventually I called 911 about the woman next door and her early morning tirades, drunk or not. But the deputies, as usual, would never see it or hear it as they would take at least an hour to get there. If they "didn't see it or hear it then it didn't happen". That made me, as usual, a liar and a "troublemaker" according to them. They'd say "We think you're making it up." She would be disturbing the peace, public drunkenness, excessively loud noise, and too loud music, besides the disorderly conduct. But in Vanderburgh County she had done nothing wrong. As usual deputies would say that me, myself, and I had done something wrong because I had reported her, I had called 911, and they then had to drive to that location. "The only reason we ever have to come out here is because you call for us," they'd say. "Nobody else ever calls." And "If it wasn't for you we'd never have to come out here."

One of these times a deputy asked me where I was from. He said it was "a culture-shock" for me and I needed "to learn to adjust to this different culture." It was an uncivilized culture compared to other places in America, and I was never able to adjust to it, during what was going to be an ugly and miserable six years. I did my best to change it, but almost everything seemed out of my control. I was in a situation I couldn't seem to get out of, or away from. So I was a victim of circumstances beyond my control for more than six years. For too many years, because nobody wanted to buy my home there.

Next door the neighbors from Hell had been putting their miniature dachshund on the front porch to bark constantly, non-stop, every two or three hours, day and night, because I had asked them not to. After about four years the barking stopped because the dog died, and then they moved away. They were truly white trailer-trash in many ways, and I never got used to them, not remotely.

Starting in the third year that neighbor woman would repeatedly call 911 when I drove away to falsely report I was driving drunk, or drinking and driving. For the next year deputies stopped me eleven times as a result of her lies about me, saying "Have you been drinking and driving?" I would say "Never in my entire life. Isn't it against the law for someone to call in false claims about someone?"

My neighbor's daily and nightly retaliations and harassments had no let-up for those four years they lived next door. It was proof they were demented and mean people, white trailer-trash. But they were not alone. In the park there were many other sociopaths, psychopaths, psychotics, drunks, criminals, and white trailer-trash. They had a lot of company. It was a community of many strange and odd people. They were misfits, but they fit in well into this particular mobile home community.

The drug dealer across the street got Disability or SSI. That neighbor woman had applied for SSI. She said she had gotten a lawyer first to guarantee her SSI application wouldn't be rejected, and then she applied for SSI because they needed a car. She said she lied about her health problems to get it. She said she would eventually use the nine months of back payments from SSI, that would start with the day she applied for it, to get a new car. That was her plan she told me about a few days after she had moved in next door. After that her friendliness disappeared and she became mean and vindictive instead.

If she could honestly qualify for SSI it would have been for psychological reasons, as she was a psychotic nut-case, and not for the COPD she said she had been chain-smoking in order to create it for the medical exam by the physician her lawyer had told her to go to. He had to make sure she would get SSI and not be turned down, in order to get his percentage, so he referred his clients to his preferred physicians. His TV advertisements guaranteed success. She said they needed that new car that they had already picked out at the car dealer's lot. After the SSI started her plan was to quit smoking. After all, she didn't want to have COPD for any longer than was absolutely necessary.

The park was full of the same kind of people, mixed with some old and retired people, and some people who had been there for many years because they didn't want to lose their investment in their mobile home, as they had never gotten a title from the park owner and therefore couldn't sell it. They, like thousands of other people since after 1982, had unknowingly bought a mobile home with no title. Their only choice was to walk away from it when they wanted to move, with a large financial loss after having done expensive improvements that had been required for them to do as specified in the sales contract. Then the park owners would get it back again for free in improved condition, with at least $1000 of repairs done, to sell again at a higher price and continue the endless cycle of profit with no investments on their part. Sometimes those people would give their mobile home to a relative or friend instead, especially if they had finished making the payments on it to "own" it.

For six years, every night and every day any time 24/7, drug dealers in the park would play CDs with the bass turned up too loud so there was a constant rumbling and blasting bass noise, "Boom! Boom!" thousands of times anytime 24/7 coming from their large three foot high speakers. Other people living in the park were bothered about it too, even though they were 100 feet away from it, not just 15 feet away like me. But they were afraid to call 911 about it or complain to park management or owners about it. They were afraid they would be evicted, with the usual "You're a troublemaker. We don't want people like you living in this park. You're evicted." Then the people paying to "own" their home would be homeless and have lost their $1500 to $3000 down-payment on their home. Nobody complained about the park or the drug dealers if they knew about this.

So tenants just endured the endless problems, knowing very well that the drug dealers would never be evicted no matter what they did, but tenants *would* be evicted if they complained about them. Drug dealers were always protected and served by the deputies, by the Sergeants, and by the park owners and park managers. It was a safe-haven for drug dealers and their customers, for buyers and users, and for the drug bosses, the crime bosses. It was a drug culture, a system that had been perfected over time, in place for about 20 years.

Deputies always said the drug dealers had a right to do whatever they wanted to do when they wanted, inside or outside their home. "They can play *their* music as loud as they want to anytime they want to." I would say "*I* have a right to not be forced to listen to it." Deputies would say nothing, and walk away, get in their cars and leave. Or, they would make some sarcastic remark, then walk away and get in their car and leave. It was the usual deputy pattern of indifference for the 911 caller and protection of and service for the perpetrators, the drug dealers.

In retaliation, and because of the deputy support, the drug dealers and white-trash tenants continued to do those too noisy things more often and louder, every day and every night for six years. I was never able to "adjust to it", like more than one deputy had said I had to do. It seemed that civility and kindness were foreign concepts for almost everyone in Vanderburgh County, including the owners of the eight parks in the county, who had ruined the dreams of many of the buyers of their homes and made their lives miserable. This had been the reality for at least a thousand people.

The standard response of the deputies was always "You have no proof," even if the drug dealers had shouted at me what they had done. They always wanted recognition, knowing deputies and park owners would support them. Or deputies would say "You have to have a video of them doing it", which was an impossibility since vandalism would be done after I drove away, when I wasn't there, when I was gone. The deputies would always say to me "We don't believe you ", or "We think you're making it up", or "Don't be calling us anymore", or "When we get here we never see what you called about. If it wasn't for you we'd never have to come out here."

I'd always say "What do you expect? It always takes you an hour or an hour and a half to get here!" It was a never-ending struggle with the Sheriff Department and the deputies, and the occasional Sergeant. After living in 55 places In 15 different states these were the worst neighbors I had ever lived next to or near in my entire life. And they were the worst deputies and Sergeants and police and law enforcement I had ever dealt with in my life. They always protected and served the perpetrators, the drug dealers, and never, not once after about 150 calls to 911 in those six years, protected or helped me. It was very much a pattern for all those stressful and stupid years.

When I had first moved to Vanderburgh County a woman at a grocery store checkout counter said she and her husband were moving from Evansville the next day and were extremely glad to be getting away from it. I asked her why she felt that way. She had said that "Once you get on the radar of the deputies and police they never let up, they just keep harassing you, they keep stopping you, giving made-up tickets, especially if you're poor and have an old car." She said both she and her husband had been experiencing this and she couldn't wait to leave Vanderburgh County.

Little did I know that the same thing was going to happen to me a few minutes later. As a matter of fact, when I left that store, and before I got back to my newly purchased wretched mobile home, a deputy stopped me and said I had "turned in front of a car without signaling, cutting off the car." It was a complete lie, as a car had been more than a block in front of me and I had definitely signaled before I turned into a store's parking lot. He didn't give me a ticket. This was the first in an endless series of deputy and police harassments that greatly increased after I sent letters to authorities and officials about their harassing intimidating behavior. Retaliation was a big part of law enforcement in both Evansville and Vanderburgh County. Like the woman in the grocery store had said, once you got on their radar they never stopped harassing you. It was some kind of ugly game.

Living in Vanderburgh County was a nightmare that never let up for the six years I lived there. Equal rights and equal justice under the law were missing in that county, as they probably also were in the worst cities and towns that I had avoided for many years. Mean people were just part of the status quo. It seemed that people had no civil rights. Several lawyers agreed with me about this.

For years, since the first week of living there, every time I went someplace as I would drive away or drive back I would expect to see my property damaged somewhere, inside or out. Or my front door wide open, as eventually happened 40 times until I had a deadbolt lock put on the door. I finally gave in to the paranoia that was unwanted but inevitable. Positive thinking was useless.

During the second and third year my home had been broken into 40 times. My front door would be wide open when I would return from wherever I had been. Nothing would be stolen, but things would have been moved. This breaking and entering didn't interest the deputies unless something was stolen. Vandalism was just a part of the culture of Vanderburgh County. They always refused to take fingerprints off the door handle. So I called 911 only a few of those times because I knew they would do nothing. It was better to avoid the deputies if possible.

So how did I stop the breaking and entering, repeated 40 times in three months, since the deputies and Sheriff Department did nothing to stop it? After the 40th time the deputy said the usual "You have no proof" and "Why do you think he does this to you?" As usual, he refused to take fingerprints off the doorknob. Clearly they were always protecting and serving the criminal, the drug dealer, across the street. He must have been giving the deputies drugs or money. That's what everybody would always say to me, whenever I brought it up in conversations. And it was common knowledge for people who lived in the park that deputies were paid-off in exchange for protection.

When the deputy asked me the usual "Why do you think he does this to you?" I answered with my usual response. "Because he's psychotic, a nut-case, and a drug dealer." This time the deputy was nicer than usual. He wrote something down on his notepad. I said "This is what I'm going to do. I'm going to buy a gun at a pawnshop. I'm going to come back here and hide my car. After I hide my car I'm going to come back here and sit and wait. Right there." I pointed to a chair facing the door. "Then, when he walks through that door, I'm going to shoot him in the face."

He looked surprised. He said "You can't do that! That wouldn't be a good idea to do that at all!"

I said "Then you deputies would have your proof. He'll be laying there on the floor. You deputies are always saying there is no proof. Well, there he'll be, laying in front of my door." I pointed to the door, and then to the green marble tiled kitchen floor in front of it. "You'll have your proof. Breaking and entering is against the law here, isn't it? I have to take matters into my own hands because you deputies, the Sheriff's Department, won't do *anything* to help me."

This particular deputy was nicer than the other ones had been because he wasn't the usual antagonistic, belligerent, sarcastic, rude deputy like all the other ones had been. I wondered if this would be an advantage for me or not. I knew some deputy, or someone else with the Sheriff Department, would tell the drug dealer across the street what I had said I'd do to him. I knew they'd warn him, even though for years they wouldn't even tell me his name, or answer any questions about him, or help me in any way, but instead made things difficult for me. Like they got some kind of perverse enjoyment out of it, or it was their standard and taught responses.

From the beginning they had told him my name and that I was the one who had called in the complaints to 911 about his conduct, his actions and words shouted at me while he would be standing in the street or in front of his steps, or on his driveway. Yelling at my home "fat fucking whore" and "fat fucking bitch" over and over again, hundreds of times in those two years, while I would be inside, sometimes looking at him out of the window. He would shout "How do you like your phone lines?" after he had cut them, a Federal crime. Or, "How do you like your door?" after each of the 40 times he had broken in and left it wide open. It seemed like he was always drunk or high on one of the drugs he sold in his little illegal drug business across the street. Or maybe he used both at the same time. Obviously his Disability payments weren't enough to support his habits, his drug and alcohol habits. And his free Medicare paid for all of his health problems that would be caused by those bad habits.

Out of desperation I had to take matters into my own hands. And it worked. Never again was my door unlocked and left wide open, or open at all. To protect him the deputies had obviously told him what I had said I would do to him. So I had changed the dynamics, solved the problem, myself. This was not the way law enforcement was supposed to operate, but it was the way I made it work after years of misery and no help from deputies who got paid to serve and protect. As always, I hoped that soon I would be able to move from this God-forsaken place. But it had become more normal, more like other places in the United States, because of all my many efforts for so long, and because of some changes in the Sheriff Department. I had been an unwilling catalyst for improvement. Life is strange.

One week later the protected white-trash criminal across the street moved from his mobile home, renting it to his cousin, and moved in with one of his girlfriends in the park. After years of huge stress, and monumental effort because of the deputies/Sergeants not co-operating, the neighborhood was mostly peaceful. Even though they were hired and paid to provide help, 99% of the time help was never there from the park management or the owners of the park, or from politicians, authorities, and law enforcement, the deputies and the Sergeants.

Sometimes it seemed like it was a parallel universe that I was living in, of strangely different people than anywhere else in America that I had been to, different than in most of the rest of America. It was the peculiar loud people, the peculiar deputies and police, the peculiar authorities and that were supposed to be pillars of the community, and the peculiar rude white-trash, all so common in that County. And of course the repulsive white-trash drug dealers, who were a drain on society, never contributing anything of value to society. They had no jobs and were supported by Government SSI, Disability, food stamps, welfare, etc., and were supported by the owners of the park, giving them free homes, free electricity and gas, free lot rental, free Cable TV, property taxes paid for, free Sprint Family Plan phone service, and free phone-hacking equipment for their invasion of privacy, against the law and a Federal crime with 2 to 5 years in prison. The deputies were always amused and/or indifferent about it, and the Sheriff obviously never reported it to the FBI like he was supposed to do. Or maybe the deputies and Sergeants never told him about it, like they were supposed to do, so the FBI could investigate it and tell the U.S. Federal Marshalls to make arrests.

Drug dealers got by with breaking the law anytime 24/7. They knew everything their neighbors said on their phones 24/7, like whenever they called 911 about them. The deputies, their friends, were indifferent, always saying "We don't enforce Federal laws", and then usually smiling. This was just one of the many and endless lies of the deputies and Sergeants done to protect the drug dealers, the suppliers, the users and buyers, and the drug bosses, the crime bosses, for those six years, and probably for 15 or 20 years before that. Illegal drugs were their government-supported m.o. Half the people in the park were their repeat customers, according to the deputies. It was a built-in ready-made customer base that the deputies and Sergeants had been ignoring and allowing for many years.

Of course it was very stressful and ugly to live next to and near these drug dealers, besides being an invasion of personal space and an invasion of privacy. Even the weather was stressful with extremes of wind velocity, and frequent tornado warnings with the siren blowing, and too high temperatures and high humidity in the summer, considering that it was so far north. Extreme storms were more common, compared to the rest of the United States. It was the geographical location.

I was stuck in a no-win situation from which I was unable to escape because of circumstances and conditions beyond my control. Like Al Gore said in 2000, "Even if I win, I can't win."

During this same time millions of people in Iraq were trying to escape from American military forces of destruction. The United States military had been destroying where they lived, destroying their social structures, their society, their homes, their businesses and churches, and destroying their livelihood, their means to make money and support themselves. Worse than that was destroying the lives of, killing, at least 500,000 innocent Iraqi people of all ages who were civilians, not soldiers. Innocent men, women, children, and babies. And causing an unknown number, probably millions, of injured and suffering Iraqi civilians, millions of people who had had no way to protect themselves against American soldiers and military forces. These were innocent men and women, old men and old women, and women and children and babies who had no way to protect themselves against the invading and attacking American military forces. In comparison, how could I complain? In comparison, living in any part of America was a luxury.

I was an American, born in America, and had had about 50 years of social conditioning and propaganda telling me that America was the best place to live in the World. I knew it wasn't true, but I knew I had a right to find a better place to live In America. It was my social conditioning. It was my inalienable right as an American, as a citizen of America. It was part of the American Dream.

An article in the Evansville newspaper said that Vanderburgh County law guaranteed that people had "a right to a peaceful environment." However, the do-nothing deputies and the worthless Sheriff Department did not protect and serve like they were supposed to, and refused to provide a peaceful environment. In reality there was no County law about disturbing the peace or excessive noise. Once again the city newspaper was wrong, and a source of ongoing propaganda.

A deputy said to me "That *sounds* good but that's not what happens. We don't have to do that. No one In Vanderburgh County has a right to a peaceful environment." So instead, by doing nothing, the law enforcement supported the perpetrators and encouraged repetition of the problems or crimes. Living in Vanderburgh County was stressful, depressing, and ugly. It was the opposite of the peace, truth, and beauty that I had been searching for in one place, for five years. Was it destiny, karma, or just bad luck that forced me to live in the opposite of what I had been searching for?

Retaliation was a fact of life in that park. You could count on it. As a matter of fact, it was the only thing you could count on. Park management and the park owners couldn't be counted on for anything. They ignored tenant complaints about problem tenants and evicted whoever complained. The many pages of lease rules, the park rules, were never enforced against the problem tenants and the drug dealers living in the park. Never. They were always protected, just like law enforcement protected them and ignored complaints about them. So people usually would not call 911 again. They were afraid to report the crimes and the criminals. It was too much of a risk, too much trouble that would continue for days or months or even years.

After more than a year of no deputy co-operation stopping the drug dealing, the harassment, the trespassing, the threats, the blasting "Boom! Boom! Thud! " on huge speakers from cars and homes anytime 24/7, and the public drunkenness, drunk driving, and other disorderly conduct I took matters into my own hands and got the license plate numbers of 25 cars, vans, SUVs, and pickups that were visiting the drug dealer across the street during just two days. I then called the Drug Enforcement Department at the Sheriff Department and asked for the Supervisor. I told him about the many problems, and gave him those 25 license plate numbers. He was very co-operative.

I said "Make sure something is done about this illegal drug activity. The deputies are public servants and that's their job, but they do nothing. It's so frustrating." I never saw any of those 25 vehicles again. But about two weeks later other vehicles replaced them and the illegal drug store owner was in business again with just as many customers, but with different license plate numbers. Maybe the Drug Enforcement supervisor had told deputies to divert those other vehicles and their occupants to another drug dealer in the park that I wouldn't see. The illegal drug business, after all, was all-pervasive, probably everywhere in America, some places more than others.

When the deputies would drive away the drug dealers would shout at me, again and again, 10 or 20 times, to make sure I heard them, or maybe because they were obsessive-compulsive besides being criminals, drug dealers, and drug addicts. "They believe me! They don't believe you! You fat fuckin' whore! You fat fuckin' bitch!" over and over again. This happened almost every time, no matter what the time of day or night, even if it was 3:00 or 4:00 in the morning. It seems that meth users, drug users, don't sleep much, or have trouble sleeping. They'd always do it again, whatever crime or problem they had done that I had called about before. Repetition, endless repetition, was the way they operated. After all, doing wrong things over and over and over was a part of being a sociopath, a psychopath, a psychotic nut-case, besides being lazy drug dealers with no work, no jobs.

There was a simple solution to this rampant criminal drug dealer activity, problem behavior, and deputy/Sergeant misconduct. All deputies and Sergeants had to do was tell the perpetrators "If you do that again you'll go to jail." Or, "If we have to come back here again we'll arrest you/charge you."

Then leave, walk away and drive away, without cozying up to them, without believing their lies in order to protect them. That would have stopped most of the problems at the beginning, so continued repetition would have been avoided and deputies would never have had to respond to another 911 call, saving a lot of gas and time and stupid repetition with the criminal drug dealers.

Then I would have had a more decent life in Vanderburgh County, like in the 55 other places I had lived in the United States, in 15 states. Instead of dealing with, living with, crime and criminal activity every day, anytime 24/7, for six ugly and oppressive years. It was repeatedly obvious that I, as an individual, meant nothing in the scheme of things in Vanderburgh County, Indiana. The continuance of corruption was much more important than the people that lived there. The continuance of the drug culture, that was dependent on the drug dealers, was much more important than protection and service to the law-abiding people that lived there. It very definitely was a well-established system in that County, where law enforcement allowed drug dealers to break the law.

If the strength of America is its legal system, and so many people are above the law, or can disregard the law, ignoring the law and getting away with it, it is easy to understand that this so-called strength is really a weakness. There has always been, and continues to be, a frightening abuse of the law causing misappropriation of laws and wrongful charges, wrongful imprisonment, wrongful death sentences, and many wrongful executions, combined with allowing crimes to be committed .

Senator Stevens of Alaska is an example of getting away with breaking the law and abuse of power when you are both a seasoned politician and very wealthy. He was charged with seven felonies and was convicted of none. His son, also an elected politician, wasn't so lucky and was convicted of some crime and served prison time because of it. Probably because he was new at politics and wasn't yet a rich politician who was owed favors, or had friends who abuse power and were above the law.

Billions of dollars have been stolen by financial industry CEOs, etc., since 2001, from their clients, from their customers, without any charges, convictions, or prison time. And they never had to pay any of it back. It's the American way. The financial burden for any national fiasco and national monetary loss is always on the lower class and the middle-class, never on the wealthy, the upper-class, the upper 5%, or even the upper 10%. This is not what a democracy is supposed to be like, unless it's a pretend democracy. Instead it's a modified version of a democracy.

The Republicans said thousands of times during the 2000 Presidential campaign that they were going to "restore honor, dignity, and restraint to the White House." However, the Republican Presidential campaign of 2000 was the most corrupt and dishonorable and unrestrained Presidential campaign in the history of the United States. The Presidency of Bush "W" was the most corrupt and dishonorable and unrestrained Presidency in the history of the United States. But it was dignified.

It seemed that I had a contract with destiny or fate or karma that I had to fulfill, or that I had to finish. It was like a never-ending ugly and strange "Twilight Zone" TV episode, or a bad dream that never ended. There were mean and dishonest people everywhere, even at the innocuous city libraries, even at gas stations and grocery stores. No matter how hard I tried, no matter what I did, I couldn't change anything significant about my life. Conditions beyond my control, circumstances I couldn't seem to change, kept me living in a place I hated but couldn't move away from.

My mobile home had been sold to me under false pretenses and deception. I had paid $1500 down and after making five payments of $100 I would get the title for it. Then I was going to sell it for a profit of about $5000 in a much improved condition and leave Indiana and never go back. I was going to leave for good, looking for a place that was good, living near people that were good. That was my humble little plan. But there was no title. It's against the law to sell a mobile home without a title. It's against the law to not give the new owner that title within 60 days. But the owners of the park, who also owned seven other parks in Vanderburgh County, hadn't been doing that for many years, maybe since they had gotten ownership of that park in 1982. Maybe this included all the parks they owned in Vanderburgh County, making them multi-millionaires.

When I questioned the former owner of my home as to why he had lied to me he said "If I had told you the truth about it you wouldn't have bought it from me, would you?" I had said "No, I wouldn't have." He said when he had paid it off two years earlier the park owners had said the usual "There is no title." And "What do you need a title for anyway?" Maybe a few thousand people in 30 years had been told the same thing when they paid off their mobile home, when they had made their last payment for their so-called "rent-to own" mobile homes. Maybe even a hundred thousand people had been cheated, in all of their eight parks and 1,974 homes, in the more than 30 years they had owned those parks. There probably were no records, no paper trails recorded at any government offices, like the county BMV, the Indiana Bureau of Motor Vehicles. Just like for the deputies and Sergeants, if there were no reports, no records, then it never happened. It was all an ugly game.

After getting a lawyer to help me I didn't get the title for another 2 ½ years, even though the County law said 60 days was the legal limit, the legal requirement for transference of a title. It pays to be a millionaire, or a multi-millionaire, in Indiana. Of course it has always been true that the rich and the very rich get treated differently, have special privileges, in the democracy of America. Maybe they have different laws, special laws for them to follow. Or maybe it's just that lawyers and Judges give them special treatment, special privileges, and get pay-offs in return, as a sign of appreciation.

When people bought a mobile home and paid monthly payments for the so-called "rent- to-own" mobile homes and never got titles to them after the last payment, when they wanted to move away they would lose their $1500 to $3000 down payments, and whatever it was worth after they had put costly and expensive improvements into the property as a condition of the purchase contract they had signed years before. Including whatever money, as monthly payments, they would have paid for it to "own" it. Expensive improvements were always a condition of the sale on the sales contracts and guaranteed the park owner would get them back for free in better condition than they had been sold in. This included new skirting at $40 for every three feet, new heating systems, new air conditioning systems, new roofs, new refrigerators and stoves.

Little did they know what was waiting for them in the years ahead. Eventually the park owners would be getting the home back again for free, to sell again for 100% profit, for many thousands of dollars more than they had paid for it years before, and because of the so-called "owners" expensive improvements and repairs made to the mobile home. It was a continuous cycle of ill-gotten money for the park owners and eventual misery for all the people who had trusted them, and the park managers, and bought a home from them, thinking they were going to be improving their lives.

Living in one of their parks would mean they paid too high rent for their lot, and water and sewer charges were twice as expensive as what the Evansville Water Department charged. Yet, it was against the law to make a profit from the sales of water and sewer services. In true capitalistic actions the owners bought the water and sewer services from the Water and Sewer Department and then doubled the charges for their park tenants for more ill-gotten profit. Even though it was against the law for them to make profits selling water and sewer services no one enforced that law.

Millionaires always want more money to add to their millions. Proof that the owners of the park knew the lot rental cost was too high was that the second lot for double-wide mobile homes, in their many parks, was only $15 a month, but the monthly lot rental cost for a single-wide was $205.

The owners of the parks told the mailman condescending things about their tenants like "Only stupid people live in metal boxes." That summarized their attitudes toward the hundreds of thousands of people, the tenants in their parks for 30 years, who had made them rich, first millionaires then multi-millionaires, and able to control the Sheriff, the Police Chief, the County Commissioners, the deputies and Sergeants, and maybe the Mayor.

This kind of scam and theft happens all over the United States. Anywhere in the United States where there are mobile home parks, commonly referred to as "trailer parks", that have mobile homes that can't be moved because there is nowhere to put them. No lots to buy for them, and no park to move them into because they're more than 10 or 15 years old. But white trailer-trash don't want to move their homes away from their trailer parks anyway. Especially when they are living in an environment so supportive and encouraging of their drug habits, with illegal drug stores for them just around the corner or down the street. A place where deputies just look the other way, ignoring drug activities. A place where deputies never saw anything and never heard anything. Where see no evil hear no evil was the deputy m.o., their status quo that could be depended on.

Several deputies had said to me "Half the people in this park use drugs. Why does that bother you?" I would say "That doesn't make it right," and then tell them about the endless harassment and vandalism and trespassing anytime 24/7, thousands of times in six years, that deputies and Sergeants always refused to see, all of which were legitimate and justified reasons for me to be bothered.

Most Americans seem to do the best they can with what they have, with what they've got, just like probably everyone else everywhere else in the World. Life isn't fair, but of course it helps immensely to be a wealthy American, a rich American, a millionaire, or a multi-millionaire in America, to have a better life. Money does matter. It can get you where you want to go. It can get you what you want to have. Money can get you safety and protection that poverty cannot.

Control, power, cronyism, bureaucracy, pay-offs, and insider deals happen everywhere. Was Vanderburgh County just a microcosm of the whole United States, a glimpse of what was yet to come? Or was it a glimpse of what was already in place almost everywhere, almost anywhere in the United States after the year 2000, after the turn of the century?

Eventually I sent letters to 30 authorities, to people in positions of power and influence, who could change things if they wanted to. At the top of each letter I wrote "Please give this to someone who can change these problems if you cannot." Not one of them did, and apparently not one of them did anything to improve the many problems. My letter described the endless problems with the deputies, the Sheriff Department, the County government, the City government, and the owners of the park, as they had affected many other people than me for many years. It certainly wasn't just me.

From experience I knew that I, as an individual, would mean nothing to them. In the United States democracy individuals and their problems mean little or nothing to people in power and authority. I had seen evidence of this repeatedly throughout my life, and I now had proof of this in Vanderburgh County.

I sent a letter to President Obama who, of course, wouldn't read it because he had a staff of letter readers like all other United States Presidents. But I had asked for them to refer it to someone who would help me. The Presidential response was "The Obama administration respects the sovereignty of each state." That was all. No referral to someone else. It was a wasted effort, a dashed hope. I sent a letter, a copy of the same one sent to Obama, to the Vanderburgh County Commissioners, to the Mayor of Evansville, to Indiana Senators and Indiana Congressmen. I got *one response*, from a Senator saying he always enjoyed hearing from his constituents about "how wonderful it is to live in Evansville", and he asked for my vote in the next election. The only response was a wrong response.

But there *were* changes and responses from the Vanderburgh County Sheriff Department, the deputies, the Sergeants, and the Evansville Police Department. In the following months I got bogus traffic tickets and stops, one after the other, based on lies. I had never in my life, in 40 years of driving, gotten a traffic ticket other than a set-up ticket in a small town in Louisiana, a source of easy tourist revenue for that town. So it was retaliation, it was pay-back time, apparently starting at the top with Sergeants, Lieutenants, the Sheriff and Police Chief, filtering down to the deputies and the police.

Apparently at least one of the authorities and people in power that I had written to had contacted the Sheriff Department and the Police Department about my letters, and they wanted retaliation and retribution. Usually when I would be stopped and harassed for something I didn't do, something I hadn't done, they would call one or two back-up cars, lights flashing and swirling for added harassment, as if I was a dangerous criminal, for as long as 30 minutes of detainment. Of course the bogus tickets were expensive and made my insurance rates go up. A Judge had said "I have to believe the deputies and the police. What would it be like to live here if I didn't?"

I then said to the Judge "Well, he was lying. Deputies and police lie all the time. It's ugly to live here, with corrupt law enforcement, with deputies and police and Sergeants that can't be trusted, and who give wrongful tickets that they lie about."

These wrongful tickets were real tickets for false reasons, because of deputy lies and police lies. Like giving me a ticket in a grocery store parking lot for not wearing a seat-belt, when I was taking off the seat-belt after I had parked. The deputy was so nervous his hand was shaking as he wrote the ticket. So I thought he knew he was doing something wrong, but had been told to give me a ticket by his superiors. As had happened before, my demented female drunken neighbor had called 911 to tell them I was driving while drinking, in retaliation for my calling 911 to report her actual drunk driving, her dangerous driving anytime 24/7, that she apparently never got any tickets for anyway because she continued to drive, drunk or not. She'd stand on her porch and shout at me "How did you like the deputy stopping you, you bitch." Obviously the deputies always told her I had called 911 about her drunk driving if they stopped her, setting up retaliation from her to me. For those six years deputies liked to do set-ups for retaliation and retribution from the drug dealers. It was an ugly game.

Each time the establishment in Vanderburgh County had triumphed again because of their lies. Vanderburgh County had law enforcement that was an example of the "hear no evil, see no evil" syndrome. They therefore encouraged the breaking of laws, and problem behavior, bad behavior, unacceptable behavior, and criminal behavior because they, the deputies and Sergeants, would say they didn't see or hear the problems that someone had had the courage to call 911 about. No official deputy records meant no proof, and no proof meant nothing happened. So they were calling the 911 caller a liar, saying the 911 callers were lying to law enforcement, which is a crime that drug dealers committed repeatedly, every time they lied to law enforcement, as they did every time I called 911, about 135 times in six years. It took courage to call 911 because of the retaliation by drug dealers and perpetrators, because of the deputy set-ups and protection of the drug dealers, and because of the sarcastic, antagonistic, belligerent reactions of the deputies and Sergeants. After all, they were the ones with the guns, and the authority to arrest or charge anybody illegally anytime they wanted to. Being rude and sarcastic was their status quo. That's what they called intimidation. They called everything intimidation that was really harassment. Harassment was against the law, intimidation was not.

Law enforcement that was hired to protect and serve the public are then giving special service and special protection to the drug dealers who cause problems and break the law. They provide special support for drug dealers who cause problems, and this encourages them to repeat the problem behavior, to continue it, to escalate it, because they know law enforcement will do nothing to stop them. It has given them approval for whatever problems and crimes they want to engage in. Retaliation, more criminal behavior and actions, and vandalism was then a certainty. And then the do-nothing deputies from the worthless Sheriff Department would do nothing about that. It was a vicious circle, a vicious cycle of ugliness, stress, manipulation, and potential danger for whoever called 911.

In the beginning of the first episode of "Gun Smoke" in 1955 Marshall Dillon stands on Boot Hill looking at the graves and says "People who hate peace, order, justice, make life offensive for other people." That was supposed to be in the early 1800's. It's still true, after the first decade of the 21$^{st}$ century, 200 years later. There are low quality, selfish, and offensive people everywhere in the United States, some places more than others. Money has nothing to do with it. Instead it's attitude, integrity, behavior, language, and character. But big problems happen when it's the government, when it's law enforcement, that doesn't want peace, order, and justice for everyone.

In a democracy people are supposed to be able to change things connected to their government. It's supposed to actually be *their* government. The truth is that the American people can't do much of anything to change their government because it isn't really their government. An example of this is that now, in the 21$^{st}$ century, it doesn't matter who the President is, a Democrat or a Republican.

In 2012 a Republican Senator said at a Senate meeting that it was going to be "necessary to kill a few Democratic Senators" so that a bill would be passed. It was a bad joke based on fact, historical fact. Democratic Senators have died mysteriously, usually in plane crashes that kill everyone else on the plane. A person charged with reckless driving or theft of a CD or possession of marijuana can get eight years in prison, but murdering someone can get as few as five years and out in three with good behavior. These are examples of badly written, poorly written, or stupidly written laws. Injustices can happen anywhere in America, some places more than others. Laws are wrongly written and enforced, good laws are twisted, distorted, or not enforced at all at the discretion of the officer, and the Judge. Injustices can easily occur all the time everywhere in America, known as the nation of laws.

Every year there are at least 15,000 wrongful convictions in the United States, at all levels, for all colors. It is not a white, black, brown thing, despite what the media and black leaders want people to think. In 2012 a black man in Evansville, Indiana said in a newspaper article that he had been a victim of racism and oppression because the jury at his courtroom trial had been all white. The Editor of that newspaper was also black. The victim said "It was against the law." In fact, *he* was racist, because he didn't think white people would judge him fairly.

The fact is, white people may not judge white people fairly, and black people may not judge black people, or white people, fairly. In a court room there are no guarantees for anyone, any color, that anything will be fair, truthful, honest, or right. Proper administration of justice is necessary for good government. But nowhere is there a guarantee that will happen. Not for anyone, no matter what color they are. The Constitution was written to prevent and counteract abuses of power and injustices. But equal justice isn't guaranteed in the United States. American courts exist to give the *chance* for justice, for the chance to get justice in America. It doesn't always happen. There is no guarantee.

Eventually my Small Claims Court appearance against Target happened. Target had a lying phony so-called "witness", a Target employee I had never seen before and certainly had never talked to, as she claimed that I had done right after I was forced to fall onto their large wooden cart used for moving large merchandise. The Target lawyer read one lie after another from a prepared script, including his pre-written responses. Often the sentences had nothing to do with what I had said. The Magistrate, not a Judge, always interrupted everything I said so I couldn't finish the sentence, or my train of thought. It was obviously an attempt to control me and what I said. He had dismissed the court reporter after he had asked me to approach the bench. Therefore, there was going to be no record of the proceedings. So there was something wrong from the beginning.

This didn't seem legal or right. After half an hour of lies from Target, with phony set-up photos at a different location and constant interruptions of whatever I said, I got up and walked to the back of the courtroom by the door. I said "I can't stay here any longer. There's nothing but lies in this courtroom. What happened to truth and justice? It's not in this courtroom." I reached for the door handle. The Magistrate said "If you leave now I can't give you any money."

I said "I don't have any money anyway. Target is a billion dollar corporation. They should have just given me the $6000 dollars I asked for instead of giving thousands to their lawyers, money they know is justifiably mine. That's why there are so many lies. That's why they're not showing the video they have of me falling onto their wooden cart. Lawyers told me Target had a reputation of lying in court and losing their videos. Justice isn't possible in this courtroom. I can't stay here anymore and listen to this fraud." Then I opened the door and left.

The Magistrate had never looked at me as I spoke, always appearing to be reading something when it was my turn to speak, and always interrupting me, usually stopping me from whatever I was saying. But, in obvious contrast, he had always watched the Target representatives when they spoke and *never* interrupted them. I instinctively knew that the only way to get his attention and to say what needed to be said was for me to leave, to get up and walk away.

About a week later I got a notice in the mail that I had won the case. The settlement was 1/10 of the $6000 that I had asked for, the maximum that was allowed in a Small Claims court case in Vanderburgh County. So I got $600, plus the $76 court fee reimbursed. Target had still won $5400 because they didn't have to pay $6000, minus their legal fees. I wrote complaints about the conduct of the lawyer and the Magistrate to their Indiana Boards of Misconduct. Apparently my complaints were dismissed, as I got no responses. This didn't surprise me at all. Special treatment of the rich and influential, of people with authority, is very common in the United States. It is the status quo.

Formerly I had spent about $1000 a year at Targets in the United States. I would never go to a Target again, so Target lost at least $20,000 of my business if I would live for only 20 more years.

They would have been better off paying me the $6000 settlement. It would have been the honest thing to do, especially because my being in Indiana had saved them from a lawsuit because of the three day medical legal stipulation in Indiana. If the injured person didn't go to a Doctor within three days after an accident in Indiana that was proof he or she had no injury.

I still couldn't move from Indiana because I didn't have the title yet for my mobile home so I couldn't sell it. But during the three years I waited to get it the owners of the park sold hundreds of homes with no titles, because they were above the law. Sometimes, during the third year, when I'd drive home from some place eggs would have been thrown at the front of my home and usually onto the front door. They'd be dried and stuck like glue. Eventually eggs would be thrown late at night, after I went to bed, at both my home and my car. It would stick like glue if I didn't wash it off before it dried. Two of these times I saw the drug dealer throwing them. I told him to stop throwing eggs at my home and my car. It was a direct approach to something deputies ignored.

He said "If you don't have a movie of it there's nothing you can do about it." That was like an admission of guilt, so I called 911 to report the vandalism. I knew the deputies would do nothing about his actions, a crime of less damage than any other vandalism I had experienced during the previous three years that the deputies had never done anything about. Eventually it had been more than $1000 worth of damage, for replacements, for repairs. So, as always, the fear would be that the perpetrators would do something worse the next time, encouraged by the complacency and indifference of the deputies and the fact that deputies would believe them, not me. But after that particular 911 call for vandalism something happened, because the egg throwing stopped and didn't happen again. Maybe it was just that there is an end to everything.

The Supreme Court decided in the 2000 election that "counting all votes in Florida would do irreparable harm" to Bush "W", who was the son of the President that had made the majority of them Supreme Court Judges. Most of the Judges were Republican, of course. What happened to equal justice and truth? It was tossed aside, ignored, by the highest level of court and Judges in the United States. If the Supreme Court could do it obviously it happens at all levels of the American legal system, potentially anywhere in America. So after it happened to me, just one person in the more than 300 million expendable masses, how could it matter to anyone else? It didn't, but it mattered to me.

Every year for the week before the Fourth of July firecrackers would explode somewhere in the park at least every five minutes all day and most of the night for the entire week. It was a fire hazard and very noisy, a public nuisance all day every day and night. It was another form of harassment and danger from endlessly self-centered and self-indulgent people, and another incompetence from the park management. Tenants paid for park management but got nothing for their money.

The park management, and the park owners, harassed people whose cats would get outside and walk around on the yards, in the grass that was mostly weeds. They'd say they were going to call Animal Control to pick them up off their owner's porches, or from their decks, or from the front steps of their owners, or from anywhere on their lots, threatening they'd be euthanized, killed as a result. This was obviously what the park owners wanted to happen. Local Animal Control Departments and so-called animal "shelters", even the Humane Society, everywhere in the United States are in the business of killing animals, not really giving them shelter and helping them. This and their wrongful evictions was proof the park management and park owners were bullies, and could never be trusted.

There was the constant possibility the park management or owners would knock at your door, or leave a note on your door, about some false, made-up, or exaggerated complaints that would justify eviction and you would lose your home, your place to live, and be homeless. And then the park owners would get your mobile home back for free with major improvements done. Even if you had a title to it because you bought it from a private party there was no place to move a mobile home if it was more than 10 years old. This was true everywhere in the United States, but in Vanderburgh County it was different because all the larger parks were owned by the same men. So eviction would mean your home couldn't be moved to other parks in the County, even if it was only a year old.

One day before the Fourth of July there were two louder blasts coming from the backyard of the vacant home next to mine. The previous owners had immigrated from Mexico, looking for a better life in America. Within six months of buying that home the cost for further repairs was prohibitive after having spent about $2000 to do the repairs required by the park owners in the contract they had signed to buy it. They had been required to put a down payment of $1500 to be able to move into it. They were barely able to speak English. Then when winter came and the whole heating system had to be replaced they couldn't afford to do it. After that the ceiling in the only bedroom they all stayed in fell down on them one night. The portable electric heater they had bought would only heat one room, and they were afraid to leave their little boy in a separate room with a portable heater. So they went back to Mexico, a better place to live than America, where the winters were too cold and business people were dishonest, liars, and not to be trusted.

The two separate loud blasts sounded like something had blown up. My demented neighbor, the chronic liar and drunk, was standing 10 feet from the yard barn on that lot, staring at it as if she was waiting for something to happen. The sides of the yard barn had been blown out, apparently by two firecrackers. Because of her inevitable retaliation I wasn't sure if I should call 911. I didn't want her to blow up my yard barn or my home.

The deputies, as always, would tell her, or her husband, that I had called 911. They aren't supposed to reveal the 911 callers identity, in order to protect the privacy and safety of whoever called 911. Deputies always talked to whoever I called 911 about first, before they would come to talk to me, the caller, so the neighbors would have figured it out anyway. But if these same neighbors called 911 for false complaints, telling lies and made-up complaints about me, deputies would also go first to them, to talk to them first. The consistently strange support of her wrongful actions and believing her lies gave her confidence to repeat what she had done, sometimes as deputies were just driving away. And confidence to do some other vandalism to my property. Or just confidence to scream stupid obscenities and threats at me from her porch again anytime 24/7. All the drug dealers in the park had these same behaviors and actions and deputy reactions for those six years. It was the status quo.

All of the drug dealers were supported and encouraged by the deputies and Sergeants every time for what turned out to be six years. The do-nothing deputies, their reactions or no reactions, their indifference, rudeness, and meanness to the 911 caller, their consistent sarcasm, belligerence and antagonism, saying they believed him, not me, therefore calling me a liar, was the same again and again for six years. It only ended when the drug dealers moved away from the park. Until they moved away from the park there was no peace. But then within a week other drug dealers would replace them, so any semblance of peace and a normal environment was short-lived and temporary.

It was a system entrenched and established in the park for many years, maybe 20 years people had said. The deputies would cause more problems than they fixed, just like 12 neighbors had told me when I first moved there, saying "Stay away from the deputies. They'll only cause you a lot of trouble." And "If you complain about the drug dealers you'll be evicted." Patterns indicate conspiracies, but heaven only knew what conspiracies these patterns indicated.

On this particular day that neighbor didn't even turn to look at the fire truck when it arrived to put out the fire that she had started, with the explosion of two firecrackers inside the yard barn behind the vacant home next to my home and my yard barn. She was entranced by what she had done, she was mesmerized, never looking away from the yard barn until the firemen were finished and walked away, back to their fire truck. It was her work of art, her creation, her successful crime. Then she walked back to where she lived, as other people that had gathered to watch walked away. She was a criminal at the scene of the crime, watching what she had done, and watching the reactions of other people responding to her masterpiece. I told the firemen what she had done before they left, as they rolled the giant hose back into the fire truck, but they weren't really interested. They told me to call 911.

She said she had lied to get SSI so she could get a new car, and to get money to support her gambling habits at the Evansville downtown riverfront casinos. Her husband's unemployment money was going to soon run out, she had told me when they first moved in next door. She had lied to get a lawsuit settled in her favor that gave her more than $7000.That's how she could pay $7000 cash for a mobile home, after she had purposely injured herself so that she could sue a restaurant where she had worked. A lawyer had helped her get what she wanted. If I had reported her to deputies in this latest crime obviously she wouldn't hesitate to burn my yard barn or my home, with or without me in it.

I was certain of this, as she had been obnoxiously confident and arrogant about her ability to pull off crimes and not be caught when I had first met her and her husband, after she had paid cash for the mobile home next door with her ill-gotten lawsuit settlement money. For the next five years she was right about her ability to break the law and easily get by with it. The deputies were always easily manipulated by her dishonesty and her two-faced demeanor. They *wanted* to believe her stories, her endless lies. Just like for six years they *wanted* to believe the stories and endless lies of the drug dealers living in the park. All of it was a game, an ugly game, with the odds stacked against the good and honest people living in the park, and probably everywhere else in the County, in order to protect the drug dealers, the users, the buyers, the suppliers, the drug bosses, the crime bosses. She wasn't pretty, in fact she was homely, but she knew how to manipulate law enforcement. She was a true representative of what people in the County were often like. She and her husband fit into the culture of the County.

No one can get insurance on their mobile home if it's older than 10 or 15 years. So that was not an option to use as protection against her lunacy, or any of the other lunatics, the other demented people in the park. She knew she could get by with any crime because the deputies and the park managers never stopped her or held her accountable for anything she did. Her demeanor was completely different with them, as she was manipulative and two-faced. She was a mini-version of American business corruption and American political corruption on a national basis.

For about 9 months of every year men and boys would play basketball nearby in the street for about 12 hours day and night. Until about 12:00 at night, at the basketball hoop standing on the driveway of the guy who repeatedly threw eggs at my home and my car. He obviously didn't have a job, but played basketball all day every day and night until 12:00, at midnight. Nearby tenants were forced to listen to the thud thud bouncing of the basketball thousands of times day and night, often with two or three, or even five, basketballs bouncing in tandem as a crowd of players threw their balls at the hoop and then bounced the ball until they could get a chance to throw it again at the hoop. The noise was oppressive and nerve-wracking. It was a public street, but they acted like it was their own personal street. It was disturbing the peace and getting in the way of on-coming traffic, potentially causing accidents, and it was excessive noise after 10:00 at night. Therefore it was disorderly conduct because of the time of night, a nuisance violation according to laws and ordinances for many years.

But this was an ordinance violation never enforced by the deputies. Not once, even though it happened 12:00 to 12:00 every day and night for most of the year for about four years. They'd just drive by the basketball players in the street if any one called 911 about it, often waving hello as they drove by and the players would move out of the way of the deputy car. More civilized places would enforce these excesses as violations, but Vanderburgh County deputies did not. Just like how criminals, drug dealers, and perpetrators were welcomed, encouraged, and supported to commit and then repeat endlessly actions that other places in the United States would consider unacceptable, criminal, or against the law, or against County ordinances.

Deputies accomplished this by doing nothing, by looking the other way, by ignoring it, and by cozying up to the drug dealers with concerned and intently interested reactions to whatever lies they told the deputies about the 911 callers. The drug dealers knew their lies would always be welcomed by the responding deputies, who then would use that dishonest information against the 911 caller. This was the pattern more than a hundred times in six years. It never changed.

For those six years all authorities I contacted at all levels were completely and totally indifferent to all of it, never responding in any way to the letters I sent. My 35 letters in six years got no responses, incited no changes, no improvements, no help from people that were in a position of power to change the endless injustices and criminal activities. A newspaper article in the Evansville city newspaper said that all people who lived in Vanderburgh County had a right to a peaceful environment. Deputies said "That sounds good, but it isn't true. There's no law like that in Vanderburgh County."

It didn't matter anyway if it was a law or not. The deputy and Sergeant m.o., their status quo, was to enforce laws selectively, giving preferential treatment for drug dealers, showing discrimination and prejudice against good law abiding people. Especially if they were single women older than about 25 years old. It was very peculiar and strange, and happened about 100 times to me during six years of non-stop ugliness, unfairness, and injustices, six years of discrimination and prejudices. These were their reactions and their responses that could be counted on. Justice could never be counted on.

Drug dealers and their endless customers would be as noisy as they wanted anytime they wanted, anytime 24/7. Drug dealers and their kids commonly shouted obscenities and threats, commonly shouting "fuck you", "mother fucker", and "fuck it" in every sentence, and often just shouting it into the air, to no one in particular, the stupid and offensive word "fuck", while talking to themselves, or while shouting to other people, to their friends and customers. It was the drug dealer's identifying vernacular, their favorite word, the word that united them. They always got away with breaking laws, and blasting noise and disturbing the peace anytime 24/7. In every way they were undisciplined and above the law. They were always like mean bratty spoiled small children with old faces and old bodies.

My drug dealer neighbor, the Devil drug dealer, had shouted at me about 75 times during the last two years I was there, "I'm gonna' shoot you, you fuckin' bitch", and "I'm gonna' kill you, you fuckin' bitch." And "I'm gonna do things to you you can't possibly imagine! You can't possibly imagine the things I'm gonna do to you!" Deputies would say "There's no law against talking", and then usually smile. And "If we didn't hear him say it then he didn't say it." Case closed. His repeated vandalism of my property was also ignored. They'd say "If we didn't see him do it then he didn't do it." And "If we didn't see it happen then it didn't happen." And "We think you're lying. We think you're making it up. We always believe him. We don't believe you." Or "We never believe you!"

This calling me a liar happened at least 50 times. The drug dealer would always stand close by, listening to the deputies and smiling. He looked like a caricature of the Devil, especially when he smiled.

When people's pet cats walked silently in the yards, that were mostly weeds, the drug dealers would complain to the park management and to the park owners, lying about the cats, like saying the cats were sitting on their cars, or making a lot of noise. The cats never made a lot of noise, they never made any noise at all, and they never sat on their cars. Cats don't go near people that hate them. They stay away from people that shout, repeatedly, "I hate cats/kittens! I'm gonna' kill those fuckin' cats/kittens!" He shouted that at them hundreds of times during that year while they were on my deck, my yard, my driveway. They always lied about the cats or kittens, like they lied about everything else.

Cats, and kittens, make no noise, in *huge* contrast to the large dogs belonging to the drug dealers barking anytime 24/7 that *did* make *a lot* of noise. Cats avoid people who are vicious and cruel, people who are mean and who hate them, and who have huge dogs that bark anytime 24/7. Cats avoid people who are excessively noisy night and day, with a lot of physical activity, and 10 to 20 cars moving around a lot on their driveway, coming and going all day every day, 24/7. Frenetic human activity because of using illegal drugs, and 10 to 30 drug customers every day 24/7, often arguing and yelling, was something cats would avoid going anywhere near. Unlike a dog, who would want to please the disturbed and strange people who visited his loud drug dealer owner.

As a result of this drug-induced drug dealer chaos and lies innocent and silent pet cats would be picked up or trapped by Animal Control and then euthanized. Or trapped or poisoned, or shot with pellet guns, by the drug dealers or the managers and owners of the park. Killed, murdered for doing nothing wrong and bothering no one. It was so stupid and so mean. It was so inhumane and so unfair. It added to the eternal and never-ending ugliness of the city, of the County, of the park I lived in, of the whole continuous and never-ending scenario of ugliness. Many thousands of cats and dogs, people's innocent and helpless pets, were killed every year by Animal Control in Vanderburgh County because they just existed, but no attempt, no effort, was made to stop criminal activities by the drug dealers in the County. After all, they were protected and above the law. They were the special people in Vanderburgh County, the chosen ones, protected by the law, by the deputies, by the Sergeants, by the police, and protected and financially supported by the owners and managers of the parks.

For that entire year the drug dealer's large dogs always barked day and night any time 24/7, and especially after 12:00 at night until 6:00 or 7:00 in the morning. Deputies would just drive by when 911 was called anytime 24/7. Or they'd stop and say that only Animal Control could give citations about barking, and then drive away, often waving to and saying "Hi!" to the drug dealers who had heard the 911 calls about their dogs on their phone-hacking equipment, and would stand outside waiting to see the deputies. Retaliating with vandalism, threats, etc., after the deputies drove away, was common.

Of course the County Animal Control wasn't open between 12:00 a.m. and 7:00 a.m. It was all a part of their big game, an ugly drug dealer game every day anytime 24/7, because they knew they could always get by with breaking any laws. When I told six different deputies and Sergeants about his three missing dogs and his three missing/disappearing girlfriends with their cars sitting for weeks in his driveway, and the drug dealer digging holes with his shovel in the woods, carrying the murdered dogs down the hill in the woods to the creek, or having huge bonfires in 100 degree heat, all of the deputies ignored me, and wrote down no information. Strangely and oddly, all of them were disinterested and said only "If we didn't see him do it he didn't do it." Or, "We don't want to get our shoes dirty." Then they left, drove away. The DDD always got by with everything, including murders, killing, poisoning.

One day a deputy was questioning me about my cats because the drug dealers across the street had complained to 911 that their dogs were forced to bark at my cats whenever they saw my cats walking or sitting on my wooden deck, or on my grass/weeds, or on my cement driveway. The drug dealers complained to the owners of the park, to the park manager, and to the deputies about this stupid lie. They said that my cats should be euthanized, picked up by Animal Control because their stupid dogs barked night and day, mostly barking at the air, not at my cats or anybody else's cats. The park lease said no dogs were to be left outside, but the drug dealers never followed park rules.

I said to the deputy "So their dogs bark at my cats, and my cats are supposed to be killed, trapped and picked up by Animal Control because the drug dealer's dogs bark at them. Their dogs bark at me every time they see me, when I'm on my deck, on my porch, or when I'm walking to my car or back from my car, or mowing my lawn, or walking up or down my steps. So *I'm* supposed to be killed because the drug dealer's dogs always bark at *me* every day and every night?"

The deputy smiled. "They say your cats are on their yards."

I said to him "They are lying, as usual. There is no leash law in the County for cats, outside of Evansville, but there is a nuisance ordinance against dogs barking for hours day and night, and a park rule prohibiting it. Nobody else in the park lets their dogs do that, and nobody else is allowed to keep their dogs in a pen except the drug dealers. Deputies never do anything to stop the dogs of the drug dealers barking. They just drive by. The loud barking is a problem all day every day, especially from 12:00 at night to 6:00 in the morning. Of course Animal Control can't stop it because they're not open."

The deputy smiled and said the usual "If they don't answer their door there is nothing we can do about it. Or if we don't hear it there is nothing we can do about it." Mission accomplished.

I said "Whenever I call 911 about it they hear me because they have been hacking into my phone conversations for almost a year, since they moved in next to me. That means they always are forewarned and stop what's been called about. So they put their dogs inside."

The deputy said the same thing other deputies said. "If we didn't hear it happen then it didn't happen. If we didn't see it happen then it didn't happen."

So here was another deputy calling me a liar. Again, about 60 times totally and eventually, with about 60 deputies and Sergeants. The Federal crime of phone-tapping was of no interest to any of them ever. They always ignored whatever I said about the ongoing problem of my phone being tapped 24/7, for two years, and the theft of half of my phone minutes stolen every month. It was proof of my legitimacy and the truth of my complaints, and proof about the endless problems with drug dealers that I called 911 about. God forbid that my honesty and truth should be proven and see the light of day, escaping from the fog and dishonesty of law enforcement in Vanderburgh County.

Whenever I dialed a number it would say on the screen of my cell phone "Three-way conversation", besides the incessant beeping and poor connections, especially on calls to 911. The Bill of Rights and The Constitution guaranteeing privacy and freedoms meant  nothing to the drug dealers and the deputies, the Sergeants, Senators, Congressmen, and all the other authorities and officials I had told about it or written to about it. This is the reality of our democracy in America.

It was one of their own private deputy jokes. And the incessant loud barking, as always, was allowed to continue as they drove away, and after they left. Or the drug dealer's large dogs would be put outside again in their too small and animal-abusive pens, where they would resume their stupid and incessant barking. Drug dealers taught their dogs to bark. They wanted their dogs to bark. It was music to their ears, along with their blasting CD bass noise, Boom! Boom!, anytime 24/7.

Obviously they took drugs themselves, not just selling drugs all day every day 24/7. Their kids were undisciplined, their dogs were undisciplined, and the drug dealers were the most undisciplined of all, besides being completely and totally selfish and self-serving, mean and peculiar.

Usually the drug dealers would come outside after deputies left and shout obscenities, and laugh and shout about how they were above the law. Forever and always, they were above the law. They were the privileged ones, and they certainly knew it, and wanted everybody to know it.

The incessant noise from as many as 8 basketballs bouncing at one time from the unemployed lazy drug dealers was combined with 10 to 15 hollering and shouting male voices, their drug customers, playing basketball with them for 12 hours a day. It was so stupid, so selfish and self-centered, so typically self-indulgent. It was all supported by the government who supported them, including when they bought and used and sold illegal drugs. It was better than committing crimes, but the excessive, noisy, and disturbing nature of it made it seem like a crime, especially at night until after 12:00. It's what the criminals did every day and every night, even during rainstorms and when it snowed. It was drug-induced enthusiasm, excessiveness, and stupidity every day and night, 24/7.

Like being forced to listen to blasting excessively loud stupid CD bass noise on three foot speakers anytime 24/7 seemed like a crime, and was in fact a crime in more civilized places in the United States. This is what they did when they weren't playing basketball. Excessive noise 24/7 from CD players, with the bass noise blasting throughout the park, was a necessity to the drug dealers living in the park. They craved it. They were noise addicts, not just drug addicts.

The park rule saying people who were a "nuisance and troublemakers would be evicted from the park" was never enforced for drug dealers. Never. They were always safe. For all park rules and Vanderburgh County laws enforcement was reserved for lies made up about good law-abiding people.

What had mattered to the deputies and to the park management and to the park owners for 20 to 25 years was protecting and serving the perpetrators, the drug dealers who caused the problems, who could do no wrong and were protected no matter what they did wrong. This was discrimination, prejudice, and unequal treatment  by the deputies, the Sergeants, and the owners and managers of the park against anyone who reported the drug dealers and the drug dealer activities. It was a very odd and peculiar place to live, with very odd, mean, and peculiar sociopath psychopath psychotic drug dealers.

The tenants who couldn't stand it anymore were then pushed out, being forced to move away and lose their down-payment of $1500 to $3000, that had been paid to own their home that they would have never owned anyway, because they would be wrongly evicted or there would be no title giving them legal ownership after they made their last payment. All people connected with all of this corruption were above the law. They were special.

Six months to a year seemed to be the norm, before moving away from the ugly noise, the repeated harassment 24/7, the vandalism of their property, the endless trespassing. That was part of the reason drug dealers had lived there for free, with free electricity and gas, free lot rental, free cable TV, yearly property taxes paid for, free lawyers when they needed them, free Sprint Family Plan phone and computer service. It had been like this for 20 or 25 years before I ever got there, people had told me, with no let-up, no end to it ever. It was encouraged by Sergeants and deputies, and always had been for those many years. The phone-hacking equipment was the new addition to their drug dealer and drug deputy/Sergeant repertoire since after 2008, that meant drug dealers heard *all* 911 calls.

It was that way the first day I had lived there, after moving into my wretched greatly-in-need-of-repair home amidst the trepidation, fear and despair, and the futility of living next to, and near, drug dealers who were above the law and protected by the owners and managers of the park, and by law enforcement, by deputies and Sergeants. In what eventually became six years I made 911 calls about 135 times, a tiny fraction of the actual times law enforcement was needed but would be indifferent and apathetic, making deputies and Sergeants and drug dealers always above the law. It was the entrenched drug culture, the established drug system in the County involving many thousands of people, maybe half a million people in 20 years.

The government connection was the Sheriff, a very good friend of the owners of the park, who people said had put him into office. Elections are easily rigged. That was an explanation for the very sophisticated phone-tapping, the phone-hacking done by the worthless low-life drug dealers, as protégé's of the owners of the park. It always pays to have friends in high places. That also explained why deputies and Sergeants said 50 times in 2014 and 2015 that they didn't enforce Federal laws.

So from the beginning I was determined to change the injustice s that I was going to be forced to live with until I could get away, escaping from the ugliness and injustices of Vanderburgh County. But from the beginning until the last day I was living there the only thing I could count on was injustices.

Other tenants in the park didn't report bad behavior, or problem behavior, or criminal activities because they didn't want to get involved, and because of their apathy and fear. If people complained to park management about the drug dealers, or their progeny or girlfriends and boyfriends, they would be evicted immediately. An eviction usually meant they couldn't rent or buy another place to live at after losing their home, after losing their previous investments in their home, and losing their security of owning a home, all because of an unjustified eviction because they complained about neighbors who were drug dealers or complained about the park. In stark contrast drug dealers could complain anytime and everyday about their neighbors, making up problems, lying , because they were bored, or wanted to create more chaos when they weren't dealing drugs. After all, lying was their status quo.

When I had been in Louisiana in 2008, staying with my friend Henry, the homes for sale in Vanderburgh County shown on internet websites had looked like unusually good buys, but in person they were in very bad shape. Like on the back of the house, or the sides of it, or on the inside of the house. Or they were in bad and decaying neighborhoods. How did the camera make them look so good? It was like the rest of Vanderburgh County. It wasn't what it seemed from a distance when you got up close and personal. Things were often different than what they seemed. When I asked a realtor about this, about how wretched the homes were in person, he said "But they photograph well!"

For four years when deputies or police would see me driving my old blue 1989 Grand Marquis they would stop me for false and made-up reasons, eventually totaling 11 times. My car was easy to notice, having been hit and badly dented after being totaled in Winnemuca, Nevada, by a woman talking on her cell phone while she was driving, with no auto insurance. Her tiny baby was thrown onto the floor because her mother had laid her on the front seat before she crashed into the side of my car while speeding.  Yet, she got no traffic tickets, no citations at all from the Winnemuca police.

But now, years later, the Vanderburgh County, Indiana deputies and police would stop me, often making illegal u-turns to get to me, then making false charges against me. Usually they wouldn't give me any ticket but this harassment, with false stops and false charges, and sometimes even bogus tickets, should have been against the law. But in Vanderburgh County police and deputies had their own laws and regulations, demonstrating both discrimination and prejudice.

I couldn't do anything to change that, or even improve it. Forces far greater than me liked the corruption. For about four years my demented woman alcoholic neighbor was repeatedly calling 911 and making false charges against me, such as "She's driving drunk",  or "She's drinking and driving". Ordinarily, making false charges, lying, to law enforcement is a crime, but the deputies in the County and the police in Evansville wanted her to do that. They wanted reasons to harass me, and to be notified as to when I would leave the park, driving away in my car, ready to be harassed by law enforcement because I had repeatedly reported the drug dealers living in the park. And because I had written to the FBI and to the Justice Department about the repeated misconduct of law enforcement in the County. Again and again for six years it was apparent, it was obvious, that the owners of the park owned the Chief of Police and owned the Vanderburgh County Sheriff, not just the County Commissioners, not just their eight mobile home parks in the County. My lawyer had said "They own *at least* eight parks in the County."

Weeks after I sent letters to authorities and politicians about the endless problems that could be fixed but instead had been going on for possibly 30 years, an employee at the BMV told me that the park manager had brought in more than a hundred mobile home titles at one time to be transferred legally to the owners of the park. So at least 100 people would then hopefully be given titles to their homes when they paid them off, instead of being told "There is no title. What do you need a title for anyway?" The tide was turning a little bit towards what was legal.

Maybe I had been a catalyst for good, for improvement, for many people who really did own their homes in the park, for things being put right even if the titles were years overdue. There would be no legal punishment or fines because the park owners were millionaires, multi- millionaires, so they were special and above the law, and they "owned" the authorities. But this would probably also be true in most of the rest of America. Wealthy people commonly get special privileges in America. They have their own social laws, regulations, and agendas. They are, or easily can be, above the law.

Eventually, after five years, most of the disgusting and deplorable men and women moved away. That act of attrition is what eventually made that part of Vanderburgh County a more normal place to live in, but for only a few weeks. Not the do-nothing deputies or the worthless Sheriff Department, or the prejudiced park management and very prejudiced and discrimination-oriented park owners. Not any of the 30 politicians and authorities who were in positions to change things, to stop things that needed to be stopped, or to just improve things, ever responded to my letters or phone calls, or changed anything. They were all in bed with each other.

There were no improvements anywhere, so their dishonest agendas continued indefinitely. Even the Prosecuting Attorney of Vanderburgh County did not respond, as his job requires him to do, to the two five page complaint forms I filled out in his office six months apart, meaning he was prejudiced and discriminatory to me because it said on the form all complaint forms were responded to within ten days. It never happened, not either time. And then there was no one anywhere that would address this obvious repeated government discrimination by an agent of the government, the Prosecuting Attorney, that was done to protect his agendas or the agendas of his government and/or non-government bosses. As always, everything is for sale.

But life goes on. I needed some assistance with formatting my book for an agent, so I called a local internet networking business and asked "What services do you provide?"

The man said angrily "What the hell services do you want?" At first I was surprised, but then I remembered where I lived. He epitomized the attitude of everyone, including politicians and authorities, in Vanderburgh County, Indiana. When in Rome, do as the Romans do.

Every year that I lived there Vectren Utilities charged me two to three times more for electricity and gas service than any of the many other places I had lived in the prior five years. Besides that greed every year they would charge me two and three times for the same energy usage, overcharging me hundreds of extra dollars each year. The only way to get a refund each year was to send a complaint to the Indiana Attorney General. Complaining to Vectren was a waste of effort, even though the numbers for the meter readings on the monthly statements were proof of their theft. I had thought of moving to Cincinnati, Ohio as they had good buys on homes for sale and it's a nice city, much nicer than Evansville, Indiana, but I decided not to when I found out Vectren was the provider of utilities there. No thanks, it wasn't worth it.

In case you don't think the United States Government and the United States military are duplicitous here are two cases in point to prove it. For eight years torture of Iraqi citizens, hundreds of thousands of men in Iraq, was classified as and called "Discomfiture Tactics", and Geneva Convention rules did not apply because the men were called "enemy combatants", not the usual prisoners of war. Hundreds of thousands of men were imprisoned for what they *might* know, not what they *did* know. Everyone and everything in America can easily be dishonest and duplicitous.

In 2012, days before Indiana Governor Daniels announced he was going to become the next President of Purdue University instead of running as a Republican Presidential candidate or for Indiana Governor again, he announced he had found more than a *billion dollars* laying around somewhere. What had he been planning to do with it secretively, on the side, that he wouldn't need as President of Purdue? One can only wonder. It was a huge budget surplus and disappearance that, oddly, no one had noticed, none of his staff of hundreds of people.

So, in the next year, 2013, Indiana taxpayers would get an extra $100 added to their tax refunds. Was it just a political ploy to help get Republican votes in the upcoming elections in November 2012? How come Daniels, a Far Right Republican, hadn't noticed the missing *billion dollars* in the months, or years, before when he was the Governor? How many other millions of dollars or billions of dollars were missing in his years as Governor that were never "found"? Or were never noticed, or never accounted for, or the public was never told about? These questions would never be answered. The truth would be hidden forever.

This was a very negative reflection on the Daniels Administration that feasibly had been happening for years, and would happen in the future, in other political administrations. Not just with Governors but with all political offices including both Republicans and Democrats, everywhere in the United States, at all levels, in the same way. All the incompetence, dishonesty, fraud, and endlessly stupid and mean problems I encountered almost every day for six years in Vanderburgh County, Indiana could easily become the norm for everywhere else in the United States, if it isn't already.

Although I paid for the title for my car being transferred to Indiana from another state I never got the copy of that Indiana title for five years. Was it incompetence, indifference, or stupidity?

Indiana is one of the few states that charges for automobile taxes every year, not every two years as most other states, and it charges twice as much each year as those states that charge only once every *two* years. Yet, when I moved there in 2008 the streets and roads in Vanderburgh County were in very bad condition compared to most other cities and counties I had been to in 45 other states. Fortunately they were much improved in Vanderburgh County and some of Evansville after 2010. Finally, after too many years. So where had all the tax money been going to for those many years? Who got it, and why? As usual, as always, no one knows for sure except whoever got it.

Indiana is one of a few states that has yearly taxes for mobile homes on rented lots in mobile home parks. They say it's just 1% but you end up paying 3% to 5% after the other fees and other taxes are added on. This is another additional tax you end up paying if you live in Indiana instead of most other states. Do all the additional taxes and add-on fees make it a better place to live? Absolutely not.

For four years every necessary repairman was an exercise in futility and frustration. An air conditioning man was going to charge $155 for just 30 minutes of his time and putting in a few screws. Another air conditioning man turned out to be a roofing man instead, as it said in big letters on his truck. He had no tools for, or knowledge of, air conditioning. A so-called handyman from an ad in the newspaper was going to fix a hole in the insulation under my home. Later I found out he had just taped a piece of cardboard over it and charged me $35 for that. Ten minutes after he left it fell off, and he refused to return and fix it when I called and told him about it as he was driving away to his next job, to possibly his next victim.

Incompetent repairmen are everywhere in America but I had never encountered it all the time, every time I needed one, again and again for years. They would sometimes say they would come back and fix it, but they never did. So I thought maybe the secret to success was to call one from the yellow pages that was a well- known name of someone in business for many years. So I did that instead of finding one in the newspaper. However, then that man came out in a truck that had no tools on it. The truck was completely empty, and therefore he had to rent what he needed to unclog my kitchen drain. He charged me $125 for the rental cost for tools, for his drive-time back and forth, and for his inflated gas costs, besides his actual work time of about twenty minutes. A week later the kitchen drain was plugged again. I called him about it and he said he wouldn't fix it again, unless I paid the same charge of $125 again.

"So you don't guarantee your work?" I said. I couldn't seem to win with any repair man.

He said "I could tell you didn't like me, so I don't want to fix it again."

"Of course I didn't like you. You charged me twice as much as you should have," I said.

The next time I asked an acquaintance to recommend a repairman for the problem I had. He gave me the name of someone he had used before and called me back the next day to see if it had worked out. I told him the guy was too busy and couldn't come out for a few days so I had called someone else. He said that because he had gone out of his way to help me I owed him and should have sex with him. I told him he hadn't helped me at all. So he shouted a bunch of profanities and hung up. I never heard from him again. Case closed.

On Christmas Eve, an hour before her clinic was going to close, a veterinarian charged me $175 for unnecessary blood tests for my 14 year old cat and gave him an injection, a drug that had another drug in it that I had told her he was allergic to and to be sure she did not give him. She was condescending and didn't think I knew what I was talking about so she had ignored me. By that time it was just before they closed on Christmas Eve night. They were therefore closed the next few days for the Christmas holiday. His allergic reaction began before we got home, about half an hour later.

He couldn't swallow, he had trouble breathing, and he was in a lot of pain and confusion about what was happening to him. He was having an allergic reaction to the drug I told her not to give him.

The arrogant veterinarian had done nothing to help him, but she had caused him a lot of misery and suffering for that night and for the next five days until he died. I had fed him liquid food with an eyedropper, and given him water with an eyedropper, for the next five days. The receptionist had returned my call about his severe reactions to the drug injection *two* days after it had begun, but the arrogant veterinarian never called back, *never* returned my call of desperation about Boo Boo, my beloved cat. It was the second day after Christmas. The receptionist said they had the results of his blood tests that showed nothing was wrong with him. But there was something *very* wrong with him because of the wrong injection. After five days of extreme suffering he died a very painful death.

I had brought him to the wrong veterinarian, and I felt terrible about that decision and about his subsequent death. But his age had made that more likely, as a 14 year old cat is equivalent to a 98 year old human being. Incompetence and meanness in Evansville and Vanderburgh County had caused me endless problems, and now they had caused the death of my beloved cat.

About a month later another vet took x-rays of my five year old cat from Nevada, said he probably had cancer, and said he needed an MRI that would cost at least $1000 to find where the cancer was. And then at least another $2000 to try to deal with that cancer in the following weeks and months. If I had been in any other country the MRI for my cat wouldn't have cost more than $150, and the cancer treatment would have cost no more than $200. Medical treatments for animals, for pets, are cost-prohibitive in the United States, just like they are cost-prohibitive for humans.

He said it maybe wouldn't work anyway. He charged me $150, and he had done nothing to help my suffering cat, my dying cat, when he was in a lot of pain and could hardly breathe. It was the Friday of a holiday weekend again, so no vets were open on Saturday and Sunday, and not open on the actual holiday on Monday. He suffered a lot, so I brought him to the Humane Society and asked them to help him because no veterinarians were open because of the holiday weekend. They said they didn't do that, they didn't have a vet to help him, despite the fact I got monthly requests from them for donations to pay for "very expensive veterinarian costs to help animals desperately in need of help." So it was just another lie in an endless stream of lies that never ended in Evansville, in Vanderburgh County, Indiana for both people and their animals, their pets.

The supervisor said "I know what I'll do." She took him into a room and her assistant brought out the empty pet carrier a few minutes later. She had euthanized him. I was stunned, as she brought me a release form to sign for him, for disposal of his body. She said "You did the right thing. Now he's at peace." He had been an exceptional cat, a wonderful cat, and I felt terrible for having brought him there, and would never know if a different veterinarian could have saved him had I brought him weeks or months earlier to a different vet, and if it hadn't been a long holiday weekend, again. My very loved cat, who had been devoted to me and was counting on me to do the right thing, had died a miserable and painful death. I had failed him and was very sad to lose him. There definitely was a void in my life, and despair, after the death of my two loving cats, both deaths happening within about a month, and both deaths directly related to the incompetence of veterinarians.

Every year a mother tortoiseshell cat would bring her kittens to my home when they were six or seven or eight weeks old. She would stay for about three or four weeks, watching out for them, nursing them , and just generally taking care of her babies, and then she would leave, not coming back for six months to a year. For two of these years the kittens were very pretty and seemed healthy but suddenly died after about two or three weeks. I researched about this and found out there are many different viruses that kittens can contract that will kill them, sometimes within 24 hours. In fact, there are so many viruses they haven't even all been named.

The third year her kittens were bigger when she brought them to me and they didn't die within four weeks. As usual I had put in an ad, hoping to find them good homes. As usual, 90% of the calls were from, or seemed to be from, men and women who wanted kittens to use for illegal dog fights or to sell them for research. Each year I'd get about twenty calls from people like that. Often when I'd ask the usual "Are you planning to use them or sell them for dog fights or research?" they'd laugh and hang up. Or if they talked about it a little I'd tell them to call back the next day to come and see them, and that person would never call back. After I told the newspaper about this ongoing repeated problem the newspaper tried to help by adding "Free to good home" onto their "Free kittens" ads in the "Pets" section of the want ads. I appreciated the gesture, especially because it seemed to help.

I called the National Humane Society 1-800 number and told them they should put a free ad in that same paper in Vanderburgh County and monitor who called in such a way as to track down who was connected to the illegal dog fights, and to find out where the dog fights were taking place, and who was taking free kittens and using them, murdering them, at those illegal dog fights in Indiana. I knew from vast experience that if something is illegal in Indiana that doesn't mean anything will be done about stopping it. Illegal dog fights were definitely run by and attended by white-trash men and women. Maybe that was why nothing was done to stop that hideous form of pleasure for white-trash men and white-trash women in Indiana. The do-nothing deputies always seemed to be working for corruption, protecting corruption and crime. It never ceased to be strange, and wrong.

One afternoon three boys rode their bicycles down the street to the creek with their fishing poles to fish in the horribly polluted and toxic water, the stream that was always dark brown and dead, or otherwise completely dry, so it couldn't possibly have had any fish in it. A baby robin was in the street, trying to fly and jumping up and down, as his parents flew around him, trying to protect him and encouraging him to try to fly. The oldest boy, about twelve, rode his bicycle past the baby bird, circled back and rode over the baby bird, crushing it, killing it. He laughed, and circled back again and rode over it again. The parent birds were frantic, flying up and down around their baby that was now dead. The two other boys, younger, about eight years old, rode over to see what the older boy had done. The older boy was looking at the dead baby bird, crushed and bleeding, and said "It's dead." The two other boys took turns riding over the body of the lifeless baby robin.

It was unbelievable. It was beyond horrible. It was the epitome of the Vanderburgh County mentality and inherent meanness. It was white-trash at its worst, like so much of Vanderburgh County. These were the future men of Indiana, the future bad and awful men of Indiana. After all, adults are often just old-looking kids. Too often they are still like undisciplined and mean bratty kids, old kids that look like adults. I couldn't tell the boy's parents about his unbelievably demented and cruel behavior because I had no idea where he lived, and I never saw him again. Probably his parents were just like him anyway, and my talking to them would have changed nothing. Besides that, there was always the very real reality of retaliation and retribution from these low quality people. Sociopaths, psychopaths, and psychotics lived all around me for those six years.

Sometimes during those six years in Indiana I thought about how if I was living in Minnesota again, where I had lived for 25 years, none of these ugly things would have happened. Not in Minneapolis, not in St. Paul, not anywhere in Minnesota because the people there were better, more civilized, more kind, and smarter, as national test comparisons, national test results, and national polls had shown for many years, since the early 1960's.

White-trash, black-trash, brown-trash, yellow -trash, all trashy people of all ages and all colors, usually align themselves with viciousness, meanness, and stupidity. It's what unifies them, and unfortunately justifies for them, in their twisted and demented minds, whatever it is they do that is ugly and wrong to people that are good and kind, and to helpless innocent animals.

Law enforcement rarely, if ever, enforced justice for their victims in Vanderburgh County. At least 100 times they would laugh and be friendly to the perpetrators about the laws they broke, but never enforce laws and ordinances against their actions. In direct contrast, deputies and Sergeants got a perverse sort of pleasure out of believing the endless and never-ending lies of the perpetrators, the drug dealers, about their victims and then turning it all around so that the victims became the perpetrators. It was all an ugly deputy/drug dealer game repeated at least a hundred times in those six years that I lived in that God-forsaken nightmare environment in Indiana.

About 50 times in that last year deputies and Sergeants had said "We believe them/him. We don't believe you. We think you're lying. We think you're making it up." There wasn't anything I could do about it. I couldn't do anything about their endless injustices. There literally was no one anywhere that would help. They could change things, but they didn't. That was the reality.

Hypocrisy and duplicity, lying and stealing, misinformation and disinformation, unscrupulous actions, apathy and indifference, vulgarity and vulgar people, greed and corruption, deceit and deception, and crabby, sarcastic, and rude people can be found anywhere in America. Not to forget the usual selfishness, meanness, dishonesty, and self-centeredness so common to humanity in general. It was all there, in all its tainted glory, in Vanderburgh County, Indiana.

But finding one of the worst places to live in was no consolation for not finding one of the best, or the best, place to live in America, my original goal. I had never been looking for the worst, or one of the worst. But that's where destiny had landed me and strangely, oddly, kept me there for six years due to circumstances beyond my control.

Oddly, strangely, it often seemed that people in Vanderburgh County Indiana didn't have a conscience. At all social and cultural levels, the highest to the lowest, there was a common void of conscience and consideration, and often an unwillingness or inability to respond to the problems and concerns of other people, of other living things. In general, people there did not react or respond to problems as presented, preferring to ignore them and pretend problems and injustices were not there. It was a variation of the "hear no evil, see no evil" syndrome, not just the indifference and apathy common throughout most of America. There are always exceptions to everything, of course, but, in general, this was the way it was. Maybe that's why the deputies were the way they were.

As I had been typing the last three pages of my other book, "American Expose", that had formerly been named "American Sins, American Glory", onto a flash drive at the downtown Central Library computers the whole manuscript disappeared. Except for the cover that someone had done for me that mistakenly said on it "a *novel* by …." Some things in it were true and some things were fiction and I hadn't decided if that made it a novel, so I had told her to take off the word "novel", but she refused to co-operate. Some grey-colored words and many numbers and many letters, hundreds of them, flashed across the screen over the page I was typing and then the entire book, the entire manuscript, disappeared. It was gone, permanently gone. A week later a library technician told me Homeland Security had stolen it because of the title, that a library employee had reported it to them.

The word "America" was a red-flag word for the Neo Con agendas after 9/11 in 2001. After almost three years of daily effort my entire manuscript disappeared, was completely gone in a few seconds. I had written it to make money with it. I had planned to do a back-up copy when I finished those last three pages. Agents and publishers don't accept hard-copy manuscripts since about 2001. I had a book agent and a publisher waiting for the flash drive to be e-mailed to them. This theft by the Government was unbelievably mean and unfair. It shouldn't have happened in a democracy.

Homeland Security, and any other Government agency, would find the contents of my book useless, and would have to manipulate the contents of it for their own purposes, whatever that was. An unknown number of writers and journalists in the United States had experienced that and disappeared, or were fired, or were accused of doing things they didn't do, since after 2001. They were imprisoned without probable cause, without charges, and without legal representation for indefinite lengths of time, sometimes in solitary confinement. All of it was insane, insanity in a democracy. That is what I was afraid of. It caused some insecurity and anxiety.

The national Government computer spying network, Federal Government computers spying on hundreds of millions of computers that had billions of entries every day 24/7, was experienced myself up close and personal in 2010. After three more years of writing a non-fiction book, this book, I started to rewrite that book that was stolen, using the third draft instead of the final version that was stolen, and decided at last it really would be a fictionalized account of things I had experienced during my life that other people would find funny and sad, or just interesting. So that meant it was mostly fiction, but not really a novel after all. So it was a non-fiction novel.

It's ridiculous to have to fear your own Government in a democracy, like it's ridiculous to have to fear the unjust and mean actions of deputies and police in a democracy. Often they don't serve and protect, just like the government often doesn't serve and protect the people it represents and who pay their salaries and who elected them.

I did some investigating on the computer, and into my account at Yahoo, and found out Homeland Security and people named "Newman", "Turkey", and "Roger" had been hacking into my e-mail account repeatedly. Then Yahoo sent a message to my account saying someone had been hacking into it. After that my entire yahoo account was frozen, then it all disappeared. My 57,800 e-mails, 99.9% of it being advertising, was gone. I was able to determine that the only part that had been saved onto somebody else's computer were my personal e-mails I had sent and received, like to my daughter and to my friends. There was nothing of any interest to anyone on any of those that had been saved and transferred to someone else's computer. It was an invasion of my privacy, and theft.

But a violation of my Constitutional right to privacy was just the norm in Vanderburgh County. Months later an undercover Homeland Security woman confronted me at a neighborhood library. Obviously someone at the library had notified them I was there, and was using one of their library computers. It wasn't just a coincidence. At first she pretended to be someone else, something else, other than what she was. Having nothing to hide and seeing through her demeanor I handed her the page to my book that I had just typed on the computer so she could read it. I answered her questions and told her I knew she was from Homeland Security.

She told me the reason my manuscript on a flash drive was taken, really stolen, was because of the people I wrote about, who I wrote about in Vanderburgh County, and what I had said about them, about the experiences I actually had with them. They were important people and I was not. What happened to equality and equal rights in America? What happened to free speech and freedom of expression? What happened to liberty and justice for all, the rights of all people living in America?

They all began secretly disappearing during the Presidential elections of 2000, then disappearing as a result of Bush "W" and Cheney, and their Neo Con Administration for eight years, and the Neo Con's Patriot Act of 2001, signed into perpetuation by Obama on December 31, 2011. The loss of freedoms in America has been the collaboration of both Republicans and Democrats in power, both elected and not- elected, since the chaos of the elections in 2001.

Computer technicians at the Central Library worked with my now-empty flash drive to see what they could retrieve of my book. One said "This is the best I can do." There it was on the screen, all on one page, pieces of it, all scrambled and highlighted, words capitalized and italicized, all words running together. It was a mess that I couldn't possibly fix. Government computers had isolated red-letter words and ideas and destroyed the rest of the manuscript on the flash drive.

After five peculiar and miserable years living in Vanderburgh County, Indiana my right shoulder, neck, arm, and hand still hurt constantly from that fall at Target five years before. If I had been able to leave Indiana at the beginning, right after I fell, and gone north to Canada I would have gotten *superior* healthcare immediately, free Universal Healthcare available to everyone in Canada without having to be a legal resident, that would have alleviated the constant pain I lived with those five years because of non- existent healthcare, or inferior but very expensive healthcare, in Indiana.

They always made mistakes, thus they were inferior. I would have been able then, as a result of immediate and ongoing competent physician help, to have gotten a lawyer to represent me so I could have gotten much more money than the measly $600 dollars as a small claims settlement, instead of being in Indiana that said I had no lawsuit because I wasn't able to see a physician within an unreasonable three days after an accident.

Because crime in most of Canada is practically non-existent compared to the United States, and because Canadians, in general, are more polite and nicer people, I am sure I would have been able then to live in a much better, less crime-ridden, place with better quality people. Because I had been to cities in east, west, and southern Canada there was no question, no doubt in my mind at all, that life would have been much better had I been living in Canada instead of Indiana. I thought the most desirable cities to live in in Canada were Victoria, Winnepeg, and Quebec.

People in Canada were like people in Minnesota, meaning better people, more intelligent, more civilized, better quality character. The cost for becoming a citizen in Canada was $6000. If I had gotten an honest settlement from Target at that small claims court fiasco, the maximum of $6000 that was allowed in Vanderburgh County, it could feasibly have paid for that.

After four years the neighbors from Hell next door sold their home. They sold it to a drug dealer, with well-established clientele, with an already thriving illegal drug business in the park. He was extremely loud and noisy anytime 24/7, with CD bass turned way too loud, and when he was talking to the 10 to 20 people that would visit him 24/7. He would talk very loudly about everything, including how the father and son who owned that park and all the other parks in the County didn't dare to charge him for monthly lot rental where he lived, or he would tell their secrets to authorities. He was loudly boastful about it. He, like all the drug dealers, got free electricity and gas, free lot rental, a free home, free cable TV, and free Sprint Family Plan phone and computer service, yearly property taxes paid, and a free lawyer when needed. They gave all the drug dealers free phone hacking equipment to tap into any phone they wanted to, while hearing those conversations on their special cell phones.

He was the Devil drug dealer, very much protected, served, and supported by deputies, Sergeants, Lieutenants, and the owners of the park and the park managers. He managed to manipulate all of them with his endless lies. Starting from the first day and night he lived there I called 911 about his excessively loud CD bass noise anytime 24/7 on large three foot speakers. And about his four foot air compressor and electric power saw and drill on his front porch that he left turned on from 1:00 to 4:00 in the morning, and about his shouting obscenities and threats at me anytime 24/7. Worst of all, the first week he lived there he poisoned my two eight week old kittens that were perfect in every way, and their mother and father, also wonderful and special cats. He was the lowest of the low. Human garbage.

Days after he moved in next door he sprinkled poison on my lawn in front of me, while smiling like a crazy man. Then he said loudly while standing behind my car, "Your God damn fuckin' cats were so loud, they made so much noise, I poisoned 'em." All the while smiling his crazy-man smile. They were indoor cats and he had poisoned them when they were outside on my deck. It would have been easy to do, just mixing poison into some food that they would innocently eat, not knowing that he was a horrible human being, a piece of human garbage that was murdering them, trusting and helpless and loving little kittens and cats. They brought beauty and love and affection and joy into the World and he, the Devil drug dealer, brought misery, pain, suffering, and death to my trusting pets and to me. I was a victim of circumstances beyond my control, and my beloved cats and kittens were victims of circumstances beyond my control, but not out of my control. An unknown number of people he sold drugs to, thousands every year, were also his victims, but they were willing and happy victims if they never had bad reactions to those drugs.

When I called 911 about him murdering my cats the responding deputies said "We didn't see him do it, so he didn't do it." And "We didn't hear him say it, so he didn't say it." Case closed.

I said "If he killed me, if he shoots me like he has threatened to do repeatedly, you wouldn't do anything to him would you?"

The deputy smiled and said "Not unless we had piles of evidence." Then they left, drove away.

The deputies loved him. He was the darling of the deputies. His lunatic harassments anytime 24/7 were allowed by the deputies, and by the government that supported him by giving him monthly SSI payments every month for 12 years because of some stitches on his head after falling off the back of a truck when he was drunk when he was 18. Deputies always gave him support and protection, lying for him, which then encouraged him to continue and repeat his deplorable criminal behavior towards me.

It was also done to make me give up, to stop calling 911 about him, to move away, because of the futility and struggle with the deputies and Sergeants who refused to do what they were supposed to do. They'd say to me "Don't you think you should move?" Or "Why don't you just move your home to someplace else? You own it don't you?" The cost for that would have been several thousand dollars, and there was nowhere to put it because it was more than 10 years old.

They would always lie for him, being deceptive and deceitful for his benefit, always making excuses for him and his behavior. They didn't care that he was a menace to society, a malicious menace causing malicious harassment, legally labeled "a malicious nuisance". They didn't care that he was a drug dealer, established as a drug dealer in the park for 10 years, because the deputies and Sergeants allowed it, encouraged it, and "didn't see it". The owners of the park and the managers didn't ever enforce park rules about "nuisance and troublemaker" tenants being evicted when the drug dealers were the daily and nightly nuisance and troublemakers. But tenants who complained about them were evicted. Equal justice did not exist in the park. It never had. Instead it was tyranny.

Making too loud noise with or without malicious intent anytime 24/7 was harassment, repeated thousands of times during that year. Shouting threats to shoot me, to kill me, and "I'm gonna' do things to you you can't possibly imagine" a few hundred times anytime 24/7 during that oppressive two years was disorderly conduct and harassment. Deputies insisted it was "intimidation", that wasn't against the law. Not harassment, which was against the law. They were always there to protect him. The only official report deputies ever made, as a result of my more than 100 calls to 911 and my more than 80 requests for them to make an official report, was just one official report on record saying all of it was "intimidation". Once or twice would qualify as intimidation, but 75 times and 1000 times was "harassment". Each of those times was a crime he knew the deputies would do nothing about.

They never wanted to hear the truth from me. But they always believed his lies, and would always tell me they thought I was "making up" whatever I said he had done. Rude personalities were common in Vanderburgh County, all ages, all social status. Being rude was the status quo, the normal behavior, so the deputies merely represented the norm, what was normal for that location, for that city, for that county, maybe even for that state, unlike most other places in America.

I called 911 every day or night about these problems for the first 90 days, starting with the day he moved in next door. Ten deputies had told me to "Keep calling us, and maybe we'll catch him doing it again." But eventually the bad deputies, by far the majority of "the Sheriff's men", said I had been making "false complaints about him." They told me there were no records of deputies ever seeing or hearing whatever I called 911 about. Not one report was ever made for those 90 days and nights, despite the fact I had asked 43 deputies to make a report and they said they would. So after 90 days deputies and Sergeants told me I would be charged with "making false complaints" if I called 911 about him again, including about his repeated anytime 24/7 threats shouted at me that he was going to shoot me. "I'm gonna kill you, you fuckin' bitch!" And "I'm gonna shoot you, you fuckin' bitch!"

He had poisoned my four cats, the good-natured mother cat and the adoring and protective father cat, and their two beautiful and especially smart orange and white kittens, causing them to die excruciating and agonizingly painful deaths on my deck, on my porch. In order to poison them he had to be trespassing again onto my yard, onto my deck, as the cats never went off of my deck. I had left them alone to answer my phone inside for only about 15 minutes. I had asked deputies repeatedly to tell him to stay off of my yard, to stay away from my lot and my car, to stop the trespassing he did anytime 24/7, starting on day one and never ending until I could eventually sell my home and move away. I had done everything I could do to stop his crimes, but the deputies had done nothing.

For years people responding to my "for sale" ad in the newspaper would say things like "We don't want to live in a place like this, with all that noise and drug dealer stuff going on" when they came to see it. And "We don't want to live in Methbrook", when I told them where it was located when they called. The park had a bad reputation that was known throughout the County.

I had to tell the truth, to answer their questions with honesty. After all, it was the dishonesty and lies of the guy I bought it from that had gotten me into this mess in the first place, a nightmare that took six years for me to get out of, to get away from. He had said "If I would have told you the truth about the problems in the park, and about all the things that were really wrong with this trailer, and that I had no title, you wouldn't have bought it."

He was right of course. It had been a typical "buyer beware" situation. So I adapted. I just didn't answer their questions about where I lived. I didn't lie, I just would change the subject. I put a "for sale" sign on the front window and hoped, instead of running expensive newspaper ads with futile ad response conversations. After more than five years of stupid anytime 24/7 struggles with drug dealers and mean people, etc., that was the only way I was able to escape from the endless nightmare of where I lived. Besides eventually selling my home for half of what it was worth, just so I could get away from Vanderburgh County and all the problems it represented.

From the beginning deputies always thought whatever he did was funny or cute. Or clever and smart. Always laughing with him about his endless false stories and lies about me, or his endless stupid and mean lies about my cats. They were always very friendly to him, very courteous and polite, patting him on the back, or squeezing his arm, talking loudly and in a very friendly manner to their friend the drug dealer from Hell that had been dealing drugs in the park, while living in other homes in the park, for about eight years. Their friendships with him spanned as much as those eight years, and I was a woman older than 25 who never bought drugs from any of the resident drug dealers in the park. The odds were stacked against me from the beginning, and never changed. Deputies "serving and protecting" people was selective and prejudiced in Vanderburgh County.

A policeman I had talked to in Evansville about the obvious discrimination, incompetency, and meanness of the Sheriff's deputies and Sergeants had said "We don't like them either," and smiled.

The deputies obviously knew him well and liked him a lot, at least 50 deputies making two visits during that ugly two years that I called 911 more than 150 times. Only four of those times, from two of the same responding deputies, did I get any help at all, an honest concern and attempt to do some actual deputy/police work. About eight years earlier almost all of the Vanderburgh County Sheriff Department deputies had been fired after ongoing and thorough outside investigations about their conduct, misconduct, etc. Their replacements had been initiated with the drug dealer from Hell at about the same time he was beginning his tenure as a drug dealer in the park. Their mutual friendships and assistance to serve him and protect him had been going on for those eight years, as they all "grew up" together, the deputies, the Sergeants, and their friend the drug dealer from Hell.

About two months after he had moved next door to me he had let the air out of my tires. They were flat when I got up in the morning, and then, a few days later, he slashed my back tires with a knife, meaning I had to buy new tires. On that particular morning he had shouted at me while he stood on his drug partner's yard as I drove away "I don't think you're gonna' get where you're going!"

The tow truck for that slashed tires incident had caused me a lot of misery and pain that lasted for about a year because of an accident resulting in 10 stitches in my elbow, with two inches of the blacktop parking lot sewn permanently into my elbow, and a severe blow to my head, a form of subdural hematoma. It had been raining and the tow truck steps were wet, besides being two feet apart. My foot slipped off the slanting top step, causing me to fall backward onto the blacktop parking lot. After getting the new tires put on I spent five hours in an Urgent Care getting incompetent and very painful service, causing medical problems that lasted for years. It was like 19th century medicine, not 21st century medicine, even though the facility was only a year old. The façade, the new and expensive outside of the facility, did not represent the incompetence that went on inside.

Eight hours later, when I drove into my driveway in the dark, the Devil drug dealer living next door, the Satan incarnate, was standing on his front lawn like he was waiting for me, staring at me as I got out of my car, while I hurt a lot all over. It was visible evidence for him that his criminal activity had reaped added and unexpected benefits for him, beyond his planned crime of slashing my tires.

When the tire guy had spread apart the knife cut it was very smooth and straight and shiny black, not like the outside of the tire. New $100 tires had replaced the tires he had slashed with a knife. Like other criminals he liked to admire, to look at, the damage he had done, the crimes he had committed and gotten away with, and to see how the victims reacted. The Sergeant I had talked to at the clinic when I was done there, about his slashing my tires, must have called him and told him I had left the Urgent Care place. Or he told a deputy and the deputy drove there to tell his friend the drug dealer, or called him. After I got out of my car and went inside my home the Devil drug dealer went over to my car and shined a light on the new replacement tires, trespassing again, to admire his crime.

I was charged $2800 for their many mistakes and a lot of unnecessary misery at the Urgent Care Clinic. They had given me nothing, not even an aspirin costing them a penny, for my extreme and extensive unrelenting pain during the five hours I had been there, and only used an inferior anesthetic, the topical Lidocaine, for the 10 stitches on my elbow. Despite the fact I repeatedly asked for something better, a different and better anesthetic. The Doctor left two inches of black tar from the parking lot stitched permanently into my elbow, that of course I couldn't see as he was doing the damage because it was, after all, on my elbow.

I had told them several times the pain was worse because I had Lupus and RSD, Reflexive Sympathetic Dystrophy, from previous injuries years earlier, but the physician was absolutely indifferent to me and never acknowledged what I said. He ignored me, except to say several times "You're too old to act like that about pain." Their Hippocratic Oath, "Physician do no harm", meant nothing to him.

For about 60 days and nights the drug dealer next door had been forcing me to listen to his endless too loud CD bass noise anytime 24/7, and his electrical power saw, his power drill, and air compressor from 1:00 to 5:00 in the morning, besides his repeated vandalism of my car and the tires, letting the air out, slashing the tires, breaking the valve stems, and pounding shiny new nails into the new tires. I told deputies he was trying to kill me with my own car, by doing things to my tires. They were indifferent, and smiled. They did everything they could do to help him succeed.

No matter what he did he was the darling of the deputies and, according to them, because they never heard him or saw him do any of this they said he didn't do it. It was always the same. "If we didn't see him do it he didn't do it." And "If we didn't see it happen it didn't happen." So they were calling me a liar, eventually more than 100 times in those ugly and very noisy crime-dominated and drug dealer-dominated two years. This wasn't supposed to be happening in America.

Often they'd say to him loudly "Don't worry! We *never* pay attention to her anyway. She's just a stupid old lady!" Or, "She's just a crazy old lady. We never pay any attention to *her*!", then laughing and smiling at him. They usually thought it was funny, a joke, whatever he would do to me, to my car, to my house, to my cats. Or to the wild animals that lived in the woods five feet away from his home. The fact that he had killed them, poisoned them, was a big joke to some of the deputies. The drug dealer from Hell slashing my tires with a knife, and then me subsequently falling off the tow truck steps and getting 10 stitches on my elbow, was a big joke that they shared amongst each other with the Devil drug dealer, laughing with him about it, and always laughing at me. Or they would be rude, sarcastic, belligerent, and antagonistic to me. Or say to him "How've you been? We haven't seen you in a long time. We've been worried about you." And "We're glad to see you got out of prison. Did they treat you right?"

After months of living with deplorable conduct, with the endless deceit and deception and lying, I gave up. I couldn't continue their stupid ugly mean game. The deputies and the Devil drug dealer, not to forget the park owners and management, had won their never-ending game to push me out, to force me to move away, to give them all an unhindered base of operations for their drug dealing and other nefarious criminal conduct, so they could continue breaking park rules anytime 24/7 without interference from me. To get rid of someone, me, who repeatedly let authorities know about their deplorable and unjust conduct, their criminal behavior. Apparently *I* was the problem for them.

Evidently to authorities I had contacted in Indiana I was the problem, because I didn't conform, because I reported problems to authorities who were supposed to help but never did. The government employees, the Sheriff Department, the deputies, Sergeants and Lieutenants who perpetuated problems and allowed them to continue weren't the problem. Either were the authorities, the officials, or the County Commissioners and politicians who fostered it, perpetuated it, ignored it, and therefore encouraged it. Drug dealers and their drug buyers and users, their customers, could have easily been stopped by deputies and Sergeants, apprehended, charged and convicted many thousands of times during those six long and ugly years, but they weren't because the whole illegal drug system wanted the illegal drug culture to continue indefinitely. They allowed it to happen, saying they never saw it or heard it. It was always the see no evil hear no evil syndrome, repeated for six ugly years of stupid problems.

That is a big part of why the drug system everywhere in the United States continues, why it isn't stopped, and will continue indefinitely. Too many people in too many places are making too much money for it to be stopped. The illegal drug culture in America is here to stay, involving many millions of people who want it to continue. For better or for worse, for the rich and for the poor.

Maybe that was why I, as just one individual, was ignored by authorities who could easily have stopped all of it. In the scheme of things I meant nothing. I wasn't a part of their system.

I couldn't fight it anymore, I couldn't struggle anymore, to have a decent place to live. So I put an ad in the local newspaper again to sell my home. I hadn't been able to fix these endless and many problems before I sold it to someone else. As a result, they would probably have the same ugly endless problems with the drug dealers, the deputies, the park owners and the management. People living in the park paid for management but got none. I had to get out as soon as possible, away from southern Indiana. Almost anywhere and everywhere in America was a better place to live.

The day after the Devil drug dealer and his belongings had been moved into his free home by the park maintenance men, from another place in the park, the two owners of the park had come to see their favorite drug dealer. People said he had just gotten out of prison, and his old drug dealer job in the park was waiting for him because he had protected the owners of the park and gone to prison without incriminating them. But nobody knew for sure. They had given him $3000 to buy the home from the unwilling owners who wanted $7000, not $3000. They were one of the few lucky ones living in the park who actually did have a title, having bought it from a person who had been the original owner when the home was moved into the park years before. So, unlike most tenants, they legally owned their home.

As the park owners stood on his porch they said to him "Bother her as much as you can. Disturb her as much as you can. Harass her as much as possible. Make as much noise as possible to force her out." That was to be his special assignment, his special mission, besides being a drug dealer in the park again for the ready-made and waiting clientele, the more than 100 tenants in the park, who knew him from before and had bought from him for years before.

About 50 of them showed up at his front door the first two days he was there, walking over to his new old home. Some would ask "How come you moved over here? Didn't you like where you were?" And "Do you like it better here?" He'd usually say "They gave me the money so I bought it."

For the next 14 months he never let up on trying to fulfill his special mission, obviously because he enjoyed it so much and it was so much his true character. It wasn't a role or a part that he was playing. It was just being his natural demented sociopath psychopath psychotic self that he was getting paid for by the owners of the park, to "bother her", "disturb her", "make as much noise as possible." He was very happy, truly in his element, walking around smiling all the time, anytime 24/7.

He had shouted at me about 50 times on 50 days "I'm gonna' do things to you you can't possibly imagine! You can't possibly imagine the things I'm gonna' do to you!", then always smiling his crazy-man smile. About 80 times he ran at my car as I was backing it up into the public street from my driveway, shouting "Get off of *my* street you fuckin' bitch! I'm gonna have you arrested! Mother-fucker! I'm gonna have you evicted!", shouting that at me again and again as I would then drive away from the lunatic drug dealer running next to my car. Deputies always said they didn't believe me.

For many years deputies and Sergeants had discriminated against neighbors of drug dealers by doing nothing to stop the endless problems, criminal behavior and criminal activities. And by telling 911 callers they were "lying" or "making it up", and by taking up to 1½ hours to respond to 911 calls. And by never making official reports about the 911 calls, and then by lying in the few official reports they did make. They *never* did any actual deputy/police work about the drug dealer problems. Not once.

This long-established pattern protected the drug dealers, the suppliers, the users and buyers, and the drug bosses, the crime bosses. It explained why illegal drugs were a huge permanent industry in America, involving many millions more people than in any other country in the World. The only way to end the endless corruption and crime, the endless social problems, was to legalize the illegal drugs. Then the illegal drug industry would come to a screeching halt. But that will never happen. The endless drug corruption is here to stay. Too many people at all levels are making too much money for it to be legalized. It had been intensified and popularized to high-definition in the 21$^{st}$ century.

The slide into decadence is easy. Sometimes exposing it to the light of day makes it shrivel and die. Thus a truthful media and truthful honest journalists have always served a useful and necessary purpose. Now, in the 21st century, they are becoming increasingly a thing of the past. The official news is created and controlled by the powers that be, by the military, and by the government everywhere at all levels. More than ever before corruption at all levels everywhere is allowed to flourish.

Above the entrance door to the Supreme Court Building in Washington, D.C. it says, in huge letters, "Equal Justice Under The Law", like it was a guaranteed right for all Americans. But it rarely happens. Instead injustice, tainted justice, is often the norm. Even though injustices happen on all levels of society the illusion of justice for all prevails. Americans seem to think it's guaranteed, that they can count on it, until they too are victims of the delusion. The American Democracy seems to be built and maintained on illusions and delusions that touch all facets of life. For most Americans.

An example of this is that about five million Americans are currently diagnosed as being clinically depressed. Physicians give them prescriptions for legal drugs to give them the delusions of being able to control or eliminate the problems. These legal drugs have the potential for making the depressed person suicidal, for making the depression worse, and for causing many negative side effects to their general health. Most suicides in the military are caused by the legal drugs they are prescribed for post-traumatic stress syndrome and depression. More deaths among soldiers have been a result of suicide than by military action and enemy combat since the wars in Iraq and Afghanistan began in 2003.

Another example is that all businesses and government offices at all levels can easily be "cooking the books", changing numbers and facts to accommodate and justify corruption, deceit, deception, dishonesty, theft, and greed. Anyone who goes public about any of this is commonly set-up for retaliation and revenge, or they are fired from their jobs. It's the American way.

One of the endless examples of this was how the New Orleans levees were poorly designed, poorly built, incorrectly designed, incorrectly built, or not built at all, leaving gaping holes and no continuity of protection in the many miles of levees. For many years nobody said anything about it, apparently because they didn't want to lose their easy well-paid jobs, with great government benefits on the side. In 2005, after an inexcusable more than 45 years of building them and never getting them finished, the New Orleans levees were still incomplete, with gaping 50' to 100'open spaces. Despite having spent and invested hundreds of millions of dollars of Government money to build the levees there were still huge holes and huge unfinished spaces in the poorly built levees before Hurricane Katrina made landfall in August, 2005. Those were the facts, not reported by the media.

The responsibilities and the faults for this man-made disaster were the highly paid and heavily compensated Engineers working for the Corps of Engineers from the beginning, and the United States Government that did not oversee them, and the United States Congress that did not monitor the appalling lack of progress for each of those more than 45 years. The fault for the levees breaking was not Hurricane Katrina, but rather United States Government-related mistakes and incompetence, especially by the Corps of Engineers. It was a man-made disaster just waiting to happen. Every year the New Orleans newspaper headlines would ask "Is This The Year The Levees Will Break?" But the truth always was that they were *already* broken, or hadn't even *ever* been totally and completely built.

Despite the responsibility of the United States Government for the disasters that followed Hurricane Katrina the Federal Government didn't help *any* of the 500,000 people in New Orleans, and the surrounding parishes, that were victims of these Government mistakes and incompetence. Not even by just providing the basics of food and water for the many thousands of victims left homeless. And never giving financial help or actual services to rebuild, repair, and replace their homes that had been destroyed and left them displaced and homeless. This involved at least 300,000 homes and residences in both Louisiana and Mississippi, and at least a million victims, who were mostly homeless people.

These were the same problems at the same time for hurricane victims on the Mississippi coast who were left displaced and homeless, also with no food and water for weeks before being helped by church groups from the northeastern part of the United States, who traveled there to rebuild and repair homes because the owners had no flood insurance. Hurricane insurance yes, but flood insurance no. And because their Government, the United States Government, wasn't helping victims in Louisiana and Mississippi in any way. The Federal Government was doing nothing for the million victims so, unbelievably, the first rescuers were the Canadian Mounties who came to their rescue in whatever limited ways they could. Other countries, like the President of Chile Hugo Chavez, offered to send food and water and other help, including money, but Bush "W" refused to accept any of it. The United States image of being "the rescuer" was already tarnished, and now it was falling apart. The reality was, the truth was, the United States Government didn't rescue its own people, a million hurricane victims.

People everywhere said the United States cared more about helping foreign people and foreign governments than helping Americans. Bush "W" said there was no money to help them because all United States Government money had been spent in Iraq, for killing people in Iraq and destroying their homes and their society, their businesses and their infra-structure, under the cover of allegedly killing terrorists for the war on terrorism. There was a disturbing parallel here for anyone who cared to look for it, for anyone who paid attention and wasn't allowing themselves to be manipulated by the words of the officials of the Federal Government. But the cover this time was Hurricane Katrina. It was the fall-guy for the United States Government to say it was a "natural disaster", meaning they had no responsibility for what happened to the levees and it was out of their control.

Philanthropic groups in the United States, that get hundreds of millions of dollars of free grant money from the U.S. Government as taxpayer's money every year, were strangely and noticeably silent and absent, nowhere to be seen. The first responders to help the victims in New Orleans were the Canadian Mounties from Vancouver, Canada, 3000 miles away. They said they "took the ferries" to get there, as both the New Orleans airport and highways were broken and closed. There were as many white victims as black victims of injustices that should never have happened, but the media centered on black victims. The Government, their Government, did nothing to help any of them, white or black. And the infamous Homeland Security was a miserable failure in every way.

But at that same time there were **billions of dollars** of Government money available to give to Blackwater, a subsidiary of Vice President Cheney's Halliburton. They were paid $250,000 every day by the United States Government, from 2005 to 2008, as contractual payments for Blackwater's alleged and dubious and non-existent reconstruction and rebuilding services in New Orleans after Hurricane Katrina. None of the actual hurricane and levee victims benefitted in any way from the *many billions of dollars* given to Blackwater by the United States Government.

This was similar and paralleled what was happening, or not happening, with Blackwater and the United States Government in Iraq at the same time. Both of them were man-made government-made disasters. None of the victims, the expendable masses in either scenario, in either location, ever benefitted in anyway. The **hundreds of billions of dollars** given to private contractors was more than wasteful spending. It was theft, under the auspices and protection of the United States Government.

Another **$8 billion dollars** of Federal Government money just "disappeared" and was never accounted for during that same time period. Of course somebody somewhere got it, so it was really stolen. That same wasted and stolen money could have been used to rebuild, repair, and replace homes for all of the million Americans left homeless and displaced after Hurricane Katina. And used as disaster relief to clean up, rebuild, reconstruct, and restore business properties and downtown areas along the coast of Louisiana and Mississippi, including New Orleans. Instead private contractors, etc., got very rich, and became multi-millionaires because of the grief and suffering and death of at least a million people, because of the failure of the Federal Government to do what it has always supposed to have been doing, protecting the people, protecting Americans in America.

More than 200 other levees and dams throughout America are supposed to have dangerous and deadly flaws, disasters that will eventually happen. People in America expect their Federal Government to help them and protect them. Since after World War II the United States has had an international reputation of being the rescuer of people in foreign countries after natural disasters and after wars with the United States, with the U.S. military usually occupying those countries for years. American generosity, trillions of dollars given to other countries and their people, has been world renowned for more than half a century. But that was done by the American Government, not by the American people.

A democracy without justice, that encourages what is wrong to continue, that ignores injustices, is not a true democracy. This kind of democracy needs to get rid of people that inform the public about the truth. It is dangerous for one person, alone, to try to get rid of injustices when a democracy is disappearing. It is dangerous for groups of people to organize to try and get rid of injustices in the American democracy of the 21st century. But this is not really new. It began to be dangerous in the latter part of the 20th century, starting in the 1960's.

In 2013 a woman who had lived for years in the park knew that a man living across the street from her was selling drugs, a drug dealer. She talked to her neighbors about it. They were all afraid of the drug dealer and of the deputies so none of them had ever called 911 about his nefarious illegal home-based business. She was fed-up with the whole problem and called 911 to see what would happen.

The two responding deputies told her they needed proof. She was told "If you buy some drugs from him we'll have the proof we need." She was surprised the deputies were so nice, so she helped them get the proof they needed. She walked across the street, knocked on the door, and bought some drugs from the drug dealer. When she walked back across the street to her home and showed the drugs to the deputies they arrested her for possession of drugs. They drove her away in their Sheriff's car, to jail. That was just more of the endless deputy and Sergeant deceit, deception, dishonesty, and lies. The 911 caller, the innocent woman who was trying to do her duty as a citizen in the democracy of America, who was trying to do the right thing, was another victim of the legal system, the law enforcement system, the justice system. A victim of the tyranny of the illegal drug system in Vanderburgh County.

The first week I had lived there people living in the park had said to me "You moved into the drug end of the park. Don't complain about the drug dealers or you will be evicted." And "Stay away from the deputies, or they'll make a lot of trouble for you." And "The deputies can't be trusted." They had been exactly right. Without the encouragement, complicity, support, and protection of the deputies there would have been no drug dealers, no drug system continuing endlessly and without interruption, if they had been doing their jobs right, what they had been hired to do, what they were paid to do.

The deputies and Sergeants were a necessary part of the equation to not stop it, like they were supposed to do. Like deputies and Sergeants in other places in America did. Some of the drug dealers eventually moved their illegal drug stores to another location in the park, to a different home, to continue their flourishing 24/7 businesses so I wouldn't call 911 about them anymore, or write to politicians and authorities again, who may or may not bother their drug bosses.

The 10 to 15 drug dealers were constant nuisances and troublemakers that park rules said would be evicted, but people who complained to park management or park owners about them would be evicted instead, being told *they* were the troublemakers and the nuisance. Half the park was empty, so half the homes were vacant most of the time, for the traditional revolving door of mobile home trailer park sales and minimum $1500 down-payments. It was a racket and a fraud, just like the drug system in the park was a racket and a fraud. The 10 to 15 drug dealers, the low-life scum, were the kingpins of the drug system. Without them nothing would happen, no money would be made, so they broke park rules 24/7 and broke laws 24/7, and nothing ever happened to them. They were always safe.

The drug dealers knew they were always safe, no matter what they did wrong. No matter what crimes they committed they would always be given special protection by the deputies, the Sergeants, the Sheriff, the police, the Chief of Police, making them all accessories to crimes. Like the two Sheriffs not reporting the phone-hacking to the FBI for 2 ½ years. It was a special world they lived in, a haven from harm and accountability and responsibility, a drug system Heaven of corruption. They all had a cozy relationship, involving thousands of people, including at least 100 law enforcement men. It was no-law enforcement that had allowed the drug system to continue for about 25 years.

People would say "It's like that in *all* the parks, isn't it?" And, "It's been that way for *many* years." The drug system was a tradition in the County, and would continue for many more years. Drug dealers and drug bosses and drug users, their customers, were a permanent part of the culture in the County. People knew they couldn't do anything about it, about stopping it, so they didn't even try. They lived in a drug culture democracy, in the 21st century.

People would say "Isn't it like that everywhere in America?" Maybe yes, maybe no. No one can possibly know the actual true extent of the illegal criminal world of illegal drug corruption in the United States now, in the 21st century. Lies yes, but not the truth.

It seemed that no one wanted to live in what people called Methbrook. At least that was what people who had responded to my "for sale" ad had told me, a reason why I hadn't been able to sell my home and escape. Besides the fact that I wasn't selling it on time payments like the park did. I had to have cash for the total amount as I was going to move to another state. Any state would be better than Indiana, any County would be better than Vanderburgh County. Whoever moved into my home, whoever bought it from me, would be forced out by the DDD, who had shouted from the first day he lived there that the drug-end of the park was going to belong to him, that he was going to force out everybody who lived in that end of the park. So I had to have the total paid in cash, no-time-payments.

In America people have to fit in and go with the flow, not rock the boat, not tell the truth about what they experience or what they know, or they, and possibly their families, will suffer the consequences. Retaliation, retribution, set-up "accidents", loss of jobs, set-up suicides, murders, assassinations, disappearances, evictions from homes, vandalism, hacking phones, or harassments done to make them move to a different location. Or theft of manuscripts off of computers, off of flash drives.

But this is not what happens in a true democracy. This is not what America is supposed to be like.

Cable TV news, especially FOX News and CNN News, and the biggest newspapers have been bought-off and paid-off by politicians and by the very wealthy, by the elite in America, by the rulers of America, beginning with Bush "W" in 2001, who paid-off newspapers with at least a billion dollars in order to control what they printed.

They have all helped in creating this apathy and dumbing of America, the planned dumbing of Americans in the 21st century, planned and carried out by the Neo Cons in power in America after 2000.

Was it destiny, karma from a past life, or just bad luck that never ended for six years for me? I will never know. That's what life is. Never knowing, no explanations, no mysteries of life and death ever solved or explained, or answered. No answers, just guesses.

But one truth of life glaringly stood out. It is necessary do what is right, to do what is good. If something isn't good and right then don't do it at all. If only people in Vanderburgh County knew that and did that life would have been a thousand times better for those what-turned-out-to-be more than six years living in Vanderburgh County, in Indiana.

If only the entire population of the United States, and all the levels of American government everywhere, and all of the people who rule America, both elected and unelected, if only they all knew that simple truth and followed that simple but important concept America would truly be a force for good in the 21st century. But they don't. People just do not operate on that principle.

People at all levels everywhere have to look out for themselves and that means they can justify anything, any behavior, any words, any actions, any dishonesty and lies. That's life.

So what is special in America? The National Parks have long been a special part of America, unique to America, but since 2001 Republican politicians haven't thought they were worth preserving and taking care of. Instead they drastically reduced yearly funding to National Parks for their operation and maintenance. As a result, continuance of the National Parks as they have always been cannot be counted on. Since 2001, when Bush "W" was President, some of the parks have been being slowly destroyed while depleting their natural resources for profit. For Republicans, in general, everything comes down to money, to making money, to greed and power and control. And ego.

Because the National Park system has been purposefully and drastically underfunded by the U.S. Government since 2001 this has resulted in a deficit of *$12 billion dollars* of necessary and past-due maintenance of *all* parks by now, in 2016, the 100th anniversary of the National Parks system. But the more than 100 million park visitors every year have paid this deficit, as entry fees, lodging, etc. to explore and visit each park. In fact, they have raised at least $15 billion dollars in the 15 years since 2001 to 2016. Where did all that money go to? Who got it, who gets it now? Not people who are interested in the preservation and maintenance of all that is beautiful, good and right, about United States National Parks, and the benefits and welfare of their many millions of visitors every year.

Since 2001, people have become millionaires by stealing money from the U.S. National Parks yearly funding and yearly profits, and from the exploitation of resources, like taking immense quantities of timber and wood from the park forests since 2001. This exploitation, stealing and theft, was not stopped by Democratic President Obama from 2009 to 2016, proving complicity with the previous Neo Con Bush "W"/Cheney Administration. This decimation of the U.S. National Parks, our heritage, that belongs to all Americans, has happened secretly, hidden but out in the open, involving thousands of people, starting at the top with both United States Presidents. But one man's conspiracy is another man's political consensus of opinion. One man's loss is another man's gain.

The Democrats in power often don't stop the endless Republican greed, lies, and their powers of destruction so they, too, are responsible for the diminished preservation of our National Parks. So they too are responsible for all of the endless problems created by the Republicans in power at any given time, because the Democrats in power do nothing to stop them. Divisiveness and lying is the Republican way since 2000, and submission is the Democratic way since 2001. Perhaps the most powerful Democrats in power, like Vice President and Presidential candidate Al Gore, were paid off, threatened, bought off, scared off, forced off, and/or instilled with fear, during and after the elections of 2000. It seemed then that they became something other than true Democrats, modified by the take-over Neo Cons in power at that time. They seemed to be subservient and submissive politicians.

In January 2016 the mobile home parks were sold to a mobile home community investment corporation in Kentucky already worth millions of dollars. Kentucky newspaper articles about lawsuits against them, about dishonest management in their 17 parks in Kentucky, was proof this corporation was very much like the previous corrupt corporation of park owners since 1982. The drug dealers in the parks had new bosses, and the problems with living in the parks continued, and became magnified and just as dangerous. Complicity with crimes continued with the newest Sheriff and the new owners of the parks, SSK. It continued to be an ugly, dishonest, and dangerous place to live.

In February 2016 a deputy told me to tell the new owners of the park everything about the 24/7 bad behavior, the 24/7 criminal drug dealer behavior, of the 15 drug dealers for those 6 ½ years. But especially the last 2 ½ years, with the drug dealers from Hell, the Devil drug dealer and his woman partner living next to me. So I wrote a letter to them in Kentucky, and called the newest Sheriff to ask him if I could send him a copy of that letter. He said "I'll see if I can do anything about the problems."

I knew the drug dealers would be listening to my conversation with the Sheriff, and I knew the Sheriff knew the drug dealers were listening to us. So he was talking to them too. I also sent the

Sheriff a copy of the Vectren response a week before to my request for proof of who had been hacking my phone for more than two years. My first request, in 2014, had been ignored. Their response now was that I would need a court order, a subpoena, to get those records, the proof of phone-hacking by my drug dealer neighbors and their drug bosses. Vectren had to protect its liability because Vectren, after all, had been hacking into **all** of their customer's phones since after 2001.

Two months passed and nothing changed. There was no improvement, nothing got better. Of course the nearly new Sheriff didn't do anything about the endless problems, the endless crimes. In February I had gotten a bill for water and sewer four weeks *before* I used it, for twice as much as I was normally charged. Of course SSK employees never read the meter, they just guessed, like the previous owners, who also charged a $4 service charge for *not* reading the hundreds of meters in the park.

Corruption feeds on corruption, always and forever. So I sent letters again about the corruption, the endless corruption, throughout the County to the DEA, the FBI, the Justice Department, and the ACLU. I assumed they would do nothing, again, to stop the endless corruption and problems and drug crimes. A Justice Department Chief Investigator sent me a letter again saying "Thank you for your information. We depend on people like you." Not from the same Chief Investigator, because he had been fired, after corruption charges were made against him about illegal drugs. Maybe that was a set-up, a retaliation against him. Nice people never last long in high positions in politics and in law enforcement, in government jobs and in non-government jobs. Crime is a business of bullies.

Innocence only gets you so far in the United States, in local, state, and Federal legal systems. Preferential treatment, lies, and distortions of the truth are easy to do, and are often necessary to get a verdict of innocence and freedom for guilty people. So I wasn't looking for evidence, I was looking for justice. Evidence can easily be twisted, distorted, lied about, made-up, changed, suppressed, and/or altered to fit deceitful agendas. This is a reality, this is the truth.

During those ugly 6 ½ years there were only four honest deputies, and no honest Sergeants or Lieutenants, out of the at least 75 I saw or talked to, anytime 24/7, most eventually responding two or three times, for at least 150 times. This was a sad and sorry record of no help, except from those four male deputies, two black and two white, who stood out as being what law enforcement is supposed to be like and supposed to do. Two white female deputies had also been honest, but the drug dealers had laughed at them and made fun of them after they drove away. In contrast, the male deputies and Sergeants were their buddies, their partners-in-crime, deceit, and deception.

The four honest male deputies had been like lights at the end of the tunnel. Fleeting and temporary lights lasting minutes or hours, replaced with the much more common darkness of deceit, deception, dishonesty, and lies lasting for years. The denial of civil rights and civil liberties meant the whole 6 ½ year nightmare had been un-American. Also, I had paid for management in the park for 6 ½ years but had gotten none, including from the new and not-improved owners. The deceitful, deceptive, dishonest old park owners, Amar Corporation, had passed the ball to SSK, the new deceitful, deceptive, dishonest park owners in 2016. Just like the old Sheriff, put into office in 2008, had passed the ball of corruption to the new Sheriff in 2014. It was more of the ugly lying and corrupt same old same old that can happen everywhere and anywhere anytime. But most Americans in the 21st century don't care. They aren't interested in the truth. Cable TV entertainment, fantasies, and fiction are all they really want. It makes life easier.

For about 25 years drug dealers had been getting special treatment by the owners of the eight parks in the County owned by the drug bosses, and by deputies, Sergeants, and successive Sheriffs and Police Chiefs, who always made sure they were above the law. They were the privileged few, all partners-in-crime. The drug system was simple, easy to do, and easy for law enforcement to ignore, to allow. Lying, and twisting and distorting the truth, were so common, a drug system tradition.

This can and does happen anywhere in America. This can also easily be stopped anywhere in America. There is nothing complicated about illegal drugs in America, ignored and allowed to continue by corruption, starting at the top, filtering down to the sub-human inhuman low-life psychotic psychopath drug dealers, all with no conscience, the scum of America, protected and helped, encouraged and supported, by law enforcement, because they are privileged. A Senator had written to me in 2014 "If deputies and Sergeants and police don't enforce laws then nobody anywhere will." As a result, the drug dealers were easily serial killers of girls and women and people's pets, killing women and girls, dogs, puppies, cats, and kittens and easily getting by with it.

All my efforts to prove otherwise had been futile, had failed, for those more than six years. The President of the United States had responded "The Obama Administration believes in the sovereignty of each state," when the drug system was inter-state, meaning the FBI and the DEA should have been notified by the Presidential staff. For 25 years they had been one big happy tightly-knit drug-induced family, of many thousands of people, as users, buyer, sellers, and management and bosses.

The deranged demented dishonest lying drug dealers were never, and had never been, held accountable for their 24/7 criminal actions. Like dealing drugs 24/7 for 25 years and hacking phones 24/7 since 2013, a Federal crime, a Federal law that was NEVER enforced. Never. Fifty deputies had said 50 times, smiling, "We don't enforce Federal laws." By law they were required to tell their Sheriff. The Sheriff, by law, had to report it to the FBI to investigate, and tell U.S. Marshalls to make arrests. What the FBI didn't know about they didn't investigate. The Sheriffs and the Police Chiefs had been protecting the drug system in the County for possibly 25 years. It was the business of crime.

A Sergeant had said to me in 2015 that it was "very sophisticated government phone-hacking equipment." It was markedly improved within a week after the newest Sheriff took office in 2014, after the other Sheriff quit to become the Senior Vice President of the largest local bank. There was much less static, much less distortion, especially on my calls to 911 about drug dealer crimes and illegal activities, eventually about 150 calls to 911 in almost three years that NEVER, not once, stopped them or helped me in any way.

For many years deputies and Sergeants would always say "We didn't see him do it so he didn't do it" and "We think you're lying, we think you're making it up," to whoever reported drug dealer crimes and problems caused by drug dealers. It was common knowledge that for 25 years drug dealers were privileged, and special. About one out of twenty black men in America are killed by other black men, usually in drug-related crimes. When the same is true for white men maybe drug systems in America will be destroyed. Maybe, maybe not. Maybe yes, maybe no.

It is surprising and unexpected that probably 99% of Americans can't do anything about the disappearance of any of their civil liberties and civil rights, and the dishonesty, lies, stealing, cheating and theft from whoever they rent from, especially corporations. About 300 million adults in America can't change or stop much of anything of social significance, except in small and inconsequential ways. This makes being an American in America a life of delusions and illusions, now in the 21st century. But the truth is, the reality is, most Americans don't care. Most people in America aren't interested in the truth. They want entertainment, or nothing at all. Controlled Cable TV and controlled national and local news, and a controlled media in general, including hundreds of inferior mass-produced movies and inferior weekly TV programs every year, contribute to this demand for endless entertainment. After all, giving people what they want is a secret for success.

There are great things in America. I just never found them. Except some of the National Parks that are grand and glorious. Looking for America has to include both the present and the past, the history of America, including when what is history happened only last week or last month. The rest of this book is about the present in America, about the recent past, and about American history going back to its beginnings, for better and for worse.

# CHAPTER TWO

## Americans In America

There's been a collective American personality shift since the turn of the century, starting about the year 2000, after Bush "W" became President. And it hasn't been for the better.

Recent studies have shown people are more likely to become what they want to be, achieving what they want to achieve, live like they want to live, if they live in other countries. Especially other democracies like France, Australia, Canada, England. People in America are more likely to achieve all parts of the American Dream in these other countries. Not a good development.

Upward mobility is more likely in these other countries. Conversely, downward mobility is more likely in the United States. Unlimited opportunity is a thing of the past in the United States. Americans are more likely to achieve all parts of the American Dream, and more and better, in at least 23 other countries, in those 23 other Democracies in the World, and not in America. Almost 150 million people, about half the people in the United States, are living near the poverty level, at the poverty level, or below poverty level. The other 23 Democracies aren't remotely like that. Besides that, it appears that America is becoming something different than a democracy.

The United States guarantees nothing for its citizens that is good. Other democracies guarantee free high quality health care for everyone, free high quality education including free college for everyone that wants it, a guaranteed two to four week paid vacation every year, and a guaranteed paid retirement, which is guaranteed financial security for all of its senior citizens. The United States has none of this. It falls woefully behind all the other 23 Democracies. Even freedom of speech, freedom of expression, and freedom to organize publically are no longer guaranteed.

The upper 10% of the United States population pay little or no taxes on their income, using tax loopholes, tax evasion, tax write-offs, typically paying no more than 1% of their millions of dollars or billions of dollars in yearly income, if they pay any taxes at all. The IRS, not a government entity, guarantees if poor Americans and middle-class Americans do not pay all of their taxes, taxed up to 35%, they will be harassed and threatened by the IRS and fined or imprisoned. As a result, the middle class and the working poor in America made the United States Government the richest in the World. Not the millionaires and billionaires, who always hoard their money.

There is something very wrong with this picture, with this reality that Americans were and are powerless to change. The majority of Americans have been powerless to change anything in the United States, increasingly more so since the 1960's. Voting for politicians who say they'll change or improve anything means little or nothing as they rarely do what they say they will do. Words are cheap, but they help politicians win elections because that's the sum of what they have to offer. Unless you're a Republican, especially a Far Right Republican or a Neo Con Republican.

Since 2001 Presidents, Senators, Congressmen/women, officials and politicians, elected or not, have not represented the people. They represent banks, corporations, the Federal Reserve, the IRS, the military, the IMF, the wealthiest people in the United States, the oil industry, and themselves.

Also the pharmaceutical industry, the financial industry, the insurance industry, the medical/sickness industry, besides the **30,000 lobbyists** in Washington, D.C., who give them a lot of money and very expensive gifts. The rest of America is just an afterthought, until election time.

In America, in politics and business, whoever manipulates the people best wins. Obama campaigned for an unprecedented three years when he was supposed to be an Illinois Senator. Being a Senator gave him credentials to run for President, but he wasn't elected to be a Senator, he was appointed, because he ran unopposed. His opponent dropped out of the race unexpectedly. Was she paid off? What and who was the political influence that pushed her out?

Then, after three years of campaigning, instead of the usual two years, he was a household name and people were used to seeing him on the media and in the news. In order to be the first black President the majority of people had to get used to him, to the new reality, to vote for him and make him President of the United States. By that time they even expected to see him, when election time came. The people of Illinois had paid for him, supported him and his family, while he was campaigning for those three years. After all, voting and marking a ballot often comes down to name recognition, not who is better qualified. Or, like in the corrupt and dishonest Presidential election of 2000, it comes down to who has the most corrupt political support and the most corrupt manipulative campaign plans, not just the most campaign money.

Black people in America have made a reputation for themselves for doing as little work as possible to keep their jobs. Usually black people can't be fired, unless the employer wants a lawsuit on their hands. They get preferential treatment about getting hired for jobs. On civil service exams they've gotten 15 to 20 extra points for many years just because they are black. Obama made use of social and cultural advantages just for black people in America when he ran for Senator, was appointed Senator, and then ran for President, and became President.

What's happening to America? World-wide it used to be known as a force for good, a key to a better future. The land of the free and the home of the brave. Since World War II until the election fiascos of 2000 that was the reputation of the United States. But it's been replaced with loss of dignity and decency, loss of honesty and integrity, corruption and lies. Greed, lies, theft, fraud, and corruption at all levels of society everywhere are common. Since 2000 it seems Presidents are appointed, as are other people who are in power at any given time. Many hundreds of unelected and appointed people are in political power and influence at any given time. It's all a big secret, a big game. Why all the subterfuge and corruption? For control, money, power, and personal gain. It's a game of power, greed, and control that the democracy of the United States allows to happen.

In the United States capitalism trumps democracy. We live in a country that enriches the few at the expense of the many. That is not a true democracy. On the federal level the United States is run by the largest banks, by the massive and all-pervasive oil industry, by the biggest players in the financial industry, by huge corporations, and by the very powerful and very rich pharmaceutical industry. Not to forget the hugely profitable medical/sickness industry with its very over-priced physicians and very over-priced medical specialists, with its hugely over-priced and greedy hospitals and every other part of the medical sickness industry. And last but not least, the hugely over-priced and greedy health insurance industry. There's nothing altruistic about the American medical system, unlike the medical systems in other democracies. More than anything it's motivated by profit and money. Lots of money.

The wealthiest people in the United States, the upper 1%, run the United States politically and economically, besides the medical system. Elected politicians, especially Republicans, represent all of them instead of representing the American people comprising the expendable masses.

Don't forget the unelected secretive so-called Shadow Government that's been around since at least 1970, apparently run by the Neo Cons since its beginning attempts and plans to control the world, after first controlling the United States. Thus Bush "W" was appointed President with the illegal control of the Supreme Court. Despite the vast illegal voting enterprise efforts engineered by Republicans and Neo Con political forces to make him President, like a dictator, Bush "W" would not have legally become President. Despite all the lies, dishonesty, and subterfuge Bush "W" still didn't get as many votes from the American people, popular votes, as Vice President Gore did in 2000. If it had been an honest election Gore would have won by a landslide. And there would have been no attacks, invasions, and wars in Iraq and in Afghanistan. And no 9/11 in 2001.

Since after World War II United States foreign policy has been globalization of United States super-power. The United States is like a totalitarian form of a democracy manipulated, distorted, and corrupted by elected and unelected officials and politicians. This includes the self-serving and very over-paid very secretive paramilitary and the self-serving and corrupt Shadow Government, the silent, hidden, secret government.

Corruption is allowed in the United States. It becomes legalized corruption. It's expected. Political corruption has become the norm. Law enforcement corruption and military corruption have become the norm. Corporate, legal, lawyer, Judge, and Magistrate corruption has become the norm. Looking the other way, ignoring what is wrong, are common reactions. In many cases it's expected, it's part of the job description, like for deputies and police, for politicians, for the military. Looking the other way, ignoring what is wrong, is actually a part of being an American, in some places more than others.

The individual American is powerless to change any of this. Since The Patriot Act of 2001 groups of people in America are powerless to change anything by protesting even if they are allowed to protest after getting permits. When thousands, even millions, of Americans protested in Washington, D.C. during the Viet Nam war nothing of any value was ever changed anyway. Since the 1960's protests have been ignored, the people in power have looked the other way.

Thomas Jefferson said "In a democracy citizens who have integrity will criticize their government, not trust it." However, while the United States Government has been forcing democracy on other countries it has been eliminating, taking away, civil liberties and freedoms at home. In 1971 seven students were murdered by Government police, the National Guard, because they were expressing freedom of speech and freedom of dissent and protest. There was no way they, or the student protests, were a threat to the Federal Government, or to anybody who worked for the Government. But nobody did anything about these murders and shootings of unarmed defenseless college students at Kent State University, about these crimes by the National Guard killing, murdering, shooting college students who were criticizing their Federal Government, demonstrating against U.S. Government actions in Viet Nam, Laos, and Cambodia. They were expressing their Constitutional rights.

No charges were ever brought against anyone in the National Guard. The entire incident was proof of the loss of freedoms and Constitutional rights in America, that no American could do anything about, or change or stop in any way. It was the first proof of a loss of democracy in America.

Other Democracies, 23 of them, exist to improve the life of all their citizens, to help them have a life of freedom that's as good as possible. The American Democracy, the American culture, has been completely different from the beginning. After many millions of Native American Indians were killed, tortured, and murdered for more than 250 years, and the rest of them were forcefully driven from their homes to relocate on Reservations, their domination was complete. But ongoing problems and murders never ended between Americans in America who were English, Irish, Swedish, Norwegian, Russian, African, German, Chinese, Japanese, Mormon, etc., until after World War I ended in 1918.

*Every year* about ***five times*** as many people are murdered in America as American soldiers died in Iraq in the entire American occupation and war of eight years. This is many more murders and many more homicides each year than in any other country in the World. In 2012 to 2014 more soldiers committed suicide than died in combat in Afghanistan.

Violence is a big part of the American psyche, a big part of the American society, and has been for many years. It's a big part of the American culture, and accounts for the great popularity of violence in video games, movies, computer games, on DVDs, and on cable TV programs. Especially among the male part of the population, all ages. It glamorizes using violence and intimidation to get what men want. But the biggest reason is the accessibility of guns. There are more privately owned guns in America than anywhere else in the World. Hundreds of times more. But most murders are committed with borrowed or stolen guns, and most murders are never solved.

In every other developed country and democracy the yearly death rate caused by guns, murders committed with guns, are between 50 and 200 people every year. In huge contrast, in the United States it's always about 15,000 people murdered with guns every year. It's a culture of violence, way beyond any other country, any other culture, with hundreds of millions of self-righteous owners of guns and rifles, and a high percentage of them, maybe millions of them, being deranged, or angry red-neck, or trigger-happy owners of registered and unregistered guns and rifles who like to shoot at and kill living things. The United States is a dangerous place to live in. Besides that, most murders are never solved.

Detroit always has one of the highest murder rates in the United States. Across Lake Erie, north of Detroit, is Windsor, Canada, with a population of about 400,000, about half of Detroit's population. Their yearly murder rate is zero. No murders. Possibly one murder every 10 years, usually committed by an American from Detroit. It's obvious Canada is much more civilized and a much, much safer place to live. That is part of what makes Canada a better place to live. Different attitudes, more civilized.

Canada has almost twice as many guns registered per person as in the United States, with 7 million registered rifles and guns, and about 200 people murdered each year. In comparison, the United States has twice as many people and more than eleven million registered guns and rifle, and the United States has at least 15,000 murders a year. So Canada has about *twice as many* registered guns and rifles per person as the United States does. Canadians obviously are nicer, kinder, more disciplined people.

What makes America the murder capital of the World, thousands of times worse than anywhere else in the World? It's the attitudes of the people and their culture, their reactions to frequent violence in movies and on TV, their upbringing and their environment, their parent's attitudes, their lack of education including getting passing grades without qualifying for those grades, and the No Child Left Behind program that was invented and continued for the benefit of black students to graduate from all grades and from high school without having really passed any grade. Lack of accountability and personal responsibility both in school and at home, and then in society, creates problem behavior. Last but not least is lack of discipline, beginning with parents and then from school teachers who will be fired if they discipline students. In the 21st century it's become dangerous to discipline kids anywhere, any time.

If their parents aren't disciplined people themselves it's unlikely a child will become a disciplined person. More than anything, parents teach by example. Not to forget inherent male aggression.

Take away testosterone and selfishness and most of the problems in the United States, and in the entire World, would disappear. More than half of the kids in America are illegitimate and grow up in single mother homes. More than half of all kids in America from legitimate births, when the parents are married, end up in divorced families. All of these reasons are conducive to development of kids with possible criminal tendencies and aggression leading to violence and murder. Increasingly, white-trash, black-trash, brown-trash people of all ages are a menace to society and account for most of the crime.

In 1964 "Freedom Summer" was a movement using volunteers to get black people in the South registered to vote. At that time only 10% were registered to vote in Mississippi. A 24 year old white man and his 21 year old wife were recruited to organize volunteers to knock on doors in Mississippi to encourage black voter registration. In that part of Mississippi there had been 80 registered Ku Klux Klan men. Suddenly the KKK there had *8000* registered members recruited to stop the young white couple from organizing volunteers for black voter registration.

They conspired with the Sheriff to stop the car and illegally detain the 24 year old white man and another 24 year old white male volunteer also in the car, and a 22 year old black male volunteer, also in the car, on false charges and put them all in jail for the night. They were to be released the next morning at a specified time so the KKK men would be waiting for them, then stop them, and then brutally kill them. The KKK men then buried the three bodies in a landfill.

They weren't charged for anything, no criminal actions of any sort. They went free after it was discovered. The state of Mississippi ignored the three murders until 41 years later. In 2005 one of the guilty KKK men, the only one still living, was charged, tried, and then finally convicted of the three murders. He died in prison a few years later.

This case exemplified the meanness, the self-righteousness, and the viciousness of Southern white men in Mississippi, including Judges and politicians who justified killing white people if they helped black people exercise their legal right to vote, and justified killing black people if they tried to register to vote. As often happens in murder cases they had no guns to defend themselves with. Against white Ku Klux Klan men who did have guns, and wore white sheets to hide their identity and give them cowardly confidence to kill anonymously. These men, including the Judges and the so-called law enforcement, were a disgrace to other white people everywhere in America, except to other members of the KKK.

From about 1550 to about 1850, about 300 years, a total of 12.5 million black people were shipped from Africa to be sold as slaves. Only 450,000 of them ever went to America to be sold as slaves, mostly for the American plantations in the South. That's less than 1/30 of the total. This is proof that slavery of black people was more popular in other parts of the World, like in Brazil. It was part of the African economy for at least 3000 years before the United States was even thought of, long before there was a United States of America. For thousands of years black people in Africa captured and sold other black people to be slaves, to be sold on the international slavery market. White men from America did not travel to Africa to kidnap and capture black people to be slaves in the South, on Southern plantations. Black people in Africa had been doing that for thousands of years to other black people because it was part of the African economy, exporting black people for thousands of years to almost every country in the World at one time or another to be slaves.

Since the 1980's black people in America have been socially conditioned to believe the red carpet will be rolled out for them if they get a college degree because they're "special". In fact, since then, they will be hired before any white college graduate with a much better GPA, even straight A's, and a much better resume. It's a kind of reverse prejudice that has existed in the United States since the 1980's. What happened to equality?  This policy and Affirmative Action should end.

Black people expect white people to feel sorry for them and to feel guilty still, after 150 years, about the 1% of wealthy white people in the United States, mostly on Southern plantations, who owned them as slaves to work on those plantations. The fact that millions of white people died and were badly injured during the Civil War, to make black people free, to end slavery after it had existed for *thousands of years* in the rest of the World, has been and is of no interest or consequence ever to black people in the United States. They ignore the truth because it doesn't fit into their agenda.

Special financial grants, housing, money programs, extra points on civil service job examinations and preferential treatment in hiring for private market jobs, special job programs, and, last but not least, Social Welfare programs and Section 8 and Affirmative Action have given *trillions* of dollars of Government money, from hundreds of millions of white people, to black people for more than sixty years. But they are never satisfied or thankful for it. It is their cultural imperative to complain and to be mad, to be angry and dissatisfied. It's a part of their culture in America.

A black student in high school or college with just a C average can get admittance to, and free financial assistance and scholarships to, Harvard and other Ivy League colleges, or other top colleges for undergraduate degrees, law degrees, master's degrees. A white student with a C average could not. Unless they are someone like Bush "W" whose father was the head of the CIA at that time, and then later the President of the United States, So Bush "W" went to Yale because of that connection. It pays to have powerful fathers who are rich and have connections, for all people of any color.

It pays to be black, even just 10% black, when you're going to school at any level anywhere in America in order to get privileges, special treatment, special opportunities, special grants, special financial assistance, lower standards to meet than white kids for equivalent grades, and special scholarships, all of which white students don't get and can't get because they are white. Even if they are the poorest of the poor. This has always been, and continues to be, prejudice against white kids.

President Obama had a C average in college and high school but was admitted to the highly competitive Harvard College, the most expensive college in the United States, with scholarships to pay for it. If he was white this could not have happened. A white student with the same GPA would not have been given that opportunity to go to Harvard, even if they came from an impoverished background, with parents living at poverty level like they are supposed to be to qualify for special programs. However, both Obama and his lawyer wife did not come from backgrounds of poverty.

According to politicians, and to the media and the Press, most of the black American population is living in dire poverty below poverty level, or at poverty level, and has few opportunities to rise above it. Or they always need more help, more money, more special treatment, on and on, never ending, from white people. But this is not so. This is not true.

There are about 18 million black people in the United States. About 40 million people in America live below poverty level. That's about 20 million white people, about 10 million black people, and about 10 million Mexicans/Hispanics and others living below poverty level. So twice as many white people as blacks are living in dire poverty and cannot escape it in America. They don't have those same special programs, special opportunities, and special hand-outs to escape it.

In 2010, 2011, 2012, and 2013 the usual approximately $38 billion dollars, or even as much as $58 billion dollars, was given away by the United States Government as foreign aid, mostly to countries that despise us. Most of that money goes to their militaries, as it always has. On top of that, the money for them was probably borrowed, probably at high interest rates, probably from Communist China. Why isn't the United States Government and military trying to destroy Communism any longer? Follow the money. Communist China *owns* a lot of the United States, its commercial real estate and businesses, and the United States Government *owes* many trillions of dollars to China after Bush "W", Cheney, and their Neo Con administration created a United States Government *deficit* of $11.5 *trillion* dollars by the time they left office in 2009. This was *their* legacy, after spending the *billions of dollars of surplus money* that Clinton had left as *his* legacy. One was historically bad and the other was historically good. But history depends on who writes it.

Obviously the welfare of the poor in America, especially poor white people, is not as important as United States foreign aid for foreign militaries, to be used as instruments of death and suffering and control of those indigenous foreign populations. Americans have been powerless to change any of this. Their government has long operated beyond their input, influence, and control.

The only source of critical and complete journalism has been documentaries, NPR news, and BBC news. The best, most complete and unbiased news coverage has long been the British Broadcasting, the BBC, on some NPR stations in America. It's the only excellent and unbiased coverage of world news. So, of course, the Republicans in power, the politicians, have often tried to stop yearly funding and government grants for NPR. Limiting the truth and controlling the truth is their status quo. Republicans, politicians or not, have always had big problems with the truth.

There have always been more registered Democrats than Republicans in the United States. The hard-core Neo Cons and Far Right Republicans make up about 35% of American adults. Voter turnout for them is probably nearly 100%. The Far Left Democrats make up about half of that, about 18%. So even if their voter turnout was 100% it isn't enough to counteract the Far Right Republicans. Voter turnout for Republicans is higher because they are motivated to protect their money, their power, their status, their businesses. Republicans are motivated by money and power, and the possibility of more control of more money and more power. Most democrats don't have much money, power, or status to protect or control. Most democrats want peace, truth, honesty, fairness in their Government. Little or no motivation means lower voter turnout at elections. Unhappy people are not as likely to vote.

Self-serving Congressmen and Congresswomen, both Democrat and Republican, who are elected to serve and represent the American people do not. They represent whoever gives them the most money. Millions of dollars. It's a job with huge benefits on the side. The same is true for Senators. It's difficult to be motivated to vote for the possibility of more corruption, unless you're a Republican. The Democratic President Obama, the "hope" and "change" man, changed or improved nothing. But if a Republican had been President instead a catastrophe would have been more possible.

Elections are not the answer because they are easily fixed and manipulated. Without the help of Congress to represent what Americans want and need there is no way for Americans to change or influence anything in their Government, at both federal and state levels. Letters to the President about specific acts of corruption, involving the Federal Government or not, involving politicians or not, and asking who to contact for help, will get a form letter saying "The President respects the sovereignty of each state", with no help about who to contact. If you write to a Governor, like former Governor Daniels of Indiana, about specific corruption in his state, government or not, including Sheriff Departments or Police Departments, his response will be that it is a local issue, not the jurisdiction (or interest) of the Governor, or of the state of Indiana. Apparently a Governor is powerless to change anything in his state about law enforcement. A letter about problems to a Senator or Congressmen, or to an official, will get no response or a stupid unrelated response.

At all levels it will be ignored, or it will set up retaliation if it is a complaint about a Sheriff Department or a Police Department. Complaints to the Attorney General of any state usually solves nothing. It just perpetuates the corruption. A copy of your letter of complaint will be sent to whoever was complained about. That's it. If they want to retaliate, or be dishonest or lie, no one is stopping them. Other than that, nothing is done. You are still on your own. Fighting corruption is a losing battle that is rarely actually helped and changed by complaints to the Attorney General of every state.

The controlled and biased Press and TV news media, especially CNN and Fox news, determine what Americans are allowed to know. Dishonesty and lies are part of it. Information on TV news media and the press are also controlled by who owns them. Rupert Murdock owns most major press and news media in the United States and in much of the world. It's a Murdock monopoly. An unbiased Press and national TV news media are a thing of the past. All that's missing is Big Brother,

Since The Patriot Act became law in 2001 there has been suppression of journalism and reporting, and imprisonment of those who speak the truth and report the truth. This was part of the Neo Cons plan for "A New America" in the new century. A government that has a policy of suppressing the truth is not a democracy. It's a government that has a lot to hide, and therefore cannot be trusted. The majority of people in the United States don't even know this is happening. An uniformed and misinformed public is what the Neo Cons in power at any given time have always wanted. When good people in any country are harassed repeatedly by their government then insecurity and distrust of that government spreads and increases. But that's not supposed to be happening in a democracy.

The oath of office for Congressional representatives is that they are supposed to represent the American people and that they will defend the Constitution. That is what they did not do when they voted "yes" for The Patriot Act in 2001. They should have all been replaced in the next election, except Congresswoman Barbara Lee from California who voted "no". She was the only Congressional Representative that defended the Constitution and protected the American people. Apparently all the others were afraid they would be labeled "unpatriotic" if they voted "no", and/or not be reelected. Or maybe they were afraid of the Neo Cons in power at that time. No matter what, they weren't doing the job they were elected to do by hundreds of millions of people in the United States.

As a result, some of the freedoms guaranteed in The Constitution are gone forever. The people of America are powerless to bring those freedoms hack. Most United States citizens don't even know what happened, don't even know what has been taken from them. That is, until they or someone they know tries to do something that is now prohibited, that is not allowed any more, that is one of the seven Constitutional rights that have disappeared. Then they can be fined or imprisoned by local or federal authorities. Or lose their jobs.

Elected officials, elected politicians, are supposed to represent the will of the people who elected them, who voted for them. Because they don't, especially since 2001, this partly explains why there is not always equal justice under the law in America, especially since 2001. The Supreme Court is supposed to protect and defend civil rights and civil liberties, but, since being hand-picked by partisan Republican Presidents they instead represent businesses, corporations, political agendas, special interest groups. Lesser courts throughout the United States have also been dominated by political agendas, local politics, businesses, and corporations for many years, and especially since 2001, since the beginning of the domination of America by Neo Cons.

The upper 1% in America have more money than 95% have all together. That upper 1% usually pays 1% in taxes or no taxes at all on their income. Does this sound like a democracy? Studies have always shown that when the upper 1%, or even the upper 10%, pay little or no taxes they do not use that money to create jobs, as Republicans and Republican politicians have insisted they do repeatedly, for many years, in order to justify this deplorable theft and dishonesty on the part of the richest people, the most rich people in America. The rich *are* different. They don't pay taxes like everybody else has to do.

What has happened to moral integrity and conscience? It seems to have been, and still be, missing in most of the part of America that runs the United States. And this missing moral integrity and conscience has trickled down to the masses, to the expendable masses.

For about 30 years members of the Ku Klux Klan, more than half a million white men registered mostly in the southern states, were never charged or convicted for the murders they committed of both white people and black people, or for the homes and property they burned and destroyed. Therefore, the United States justice system and state judicial systems supported their criminal behavior for about 30 years.

In the 1960's and 1970's both white and black civil rights activists in the South were killed by Ku Klux Klansmen. They were Democrats murdered by Republicans. In the United States a mean, selfish, vengeful, dishonest, self-righteous man, or woman, will be a Republican. If you find good, kind, honest, and generous people they will be Democrats. There are exceptions, of course, but rarely. And the Republicans are usually the ones with the most money.

So what is their problem, why are Republicans the way they are? A rich Democrat doesn't have the same personality type as a rich Republican does, but it seems rich Democrats often change over to the other side. They become Republicans, the party that will protect their masses of money so it won't be lost or spent for justifiable and honest taxes. Rich people, apparently, like to accumulate money, and never have enough of it to satisfy their need to accumulate more money and hoard more money. It's one of the attitudes and realities that separates the rich from the poor in America.

If people hurt other people they need to be stopped. But they usually are not. In theory maybe, but not in reality. If people, single or in groups, negatively affect other people's lives they need to be stopped. But they usually are not. Not in the United States anyway. If a government is negatively affecting its own citizens, or hurting people in other countries unjustifiably, it needs to be stopped. But in the United States Government and United States Democracy it cannot be stopped. The power of voting, of elections, is a delusion.

People have a right to be informed with the truth about their government. But the truth is often mired in the mud of lies, and is very difficult, or impossible, to find. The truth gets lost among the dishonesty and lies that are accepted by the majority of people in America.

Before 2001 there were 50 media corporations. After 2012 there were only 5 media corporations controlling American media. The 5 media corporations are owned by Rupert Murdock and the Reverend Sun Nyung Moon. This media monopoly covers the United States and also most countries in the World. Information is limited to a controlled and biased TV news media and a not-free-Press owned by these 5 corporations, influencing and controlling about a billion people throughout the World.

Objective news reporting is becoming a thing of the past. Journalism classes at colleges and universities now include information and instruction about "spin", spinning the truth, lying effectively, because it's become a new part and a big part of American culture and journalism. Lying and spin is a big part of Republican TV news media, especially FOX News, and also on CNN news, in the 21st century. Lying and spin, spinning the truth, is officially an acceptable part of American culture in the 21st century. Dishonesty and effective lying is now officially a part of the American culture, taught at many colleges and universities as a necessary part of success.

American people have come to expect lies and deception anywhere and everywhere. Lies are often acceptable to a lot of people. Expectations of telling the truth are becoming a thing of the past in the American culture. When Republican politicians lie it's expected, it's just part of the Republican agenda and style. But the other side of the coin is that Republicans involved in politics are always looking for anything remotely like a lie coming from the Democratic political side to accuse them and incriminate them about, especially during campaigns. If they can't find any lies the Republicans manufacture them. The Republicans then lie about the alleged lies.

In America, after 2001, if anyone, any citizen, finds fault with the Federal Government they are called, labeled, "anti-American" and "an enemy of America". This is ridiculous. Why are politicians, officials, the Neo Cons, the Government, so paranoid? This is no longer a Government by the people, of the people, and for the people. Instead it's a Government by corporations, special interest groups like the NRA, the oil industry, the ruling elite, the upper 10%, and by at least 20,000 lobbyists in Washington, D.C. And, of course, the power-hungry demented Neo Cons, "the crazies", as they were called in the 1980's by people in Washington, D.C. who worked for the Federal Government. A true democracy is about participation. All other democracies in the world, 23 of them, welcome and encourage citizen involvement, expression of concerns and problems, and complaints and criticism of *their* government. This has been the way, and is the way, of all other 23 Democracies except the United States, since 2001.

In 2003 Phil Donahue hosted the most popular and the highest rated TV show at that time. He criticized Bush "W" and Cheney, and their plans for a war in Iraq. He had guests that also criticized Bush "W" and Cheney, and their plans. Three days before the attack and invasion of Iraq his show was unexpectedly and mysteriously cancelled. Immediately he disappeared from the public limelight and never had a TV show again.

Truth in a democracy is a good thing, not something the Government is supposed to control and be afraid of. Therefore, this was a very big sign that things were going wrong, that the national Government was going in a wrong direction, away from the American people who had elected them to represent them. In a democracy citizen involvement and knowledge is a good thing, a necessary thing. Forcing the cancellation of the very popular Phil Donohue show, watched by many millions of people every day, was proof the Bush "W" and Cheney Neo Con administration thought they were not accountable for what they did or were going to do. And that what they were going to be doing, attacking Iraq, was wrong. It was proof that what they were going to be doing could not stand the light of day. It was proof their actions for an indefinite future time would not be able to stand the light of Donohue's daytime TV show, the most popular show on TV watched by many millions of people in 2001.

What Martin Luther King called "the madness of militarism" in 1967 is dependent on deception, lies, manipulation, dropping bombs and killing defenseless and innocent men, women, children, and babies in the name of freedom. In the 1980's then-President Reagan said America was "like a shining city on a hill". After World War II the international image of the United States for about 60 years was that it represented hope, that it would do great things for humanity, not just for the United States itself. But what it became was a very costly military, DOD, and CIA , and other secret services that policed the rest of the World and set up permanent military bases in at least 40 countries in an attempt to control, to spread and maintain its global super-power at very inflated costs, not because those foreign countries wanted them there. Militarism became a part of United States indirect imperialism and expansion. It never has been imperialism.

The United States gives billions of dollars every year to other countries to buy weapons made in the United States as part of their yearly foreign aid program. This money mostly goes to countries that are in much better financial condition than the United States. And, to make matters worse, since 2001 this money to give away as foreign aid is borrowed money, mostly from China. So it's a form of subsidizing United States production of weapons, planes, helicopters. It's welfare for weapons. It's welfare for Boeing, Lockheed, etc. It's extremely expensive welfare for the defense industry and for the Department of Defense.

Washington, D.C. politicians have been stealing the *$2 trillion dollars to $4 trillion dollars* yearly surplus from the Social Security Fund for their secret purposes since 2001. When they tell the American public Social Security is, or will be, insufficient, depleted, bankrupt they know this will happen because they made it happen. Where did it go? What did they do with it? They will never return it, or explain what happened to it, as it is "classified" information, meaning "secret".

As a result, there have been endless lies and dishonesty to force privatization of the Social Security Fund, that would then create even more profit for the already wealthy, the already rich, by forcing hundreds of millions of people to invest in stocks, bonds, annuities, mutual funds, and securities that they would never invest in if they were given a choice, and that have a high likelihood of failing. This would give billions of dollars more, for an indefinite future time, to the financial industry that had already hugely profited dishonestly from the multi-billion dollar Federal Government bail-out, a rescue that gave them money that really belonged to *all* Americans. It was the capitalism reality of more wealth for the few at the expense of the many.

The Republicans have always been jealous of and resented the huge success of the Social Security program started by President Franklin Roosevelt and his Democratic administration after World War II. It has been a major triumph for the Democratic Party, and for everything it represents for all American people. For years Republicans and Neo Cons in power have tried to destroy it, or privatize it. This would eventually force hundreds of millions of Americans into immediate or eventual poverty, greater poverty, or destitution because of the inevitable failure of the privatization of the Social Security program. Dependence on Wall Street would lead to failure.

This possible failure of an absolutely necessary American institution would only happen because of theft by the few at the expense of the many, and because of the meanness, greed, and power to destroy by the Republicans in power at any given time. Since 2001 the Democrats in power do nothing to stop it. Meanwhile, Neo Cons have gotten extremely rich taking, stealing, *trillions* of dollars from the Social Security Fund, and the Democrats in power have let them, since 2001. Maybe the Democrats in power have gotten extremely rich too. This theft has taken place as the American public, the average American , has gotten poorer mostly because of the actions of politicians and officials in power, elected or not. It's the Robin Hood thing in reverse.

Voting and elections are not the answer to problems in America. Votes and elections have been, and can be in the future, fixed and manipulated. Americans let themselves be pawns in ugly political games. But nothing can be done about it anyway. Complaining, protesting, and demonstrations never changed anything anyway since about 1963, since Kent State University students were gunned down by state police as they carried their books to the next classes and stopped to protest national government and military actions in Viet Nam. Delusions and illusions are necessary, especially in 21$^{st}$ century America. Since 1963 being informed has consequences, even including being murdered, gunned down by local, state and national police.

Socially it has become acceptable, even expected, to lie in everyday America, not just political America. Keeping Americans in the dark by a secretive and dishonest Government has been called "the dumbing of America". To do this it has been absolutely essential to lie, starting at the highest levels. On the whole, Americans like it, and allow themselves to be pawns in the game, victims of the manipulations and distortions, the twisting of the truth, and the endless social and government dishonesty since 2001. Since the takeover by the Neo Cons during the Presidential elections of 2000, as was planned since the 1970's.

People lie to protect the ones they love and to protect themselves. But this social lying so common in the 21$^{st}$ century is a deception, something different than protection. People expect politicians to lie. But people portrayed in movies and on TV shows, spokespersons on Fox News and CNN, and the press are as likely to be dishonest as honest since 2001. It's become socially acceptable, not just politically acceptable, in the 21$^{st}$ century.

In general Americans think they are superior people, and that America is a superior country because that's what they have been told by politicians, especially Presidents, all their lives. On international behavior tests Americans always rank at the top of all countries for confidence, and always rank near the bottom for intellectual capabilities and accomplishments.

Americans seem to think their country is the only one blessed by God, therefore they are uniquely blessed by God. Especially Republicans, the Far Right, Fundamentalists, Neo Cons, and

Evangelicals think this is true. Politicians, many of whom are self-serving and prone to lie as part of their jobs, tell Americans this. Religious leaders, whose beliefs are dominated by fantasies and belief and faith in things never seen and never heard, tell them this. One delusion follows another. This belief is based on something that can't be proven or disproven, the blessings of God and the truth or fantasies and myths of the Bible, the supposed words of God.

It's all a grand illusion, perpetuated by social conditioning, American culture, businesses and advertising, movies and TV, United States politics, and lies. It used to be that two-faced white people were common in the South. It was a Southern tradition, a Southern trait, but no more. Superficially nice and genuinely mean, rude, selfish people are common everywhere, some areas of America more than others. Foreigners have long regarded Americans as obnoxious. It's the American super-confidence. Humility is not an American trait, except for the at least 100 million people living near poverty, at poverty, or below poverty level who live with humility and difficulties because of that poverty, 24 hours a day, 365 days a year.

Politeness and courtesy are disappearing, as vulgarity and selfishness have increased at all levels of society. It is tolerated, therefore encouraged, among children of all ages, even starting as early as preschoolers as they mimic and copy their parents, and, of course, it's common among teen-agers. Dignity and integrity are disappearing. Rudeness is the new common character trait and kindness is becoming a thing of the past. This all seems to be the new American general psyche in the 21st century, the American general personality for all colors of people. The national school program "No child left behind" increased this problem immensely, starting in the 1990's, when the negative fallout began to be apparent.

Meanness, condescension, and arrogance to white people coming from black teenagers and black adults in America was a direct result of this school program and of other social programs that were targeted for black people, both adults and kids. Disdain for white people was one of the direct results. Black kids and young adults could get better and go farther than white kids and young adults by doing nothing, by being lazy and taking advantage of the system that was pushed on them because of some stupid collective white guilt about black slavery hundreds of years earlier. It has been a social triumph for both black adults and black children, even if they were only a small percentage black.

In America it's not what you know, it's who you know. An example of this was that before filing for bankruptcy many, if not all, financial businesses, banks, mutual funds, etc., gave their client's money that was deposited with their banks, etc., to other businesses in order to hide that money with someone they could trust to conceal it. These were illegal transfers of money, millions and billions of dollars, for which they were never held accountable.

In 2001 more than *$70 billion dollars* of taxpayer's money was given by the Federal Government to America's biggest banks because of their mostly non-existent losses, really paper losses, exchanges of money, not losses of actual tangible money, and because of their extremely poor but purposefully deceptive mismanagement practices. The losses were not really in sub-prime loans, as these banks had always sold their sub-prime loans and mortgages to investors because banks don't like to take risks. They don't take risks because they are in the business of making money, not helping people.

The United States Government gave them bailout money that belonged to the taxpayers, *$70 billion dollars* of taxpayer's money for those bank's mistakes and wrong decisions in investments. But the banks had actually made huge profits, *billions of dollars* from their bad investments, by hedging their bets, their investments, and by using other legal maneuvers. In 2009,when banks were told they could no longer sell their sub-prime loans and mortgages to investors, banks stopped giving sub-prime loans, and to nothing with less than an A rating. They hoarded the more than $70 *billion dollars* that had been a Federal Government gift, actually a theft, from poor Americans and middle-class Americans given to the already wealthy. It was more perpetual wealth for the few at the expense of the many, which is what capitalism is about.

Before Bush "W" left office in 2009 he gave them a *few billion dollars* more, with no media coverage, as a parting gift to some of the people who had put him in office for eight years. Obama, as the new President, also gave them $70 *billion dollars* of taxpayer's money, with a lot of media coverage, as a gift from the new incoming President. When in Rome do as the Romans do.

Once again America stopped being by and for the people under both Republican and Democratic rule. It was for the already wealthy, as has happened repeatedly in United States history, especially since the 1980's, since Reagan was President, and corporate America and the largest banks in America began to rule America. They began to rule Americans.

During any exaggerated crisis these mega -banks always had *trillions of dollars* of money hidden in tax-havens in off-shore countries like Costa Rica. Not billions. Trillions. Starting in 2009 why did the Democratic Obama allow this huge Republican betrayal to Americans, and the huge theft of their money, to continue? He must have gotten something in exchange for his co-operation. After all, political pay-offs are so common.

Since the United States has occupied Iraq the United States has taken *billions of dollars* of dollars of yearly profits from oil production in Iraq. Where has that profit gone to? Lack of accountability and dishonest accountability has been a hallmark of the United States war and continuing occupation in Iraq.

The United States Government operates on the principle that the people, the expendable masses, don't need to know what's happening. They don't need to know what their Government is really doing. The United States Government, politicians in power, use taxpayer's money for their own personal gain. It's like gambling. It's the same thing the financial industry did. They used customer's money for their own personal gain.

In 2008 there were no criminal charges made for their misappropriation of funds, for their theft of billions of dollars of client's money. It pays to be a favorite of the Federal Government. The Government bailout meant many involved got million dollar and multi-million dollar bonuses, even *billion dollar* yearly bonuses, that year for "a job well done" for their employers, that was really a job poorly done for their clients. It was a gigantic financial reward for bad behavior. They were paid for *their* so-called losses and didn't pay their clients for *their* real and actual losses.

About 40% of the United States economy is dependent on the financial industry. The financial industry manipulates the market for their own gain, for their own financial benefit, not their client's benefit. An economy based on financial investments is not a productive economy. It's a gambling economy. It resembles organized crime, gambling with the United States economy, gambling with the taxpayer's money, hedging their bets so they win either way, with greater wins and bigger profits resulting from *bad* investments. "Losing" is where the most money is found, not in "winning". So losing is really winning.

The financial crisis of 2008 was a Federal Government give-away of **$150 billion dollars** to financial companies and corporations, with million dollar and multi-million dollar bonuses, and even **billion dollar** bonuses, given at the end of that year to leaders of financial companies as yearly bonuses for their incompetence and dishonesty. An example of this was the head of Freddie Mac, a United States Government Department for housing loans, etc., who got a bonus that year of $153 million dollars for his incompetence and dishonesty, for his theft and manipulation that caused millions of people in the United States to lose their homes, bringing unnecessary and avoidable life-changing misery into the homes and lives of millions of people in the United States. He was a black man with authority and influence that abused that trust, and became rich in the process, a multi-millionaire illegally.

That new kind of illegitimate "talent" was very well rewarded again and again. The American Government rewards both business leaders and government leaders who cause misery for millions of Americans. The more the better, the bigger the reward. It's the American way. There are at least a hundred million more poor white people than black people who are poor in America. But clearly the media and advertising think black people, especially half-black and half-white like President Obama, are more important than white people who are also deprived and live in deprivation, who are poor.

At least 80% of the actors on TV commercials and in print advertisements, etc., are half-black, half-white, including commercials for non-profits and government organizations asking for help, for money. Clearly the message is that black people, 15% of the population, are more important than Mexican people, Oriental people, white people, and everybody else in America. The voice-overs on commercials on TV and radio are also about 80% black speakers. It's the selling of, the propaganda of, black influence being more important than any other racial influence in America. One can only wonder what the reasons are, what the rationales are, behind all of this promotion of people who are a combination of black and white in America, since Obama was elected President.

For almost four years President Obama was on the same TV commercial for "Feeding America, org.", asking for donations to feed people in America, millions of people in America who go hungry every day because they don't get enough to eat. Why hadn't he done something about it in those almost four years, about fixing that problem that is so easily fixed? If the President of the United States can't, who can? It's not that he can't, it's that he doesn't. In the so-called richest country in the World, that has the biggest national debt in the World, one in eight people go hungry at the end of any day. That's what the TV commercials said, for years.

Civil service employees can't be fired no matter how poorly they perform their jobs. Black people, 15% of the American population, have been 40% to 60% of civil service employees for many years, for at least 60 years. Since the 1950's they have always gotten at least an extra 20 points on State and Federal Government employee entrance tests because of the color of their skin, their ethnic background. This has never been equal rights for white people on a national basis. Non-government jobs have been subsidized by State and Federal Government programs if black people are hired instead of white people, paying as much as half the salary.

It's like how black students have been paid to go to school and are paid for each test they take and pass, hundreds of dollars each month. Yet, white or Mexican or Oriental students don't get paid anything if they go to school every day, work hard, and get A's for their grades. This has never been equal rights for all other students of all other races. Unequal rights has been the norm since Affirmative Action and preferential treatment for black people became the norm in the United States since the 1980's and 1990's. It was a cultural regression for everybody else.

Lack of ethical behavior began with the Puritans from England at the beginning of a new America, and it continued with the newly formed United States Government and United States military as they continued their supposed "manifest destiny" by killing millions of Native American Indians for at least another 250 years, until white dominance was complete. The subjugation of indigenous people throughout the world had happened throughout history by all colors and races of people. This wasn't something new or unique. But it was a tragedy, wrong, and not excusable.

The Indians were forced to live on Government-run reservations that had inferior land, or useless land, making them unable to live like they had for centuries, or even for thousands of years. They couldn't escape the destitution, the poverty, on the reservations. The United States Government controlled them by controlling their economy, their ability to support themselves and live, and their supply of money. This was similar to how the United States Government, the IMF, and the World Bank control the economies of other countries in the 21$^{st}$ century, by controlling their money through the International Monetary Fund and the World Bank, and by the demands and conditions they make on their huge loans to these countries.

In 2012 Asians made up about 3% of the population and were in movies, commercials, TV shows and in advertising photos about 1% of the time. Mexicans make up about 18% of the population but are in only about *5%* of the movies, commercials, TV shows, and advertising photos in the United States. Blacks are about 15% of the population but are about 65% of the judicial Judges that are appointed and are in about 65% to 75% of commercials, TV shows, movies, and advertising photos. Whites are about 50% of the population and are in about 50% of the commercials, TV shows, movies, and advertising photos. If the President of the United States was Asian or Mexican or Native American Indian it is likely they would also be represented 65% to 75% of the time in the media. Manipulation is a big part of the American culture.

The richest man in the World is Mexican, living in Mexico, worth $37 billion dollars. This is proof that people who have the most money do not create jobs. He certainly hasn't. For many years Mexicans have risked their lives to come to America to get jobs, and to get welfare for Mexican women with children. They pay up to $6000 for transportation that hides them so they can cross the border and be in the United States illegally, so they can try to get a job. For many years there has not been enough jobs in Mexico to support the Mexican population. Obviously the wealthiest man in the world, a Mexican in Mexico, has done little or nothing to help, or to provide jobs for, his fellow Mexicans in Mexico that are poor and need help.

It is the same way in the United States. In the 21st century the wealthiest people in the United States have not created jobs for the masses of people, at least 40 million of them, that need jobs or better paying jobs. How many jobs have they created? Probably none. Most of the upper 10%, especially the upper 1%, made their money from financial investments. When Republican politicians chant their mantras, their tired old mantras about how if the wealthiest people are taxed more they won't be able to create as many jobs, they are lying for that elite, for their benefactor's benefit. And for their own benefit.

Proportionately there are more black millionaires and multi-millionaires in the United Stated than white millionaires and multi-millionaires. How many jobs have they created? Probably none, like the white millionaires and multi-millionaires probably haven't either. The more wealthy a person is the less likely they are to create jobs, or better jobs, for the unfortunate masses, the at least 100 million people living near, at, or below poverty level in the United States at the beginning of the 21st century. This is probably true for most cultures throughout the World because it is common for extremely wealthy people to hoard their wealth, or to use it for more investments, not for altruism.

America isn't special just because it's America. Just like parents aren't special just because they're parents. Because of politicians and officials, especially Presidents, saying "America is the best country in the World" year after year, decade after decade, generation after generation, Americans, in general, think that it's true. They believe that, even if they've never been beyond their own state or limited area of the United States. Or no matter what their life experiences have been that disprove it. Just saying it doesn't make it so, but, in general, people in America want to believe it. It's American propaganda.

There isn't a best place to live in America. Every place has problems, just different problems more problems, or fewer problems. Most of the better places to live in the United States are too expensive, regarding real estate, for half the population in the United States to live in modestly, or live in at all. Thus the Mexican immigrant solution of several families living in each house, of several people owning the same house together. This is partly what drove housing prices up so high in California before the American real estate collapse began in 2005 and 2006. This also explains why poor people in America move much more often than the upper-middle class and the upper class, as they search for a better life, a better standard of living, a better quality of life.

There is political corruption everywhere, at all levels. Power and greed are the motivating reasons for American corruption, at all levels, from the poor to the rich, just like everywhere else in the World. On a radio show about marriage someone somewhere aptly said "Cheaters need to stop their cheating, creating chaos, misery, and pain in other people's lives." This applies to all corruption everywhere, by anyone, at all levels.

Waking the collective conscience, the collective consciousness, was of no value in the 1960's and the 1970's."No more blood for oil" was commonly seen on signs at public and mass demonstrations, at public protests, but they changed nothing. Since 2003 it's been the same, more blood for oil, but with no photos, videos, or unbiased news coverage to inform the American people about what was really happening in Iraq and Afghanistan, as America was becoming a closed and controlled society.

82

Americans haven't had power to change anything since the 1960's, since the war in Viet Nam began, since immediately after President Kennedy was assassinated. But protests and demonstrations, with up to a million people participating each time, gave the demonstrators the feeling they were changing things, changing national Government policy. Taking away the right to protest changed nothing anyway, as the United States Government never paid any attention to what the protestors wanted, and never changed any Government actions or policies as a result of those protests and demonstrations and marches in Washington, D.C.

To do the right thing, the humane thing, for many millions of innocent South Vietnamese civilians and for American military men in Viet Nam was beyond the scope of the United States political agenda in Viet Nam for more than a decade. The eventual death of 58,000 American soldiers was expected. The eventual death of millions of civilians in Viet Nam, Cambodia, and Laos was expected. The lives of the expendable masses in all countries were not important.

The eventual death of millions of Vietnamese and Cambodian civilians was regarded as "collateral damage". Vietnamese and Cambodian civilians of all ages, including babies, were tortured and killed by American soldiers, who had been shown by their superior officers how to murder all ages of people with unbelievable cruelty, repeatedly telling them Vietnamese and Cambodian people were not humans, that they were just animals who needed to be killed by American soldiers. The Marine chant was "Kill! Kill! Kill!" And, "If you don't kill them they will kill you." This was the justification for killing of civilians who had no weapons and no way to defend themselves, and for burning hundreds of entire villages. The soldiers were there to defend South Vietnamese people from Communism, but soldiers were often working against those people.

The Viet Cong soldiers were ruthlessly killing American soldiers who didn't want to be there, invading Viet Nam and fighting the Viet Cong Communist forces. American soldiers fought to protect and defend their buddies, their friends, their fellow soldiers, and because that is what they were drafted into mandatory military service to do and taught to do. It was always kill or be killed, because that is always what war is about.

During World War II soldiers were in combat an average of 10 days a month, but for the war in Viet Nam and later in Cambodia, from 1965 to 1975, American soldiers were in combat an average of 240 days a year. LBJ said America was in Viet Nam to fight the spread of Communism. For that reason American soldiers were motivated to fight to supposedly protect America, 6000 miles away. Viet Nam, Cambodia, Laos had no militaries, no military planes to fly 6000 miles to America, no abilities to bomb America, or do anything to the American people. That alone was justification for the draft dodgers in America, in the 1960' and the 1970's, for not wanting to fight, kill, and die in the longest undeclared war in U.S. history.

In 1971 students at Ohio State University were demonstrating against Nixon invading Cambodia and four students were shot and killed by the National Guard. One of the students was just walking to her next class, not involved in any way in the demonstrations near her. Nine more students were shot and injured. No one in the demonstration was carrying a gun or rifle, just school books. Not even a club, like law enforcement always uses to hit any person near a demonstration. They were expressing freedom of speech and the freedom to demonstrate and protest the actions of the United States Government, all Constitutional rights, all "guaranteed rights" that weren't guaranteed, rights that disappeared when the people that rule America wanted them to disappear. It was so easy to do. None of the National Guard murderers were charged with anything. They were just "doing their job".

Americans are unified in their political disunity, their lack of political unity. Elections and politicians everywhere, at all levels, are bought and paid for. No one anywhere takes responsibility for anything that is done wrong, for any bad consequences of wrongful and even illegal actions. And almost everything that is socially wrong is rarely if ever changed.

When you can't win even if you've won is what happened during and after the Republican election fiasco of 2000 in Florida. At that time Vice President Gore said "Even if I win I can't win." He was rich and famous, and had the vast majority of Americans voting for him and supporting him to be the next President. He had gotten the majority of votes in the national election, even though the Diebold voting machines had been fixed so **10 million** votes for Gore would register as a vote for Bush "W", and **18 million** votes weren't even counted in Ohio and Florida.

But still he, and his campaign members, couldn't stop the force of the Republican modus operandi, the hate and the ego, the dishonesty, the lies, the manipulations of Republican politicians and Republican officials in power, elected or not. This was an immovable Republican force, finalized by a Republican majority of Supreme Court Judges predisposed to decide in favor of any Republican, but especially in favor of Bush "W", the son of the President that had put several of them there, as Supreme Court Judges. It was high-end job security for the rest of their lives, as it is a life-time appointment. They had to, and did, show their gratitude.

This was a perfect example of how laws and rules can be twisted and distorted for unethical purposes by a minority in the United States, and the majority is powerless to change it to something ethical, fair, and right. That which is illegal becomes legal.

So Bush "W" became President by appointment in 2000. Then in January of 2001 the nightmare was complete, after the Republicans and Neo Cons in power, elected or not, manipulated the American public and the United States voting system in 2000, then manipulated the Superior Court Judges and the Constitution, bending and breaking laws, rewriting The Constitution for themselves, for their ulterior and unlawful motives. This controlling Neo Con behavior continued after he was appointed President for a total of eight years. The biggest and the worst actions were changing The Constitution by eliminating seven of the rights of all Americans that they had had for about 235 years, designing and allowing the 9/11 tragedies, and stealing an unbelievable total of **$20 trillion dollars to as much as $40 trillion dollars** from the Social Security Fund surplus *every year* that Bush "W" and Cheney were in power.

There have been many ways of proving these almost unbelievable and illegal actions committed on all American people, that eventually led to the United States military and privatized military killing, torturing, and wounding of at least a million Iraqi people, and the death of about 3000 American soldiers. But no one dares to do anything, to say anything, to publish the information and the proof, except documentaries produced by brave people in America who risk everything to tell the truth. This is not what a Democracy "by the people and for the people" is supposed to be like. But the people of the United States are not united enough to change anything, to demand changes for anything, to demand the truth be told about anything. Let alone the truth about these unbelievable atrocities and illegal actions of their Government and their military, besides the theft of their money and the endless lies.

Being in the dark and the dumbing of Americans became the status quo for the 21st century. When the 9/11 Commission requested all e-mails sent from and to the Whitehouse for a designated period of time before and after 9/11, and all e-mails sent from and to Bush "W" and Cheney, *all* of these e-mails were destroyed, many *millions* of them, and *none* were given to the 9/11 Commission. This was proof they had a lot to hide. But nothing happened to them for not co-operating after committing these crimes. They were above the law. All evidence of their crimes had been destroyed. There were no charges, no legal actions, no investigations. The average American would not and could not be given such leniency.

Greed, money, and power trump honesty in America. Greed, money, and power trump everything in America. Maybe it's the same everywhere in the World, making it just a human shortcoming, a human flaw potentially for all humans in general. These are the reasons for most of the misery perpetrated in the World, usually by very flawed human beings, and always by very selfish human beings. It's a major flaw of humanity.

In the 21st century it's all-American and OK to be mean, vicious, self-righteous, two-faced, arrogant, vulgar, to lie and be selfish. Apparently Americans have always been these ways. It's just an American tradition since America began. The Republican Right personifies that. There was a shift in that direction starting in 2000. It's become the American way, maybe even for the entire 21st century. The Bush "W" Neo Con administration had a lasting influence that was bad for some, even terrible, and was good for others. That's America. It's always divided, the population is never united, in the United States of America.

At the beginning of America Puritans from England killed, murdered, entire Native Indian tribes, who of course had no guns to defend themselves with against the treacherous, murderous, well-armed Puritans who had guns, rifles, shotguns, and bullets they had brought with them from England. These very religious people had relocated to a new country to have freedom of religious expression, to have a pure and untainted religion. They called themselves Puritans as proof of their personal purity for God. However, the Ten Commandments didn't mean anything to them when they were invaders of the foreign land, occupied by Indians for thousands of years. If possession is 9/10's of the law then the Native Indians owned this new/old foreign country the Puritans were taking over for their own.

"Do unto others as you would have them do unto you" and "Love thy neighbor" and "Thou shalt not kill", part of the Ten Commandments in their sacred Bible, obviously meant nothing to them and were ignored by these highly religious and self-righteous people from England. Native Indians had helped them from the beginning, and had never hurt them, giving them food so they wouldn't starve during their first winter in a new and harsh land, and giving them seeds and vegetables to plant for food for the coming year. From the beginning they had been friendly and kind to these white invaders of their ancestral land, helping and sharing with these white foreign invaders in every way they could.

White people have been selfish, paranoid, vicious, arrogant, violent, mean, and intolerant in what became America since the very beginning. It continues in America in the 21st century.

Their legacy continues. From the beginning of America white Americans have said one thing and done another. Hypocrisy has been part of the foundation of America. First the English from England, and then every other race and foreign culture in the World, became acclimatized to this prevailing attitude in the new and growing country of America.

For centuries the Government of England, of Britain, had been trying to conquer and control the World, using brutal and cruel methods of subjugation towards native foreign cultures and populations, while maintaining a mostly extra-civilized stiff upper-lip attitude as they would say one thing and do another, appear to be one way and act another. That was the heritage, the legacy, that the English settlers, the settlers from Britain, brought with them that lasted for the next 250 years. It was a major influence on the development of America since its beginning that continues today. There is no reason this British inheritance and tradition will ever stop.

In a country where everybody's relatives are immigrants, except the Native American Indians, Americans have usually not liked or accepted immigrants, millions of them decade after decade, since the beginning of America, and not accepted the usually welcoming Native Indians from the very beginning. This attitude is the opposite of the other 23 Democracies where the individual is important and matters. A lack of freedom and fairness has always been part of living in America. People in the other Democracies are more friendly, more tolerant and accepting.

Some of the most cruel, violent, vicious, and inhumane people in the World have been Buddhists, throughout a few thousand years of history. These men from Japan, China, Korea, etc. do not believe there is a God to guide them, to punish them, to be held accountable to in the after-life, after death. For thousands of years hundreds of billions of people, even trillions of people, have believed in and followed the teachings of Buddha, espousing peace, kindness, and serenity in life, but justifying cruel and inhumane treatment and torture of their enemies. Besides their ruthless killing of hundreds of millions of their self-proclaimed enemies during those thousands of years, people who did not believe in the Buddhist religion.

Belief in one God, like in Christianity and for Muslims, and their belief in Jesus and Mohammed respectively, hasn't produced better people, better men specifically. As an example, the treatment and torture of enemies by British soldiers throughout history has been deplorable, awful, and inhumane. Notoriously, American soldiers have been less cruel to their enemies than their English counterparts, but since the occupation of Iraq, with their cruelty and torture of prisoners in prisons, this reputation has changed. As a result there's been Eastern hypocrisy and Western hypocrisy throughout history. Both the East and the West have tried to rule the World, or at least to control other countries, often using violent and cruel methods in the process. Religions of any kind haven't stopped people from doing bad and inexcusable things anywhere in the World when conquest, power, money, and control have been the motive.

Which is right, one God or no God? There are more than a *thousand* religions in the World. Obviously they can't all be right. The majority of people in the World are Muslims. Early Christianity included belief in several gods. Biblical scholars, archaeologists, professors of biblical history, and professional explorers in general searching for the truth about the Bible, have tried to prove the accuracy of the Old Testament for centuries and have failed to prove that any of it really happened.

Even the reigns of Kings, written about in the Old Testament, are depicted as being in the wrong century than when they *really* occurred. A century is a very long time, a mistake of one hundred years is a big mistake, during which time any civilization will change substantially. But this epitomizes the whole Old Testament, which has never been proven and is mostly, or all, myths and stories written mostly 100 years after, and often *300 to 500 years after,* they were supposed to have happened. The same things can be said, in general, for the New Testament.

This all means, in reality, that Christians and the Bible are sources of myths and hypocrisy, based on hypocrisy, stories, and myths. Religions civilize and unite people, so the World would have been even more of a mess without the nearly 1000 religions in the World, even if all of them are based on myths. Religions have always given people something to belong to, a reason for them to come together with good intentions. A goodness to aspire to, with unintended consequences if they don't. Religions hold people to higher standards.

But throughout history most of the cruelty in the World that results in wars and conflicts has been because of religions. Throughout history most of the inhumanity and cruelty in the World has been connected to religions. Buddhists believe there is no life after death so their religion isn't based on fear, like Christianity is. Perhaps Buddhists have less of a conscience because of that.

Historically, the United States Government does not believe the majority is right, or that it should do what is right for the majority, for the expendable masses. Or that they have the same civil rights, the same human rights, as the upper 5% or 10%, and especially the upper 1%, despite the fact that the United States is a democracy, and based on Christianity, with a foundation of Christianity.

The Congressional oath of office, like the Presidential oath of office, is that they will defend The Constitution. "I promise to preserve, protect, and defend The Constitution" is the Presidential oath of office. Passing the Patriot Act in 2001 was a major violation of that oath. What incentive do they have to follow that oath? None. No citizen can do anything about them not following that oath. The Government cannot be sued. Integrity is not a requirement, nor is it a political concept that is always adhered to. Lying is common.

As an example, just one of many examples, Congress protects CEO's of large corporations. These CEO's get paid millions of dollars, even billions of dollars every year, and often pay no taxes on it, or very little taxes on it, say 1%. Senators and Representatives of Congress get their payoffs on the side so they will give allocations, subsidies, and favors in exchange, in return for looking the other way. Congress does nothing about this theft, so this cheating that has been the historical norm.

Yet Congress has always been the only hope for good and honest Americans to maintain an open society and to protect United States citizens from loss of their civil liberties, their civil rights, and their freedoms guaranteed in The Constitution. But, in many ways, Congress has miserably failed Americans, the citizens they represent who put them in power, who voted for them, or not. They might just as well be appointed. Elections are becoming a useless and unnecessary part of the equation. Elections make people think they are in control of their Government, participating in their Government, their country, giving them a feeling of being a part of the United States. Leaders who are for peace, truth, justice, who don't want to exploit the poor, and are for a real democracy, never last very long. They are eliminated, one way or another, either figuratively or in actuality.

There were about 150 million people in the United States in 2013 who were living near poverty level, at poverty level, or below poverty level. That's almost half the population in the United States.

To ignore this many people, for a Government to not help this large of a percentage of its population, is proof that the United States is no longer a democracy. Besides the proof evident in the partial destruction, the desecration, of The Constitution and Bill of Rights in 2001 by the Congress, by the Senate, and by President Bush "W" and Vice President Cheney. No other democracy, of which there are 24 in the World, has ever done this to their people, to their citizens. Just the United States.

In 2000 Democratic Senator Carnahan of Missouri was being challenged by Ashcroft, the Republican candidate in a re-election campaign. Carnahan's plane mysteriously and for no apparent reason crashed on October 17, 2000, a few weeks before the election. However, even though he had died as a result of that crash, as had his son who was the pilot of the plane, Carnahan won the election instead of Ashcroft. People didn't want Ashcroft as Senator so they voted for Carnahan anyway. As a result, his wife was then appointed Senator to replace her deceased husband. She said "He was a good and honest man, for justice and freedom." No wonder he was eliminated.

Ashcroft was then appointed Attorney General of the United States by the new President Bush "W". Thereafter Ashcroft did things, made decisions for years, which caused misery for millions of people, even though he was a former Pastor of a church and supposedly had more integrity than a politician would have. Religions have been the indirect cause for a lot of misery in the World.

Democratic Senator Wellstone of Minnesota was known to be a good and honest man, with a majority support, who was also in his plane when it mysteriously crashed in September, 2004, just before his election. He died, as did everyone else who was in that plane crash. It was too late to put a Democratic replacement on that ballot so, of course, his Republican opponent won the election because there was no one running against him. He won by default. It had been a planned "accident".

In order to run for President the background of George W. Bush had to be hidden and altered in order to qualify as a candidate. Bush "W" had four security violations with the Security and Exchange Commission. Later, Martha Stewart had one violation and went to prison for a year because of it. Too bad her father wasn't a former Neo Con President. Bush "W" had made a profit of $846,000 days before a stock dropped precipitously to $4 a share. Insider information, insider trading, is illegal for other people. But Bush "W' was not charged because he was "special", above the law.

He also had a drunk driving violation. These illegal and law breaking actions, crimes, should have made him exempt from running for President, and certainly from then becoming a United States President, but the Supreme Court Judges, the highest court in America, came to his rescue and ignored this, just like they twisted and distorted United States laws to make him, to appoint him, the United States President in 2000. His lawyer, Alberto Gonzalez, had gotten the drunk driving crime taken off his record before the election. So, after his illegal victory was made legal by Supreme Court Judges twisting and distorting laws, after Bush "W" then became President, he appointed Gonzalez as the new Attorney General of the United States. It pays to have friends in high places.

The Supreme Court Judges that had been appointed by his father, former President Bush, made the difference in the final decision to bend laws for just this one time, never to be repeated again in United States history it was decreed later. Neo Con Bush "W" was forced on the majority of the American people, that did not want him to be the President of their country, by manipulating the national and state voting systems in ways unprecedented in American history. In America connections and money are everything in the political boxing ring.

As the President, Bush "W" tried to appoint his cleaning lady to be a Supreme Court Judge. Just how "supreme" are the Supreme Court Judges, for the highest court in the United States? Apparently not much. No wonder Bush "W" thought he was chosen by God to be the President, and that God spoke directly to him. He was above the law and he was "special" because he was protected by the Neo Cons in power that were elected and not elected. They were going to make him President no matter what. He was going to be their spokesperson no matter what they had to do to get him there, against all odds. And Cheney, as Vice President, would be the one calling the shots, the director of "the decider", as Bush "W" called himself.

An uniformed public is what the Neo Cons wanted. The people of America don't need to know the truth. But suppression and hiding the truth about the Government is not what a democracy does. No other democracy in the World, 23 of them besides the United States, has done such a disservice and dishonesty to their people. The United States is number one.

The Neo Con agenda, 2000 to 2009, stole **trillions of dollars** from Americans in order to further their secret Neo Con agendas and to bankrupt America. After that, for years, Republican politicians had repeatedly accused Democratic President Obama of excessive national Government spending when, in fact, they were the "wrong-doers" before he got there, that was done in a manner, with an excess, never seen before in United States history. Making sure a Democrat became President was their fall guy for the Neo Con's huge financial mess, their theft and disappearance of trillions of dollars of American government money for eight years duration.

Obama was a done-deal before election day. Lack of accountability, not taking responsibility for what they do, is a Republican tradition. A Democrat for President meant they could shift the blame and the actual real financial burden of *$11.5 trillion dollar s of national debt* that the Republicans in power for eight years had created, after President Clinton had handed Bush "W" a balanced budget and a *$20 billion dollar budget surplus* dollar budget surplus for the first time in United States history. But the biggest national budget surplus in history quickly disappeared, was stolen, when the Republicans got a hold of it, and it was never accounted for. Instead the Republicans in power left the biggest budget deficit by far in U.S. history when they left office eight years later. Greed and theft, and lying and dishonesty, had become the American political way. Especially for the Neo Cons, for the Far Right, for the Republicans.

The United States Government is supposed to serve and protect the citizens of America. This is impossible because of wasteful multi-million dollar or billion dollar projects, massive corruption, theft, and incompetence. Also, it's impossible because of serving special interest groups and lobbyists, more than 30,000 of them, instead of the welfare of its citizens. All of this results in billion dollar, and trillion dollar, losses of American's money being wasted and stolen every year by their Government, by their elected politicians and appointed officials, especially since 2001.

When Republican politicians say Social Security and other entitlement programs have to be cut or eliminated they are **lying**. What has to be cut or eliminated is the secret huge Government theft and politician theft of *trillions of dollars* from the Social Security Fund, the usual twisting and distorting of the truth, the common lying and lies, and stopping the dishonesty to the people they are supposed to represent. No good has ever come from government theft, secrets, and lies.

The people in the United States, the American public, are *managed* by the United States Government, not served by their Government. Politicians elected to serve the public usually do not serve the American people. They serve themselves, banks, CEOs, corporations, the 1% elite, the upper 10%, oil corporations, the military, the lobbyists (more than 20,000 of them), and special interest groups. The American public, the expendable masses, are just incidental. They are the people who pay their salaries with their taxes, but out of sight out of mind.

The United States is the only free country in the World, for many years, that doesn't have a budget in its Federal Government for a free national, or universal, health care system for everyone. Instead, sickness is Big Business in America, a mega-industry in America, that is always one of the top three most lucrative industries every year for about the last 25 years. It's been medical industry greed and corruption for about 50 years.

A healthy nation became secondary to the profits of the pharmaceutical industry and chemical industry, and physicians became certified pill-pushers. *Very* highly paid pill-pushers. More than 100,000 available pharmaceuticals (pills and injections) and more than 100,000 artificial chemicals, all produced in America, mean actual health is impossible, an impossibility. Sickness is inevitable and is a guaranteed source of income for the United States economy, for businesses both large and small. Health problems are a big part of what it means to be an American, an important part of being an American in America, and thereby contributing to the health of the American economy.

One of the top three most lucrative industries for the last 25 years is the insurance industry. Health insurance is really sickness insurance. Life insurance is really death insurance. Mandatory health insurance plays right into it, as the health and welfare of Americans is secondary to the unbelievably greedy profits of medicine in America since before 2001, but much more so since 2001.The rest of the World charges 1/10 to 1/1000 of the prices charged for medical procedures, hospitalization, drugs, etc. in America, for the same quality and for better service than in America.

In other countries serving people and helping people to be healthy are the reasons for their medical systems, not for the reason of making *huge* profits like in the American medical/sickness industry. In 1946, after World War II, the United States national debt was $200 billion, 122% of the GDP. In 2011 the national debt was almost*$12 trillion dollars,* a lot more money, a much bigger debt, than ever before in United States history, but about 89% of the GDP. The cost of living in 2011 was about 20 to 25 times more than in 1946, depending upon where you lived in the United States. Minimum wage was only 40 cents an hour in 1946 and was $7.25 an hour in 2011. These are the worst years for national debt in United States history, until the debt will be worse in following years.

In 1946 politicians fixed the problem by doing what they were supposed to do, what they were hired to do by the people who elected them to represent their interests. Politicians in 1946 made more cuts to entitlements and gifts to special interest groups than ever before, and cut costs and raised taxes for everyone, including the most wealthy, the upper elite, without touching Social Security. There was unity of purpose then in 1946, for both the Government and the American people. This is the opposite of today's politicians and today's America. In 1946 there was much less tax evasion by corporations, by banks, by the upper 10%, etc. Yet, tax rates were higher than ever before and higher than now, in 2014. The rich paid their fair share, without cheating, without tax evasion and write-offs, or hiding their money in off-shore accounts, etc.

The results were positive, restoring what was right about America, not just eliminating the national debt, the budget deficit. There is no real reason other than greed, dishonesty, devisiveness, corruption, lies and selfishness that the same things can't be done, that the same methods can't be used, to fix the national debt now and anytime in the future. But today's politicians don't want to copy success. There is a prevailing arrogance. The massive financial failure of the United States Government during 2001 to 2009 was part of the Neo Con's plan for "a New America". Common sense was not part of the Neo Cons plan for "a New America". But increasing the gap between the very rich and everybody else *was* part of their agenda, a part of their plans made years before.

Cuts to entitlement programs means greater poverty and decreased standards of living for most Americans. An impoverished America is a Neo Con America, for purposes of control. The rich keep getting richer, the poor keep getting poorer. This very unbalanced situation could easily be fixed just by the upper 20% actually paying their taxes, *all* of it that is due, not using tax evasion and tax write-offs, etc. Raising taxes for the very rich to be the same as for the middle-class and the poor, and then actually *paying* their taxes, would balance this unbalanced situation even more. But first the corruption, lies, selfishness, and dishonesty need to be stopped. But of course that will never happen.

Nearly perpetual wars for about 60 years have provided cover for theft of many **trillions of dollars** from the American people, stealing and depriving Americans of a better life for everyone for about 60 years. But that pales in comparison to what has been happening since 2001, since 9/11 happened, since after it was allowed to happen by the Neo Cons in power at that time. That was the ultimate cover of covers for radical change in what had formerly been guaranteed freedoms, and for the theft of at least **$100 trillion dollars** stolen from the American people in the following 10 years by their Government, with the DOD probably being the most guilty. This includes the *yearly* theft by politicians of the at least *$4 trillion dollar yearly surplus* in the Social Security Fund since 2001. Wake up America! Politicians have lied about this every year since the theft began after 9/11 in 2001. All of these many *trillions of dollars* stolen from the Social Security Fund need to be returned to the American people. But of course it won't be. Not now, not ever.

The *yearly* theft of at least *$4 trillion dollars* from Social Security since 2001 needs to stop, but it won't be stopped. First politicians and officials would have to admit what they have done wrong, which will never happen. Because at least **$100 trillion dollars** will have "disappeared" mysteriously, and because they are above the law, they will not have to return it. Petty thieves go to prison for up to 25 years for stealing something worth $1 to $1000. But the wealthiest thieves in America are above the law, or have different laws just for them. Or they use the "I don't remember" excuse, and then have no legal responsibility because they are the elite, and they are allowed to have convenient memory loss, unlike other Americans, who would then be accused of lying. The rich *are* different. They have more money, and they are above the law. Or at least they have their own special laws.

There will be no charges, no convictions, no imprisonment for these million dollar, billion dollar, trillion dollar political, DOD, military, and Government theft because they, like CEOs, have a license to steal. The rich are indeed privileged. Money drives American politics, not the American people and their hopeful voting at elections. Especially since the pivotal changing points of 2000/2001. There's no going back to anything that used to be.

There has always been a solution for eliminating the at least *$11.5 trillion dollar debt* that Bush "W" and Cheney left behind for the American people to pay for, and to stop the at least $1 trillion dollar yearly interest payments on that debt. That solution was across the border, in Canada. However, because of the arrogance of the World's "super-power" United States politicians and the people that rule America this could never happen.

Canada has a Parliamentary Government. When Canada had an economic financial crisis of excessive national debt after 2001 their Parliament raised taxes for all Canadians and eliminated unnecessary spending and programs, and money to special interest groups. This was common sense, and no one could argue or object about it. Canada's Government is not divided, never having constant political arguing, or fear-mongering, manipulation, posturing, and division, like in the United States Government, especially in Washington, D.C., in the Senate and the House, especially in the 21$^{st}$ century. The common sense approach used by the Canadians has always worked very well, very effectively.  American politicians would rather argue endlessly, and refuse to follow another country's success formula because of their pride and arrogance, because of their assumed superiority. Pride and arrogance and superiority about what?

The financial crisis in Canada was stopped and replaced with economic growth and prosperity and a large increase in jobs nationally. This has continued for more than a decade, therefore it is a legitimate formula for success. Successful countries follow proven success, just like successful people usually have followed, or copied, somebody else's success.

In 2012 seven leaders of Latin American countries that have had unsuccessful attempts made to assassinate them for years had all gotten cancer in 2012, all at about the same time. They said publically that they thought the United States CIA had done something to give cancer to them in the hopes of killing them that way, since previous CIA assassination attempts hadn't been successful. All of these leaders are, or were, very loved and supported by the majority of people in their countries. But not by their military leaders or opposition leaders that are bought and paid for by the United States, to the tune of a total of $38 billion to $58 billion dollars paid each year as "foreign aid", given mostly to their militaries by the United States.

The United States medical/sickness industry and the cancer industry have known many ways to cause cancer for many years. Perhaps that's why the cancer rate in America in 2014 is one out of eight people, not one out of 500 people like it was 50 years ago. Creating cancer, causing cancer, greatly increases the profits of the medical/sickness industry, of which the cancer industry is the major contributor each year. Also, an oppressed and sick population is easier to manage, and pays much higher health insurance premiums. The insurance industry is always one of the top three money-makers, the top profit-producing industries in America each year for at least the past 30 years. In order to find the reasons for things, the motive for almost anything, follow the money.

As a result of Government-subsidized corruption, price-gouging, and oil company corruption, the oil industry has been one of the top three money-making industries in the United States for at least 40 years. However, since about 1980 the United States Government prints money continuously to give as subsidies to oil companies like Exxon and Mobile, now Exxon-Mobile. It's welfare for the extremely wealthy oil industry. Every year since about 1980 the United States Treasury deposits this money, hundreds of millions of dollars, directly into banks for oil companies as subsidies, as oil welfare payments. The media has always reported oil company profits as "millions of dollars", but yearly oil company profits since about 2000 are about *$40 billion dollars* each year. The media lies. Again and again, and as always.

The United States Treasury, the United States Government, could do the same thing to pay off part of the United States *$13 trillion dollar debt* to China, England, Russia, France, Japan, etc., that the Neo Cons and Republicans caused in 2001 to 2009. The *interest paid* on the accumulated debt in 2012 was more than *a trillion dollars* by itself. Stealing from America has always been easy to do because of political and Government complicity and approval at all levels. The finger has never pointed to just one person, but often involves hundreds of people inside the Federal Government, or outside of the Federal Government.

Democrats are for all the people, the poor, the rich, and the average American, and for honesty. At least this is what they used to represent. Republicans are for big business, the rich, the upper 10%, especially the upper 1%, corruption, lies, and greed. Not to forget meanness. So a Democratic President, or a Democratic majority in Congress, should have stopped this massive government-approved oil industry theft of billions of dollars in 30 years. But it has been a Government secret, a mutual two-party theft, a mutual Republican and Democratic political shared guilt and corruption responsibility. Most Americans have always needed this financial gift *much* more than the oil companies did, who really didn't need it at all. But the American people have always been powerless to stop it, like they have been powerless to stop the many *trillions of dollars* stolen from their Social Security Fund since 2001. Most Americans don't even know about it.

There have been alternative solutions for natural energy and fuel alternatives for many years, all of them independently developed and perfected. But not supported financially or in policy by the United States Government. Solar energy, geothermal steam energy, wind-power, hydro-steam, and growing algae for oil have been developed and perfected for years. Nothing needs to be discovered, invented, or patented. No research is necessary, like Obama repeatedly said was necessary in 2009 to 2014. But the best source of free energy, that would improve the lives of everyone in the World, is separating hydrogen from oxygen for fuel. This has been known about for years.

It is clear the United States Government, the powers that be, do not want Americans to have as good a life as possible, but, instead, want to control the expendable masses. Controlling, greedy, and manipulative Republicans in power and the weak apathetic Democrats in power in every Presidential Administration have made sure this doesn't happen. They have made sure the United States remains controlled and manipulated by the oil industry, a slave to the oil industry.

Iceland, a democracy, uses natural geothermal steam from the Earth to provide heat and electricity cheaply for everyone in Iceland. If the United States Government, including politicians elected or not and officials elected or not, wasn't so arrogant, controlled by the oil industry, Neo Cons, the elite, the Far Right, and politicians who get huge financial pay-offs from the oil industry, the United States population would have benefitted and profited immensely from copying Iceland. But politicians in America were, and are, bought and paid for by the oil industry. Some of them owe their political careers to the oil industry. So their allegiance has been to the oil industry, not to the American people who elected them and pay their inflated $150,000 yearly salaries. The American people have been powerless to change any of this. Voting and elections have never been the answer.

As a result of Hurricane Katrina oil spills covered New Orleans. But the oil industry in New Orleans, in Louisiana, didn't pay a dime for damages to property and people, or for deaths, including the deaths of at least 10,000 pets, caused by those oil spills. Or for the cleanup necessary for most of New Orleans. It pays to be a favorite of the federal and state Governments if you want special treatment. If you want to not have to pay hundreds of millions, even billions of dollars, in reparation because of incompetence, mistakes, indifference. If you want to be like the oil industry in America.

Oil prices are manipulated by decreasing and limiting the supply of oil, and then using that controlled decrease in supply of oil as a justification to increase prices. Actual supply and demand have nothing to do with it. Melting of the icecaps helps oil companies to find oil there, to more easily drill for and discover new sources of oil there, in those newly accessible locations that don't have rules, regulations, and restrictions for drilling. This is one reason the United States Government and Republicans do not admit to global warming, endlessly arguing it isn't necessary to make changes to stop it, to stop the global warming that they want to happen for financial profits, for more money.

Houston generates all of its energy, all of its power, from wind power, from windmills. There's no reason that this can't be done everywhere in the United States, except for greed and collaboration with, conspiracy with, the oil, gas, and coal companies, that are like pay-offs for co-operation. School buses in Las Vegas run 100% on biodiesel fuel. There's no reason that same thing can't be done everywhere in the United States, but it isn't done anywhere else in the United States. Politics even drives school buses.

Destroying the atmosphere of the Earth and destroying the health of people throughout America and the World with cancer, asthma, diabetes, heart problems, diseases, and forcing them into poverty and keeping them in poverty, has been the impact and result of the oil, gas, and coal industries 100 year monopoly of economies. Obviously this is what the United States Government wants, and has wanted for many years. Of course it inevitably points to complicity.`

To sustain life on Earth carbon dioxide has to be reduced drastically. All other democracies have plans and actions to accommodate that. As an example, Sweden will use no oil or gasoline after 2020, allowing and using only biodiesel fuel. Some other democracies are following their example.

It is possible that, from the beginning, alternatives to oil and gasoline have been eliminated by Americans representing the oil and gasoline industry. In about 1870 Rudolph Diesel, in Germany, invented film with sound. It wasn't invented in America, like Americans think. In general, it seems Americans think everything was invented in America. Later he invented a diesel engine that would run on peanut oil, not crude oil and gasoline. He was murdered in 1903 while traveling on a ship to the World's Fair exhibition of this invention, of his diesel fuel engine. Biodiesel fuel and diesel fuel are named after him. Was the oil and gas industry in America responsible for this murder? If so, it was never revealed to the American public. But for most people, no good ever comes of secrets.

Henry Ford designed the Model T to run on ethanol. J.D. Rockefeller, founder of Standard Oil, funded legislation to *begin* Prohibition, to create Prohibition, making all alcohol, including ethanol, illegal. Transporting millions of gallons of ethanol then stopped, replaced by millions of gallons of oil and gasoline for cars and trucks that then ran on oil and gasoline only. After Prohibition ended domination of oil continued because cars running on ethanol had been eliminated, destroyed.

In a similar manner, almost 100 years later, electric cars were eliminated in the United States by the United States Government recalling them and then destroying them, within about three years after they were sold to Americans in the 1990's.Therefore, none were allowed to be sold as used cars. They worked so well they were a threat to the oil and gasoline industry. This Federal Government action was not an action of a true democracy. The very satisfied owners of the electric cars were powerless to stop it, or to keep their cars that were then taken from them by the Federal

Government and destroyed. It was something that wouldn't happen in a true democracy.

The United States Government has long been run by the oil industry, by the medical/sickness industry, by the pharmaceutical industry, by the insurance industry, by the defense industry and the United States military, which are parts of the vast military industrial complex, and by special-interest groups, by lobbyists, more than 30,000 of them in Washington, D.C., by the CIA, the FBI, the IRS, the NSA, the IMF, and by huge corporations, and by the upper 1% in America , the elite. There's no room left for anyone else. The expendable masses are just an after-thought.

Since Reagan, since the 1980's, about a *million dollars* would have been saved in electrical costs at the White House if President Reagan had not taken off the solar panels on the White House installed under the order of President Carter before him. The Republicans would not, could not, allow that to happen. It would be an example for the rest of the nation, for the rest of America, an example and motivation from the top to convert to solar power, thereby depriving the oil industry of maybe half of their ill-gotten gains. Corruption is the American way, and has been for a few hundred years. It must be perpetuated and maintained in order to continue control, power, and profit for the elite.

In 2012 the United States was exporting oil because it was producing a surplus of refined oil. At the same time prices for oil and gasoline went up about 50 cents a gallon in America. Obviously the American oil industry, oil refined in America, is not for the benefit of Americans. Obviously prices have nothing to do with supply and demand. At the same time President Obama was campaigning heavily in the United States about pushing for alternative energy cars and trucks to be made in the United States, just when the need for them was lessened.

Perhaps the oil games meant prices would continue to go up as America would continue to export more refined oil than ever before indefinitely, and as Americans continued to drive less each year. The oil industry has always been a game of manipulation and lies, having nothing to do with American national and international (Middle Eastern) supply and American demand, contrary to what the media has always said. It has never been about supply and demand as the supply has always been manipulated, making many people very rich.

Changing to a new economy based on using sustainable energy, renewable energy, free energy, and stopping the forced dependence on fossil fuels would also greatly lessen waste production and accumulation. Every day corporations pour millions of gallons of poison, of toxins, of waste, into the streams, rivers, and oceans of America. Poisoning the oceans, rivers, streams, polluting the atmosphere, exhausting the soil, destroying the forests and land to search for and mine coal, would all stop. Nobody stops the crimes against the Earth, against the oceans, streams, and rivers, and the health and environmental violations, even though it's against the law. Laws have long been in place. But they are not enforced by the people that are hired to enforce them. No records means no proof of violations of laws.

This is a big problem everywhere in the United States. Not enforcing laws that are already in place, and selectively enforcing laws. More laws don't need to be created. They need to be enforced equally. And without prejudice, profiling, and targeting.

The United States Government made it impossible to implement alternative energies nationally after Carter was President. The United States Government was in bed with the oil industry and Saudi Arabia. Nothing needs to be invented or discovered. But a clean fuel, cost-efficient economy didn't fit into the national Government's plans for Americans. Dependency on foreign oil did.

Jimmy Carter was the only President to have energy policies, reducing national energy expenditures by 25%. He had solar energy panels installed at the White House. Reagan, his successor, had the solar panels removed and ended the energy saving policies. Free sources of energy, the wind and the Sun, have been mostly rejected by the United States Government since Carter was President. In the 1980's Carter started a program to develop an alternative to oil, that was also rejected.

This was a method using algae for creating oil in months, not thousands or millions of years, not hundreds or thousands of feet under-ground. It would have saved Americans trillions of dollars and saved the environment from carbon dioxide poisoning and destruction. It meant billions of dollars, even trillions of dollars, would be saved from oil exploration, drilling, and transportation of oil, and the yearly welfare subsidies paid to oil companies by the United States Government. This kind of progress could not be allowed by the powers-that-be. That kind of progress had to be stopped.

Algae is the original source for oil discovered as a result of drilling. It's where it all began. Carter's Energy Institute developed a way to get oil from algae in only three days, the same as the oil that took as much as 1.5 million years to develop and be discovered with hundreds of millions of dollars of equipment, manpower, etc. It was a major breakthrough that would change the economy of the United States and improve the life of hundreds of millions of Americans, and everybody else in the World. It was a major threat to the trillion dollar oil industry throughout the World.

This bio-diesel fuel from algae would save the planet and stop all interest in military actions in the Middle East, and pay-offs to the Middle East. The United States gives Saudi Arabia at least $1.5 billion dollars every year, mostly for their military, and does the same for Pakistan and Egypt. These pay-offs, these yearly monetary gifts, then would have been even less justified. The United States would no longer have been a super-power, or have world-wide military domination, which is why the United States is a super-power. Poverty in America would end, and world-wide poverty would end. It would have been a catastrophe for the people that run the United States, and the people that run the World in general, in terms of maintaining their power, control, and financial status.

The Neo Cons and the Republicans in power at that time made sure these political catastrophes wouldn't happen. They made sure Carter would not be reelected. It was then determined through national polls that Carter couldn't be re-elected if he couldn't get release of the American hostages in Iran. So the Republicans in power arranged a deal with Iran to send planeloads of free United States produced weapons to Iran in exchange for their promise to not release the hostages until after Reagan was elected to replace Carter.

Reagan's campaign promise had been that the American hostages in Iran would be released if he was elected. Days after he was elected they were magically released. His campaign promise was magically fulfilled immediately after he became President. So he had a very high approval rating from the start. After that his campaign promises were mostly not fulfilled because none involved bribery of foreign governments. There's no limit to what Republicans will do to get into power. Free energy from the wind and sun, and oil from algae, were forbidden political subjects after that.

Americans have the best Government that money can buy. Elected politicians are bought and paid for. So who represents the average American? No one. Carter tried to represent the average American but the United States political system, the Neo Cons in power, wouldn't let him. Clinton, too, tried to represent the average Americans. The Republicans in power tried to get rid of him by impeaching him and creating a two year hatred campaign, led by Republican Newt Gingrich, who was having a four year affair with a married intern before, during, and after Gingrich's impeachment proceedings about Clinton's alleged infidelities while in office. Including Clinton supposedly lying about it, saying "I did not have an affair with Monica Lewinsky." Clinton's definition of affair, and of having sex, did not include doing what he did with Miss Lewinsky, but the Republican definition did.

After the impeachment proceedings ended Gingrich's wife divorced him. She then went on to become a Congresswoman. Hypocrisy never ends in the American political arena. It's everywhere and anywhere always.

It was a violation of the privacy of President Clinton and his intern by the Federal Government, initially begun by Linda Tripp as a result of her tape recordings of his phone conversations, another violation of privacy and a violation of a Constitutional right. After Republican politicians and government lawyers and Judges had two years of free advertising for their upcoming elections, during the unsuccessful impeachment proceedings, Tripp sued the Federal Government for invasion of *her* privacy. She was given an unbelievable more than a million dollars as the settlement. Later, legislation was passed so that no one could ever again get legal settlements from the Federal Government for more than the actual money lost, if they get any money at all. Favoritism for Republicans would possibly end.

During the Clinton fiasco Newt Gingrich had an ongoing affair with a married woman, as he was also married, during the entire two years of the trial. He made almost daily fevered pitches against Clinton's promiscuity on the TV news, especially FOX News, the podium for two-faced and mean Republican politicians to get their words repeated many times 24/7. The message has always been clear. Republicans can cheat but Democrats can't. After all, double standards are the American way.

If the United States is a country based on justice and laws why is there so much injustice everywhere in America? America is supposed to be a land of truth and justice. But if you actually find it and get it you are very lucky, fortunate to find that which is promised by the Bill of Rights and the Constitution for the past 235 years but can be very difficult to find in America. Maybe you will, maybe you won't. It's been even more difficult to find since after 2001. Indifference, apathy, and incompetence are three of the reasons. Arrogance is another reason. Meanness, dishonesty, and lies are the other reasons. These are probably the same reasons as everywhere else in the World.

Wrongs can be right to any policemen or deputies, any Judge or lawyer, at their discretion. Preferential treatment and unjustified tickets or charges happen all the time anywhere in the United States, some places more than others. Equal justice under the law often doesn't exist. Laws and legal procedures can favor whoever is best represented, whoever has the best lawyers, whoever is part of the upper 10% in American society, or whoever is best liked, or is the most well-known, or whoever is friends with the Judge. It's a cruel world out there. There's always a struggle between good and bad.

There are low quality and selfish people everywhere in America, some places more than others. There definitely are regional variations. White-trash, black-trash, brown-trash Americans are at all class levels, from rich to poor. America definitely has social classes. It isn't just money. It's also attitude, behavior, and character. Low quality behavior happens at all levels. Each level has their own style, their own modus operandi, to demonstrate their excessive selfishness, their greed, and their endless quest for money and power. At the top levels these behaviors can cause misery for millions of people, even misery for hundreds of millions of people.

A complicity of silence and secrecy to hide corruption happens everywhere in America, probably everywhere in the World. It's what people do in their own families, and at all levels of human interaction, at all levels of society, at all levels of business, all levels of medicine, all levels of politics, all levels of government and law. Even in religions and in the Church, especially the Catholic Church where their Church doctrine tells their representatives, their Priests, Bishops, etc., to lie if it's necessary to protect the Catholic Church. It's not acceptable, but it is a fact of life. And a fact of government.

Some of the things that are wrong in America can be easily fixed. But they haven't been and they won't be. In a democracy the people should be informed with the truth. Everyone has a right to be informed with the truth. But after the Presidential elections of 2000 being informed with the truth became a thing of the past. Most Americans can't even effectively *influence* their Government anymore.

The system of checks and balances started to be broken in about 1963, before the war in Viet Nam began. Because of The Patriot Act of 2001 any United States citizen, born here or not, can be arrested and imprisoned indefinitely without legal representation and without probable cause. Freedom of speech, the basis of democracy, is now conditional and easily taken away at the discretion of those in power, at many levels. Demonstrations are only allowed with permits for each person participating. These are frightening developments contrary to a true democracy, and not what the United States is supposed to be like. The United States is the only Democracy in the World, out of 24 Democracies, that is this way.

These undesirable major changes in American society were allowed to become part of America in an undemocratic way, by using an undemocratic process. Congress, as elected representatives of the American people, signed The Patriot Act into law in 2001 without even reading it. The 365 page document was given to them to read just a few hours before they were to vote on it, having been printed throughout the night. Why were the Neo Cons in such a hurry to pass something that would be enforced for at least the next 10 years? Because it was so deceitful, so manipulative, and so necessary for the fulfillment of the Neo Con's plans for the entire 21st century.

They had planned the war in Iraq about 8 months before it happened, and had planned at that time to end that war on September 11, 2011, exactly 10 years after the 9/11 catastrophes. This apparently was for public relations impact, like 9/11 had automatic danger significance and connection to the national emergency number 911. If any Congressmen and Congresswomen didn't sign The Patriot Act, to pass it, they would be labeled "unpatriotic" by TV news media and by the so-called free Press, and by other politicians and FOX News people 24/7. Probably they then would not be reelected for a position that has endless possibilities to make a lot of money on the side, besides connections and status and an excessively high salary of about $150,000 for little actual work. And, like Senators, with a very low percentage of participation, of actually appearing for voter participation, of actually voting on anything and truthfully representing their constituents. So it was a done deal before they even saw it. It didn't need to be read, it just had to be signed.

In a closed society anything that elevates the individual, and truthfully informs the public, is censored. This includes the Press, the media, demonstrations, dissent, protests, intellectual inquiry, books, articles, documentaries, movies. A free flow of information, a free access to all information that is uncensored, unfiltered, and unbiased, including what is in public libraries, cannot be allowed. Most people in America are not aware that their freedoms are now limited. Freedoms are now controlled. This is what has been happening in America since 2001. The Constitution and The Bill of Rights have been changed by those in power since 2001, eliminating freedoms and civil rights.

The Patriot Act was signed into permanent perpetuation 10 years later in 2011 by President Obama, a Democrat. September II is now named "Patriot Day" on calendars. If you didn't support the war on terrorism that started after that day you were labeled "unpatriotic". The tragedies of 9/11 were designed to arouse patriotism. On December 31, 2011, on New Year's Eve day, President Obama signed The National Defense Act, which authorizes indefinite detention of any American, without charges, without legal representation or probable cause, and without a trial.

Apparently The Patriot Act was not enough, or not clear enough on that account. It's not just a Neo Con thing. It's a Democratic, Republican, Far Right, and Neo Con collaboration, a collaborative co-operation and mutual effort to control America, to change America for themselves as they want it, involving thousands of people in America. It's very controlling, but out of control.

Every country has its own personality, different than any other country. Every citizen of America has all of their ancestors originally from another country. American's ancestors have always come from somewhere else. Consequently, the social structure is more diversified, with more diversity of character and temperament, and traditions. But for many people traditions have gone by the wayside. Change is a very big part of American culture. Change, however, is not always beneficial. Religion and churches are traditions that have stood the test of time and don't change.

Indifference to the welfare of and manipulation of groups of people, entire populations, has happened throughout the World, throughout history. Churches are a good example. The holidays of Christmas and Easter were created, manufactured, about 300 years after Jesus died. Church officials, mostly Catholic, mostly in Italy, decided, after 300 years of uncertainty, that Jesus was born on December 25 by a woman that had never had sex, the Virgin Mary, and that years later Jesus had been crucified and then resurrected. Never really dying meant he could control his followers indefinitely, having powers of resurrection that no mere mortals would ever have. This was valuable public relations, fourth century PR. Thus Christmas and Easter were created as holidays to celebrate those supposed and alleged "miracles", created and designed by the powers-that-be in Italy about 700 years ago.

Obviously these religious holidays, special days for worship and church attendance, special days for donations and collections of money in all Christian Churches in America, were not based on hidden facts no one knew about for 300 years. They increased interest in, and allegiance to, the Church, especially the Catholic Church, resulting in increased contributions of money, art, real estate, eventually making the Catholic Church extremely rich, the wealthiest church in the World. Separate dioceses in the United States are worth hundreds of millions of dollars individually. Like other multi-millionaires and billionaires in the United States they hoard their money and don't use it to help poor people and people in need to have better lives, or to help the United States economy by paying taxes on those riches and wealth. But this seems to be the antithesis of what churches are supposed to do.

Every year oil companies make hundreds of billions of dollars in profits, yet they have never paid taxes on it. Like churches, religions, they are privileged and pay no taxes. Unlike churches they are not, and have never been, non-profit. Unlike churches oil companies get at least $50 billion dollars in subsidies every year as gifts from the United States Government, the United States politicians. In the United States oil is the King, the oil industry is the god that politicians worship. In return, they have always gotten big pay-offs on the side. As always, the solution for questions, the answer, is to follow the money. The method to this madness, to this massive theft, is money and greed and corruption.

The oldest known bones from human beings are 3.4 million years old. Yet Christianity continues to insist that Adam and Eve were the first human beings about 6000 years ago. It's a traditional belief. The difference between the mythology and the truth of radio carbon dating is about 3.4 million years, as 6000 years then becomes a drop in the bucket. But most Christians want to believe the myth, as they want to believe other myths in the Bible, as they want to believe in the myths of Christmas and Easter.

Bad things happen to good people, good things happen to bad people. That's life. Good people don't have better luck than bad people. They aren't rewarded by the Universe, or by God. People cling to religions because they fear death and because they want something to lean on, to have a feeling of being protected from life, and death. Religions give hope, and a feeling of belonging to a group, of belonging to something bigger than oneself, of something beyond oneself, of something spiritual.

All major problems in life happen because of bad karma from previous lives, because of wrong things we did in our previous lives. All major good things in all lives happen because of major good things done in previous lives. It's all a learning experience, in order to understand and experience what was done, in a major way, to harm or help other people, during other lives. Supposedly all humans have lived hundreds of times before, or even thousands of times before, and lose all memory of these many lives when they reincarnate. Talents developed in other lives may show up as talents in this life.

Reincarnation is believed in by the majority of religions and by the majority of people in the world. The designers of the new Christian religion chose to leave it out of their newly designed religion, that was created and developed to unify and control a confused and disorganized group of people. Reincarnation was a concept of personal power and personal control that the rulers and organizers didn't want them to have. People would have to pay for their crimes in this life, and would turn to the Catholic Church and other Christian churches for forgiveness and redemption, and give money to the Church as part of the process. Churches would have a built-in profit mechanism.

After Mother Theresa died she was named a saint by the Catholic Church. But after she died her diaries revealed she hadn't prayed to God for years, and that she didn't believe prayers were answered, or that there was a God because there was too much suffering in the World. She devoted her life to trying to alleviate some of that suffering for some of the poorest of the poor, with no financial compensation for herself. But, ironically, she was given the status of being a saint by the Catholic Church even though she wrote that she hadn't prayed or believed there was a God for many years. Maybe the Catholic Church Bishops and the Pope didn't know about her diary. No matter what she believed, what she did is what counts. Therefore, she deserved to be named a saint, but it should have been done while she was alive so she would have known about her rightful recognition by the Catholic Church that she devoted her whole life to.

The DOD uses half a million gallons of gasoline every day. Every day since about 2010 at least 20 specks of metal cross the sky from one horizon to the other horizon at a very high elevation in about five minutes. These are shiny metal objects flying so high in the sky they cannot be seen, except as a moving speck of grey metal. Planes can't fly that fast, so maybe they aren't planes at all. All that can be seen is their white smoke emissions trailing behind them for hundreds of miles, leaving proof from one side of the horizon to the other, eventually covering thousands of miles like clouds across the sky.

Perhaps this is more Government secrecy, and another gigantic waste of gasoline and oil, as it helps no one. Perhaps these are a product of the secretive Shadow Government, or of the secret UFO reverse-engineering projects. Because America is a democracy the people, the citizens, have a right to know. But, as has been happening since after World War II, the people will not be told.

For what purpose, and by whom, are the obvious questions. The strange "planes" must use more gasoline than all the people driving in the cities they fly over are using below them. For years car drivers have been blamed for oil and gasoline shortages, and excessive use. The real cause has been the United States military, their planes, their jets, and now whatever it is that's crossing the sky in five to ten minutes, from one side to the other, many times a day. Let's put the blame where it belongs. But, actually, when gasoline use goes up the supply of gasoline always goes down, and then the price of gasoline and oil always goes up. That's how the oil industry, subsidized by gifts of billions of taxpayer dollars every year, controls oil and gasoline prices and controls Americans, manipulating American drivers and the economy. That's why prices for gasoline have always increased by about 25 cents a gallon every time a holiday happens every year, for at least the last 20 years. It's an American tradition, a holiday tradition.

For many years many millions of Americans have lowered their expectations so much they've given up on anything better in their lives. That's just coping, and it's a reality for even a hundred million Americans. America as the land of opportunity has only been a myth for many millions of Americans, especially in the past 30 or 40 years. So the hopes inherent in a democracy never materialized for them, no matter how hard they worked, how hard they tried. Other democracies, 23 of them, help their people in every way they can to become what they want to be, to have the best lives they can have. Their citizens actually have happy lives, unlike most Americans. In general, Americans are not happy. They are just coping. They are just getting by as best they can.

Since 2001 that's what the Neo Cons in power have wanted. The masses, the expendable masses, should not be happy. Slowly but definitely the IMF and the World Bank are requiring all countries that get loans from them, as requirements for the loans, to destroy their existing free high quality Universal Healthcare systems, to eliminate them and replace them with a privatized medical system like America has. Private practice over-priced physicians, privately owned over-priced hospitals, over-priced legal drugs from private pharmacies, private practices for medical specialists and their astronomical charges, and anything else connected with an over-priced privatized medical system, charging up to 1000 times more than what the costs actually are, making it a capitalistic for-profit free-market enterprise subject to greed.

Global capitalism is being forced on countries that get financial help from the IMF and the World Bank as conditions for, as requirements for, financial help in the form of high-interest loans they probably will never be able to pay back. In fifty years maybe there will only be a few true and actual democracies left, with a happy and prosperous population a thing of the past. Global privatized economies and medical systems and controlled unhappy populations seems to be the goal of the IMF and of the World Bank, and of the Neo Cons and everybody else in power in America. There very definitely is, and always has been, a method to their collective madness.

Countries that are given foreign aid are required to purchase weapons, bombs, helicopters, jets, etc. from United States companies like Lockheed and Boeing. It's a conditional gift that then comes back to the United States Government that is subsidizing those industries, those companies, those corporations with guaranteed business and huge income from the money borrowed by the United States to give away as foreign aid.

It's friends with benefits because it guarantees small countries are combat-ready, willing and able to engage in military actions somewhere in the World at all times. This creates international instability and opportunity for United States Government intervention and military actions. It asserts and confirms to the rest of the World and to Americans in general that the United States is still the World's Super-Power, with political and military influence in many countries. At one time the United States had military bases in 170 countries. Some of those United States foreign military bases have been closed at various times in the 21$^{st}$ century, saving hundreds of millions of dollars.

For many years the United States Government has manipulated the American public by instilling fear. The Viet Nam war was the fear of Communism, as if it was going to be forced on the American public from 6000 miles away. But the United States Government and the United States military admitted in Government documents that 90% of the reason the United States was in Viet Nam was "to save face", and only 10% of the reason was because of "the Communist threat". The Government lied to get public support, like they lied about weapons of mass destruction in Iraq to get public support for invasions of Iraq and attacks on Iraq after 2001.

Viet Nam had no capabilities to force the 50 times larger and hugely more powerful United States to become Communist, just like Iraq had no capabilities to fly to the United States with WMD or just the usual weapons of war. Both the governments and military of Iraq and Viet Nam could not have invaded the United States of America. But the American public bought the stories, believed the lies. Again and again the biggest threat to American national security has been the politicians and officials, elected or not, who run it.

The United States Government has been against the American public, in general, in many ways for many years, at least since 1963. It has been pro-American for the minority of Americans. Since the 1960's the United States Government and the people in control of America have needed to do more to help most Americans, the majority of Americans, to have better lives. That will never happen, but political rhetoric and lies will give the impression that it does.

Under Obama there were more tax cuts for businesses, companies, and corporations than ever before. But the Republicans never acknowledged that. They never spoke about that. That truth didn't fit their agenda. A Democratic President is supposed to be for the people, a Republican President is for the wealthy and businesses, especially large corporations. Obama, as President, tried to be for both. As always, oil companies continued to get four times the financial subsidies as renewable energy businesses did. But an alternative energy business that Obama was financially connected to and involved in was given a billion dollar Government loan, then it went bankrupt after producing nothing.

Who got the billion dollars that company, called Solyndra, will never pay back? How much of that billion dollars did President Obama get, and keep? Corruption is probably as old as societies have been around. It's nothing new, but that doesn't make it right when it happens. It doesn't excuse it.

For his re-election campaign in 2012 more than a billion dollars was donated to his campaign. Since most of his base supporters would vote for him just because there was no other Democrat to vote for, no matter who he was, no matter what his first term had been like, just to make sure there wouldn't be a Republican President, very little advertising was needed.

This, of course, has also always been true if the current President is Republican. Since Obama's records would speak for themselves why did he need a billion dollars for advertising and promoting himself? Where did the left-over hundreds of millions of dollars go to? Who got it? Accountability goes out the window when political finances and money are involved. Actually, accountability is sadly lacking in most, or all, of politics at all levels in the United States. It's the American way, an American tradition.

The differences between what a Republican President does and what a Democratic President does is disappearing. As an example, under Obama the total United States taxes paid in 2010 and 2011 were 34% *less* than in 2001 to 2002, when there was a Republican President, and unemployment remained basically the same. As usual, the upper 1% paid 1% for taxes, or nothing, on their total income. Therefore, the fact that the 2012 Presidential candidate Romney paid 14% in 2011 and 2012 was unusually generous and honest, not the usual tax-evasion like his opponent Gingrich had done but had repeatedly lied about. He repeatedly insisted Romney had done tax-evasion when Romney hadn't.

Just saying it happened didn't make it so, but probably all Republicans believed Gingrich, out of party loyalty if nothing else. Republicans will always say anything, lying to promote themselves at election time, even lying in competition with their own party members. Even Republicans campaigning against other Republicans can be dishonest. So Republican unity is doubtful. That's why there are Far Right and Neo Con diversions, as separate branches of the political nemesis.

Yet, the worn-out Republican mantra that only Republicans lower taxes continued in the 2012 campaigns. At that same time more people lived in poverty in America, in 2012, than ever before in both the 20th and 21st centuries. Meanwhile, Republicans continue, as they have for more than 50 years, to react as if it was a diabolical heresy to raise taxes on the upper 10%, or just the upper 1%, or even just make sure they pay any taxes at all, and not allow and encourage tax-evasion, tax loop-holes, off-shore tax havens, tax write-offs, tax-breaks, tax-cuts.

Meanwhile, corporate tax avoidance increases every year. And, as usual, oil companies continue to pay no taxes on their multi-billion dollar profits each year. In 2012 Exxon reported earnings of $430 billion. The media always reported it as "millions" in profit, never "billions", and, on top of that, Exxon under-reported their actual earnings, as it probably always has. And then, because this isn't enough theft from the American people, the Federal Government continues to give Exxon and other oil companies yearly subsidies of hundreds of millions of dollars of taxpayer's money. It's the American way. The rich must become richer and the poor must become poorer.

In 2012 at least 5000 people in America had to live in tents located throughout America because they lost their jobs or didn't get salaries high enough to pay for a place to live because of still hugely inflated rental costs and real estate costs in general. This included people living in tents in winter cold and snow, with no electricity for heat, in states like Michigan and Ohio. If they don't pay their taxes, at a rate of 20% to 35%, they will be fined or imprisoned. Prison would maybe be the better alternative, the better choice, as the United States Government usually pays prisons $50,000 to $80,000 per prisoner each year, which is obviously a huge over-charge on the part of the prisons. Life is much better in an American prison than being homeless or living in a tent in a city in America.

But the very wealthy and politicians would go to special prisons, if they were incarcerated at all. It's the American way. It's an American tradition.

Apparently UFO's and ETV's are a threat to the United States system of power. If ET's wanted to harm, take over, or destroy anything in the United States, or in any other country, they obviously could have done so for at least the past few hundred years. Paintings 1000 to 3000 years old show them in the background, in the sky behind the subjects of the paintings and murals. These other-worldly beings could have taken over, or destroyed, anything anywhere in the World for at least a thousand years because they were advanced beyond anything imaginable here on Earth, and could get to Earth quickly, apparently, from *light years* away. None of that has ever happened for those 1000 to 3000 years so the United States Government attitude and military attitude of secrecy, paranoia, and fear has always been for control of the American people by instilling fear, fear of the unknown and fear of potential harm, allowing secret reverse-engineering of anything connected with UFO's, ETV's, and ET's. But nothing good ever comes of secrecy and lies.

The American power structure cannot compete with, or be superior to, extra-terrestrial beings and extra-terrestrial intelligence and technology. But it can copy it, reverse-engineering it for Americans to use. And it can destroy, and has destroyed, UFO's, ETV's, and ET's. So secrecy and subterfuge about the recovered, and then hidden, UFO's and ETV's and ET's, and threats, lies, loss of jobs, and murders of people who don't cooperate or know too much, are an outcome of the United States Government reactions, the FBI, the CIA, the DOD, and actions from the United States military.

The supposed threat to the United States has never been seen as a threat by any other country in the World. The obvious inferiority to obviously immensely superior ET intelligence and vastly superior technology has been a threat to the United States military and to the United States Government since the 1940's. The powers-that-be in the United States have done whatever they want to do in order to hide whatever they know about it since after World War II ended. Perhaps those dots of metal trailing smoke or vapor from one horizon to the other in about five minutes, since about 2010, are by-products of that secrecy and reverse-engineering. If so, the Government response and explanation for it will be a lie. It's the American way, it's an American tradition.

In 2011 a newly revealed silent helicopter, a military helicopter, crashed in Pakistan at the living quarters of Saddam Hussein when he was assassinated by United States military forces. It was reported on BBC news that the secret technology inside the silent helicopter "were vaporized upon impact". Vaporized? What used to be science fiction is now here, as a result of reverse-engineered ETV technology. So the silent helicopter couldn't be detected by Pakistani radar. So this new development was not reported in the United States but it was reported in England, where the Government is not as secretive, not hiding information, distorting and twisting information, like the American Government does. It's the American way. It's become an American tradition since after World War II, and definitely is here to stay. No one can change it, as it is so vast and all-encompassing.

This was probably a product of the 70 year old "Black Project", the United States military secret UFO project that started in the 1940's after UFO's crashed at Roswell, New Mexico, apparently because United States radar scrambled their UFO power source. But the United States Government has always denied the existence of UFO's, ETV's, ET's, and will continue to do so in the 21st century. The name "Black" refers to "secret". Like Black Hawk, a helicopter, Black Bird, a plane, and Black Projects which are to do reverse-engineering and dismantling of UFO's, ETV's, and studying their occupants, the ET's. And like Black Water, which is at least 200,000 privatized secret army and para-military personnel in Iraq, Iran, Afghanistan, that are paid at least 10 to 100 times more than military personnel would be paid to do the same things. Stealth bombers are silent bombers, like stealth helicopters are silent helicopters. Silence and secrecy are important parts of the military.

Alternative sources of energy have often been rejected by the United States Patent Office. No patent means no funding to bring it to market, to the buying public. Many alternative methods that have been patented can't get funding or financial backing anyway. As an example, a man designed an electro-magnetic source of free electricity, free energy using magnets instead of fuel. He was put in prison for two years while he was in California, the most progressive state for many years, with no charges and no trial and no legal representation, because he was promoting and demonstrating his free-energy engine to the public. He was never allowed an appeal to the non-existent charges. If this travesty and gross injustice could happen in California it could happen anywhere in the United States.

Other invented and developed sources of free energy have been cold-fusion, the Patterson Cell electro-static motors, zero-point energy, and anti-gravity, which is the power used by UFO's and ETV's from other planets that the United States military has been recovering or shooting down since the 1940's. And then hiding them at secret and hidden places in the United States, such as secret facilities on deserts and mountains. People knowledgeable of these UFO's have always been sworn to secrecy, with death the consequence of breaking that secrecy. In other countries it's free information, public information available to anyone. For some countries, like France and England, all their information about UFO's and ETV's in their countries since the 1940s is on the internet. Not by chance and not by coincidence, the American B-2 Bombers are shaped like a spaceship and are powered by electro-gravity like an ETV, or UFO, using uranium for fuel.

Resistance to alternative energy changes, perpetuating the status quo and the dependence on oil, is for the purpose of continuing big sources of big money, big profit. Ridiculing and discrediting alternative sources of energy has happened for many years, and murders have been committed to hide and stop these alternative sources of energy, apparently by agents of the U.S. Government.

Being killed, murdered, imprisoned with or without charges, or disappearing mysteriously for what you say or write, has been a fascist government and Communist government thing for many years, and is now a Mexico criminal drug trade thing. They murder news journalists and editors for what they write and publish, or say, about them. In the United States, especially since The Patriot Act of 2001, Americans have been, and are, imprisoned for what they say publically or write about Federal Government-connected issues, especially if it's published by the so-called free Press. Or, they are just threatened or harassed, or have been threatened or harassed, by state governments or the Federal Government, by the FBI, the CIA, or agents from other privatized or military sources for secret intelligence. Loss of their jobs, inability to get another job, loss of life for themselves or their families, have been happening since after World War II. It's the Neo Con-inspired m.o. in America.

President Eisenhower and his family were threatened, including death threats, in the 1950's by the powers-that-be to not say anything to the American people about the UFO's that had been recovered after they had crashed in the deserts of New Mexico. It's still a secret 60 years later. Suppression of information, censorship and manipulation by the Federal Government and state governments, are part of the history of America, especially since World War II. Basically, a free Press is a thing of the past since after 2001. Newspapers are only the same at local levels, for the small town Press.

It is possible that President Roosevelt was murdered, poisoned, at his vacation home in Georgia because he said he was "going to talk to the American people about the recovered UFOs after the war" was ended. The powers-that-be didn't want him to do that. Days after he said that he died suddenly and unexpectedly, after writing a letter to the leader of Russia while at his summer home in Georgia.

This enabled the very inexperienced Vice President Truman to quickly become President, and then be manipulated by the powers-that-be to do whatever they wanted to be done, like dropping the atomic bomb on Hiroshima to end World War II. But it didn't work, it didn't end World War II.

Most countries in the World have records of UFO's, ETV's, ET's and their activities in those countries. It's only the United States Government that has kept records of them hidden and secret, and has always publically denied their existence for more than 70 years. No other country in the world thinks UFO's, ETV's, and ET's are a threat except the United States, that has by far the biggest, the most comprehensive, and the most active military in the World.

The United States is the World's military Super-Power. So this is another way the American people have been controlled by their Government. Especially since after World War II.

In 2000 the French Government agency for space studies called the CNES released more than 100,000 pages of information about UFO, ETV, and ET contacts for at least 50 years in France. France is a true democracy. A good democracy is an informed democracy. People need to be informed with the truth, not half-truths and lies. The Government of France thought its citizens had a right to know. They said "The people wanted the truth." In the same way, the French people and the French Government were against the United States bombing and invading Iraq in 2003 because they knew the truth. As a result, millions of Americans allowed themselves to be manipulated by Republicans and by the media to turn against France and the French people. The truth was the enemy. And Americans, in general, are easily manipulated by their politicians and officials, and by the media and the Press.

The United Kingdom has a declassified and public website with 10,000 pages of UFO accounts that have happened in the United Kingdom. It's another democracy that actually has freedom of all information like France does. More than any of the other 23 democracies America doesn't have freedom of information. Even though it is guaranteed in the Constitution and the Bill of Rights. The United States Government, the Department of Defense, and the military can't allow lack of control in America and in the world, and a loss of world super-power status and superiority.

It's the United States Government and the people who control America that have been afraid for 70 years, not the American people. Thousands of people in other countries have seen UFO's, ETV's, and ET's travel at estimated speeds of 3,000 to 12,000 mph. Their government and their military doesn't ridicule them, threaten them, or do set-up "suicides" and murders, like the U.S. Government has done an unknown number of times, if harassment and/or loss of jobs isn't enough to silence them. Agents of the CIA, the FBI, and the U.S. military have done this for about 70 years. Possibly starting with the death of President Roosevelt in 1945. To everybody else in the World this other-worldly activity has always been an interesting and strange phenomenon to observe in the sky. But Americans supposedly would be too afraid to know the truth about whatever their Government and their military decided they need to "protect" Americans from. As always, it's about money, power, and control of the expendable masses.

It's another form of United States Government control, both on a national level and on a state level. During World War II a UFO was discovered after it crashed in New Mexico. President Roosevelt was shown the remains of the UFO. He said first the United States had to win the war, then he would talk to the American people about it. He said the United States didn't have the resources then to reverse-engineer its technology. Soon after that he died. He was not going to keep it a secret.

Was he murdered, poisoned, like many other people who knew about or saw UFO's have been since the 1947 Roswell, New Mexico UFO incident? FDR was not going to keep it a secret from the American people, as he had been advised to do. He did not think it was a threat to America or Americans. Newspapers reported that he died from a stroke while at his vacation home in Georgia. Maybe they were given misinformation, disinformation, or lies. Perhaps he didn't die a natural death, just like other people who saw and/or reported UFO's, ETV's, and ET's have disappeared, or died mysterious deaths, or had set-up so-called "suicides" and other unlikely deaths. Just like 42 of the witnesses of JFK's assassination died within a few years after it happened in Dalles, Texas.

An intersected web of deceit and secrecy and theft, threats and manipulation, harassment and cruelty, wrongful imprisonment and loss of jobs, murder and assassinations, has been a pattern allowed to continue for about 70 years. Ending the secrecy, exposing the ugliness, is a way to stop it. But no one wants to deal with the repercussions to themselves and to their families, the retaliation and retribution, the murders and fear caused by the United States Government, the CIA, the FBI, and the U.S. military. That's what *has* been justifiably feared for about 70 years, not the other-worldly visitors who have never harmed anyone, ever, for a few thousand years.

Reverse-engineering of UFO's, ETV's, and information taken from captured ET's since the early 1940's has resulted in the development of MRI's, CT scans, laser surgery, fiber optics, laser weapons, computer chips, computers, laptop computers, microwaves, Black Bird planes, Black Hawk helicopters, and cell phones, to name some of the advances and results. Reverse-engineering is how free energy has been discovered by separating hydrogen from oxygen. This form of free energy causes no pollution. It would collapse the oil industry, a disaster for the United States Government and the powers-that-be, and also put a big dent in the medical/sickness industry. Americans would be healthier and have more money to live on, as would people in other industrialized nations throughout the World. And the natural environment in America, and other nations, would benefit immensely. These are improvements which cannot be allowed to happen, have not been allowed to happen, and will not be allowed to happen.

On "Star Trek" episodes on TV in the 1970's and the 1980's the Doctor on the spaceship used handheld scanners to diagnose and cure diseases, etc. Handheld scanners that diagnose and cure cancer would collapse and destroy the immensely profitable American cancer industry. That means many millions of people, hundreds of millions of people, have died from cancer unnecessarily for many years, and will continue to die and suffer unnecessarily indefinitely. That particular UFO and ETV technology will remain unrevealed, hidden, a secret indefinitely. Maybe forever. Cancer is an absolutely necessary sickness to support the American economy.

Bigwigs in Hollywood have known about the UFO's, the ETV's, and their occupants for a long time. They have been a part of the in-crowd. UFO's haven't been "unidentified" for many years, so they've been called Extra-Terrestrial Vehicles, and ET's, not UFO's, for years by people in the know.

The biggest user of gasoline and oil by far since World War II has been the military, their planes, jets, etc. Commercial planes and jets put more than 50 million tons of excess carbon dioxide into the air each year. They are responsible for much more carbon dioxide toxins in the air than cars. Because of military planes, jets, etc., that amount is tripled to more than 150 tons of carbon dioxide toxins dumped into the air each year. Using liquid nitrogen for fuel instead would alleviate all these toxins and carbon dioxide released into the air. So why hasn't it happened? Why won't it happen? Because oil is King in America, and because of the ever-present struggles for greed, money, control and power. What is wrong is ignored and therefore given approval, especially in the 21$^{st}$ century.

Now, in the 21$^{st}$ century, one out of every eight people in America has been involved in a bankruptcy. Most often bankruptcies in America happen because of medical bills, too high medical costs and resulting debts. In all other democracies, 23 of them, this would not have happened because free high quality Universal Healthcare has been available for everyone in their countries for many years. This has always contributed to better, healthier, and happier lives for people living in those countries. They have better health, no bankruptcies caused by medical debt, and more money for each person to spend because of no money spent on medical bills or over-priced legal drugs. They also have better social security, a higher rate of home ownership, less stress, a Government they can trust to be honest and to be looking out for their welfare, and much fewer divorces than in America. Most divorces in America are caused by financial problems. As a result of all these many advantages there are increased opportunities for a happier life for anyone living in *any* other democracy in the World.

In general, better lives and happier lives have always happened in 23 other countries that are Democracies, but not in America. Even though the pursuit of happiness is a right all Americans have it's been difficult to find it in America since its beginning. Unless you were lucky enough, are lucky enough, to be in the elite, the upper 10%, or, better yet, the upper 5% or upper 1%. Money does promote a better life, allowing creation of a better life and more happiness as a result.

Lack of justice, not allowing "life, liberty, and the pursuit of happiness", began with the native American Indians because settlers, and then American soldiers, murdered entire tribes of Indian men, women, children, and babies, when they had no weapons or ways to defend themselves as they of course had no guns. Eventually Indians had gotten stolen guns from white men in order to protect themselves from the savage white soldiers and settlers. After murdering many millions of Indians, the original inhabitants of what became America, for an unbelievable roughly 250 years, the Indians were forced onto Government Reservations to live in substandard housing for generations. They had few sources of income and the land was usually so poor it was unable to be farmed. That was the first Government-enforced poverty, continuing for generations, in America.

The problems and well-known complaints of black slaves in the American South have been well-covered by the media and in books for at least the last 60 years. However, *just ½ of 1%* of the population in the South owned slaves for about 200 years. *Millions* of white people died, and were injured, in the Civil War so that slavery would be ended in the South. Obviously those millions of white people, mostly men, were also deprived of "life, liberty, and the pursuit of happiness".

Migrant Mexican farm workers, many millions of them, have been contributing and working in America for more than 60 years but have sometimes been denied access to restaurants and movies, and sometimes denied justice from law enforcement and in American courts. They have always paid into Social Security but can't get it back, even though they paid into it. But some Mexicans from Mexico have gotten million dollar settlements from American courts in lawsuits during the last 20 years.

Millions of underpaid white workers, including children, worked 12 hour days in substandard conditions in factories before the 1950's. Eventually this injustice propelled America into industrial and international prominence because of this cheap labor force hugely increasing profits.

This wealth contributed to the Industrial Revolution in the 1800's and early 1900's.Unions were forced into existence to prevent, or to control and stop, the common and widespread abuse of human rights in early industrial America, as it became the wealthiest country in the World.

For about 250 years white women, or women of any color, couldn't vote. They had few rights in the male-dominated American culture. But many injustices are found throughout the history of America, usually with the public protesting and demanding conditions be changed.

Since after World War II none of the countries attacked and occupied by the United States military ever had the capabilities to attack the United States, or to take freedom away from America or Americans, unless leaders of the United States Government wanted them to, like on September 11 in 2001. Some of the countries attacked, invaded, and occupied by the United States military have been Viet Nam, Korea, Panama, Egypt, Kosovo, Chile, Cuba, Iraq, Iran, Libya, Syria, and Afghanistan. All countries much *much* smaller than the United States. Therefore, the United States international reputation as a bully has always been justified.

Become an informed citizen. Watch these very well done and very informative documentaries on DVD's that were made by courageous and intelligent people who took very real risks to produce them. They are "The End of America", "Redacted", a drama by Brian de Palma that has a special features part of actual photos taken of the war in Iraq, "No End in Sight", "The Dark Side", "Un-Constitutional", "Uncovered", "Zeitgeist", and "Inside Job". You'll be glad you did. Being informed with the sad and ugly truth, being fully informed with the truth, is the responsibility of all American citizens. Often the truth has become the enemy to the leaders of the American Democracy.

In the 21st century America has become a controlled democracy, with limited and controlled freedoms. How much of the American Government in the 21st century, for both national and state governments, is actually against its own citizens? Is that what the Neo Con's "Plan For A New America In The 21st Century" was supposed to do, supposed to be, both anti-American and anti-democracy? In many ways America stopped being a democracy in 2001 and 2003, but actually was going in that direction for many years before that. The system of checks and balances started to be broken in about 1963, before the Viet Nam war began.

Because of The Patriot Act of 2001 any United States citizen, born here or not, can be arrested and imprisoned indefinitely without legal representation and without probable cause. Freedom of speech, the basis of democracy, is now conditional and easily taken away at the discretion of those in power, at many levels. Demonstrations are only allowed with permits for each person participating. Millions of marchers means millions of permits, so it's unlikely to happen. These are frightening developments contrary to a true democracy. It's not what the United States is supposed to be like. The United States is the only democracy in the World, out of 24, that is this way.

These undesirable major changes in American society were allowed to become part of America in an undemocratic way, by using an undemocratic process. Congress, as elected representatives of the American people, signed The Patriot Act into law in 2001 without even reading it. The 365 page document was given to them to read just a few hours before they were to vote on it. Why were the Neo Cons in such a hurry to pass something that would be enforced for at least the next 10 years? The war in Iraq was already planned, and was planned to end on September 11, 2011 for PR impact and for future history books.

If any of the Congressmen and Congresswomen didn't sign it, to pass it, they would be labeled unpatriotic by TV news media and by FOX News, and by the Press, and probably not be re-elected. It was a done deal before they even saw it. It didn't need to be read, it just needed to be signed.

In a closed society anything that elevates the individual and truthfully informs the public is censored. Like a free Press, like demonstrations, dissent, protests, like intellectual inquiry that leads to articles and books, like uncensored and unrestricted movies, documentaries, and books. And like a free-flow of information and free access to all information, all unbiased and unfiltered information, is then censored, not allowed, including what is in public libraries. Most people in America are probably not aware that their freedoms are now limited. Freedom is now controlled. This is what has been happening in America since 2001.

All of this has happened before. Ideology to conform, imprisonment if you don't conform, ideology to report suspicious behavior for a common cause, imprisonment of news reporters, authors, and journalists for what they write, illegally detaining and imprisoning people with no charges, no probable-cause, or legal representation. All of this happened before in Nazi Germany in the 1930's and 1940's, and began happening in the United States after 9/11, in 2001.

The Patriot Act in 2001 and declaring a war on Iraq in 2003 made all of those actions in the United States possible.  As long as there is a war the President (and his advisors) has absolute and total control of the United States. Other countries have experienced attacks and bombings by terrorists for the past 30 years but did not institute reactions reminiscent of Nazi Germany and Hitler. Since 2001 in America there has been unlimited surveillance of all citizens, phone-tapping, seizure of records, allowing police and deputies to break into and destroy any residence they want to, like the United States military did in Iraq starting in 2003.

Since 2001 in America there has been a list of millions of United States citizens, including at that time Democratic politicians like Ted Kennedy, spiritual and religious leaders, and normal, average citizens, as potential terrorists. Since 2001 there has been seizure of billions of e-mails, library records, and medical and bank records, besides indefinite imprisonment with no probable-cause and no legal representation for an unknown number of America citizens.

For 235 years these actions were violations of American's civil rights, violations of their Constitutional rights. After The Patriot Act became law these rights disappeared, never to be regained. The war in Iraq, more than other wars, was an excuse, a cover, a front, to change America and to control Americans more than ever before, as was planned by the Republican Neo Conservatives in the 1970's. It was planned by "the Crazies", as they were referred to in Washington, D.C. by the CIA and by fellow politicians in the 1970's and the 1980's. So those same men, "the Crazies", ruled and controlled America after 2000, and ruled and controlled the Presidential elections in 2000. No wonder there was chaos for those elections.

In 2003 Bush "W" said in a TV interview with reporters "Iraq had nothing to do with 9/11." After that Bush "W" signed a new law that said a President could not be convicted of war crimes committed after September 9, 2001."The Crazies" were covering their tracks and protecting themselves from the law. After all, twisting and distorting and temporarily changing Federal laws is what made Bush "W" the President of the United States for eight years. Maybe they wouldn't be able to do it again.

Depriving people of their civil liberties was part of the Neo Con "Plans For A New Democracy In America", written before 2000. Public information is easily discredited and ridiculed, always by Republicans, especially Neo Cons and the Far Right. They just discredit or ridicule the source to silence the opposition. That's their m.o., so commonly used. Disinformation and misinformation can easily replace truthful information. Twisting and distorting the truth is easily done.

Closing down an open society happened In Nazi Germany and fascist Italy, and has been happening in America since 2001. Since 9/11 and the passing of The Patriot Act dissent can be called "espionage", a crime. Critical journalism can be called "treason", or "espionage", or "terrorism", all of which are crimes. Anyone can be called "a terrorist", a crime. There now can be arrests made with no probable-cause. All of these so-called crimes, as manufactured charges, can result in indefinite imprisonment with no legal counsel or representation as was guaranteed in The Bill of Rights and The Constitution for 235 years and is now gone, but not always.

Also, since 2001 solitary confinement of innocent Americans in 3' by 10' prison cells for months has happened an unknown number of times in the United States as a result of made-up charges. In a closed society a citizen has no rights and must conform and obey, and never speak out, or be punished by imprisonment. Homeland Security stifles dissent and uses undercover agents to deal with it. The Homeland Security in Nazi Germany did the same things, in the 1930's and 1940's, using the same name, with the same intentions. In 2011 President Obama signed "The Patriot Act" into permanent law, before it expired after its 10 year expiration date. Homeland Security in America is also here to stay. America is not "the land of the free" any longer, since immense and frightful changes began officially happening in 2001.

After 2001 the United States started to become a closed society, a controlled society and culture. The Press, the free Press in a democracy, is supposed to be for the people, not for the government, or for people like Rupert Murdock, a billionaire who controls media information for about a billion people throughout the World. He apparently is a spokesman for the Neo Cons, to manipulate the people, which is what happened increasingly after 2001. Deceptions and distortion of the truth in the Press and the media promoted and supported Neo Con political agendas more than ever before in United States history after 2001.

Without free speech a democracy ceases to exist. With free speech a person has a responsibility to speak out about injustices and wrongs. But, in the absence of truth about what a government is really doing, free speech doesn't mean much. Demonstrations and protests of all sizes haven't accomplished anything, or changed anything for the better, since the 1960's, since the Viet Nam war.

If freedom is the right of *all people*, of all of humanity, then freedoms should not be taken away in a democracy. Taking away freedoms understandably happens in all other types of government.

The Gulf of Tonkin issue never happened. It was made up, manufactured by politicians in power, both Democrats and Republicans, to justify an invasion, a war, with Viet Nam in 1964. Since the Viet Nam war, starting In 1964, demonstrations, protests, and dissent have been ignored by the Federal Government, changing nothing. Since 2001 protests and demonstrations are allowed only by getting permits from the government for each demonstrator. Of course permits can be, and are, ignored or denied. This is against The Constitution, The Bill of Rights, the rights to assemble and to protest, and the right to freedom of speech and expression. All made legal under the guise of The Patriot Act.

To insure the will of the people, to have a real democracy, allowing dissent and protests is necessary. The United States is the only democracy, out of 24 in the World, that responds to public dissent, protests, and demonstrations with tear gas, clubbing, shooting the people with shotguns and rifles, injuring and killing the people, and imprisoning people for legal actions of dissent.

Suppression of journalism and reporting, and imprisonment of those who speak the truth and report the truth, was part of the Neo Con's plan for "A New America" in the new century, the 21$^{st}$ century. A Government that has a policy of suppressing the truth is not a democracy. An uninformed and misinformed public is what the Neo Cons in power have wanted since the 1970's.Why all the secrecy? What have they been afraid of?

A revolution would never happen. White people are not united enough. Black people are united, but not white people. A revolution would never happen. So why haven't the Neo Cons been upfront about their plans and just done it, taken over America for their own purposes? That's essentially what's happening anyway, slowly, gradually. The Neo Cons are obviously control freaks who like to make people miserable, afraid, and unhappy. The expendable masses are indeed expendable.

Reporters, authors, journalists, and government employees who report the truth about what the United States Government and United States military is doing around the World, who take risks to find out and report the truth that the Federal Government doesn't want known, lose their jobs or are killed, or they die unexpectedly or in unlikely circumstances. Or have suspicious so-called "suicides". The State Department and the Secretary of State have a reputation of making public complaints about international human rights and civil rights violations in other countries, and the need for freedom of expression in those countries, but if anyone in the United States reports the duplicity and the hypocrisy of any of this they will then be victims of the same hypocrisy. They will lose their jobs or be imprisoned, threatened, harassed, or even killed. It certainly isn't worth losing one's life, or job, just to report the truth, the whole truth, and nothing but the truth.

For many years the United States Government says one thing and does another in both national and international affairs. This is no secret. This hypocrisy has permeated the social and cultural structure of all of America. You can find it anywhere in America, some places more than others. After all, copying is the highest form of flattery. And it all starts at the top. Bush "W" signed into law after 9/11 a new law that said a President could not be convicted of any war crimes after 9/11. He had said in a TV interview with reporters "Iraq had nothing to do with 9/11." Video recordings and audio recordings do not lie, but are easily destroyed or lost in the face of subversion.

An informed public should not be a threat to a democracy. It would not be a threat to a real democracy. What are "they" afraid of? Why are "they" paranoid about criticism? Millions of people publically criticizing anything in America hasn't changed *anything* in America for more than 50 years, so "their" reactions have been unfounded and very excessive. It's just another excuse to manipulate people in America, citizens who are told they are living in the best Democracy in the World.

When a democracy is disappearing, like it did in Nazi Germany, where Hitler was elected in a democratic election, when rules and laws are ignored by authorities, extremes in government, military, and law enforcement are allowed. Everything gets out of control, but yet is very controlled. The political agenda changes, instilling fear instead of security. What the public wants becomes less and less important until it disappears. The democracy disappears then, too.

The people, the citizens, mean nothing to the leaders of that country in terms of their welfare. They are there to be controlled for the benefit of those in power. At that point the democracy has ceased to exist, as happened in Nazi Germany in the 1930's and 1940's.

What made this happen? How did America get this way? The weak Democrats in power let the unbalanced, power-hungry, and greedy Neo Cons in power do it, as the Neo Cons had planned to do since the 1970's. The United States public was powerless to stop these actions. Their elected representatives allowed it to happen, so they failed the people they represented, the people who had elected them. Since after 9/11, 2001 written criticism of the United States Government is not allowed.

Also, criticism of the theory of evolution is not allowed. Hitler used Darwin's theories of evolution as justification for annihilating the entire race of Jewish people, and all handicapped people, in all of the countries that he took over, for the genocide of more than 10 million people. Since 2001, in America, if anyone publishes criticism of the theory of evolution, or if college teachers talk about it and criticize the theory of evolution in their classrooms, they will likely lose their jobs and be subject to ridicule, ostracism, and death threats. This has happened in the United States an unknown number of times, to an unknown number of teachers and professors.

Injustices and abuse of human rights, and abuse of civil rights, is found throughout the history of the United States for all people except the elite, the upper class, in America. But the United States Government has a history of injustice, killing, and the subjugation of indigenous people in America and in other countries.

When he was the President Lincoln said "When America ceases to be good, it ceases to be great." Lincoln started, and continued, the Civil War between the North and the South that became a long and brutal war, a savage and cruel war, killing and injuring millions of people, more Americans than any other war before or after. The suffering, death, and devastation of property in the South was immense. The Northern military destroyed as much of the South as they could in order to give black people freedom from slavery. All this misery and death when only 1% of the Southern population had slaves, and a much smaller percentage of that actually abused their slaves. As usual, politicians, the media, and authors and journalists have easily manipulated the truth.

Because he kept the union of the North and the South together when it had threatened to fall apart he has been called a great President. The South was forced to stay a part of the United States. But that awful war dragged on for more than 12 years, devastating much of America and all the people in America in one way or another, either socially, physically, financially, or emotionally and mentally, so it seemed to make Lincoln a hypocrit in a big way.

During World War I in Europe an inconceivable *10 to 12 million* civilians were killed, *9 million* soldiers were killed, and *21 million* soldiers were seriously wounded, changing their lives for the worst for the rest of their lives. After World War II in Europe and Japan statistics were about the same, with both wars resulting in about *25 million* civilians of all ages having died, about *20 million* soldiers having been killed, and at least *45 million* soldiers and civilians seriously wounded, with life-changing after-effects to last the rest of their lives. About *27 million* Russians in Russia were killed, both civilians and soldiers. And about *6 million* Jewish people were tortured and killed by the German Nazis. The total people suffering from injuries and from dying in the devastation and cruelty of war for both of these World Wars was about the same as 1/3 of the total United States population in 2012. These more than ***100 million people*** were victims of the most wars in any century in history.

These wars were supposed to be the wars that would end all wars. But for America it was just the beginning. Since after World War II, for almost 70 years, the United States Government and the United States military have been involved in almost continuous wars and occupations in other countries. But in comparison to the populations of other countries Americans have been protected from such carnage, destruction, and suffering and death, resulting from the madness and insanity of wars and occupations, by bringing its wars to other countries. No country has wanted to engage in a war or conflict with the United States since World War II so the United States invades them, with superior weapons, like the bully on the block or on the school grounds makes life miserable for kids who try to avoid him. But in this case the block or school grounds is much of the rest of the World.

In the 21st century the horrors of wars and occupations that American soldiers have to endure is sanitized by the United States Government and the military, and the media and the Press. So the insanity and madness of wars, and fighting for nothing except the whims and arguments and problems of the elite and of the politicians in America, continues indefinitely.

In 1999, after "The People's History of the United States" was published and sold two million copies, extolling the virtues and values of public demonstrations and organized public protests, The Patriot Act of 2001 made them against the law. Thereafter, Government permits for each participant were necessary. Government surveillance of any protests or demonstrations was greatly increased. Public protests or public demonstrations of half a million people, or a million people, or even just a thousand people, would be a thing of the past in the 21st century. It wasn't going to happen in "The New America for the 21st Century", the Neo Con's plans for a new America written years before.

The 1912 elections for President centered on popular unrest and too much Government. One hundred years later, in 2012, it was the same. There's been no improvement. During the Bush "W" eight year Republican administration from 2001 to 2009, when the Neo Cons ruled, there was more Federal Government control and interventions than ever before in the history of the United States. Yet, this was ignored by the public. Republican campaigns always lament against the Democrats because of their alleged desires for a bigger Government. The difference is the Democrats are up-front about their plans and the Republicans, and the Neo Cons, and the Far Right are secretive, dishonest, and sneaky about their methods to dominate and rule America.

In the past 30 years there has been a breakdown of morality, of values, of accountability, of behavior, and a breakdown of families, at all levels of American society. It's become a different America, a different country, when lies and dishonesty, corruption and apathy, are acceptable and expected everywhere and anywhere, at all levels of society. It's a changed America when you can't trust anyone, when leadership everywhere rarely tells the truth, when integrity is hard to find, when lack of integrity is common. It's become the American way. It doesn't start at the bottom and work up to the top, but it does start at the top and filter down to the bottom. Dishonesty and lies permeate American society. It's everywhere in the 21st century, some places more than others.

Six million manufacturing jobs have been lost in the United States since 2001, as the United States Government has given huge tax breaks to corporations if they relocate to foreign countries. This, or course, was not the will of the American people, especially those six million people who lost their jobs to cheaper foreign labor, mostly in China and Mexico. Was this part of the Neo Con plan to destabilize America? Or was it an attempt to globalize American super-power? Or was it both?

It was because of the Bush "W"/Cheney Administration, and the Neo Cons with their book with thousands of pages of information and secret plans to share with each other. Obama, as a Democratic President, should have reversed some of the vast and ugly damage done by the Republican Administration, but he did nothing. He was the new Neo Con version of a Democratic President.

The IMF is located in Washington, D.C. and is dominated by the United States. It controls and manipulates the currency and economy of, the economic policies of, the United States and other countries for the benefit of the IMF, the International Monetary Fund, and the United States. This is called predatory capitalism. The people, the public in the United States, are powerless to influence this entity. It has a life of its own and is accountable to no one. It's like the Fed, the Federal Reserve.

The collapse of the auto industry, since 2001, contributed a lot to the massive problems in the United States economy. But the collapse of the housing industry since 2001, because of the greed and dishonesty of the financial industry, and unenforced regulations, was a windfall to all concerned, all who had been involved in the collapse. It redistributed wealth, making many who were involved in it millionaires and multi-millionaires overnight because of their theft of hundreds of millions of dollars from their clients, their customers, that they did not pay back, and because of the Federal Government bailout giving them *billions of dollars* of tax-payers money. So, many in the financial industry got million dollar or multi-million dollar, or even *billion dollar yearly bonuses* as a result of the United States Government rewarding them for their gigantic, and unprecedented, dishonesty towards the American people. Corruption always follows the money.

Large corporations run the United States Government. Corporations are one of the rulers of America. So large corporations, like FOX TV owned by Rupert Murdock, who is originally from Australia, control what Americans read and hear on the controlled TV and radio news media on both national and international news. Biased sources control what Americans are allowed to know. A free Press is no more, except local news and newspapers to some extent. But they too are more controlled and manipulated than ever before in the history of the United States.

It seems most Americans like violence and meanness on TV, movies, and video games. It seems they get enjoyment from other people's misery, from vulgarity, rudeness, aggressiveness, causing pain, and arguing. FOX News and Rush Limbaugh are paid for and supported by conservative corporations, wealthy conservative individuals, and smaller conservative companies. They want them to give American viewers what they want to see and hear on FOX TV and FOX Radio News. FOX News is all about *opinions*, not actual news, 24 hours a day, every day. Apparently it gives hundreds of millions of Americans what they want. So they found a recipe for major unprecedented success.

When anything threatens the sources of income of the major corporations it is dealt with fast. An example of this, of how the truth can hurt these huge corporations, is when Michael Moore talked about Walmart's "Dead Peasant Insurance" in one of his documentary movies. Walmart quickly made a national public announcement that they were stopping this policy that was a major source of Walmart's immense wealth, helping to make them the wealthiest retail corporation in the World. Those Dead Peasant Insurance policies would be written for up to millions of dollars per person, per death. This explained why they hired old people, in their 70's and 80's, when nobody else would, and why handicapped and chronically sick people, even in wheelchairs, were hired by Walmart stores.

What looked like altruism to the public was instead greed on the part of Walmart Corporation. The real value of employees for Walmart's portfolio and future wealth were the Dead Peasant Insurance policies taken out on them, like General Electric and Proctor and Gamble had also been doing for many years about their employees. These included million dollar and multi-million dollar life insurance policies, actually death insurance, taken out on their employees without their knowledge. The best employee was a dead employee, economically speaking.

Supposedly Walmart invested in local and national products, as they advertised for years they did. It was just more of the "let's not and say we do", or "say one thing and do another", both time-honored American political traditions. For years Walmart had said they "invested in America" in their commercials. Insurance investments were the biggest and most lucrative way they did that.

Free Republic.com, a Republican internet company, vehemently opposed and viciously opposed freedom of speech and freedom of expression for years in their national rampage and battle against the Dixie Chicks from Texas, after 2001, because of the statement one of them made at one of their concerts. She said they were "ashamed that President Bush ("W") was from Texas." Because of that one small innocuous statement they received death threats and had many problems forced on them for years. What happened to the American Democracy and freedom of speech and freedom of expression? It was destroyed by vicious Republicans who were free to influence millions of their listeners by means of the internet, and on FOX NEWS, anytime they wanted, with no limitations made by any politicians, officials, etc. on their methods of expressing hatred and narrow-mindedness, using millions of words of hatred millions of times for the next few years. This was proof that freedom of expression and freedom of speech has long been for hate-mongers and war-mongers, especially Republicans at all levels, and not for Americans who speak the truth.

President Kennedy was shot by bullets coming from three or four directions, as was revealed after he was seen by physicians who saw his body in the hospital examination room where he was brought immediately after, and by the photos taken at that time. And by the testimony of at least *42 people* who saw President Kennedy gunned down by three bullets hitting him from completely different directions, as they stood close by. Subsequently there was a cover-up of truthful information by everyone involved, including the Warren Commission, military men at all levels, the FBI, the CIA, then-President Johnson, other politicians that were both Democrats and Republicans, and by the Secret Service, and on and on. This kind of orchestrated secrecy meant it all started at the top and was a coordinated effort for secrecy, with people supposedly "just doing their jobs", and what they were ordered to do. It's always the same. Threaten people, threaten their families, and cooperation is guaranteed. This isn't apathy, it's fear. Fear of the American Government, the CIA, the FBI.

History books in America have always said, will always say, Kennedy was killed by a lone gunman who wasn't even physically near there, who was then killed by another lone gunman in a crowd of about 50 people as he was being escorted by police. This is one of the major lies in history books, but it definitely isn't the only lie. History has always been just the opinion and fabrication of whoever writes it, and whoever may be interviewed for the information, or whoever wrote about the apparent history after it happened. The truth about anything can easily become secondary. It's so easy to lie.

The only job of the Secret Service is to protect the President. The Secret Service, the President's private police force, was not protecting President Kennedy at that time and, in fact, wasn't even there at all at Dealey Plaza in Dallas, Texas. The responsibility of the Secret Service, its only job, is to protect the President. It has to follow standard procedures for the security and protection of the President.

Yet, before JFK was to be in Dallas a Secret Service commander was told there was no need for any Secret Service agents to be at Dealey Plaza. So the Secret Service did not inspect the Plaza, as was *required* before JFK was going to be there. Standard protection procedures were ignored by the Secret Service. Later, after JFK was shot, it was never revealed, or even asked about during the official investigation or by the Warren Commission, *who* had told that Secret Service Commander to *not* inspect Dealey Plaza. Or who told *that* person to tell the Secret Service Commander that. Other crucial and important details like that were carefully ignored by the official Government investigation and by the Warren Commission. There were endless cover-ups and lies to protect, and ignoring them was one of the solutions.

In 1963 President Kennedy fired the head of the CIA, Warren Dulles, probably because of the Cuban Bay of Pigs fiasco that Dulles was the mastermind of. President Kennedy had indicated in conversations that the Cuban fiasco had been a set-up by the CIA. It was a CIA operation to make Kennedy look bad, to make him look incompetent. Apparently to lessen his popularity among Americans in general, and therefore to lessen his chances of re-election, which was a certainty at that point. He was immensely popular and would certainly be re-elected. Not long after firing Dulles as the Director of the CIA President Kennedy was assassinated. Maybe Dulles was the mastermind of that.

Earlier in 1963 the President of South Viet Nam had been murdered, probably by the CIA, because he wasn't co-operating with the United States Government, or with the CIA. After that, the CIA wanted an invasion of Viet Nam, a war in Viet Nam, but President Kennedy did not. He wasn't co-operating with Dulles, with the CIA. At that time the CIA was already in Viet Nam, as was the United States military, as a result of CIA interventions and actions. But President Kennedy had signed arrangements to bring all American soldiers back to America.

Days after President Kennedy was murdered his replacement was Lyndon Johnson, the Vice President, who then reversed that Presidential order so that those 1000 United States soldiers stayed in Viet Nam instead, and more United States soldiers, hundreds of thousands more, were sent to Viet Nam for the next 12 years. President Kennedy had huge public support and popularity and would have been re-elected. JFK stood for peace and for all Americans, rich and poor and everything in between. The CIA, the United States military, the Neo Cons in power, and the ruling elite all stood for war, corruption, greed, money, control, death, and lies. Eliminating President Kennedy, assassinating him, meant they could manipulate the American public, the expendable masses, and start a war in Viet Nam and continue it, based on lies, deception, and deceit for 12 years.

Then, for the next 12 years, the United States military and the CIA killed *4 to 6 million* Vietnamese civilians. No official records were kept by the United States of the deaths of people of all ages, including men, women, children, and babies, all of whom had nothing to defend themselves with, no guns, no weapons, making at least *4 to 6 million* Vietnamese civilians of all ages victims of United States aggression, cruelty, and military force. All allegedly done to protect America, *6000 miles away*, from Vietnamese Communism and the threat of Communism in Viet Nam being forced on America 6000 miles away, and spreading to other countries in the process. Even though they had *no* military, *no* bombs, *no* military planes, *no* way to get their Communist soldiers to America *6000 miles* away.

The fact that lies were perpetrated by, and forced onto the American public by, their President and his Administration was not acceptable to many millions of people in America. Especially the younger generation, millions of who protested and marched, demonstrating against what they couldn't possibly stop, including the draft and death for *58,000* American soldiers. Freedoms and rights in America had begun to disappear.

In America if one famous person is murdered it's a tragedy. If millions are murdered in other countries by American soldiers and by the United States military then it's a statistic, or just ignored. Since the beginning, starting with the Native American Indians, the United States Government didn't keep records of how many people are killed by, have been murdered by, United States Government military forces, or by privatized military forces in the 21$^{st}$ century. This, then, takes away their humanity, their significance in the scheme of things, their significance as human beings.

The night before JKK was murdered the Secret Service bodyguards for the President partied and got drunk at a well-known Dallas nightclub until 2:00 or 3:00 in the morning. This was a violation of Secret Service rules, for which they were never held officially accountable. Hours later the Presidential limousine top was rolled down. There were **no** Secret Service men in the Dallas Plaza but they were everywhere else on the planned route. This allowed the placement of at least three snipers carrying rifles in gun cases in different locations in the plaza. It allowed them to shoot at the President three times, or more, from three or four different directions as his Presidential limousine passed by.

The driver of the Presidential car changed the planned route just before the shooting began. The responding Secret Service men had no guns. Later, at the Dallas hospital, a forensic pathologist was not allowed to see JFK's body because FBI men and Secret Service men forcibly removed JFK's body within minutes after it had arrived to a waiting military transport plane (as shown on a video), not onto Air Force One as was reported everywhere in America by the media, by TV news, and the Press.

No Warren Commission investigation questioned or got an answer as to why a military transport plane was already there waiting, near the hospital. He was then flown to a secret military location. These were illegal actions under such circumstances but no one was ever questioned, or held officially accountable and responsible for these actions. After that he was flown to Walter Reed Army Hospital where records later indicated his brain was removed. Why? Again, there was no official accountability or explanation required. Then his body was flown to a Naval Hospital where two men with no prior experience or credentials did an autopsy on him.

Men who had never done an autopsy before did an autopsy on the President of the United States in secrecy. No one was ever held officially accountable for such inhumanity and so many illegal actions, all done in secrecy from the American people, and later covered by lies. Later, the Warren Commission was another fiasco. Photos of him taken at the Dallas hospital showed his skull was missing from the back of his head, as an exit wound, not an entry penetration, which was proof he was not shot from behind by the accused Lee Harvey Oswald while in the book depository. Another bullet hole was in the side of his head, another was in his lower neck in the front. All incriminating evidence of the truth about what happened was hidden and ignored then, and forever.

Military photos taken at Walter Reed Hospital did not match those photos, those same bullet-hole entries, those same locations. Even the hair looked different, like it was a wig. It seemed to be a stand-in body, a replacement body for the military photos of the violently murdered President

Kennedy. These were the photos given to the media. Was someone else murdered, a pre-selected man, in order to be a cover, a replacement for the actual body of President Kennedy? These obvious discrepancies from the truth, from the facts as they appeared, were never officially investigated by anyone, including the Warren Commission. Dulles stopped any such investigations to find the truth.

Government reports, like newspaper and magazine articles, like statistics and scientific studies, can be easily manipulated and falsified. Nobody could possibly know how often it is done, or how often and when it has been done in the past. It's so easy to change the facts, to lie. Dishonesty is the most common trait among Americans, at all levels of business and personal lives, at all levels of government. Unfortunately, it seems to be the American way, an American tradition.

More than 50 people saw at least three men dressed in grey suit coats at different locations, including two men at the so-called grassy knoll in Dealey Plaza, shooting at President Kennedy, at his limousine, after taking rifles out of their gun cases. Later, these eyewitness accounts were ignored and discounted by the Warren Commission, the FBI, and the CIA. Their home movies and photos of the assassination, before and after, had been taken away by the FBI and were never returned. One man had seen one of the men get into a waiting car behind the plaza immediately after the President was shot. Within about three years 42 of these eyewitness bystanders, innocent of any wrong-doing, were dead, having died mysterious and unlikely deaths, including set-up "suicides".

Then, almost 40 years later, in 2001, a retired Army Colonel said that he was told to "eliminate" those eyewitnesses of the President's assassination. In an interview he would not say how he "eliminated them". He said he was "not on trial" and had only been "following orders". He would not say who had ordered those murders of 42 innocent bystanders, or who had ordered a military Colonel to arrange and carryout those 42 assassinations of innocent Americans in America. The Colonel, a cold-blooded killer who said he just had a job to do, had no remorse at all about murdering those 42 innocent people who had been witnesses of the truth about the assassination of their President, a President who truly represented all of the people in America. Assassins and military Colonels are required to have no conscience. It's a job requirement.

This attitude is common among American military men, especially among those of higher rank and power and authority, because they are taught to be that way, because they are rewarded for being that way, and because they like to be that way. It is expected, and is a sign of being a real man according to the military. There is a reason former soldiers, after being in combat or in a war or occupation, never talk about their bad experiences to their loved ones or family or friends when they are discharged. The reason is that they have sworn, taken an oath and a pledge, to never talk about their ugly experiences, the ones that may give them nightmares or weigh on their conscience, about what they did, to anyone after they are discharged. Maybe all militaries in the World are like that.

The intricately orchestrated assassination of President Kennedy had to be masterminded by people on the inside, people who could control all facets of what was planned and of what was going to happen. It points to no one person. Everybody was "just doing their job", everybody was just doing what they were told to do, and got paid to do. As usual, for all corruption follow the money.

After Lee Harvey Oswald was arrested for the murder of Kennedy, and for the murder of a Dallas policemen who reportedly had been pursuing Oswald but was more likely murdered by other people as a part of obvious schemes, plans, and set-ups that played out, Oswald said he could prove he wasn't near the scene of either of the crimes. He said to reporters "I'm the fall guy for the CIA", as police were leading him away. He had worked in Russia for the American CIA, and had been at the CIA in Dallas just days before JFK was murdered. When he was in jail he said "I'm the patsy for the CIA."

No finger prints from Oswald were found on the rifle that was found at the book depository. So after Oswald was murdered, when his body was at a Dallas funeral home, CIA agents or FBI agents brought that rifle there to get his palm prints and finger prints smudged onto that rifle from Oswald's hands. People who saw this happen were told not to report it, or they or their families would be killed. Years later, when they did report it, hopefully they were not murdered too, like all other eyewitnesses who eventually were murdered and assassinated by Government and military forces.

As usual, the truth in the United States can be very dangerous, especially when it involves the Federal Government and the people that rule and control America. This is despite the fact that people in America are taught to believe America is the epitome of truth and justice, never-ending truth and justice being the foundation of America.

Oswald never had any legal representation during the 24 hours he was in jail, before he was murdered. This was, however, his Constitutional right as an American in America. But he was denied this right, just like an unknown number of Americans in America can be, are, and have been denied this same right since 2001.

In 1964, just months after the murder of President Kennedy, President Johnson announced on TV that Secretary of State Bob McNamara, also a Democrat, had told him an American Navy ship had been attacked by North Viet Nam in the Gulf of Tonkin. A war with North Viet Nam would now be justified. But McNamara had lied. There had been no attack on any American ship in the Gulf of Tonkin. It never happened. Years later McNamara said he had "thought the United States would be fighting against Communism in Viet Nam, but, instead, it was just a civil war in Viet Nam."

It was "just a civil war", *their* war, not the business of the United States in any way, that "just" ended up killing *4 to 6 million* South Vietnamese civilians and *58,000* American soldiers, most of which did not want to be there but had to because they were drafted. Years in prison was the alternative, and then an inability to get a job at home because of that prison record, besides harassment from their own Government, the Democratic Administration of President Johnson. Relocating to Canada or Mexico was the other alternative. The better alternative.

After years of dedicated and thorough research the former District Attorney of New Orleans, Jim Garrison, said "Unequivocally, Oswald was not guilty." One man's conspiracy is another man's political consensus of opinion.

# CHAPTER THREE

## The Medical/Sickness Industry In America

Average cancer treatments cost a total of $50,000 to $100,000 before remission and/or control, or death occurs. Every reoccurrence costs as much or more. Statistics have long shown that people with cancer are as likely to die during or after having cancer treatments instead of having *no* cancer treatments. As an example, chemotherapy has never worked for most cancer patients. After all, its purpose has always been to kill and destroy cells at random, causing death for hundreds of millions of cancer patients who were trusting that their Doctor, their oncologist, is really helping them, when, in fact, it has always been just a shot in the dark.

Insulin (from pigs or synthetic), Metformin, and other drugs for diabetes like Actos cause strokes, high blood pressure, heart problems and heart attacks, kidney disease and kidney failure, infections, death, amputations, etc. So diabetics will eventually need treatment and more drugs for other health problems that develop because of the drugs they've taken for diabetes.

It's a vicious circle that never ends. Health problems attributable to diabetes can be caused by the drugs taken for diabetes. The same is true for drugs taken for cancer and high cholesterol. These new sicknesses, caused by drugs used in treatments, are sources of endless money, a lot of money for the United States medical/sickness industry. People are caught up in the endless cycle of mandatory expensive doctor visits and expensive drugs, mandatory visits for prescription renewals and expensive tests, for the rest of their lives. This is just what the medical/sickness industry wants.

It is not uncommon for a patient to die of pneumonia or fatal infections in a hospital after being treated for something else. Pharmaceutical drugs *cause* pneumonia, diabetes, cancer, and many other health problems. Legal drugs are necessary to perpetuate the medical/sickness industry by *causing* health problems, sickness, even death. They endlessly add to the sickness industry arsenal. They are a way to control a national population by means of a kind of oppression. Health is happiness, sickness is for oppression and despair. Health is what everybody wants, and they will do whatever doctors tell them to do to try and get it. Unfortunately, in America it's sickness that drives the economy, not health.

Trillions of dollars of taxpayer's money from the Government given to the National Institute For Health has funded research for more than 60 years for cancer, diabetes, and high cholesterol with no cures being revealed to the public, and they never will be. Cancer is much too profitable an industry for everyone concerned, including researchers, as is diabetes and high cholesterol. For more than 30 years tests have conclusively shown that people are as likely to die with low cholesterol as high cholesterol. People who die from heart attacks are as likely to have had low cholesterol as high cholesterol. But the medical and pharmaceutical industries won't tell hundreds of millions of people that and eliminate their customers for the multi-billion dollar drugs for high cholesterol to be taken for the rest of their lives.

For more than 60 years if people don't die from their cancer treatment they die when it comes back, when it appears again, usually at another location because the former location was burned away (radiation) or cut away (surgery). But, of course, it probably never really left. It's always been the cut, burn, poison (surgery, drugs and chemotherapy) approach that's used in the United States because that's where the money is. Cancer is Big Business in America, a giant money-making industry that grows hugely and exponentially every year, ad infinitum.

For hundreds of years cancer and diabetes have been cured or managed by using herbs, nutrition, and combinations of natural approaches in other countries, like the Chinese system of medicine and herbs that's at least a thousand years old. For the past hundred years if a physician in the United States used these methods he would lose his license to practice medicine and/or be heavily fined. Like dentists that refused to use mercury in dental fillings after the early 1900's would lose their license to be a dentist, and could also be fined. Even now, in the 21st century, anybody promoting cancer cures in the United States can be fined and/or imprisoned because they are a tiny threat to the huge and almighty medical/sickness industry, especially to the almighty and immensely profitable cancer industry. It's all about control and power and money, huge profits from the suffering and sickness and death of innocent and manipulated people in America. It rarely is about altruism and their welfare. It's the American way. It has become an American tradition.

The Hippocratic Oath has been taken by new physicians for centuries. "Above all, do no harm". But for many years it has often been ignored. Especially in the 21st century the profit motive is king, allowing medical and physician hypocrisy. Mental and physical sickness is necessary to increase profits and for perpetuation of the medical/sickness industry and pharmaceutical industry. A happy and healthy population is not their goal or their reason for being.

The medical industry has complained for many years about their allegedly huge monetary losses because of lawsuits, medical malpractice lawsuits. It's been used as a reason, as an excuse, for extremely high medical costs in the United States for many years. But it's just the usual lies, deceit, distortion and manipulation from the medical industry. The standard reason given for any medical mistakes, suffering, and deaths is that it was an "act of God". Who can argue with God? Case closed. No money is paid as a settlement. The outcome was out of their hands and they can't be held responsible. After all, they are always just "practicing", endless experiments on endlessly unique individual people, their patients who must be patient. Besides that, it's almost impossible to prove a physician did something wrong. Fellow physicians will lie for their colleagues. They seem to be above the law.

Maybe it's because they are part of the financial elite and hire the very best lawyers for any lawsuits. Perhaps they have their own laws. The physician who developed the drug called Ecstacy was attempting to decrease mental and physical suffering in his patients and gave it away for free to those who needed it. He was that very rare altruistic doctor, not in it for the money and for as high a profit as possible. However, when his patients started selling it to friends, etc. the FDA shut him down. The FDA didn't buy the rights to produce and sell it because the drug actually helped people be happier and healthier, unlike all other legal drugs. No lawyer could help him fight the power of the FDA.

Many states have a higher death rate from reactions to legal drugs, prescription drugs from a pharmacy, than from any disease. Investigations have shown that teenagers involved in school shootings were usually taking suicide-inducing prescription drugs, usually for depression, or were experiencing withdrawal symptoms from prescription drugs. Deaths from reactions to or overdoses of legal drugs are the leading cause of deaths in the United States.

Stem cells have potential for improving many chronic health problems, degenerative or not. Every time a child is born stem cells in the umbilical cord are thrown away, lost when it is discarded. So why aren't they saved? There's nothing sacred about umbilical cords that are always put in the hospital garbage disposals. Millions of these should have been saved, could have been saved, and then used to help millions of people for many years. Republicans couldn't say that it's murder of a baby, a human being, like they have said for years about using embryos that couldn't be used for in-vitro fertilization and would be discarded anyway. Embryos are a long way off from being functioning human beings, babies functioning on their own as fully developed human beings. Republicans talk about it as if the embryos could become babies by themselves, independent of being in a mother's womb.

Republicans have always insisted that it is a moral issue for that reason. To them it's always been about supposedly killing a human being. This stupidity has been proliferated endlessly and often by Republican politicians and officials in America. It is typical Republican meanness, closed-mindedness, and obstructionism that hurts millions of people in America by depriving them of stem cells that potentially would improve their health problems.

Republicans argue about everything and find fault with Democrats just for the sake of making problems and getting publicity. This pleases Republican voters. It's apparently what they want from their Republican representatives as it has only increased in the 21st century. It pleases physicians and medical specialists for the same reasons if they are Republican. It would be unusual to find a physician who is a Democrat, or that stays a Democrat after they have become wealthy, accumulating both the inevitable status and wealth of physicians in America.

It isn't always that Americans eat too much. Instead it's *what* they eat that makes them overweight. That, combined with widespread blood sugar problems, means most people in America are not at fault for why they weigh too much. The reasons are thyroid problems that are usually undiagnosed, allergies that also are usually undiagnosed, blood sugar imbalances often caused by nutritional deficiencies like chromium and vanadyl sulfate, and an inability to digest the highly processed food that is available for Americans to eat, all of which result in stomach problems, digestion problems, and weight problems.

Genetically modified corn is fed to cattle. Because they are unable to digest it the corn causes more rapid weight gain for the cattle. This makes them ready more quickly to be sold and killed for meat at the grocery store and for restaurants. Corn oil, for cooking, is made from the same genetically modified corn. Corn syrup, usually used instead of sugar in most food products at all grocery stores and restaurants, is also made from this genetically modified corn.

Food that is highly processed cannot be assimilated by the body, so the body rejects it. An example is highly processed fat, bad fatty acids, that negatively affect the body, that negatively influence the thyroid, causing weight gain, indigestion, and allergic reactions because the body is rejecting it. Therefore, highly processed food causes many health problems that necessitate many very expensive and over-priced visits to physicians, many expensive and over-priced tests so they can't be sued for misdiagnosis, etc., and then many expensive and over-priced prescriptions for and purchases of pharmaceuticals to attempt to deal with those problems. Then these legal drugs usually lead to the necessity to take other legal drugs for the problems created by the other legal drugs.

It is always an endless cycle of expensive connections to "your Doctor", as TV and radio commercials have pushed for years. Everyone must have their own very expensive too expensive Doctor. It's the American way. Sickness is the American way. Many health problems are really food problems. Processed food, especially over-processed food, highly processed food, is a built-in constant money-maker for the yearly multi-billion dollar medical/sickness industry and the yearly multi-million dollar weight loss industry. Over-processed food has been a boon to the American economy for many years and probably will continue to be so for the rest of the 21st century.

In desperation to find real and lasting health people in America have made the natural food industry, the natural supplement industry, also a multi-billion dollar industry. But compensating for and overcoming the endless forces working against health, real and lasting health, cannot be done with supplements alone. There has to be huge changes and improvements in the way food is produced in America. As always, follow the money to find the reasons no changes will ever be made for the benefit of the health of all people in America. The expendable masses are indeed expendable.

In 2011 and 2012 parts of cattle that formerly had been thrown away were ground into what was called "pink slime". It was treated repeatedly with ammonia to lessen exposure to e-coli, which comes from feces and excrement, then artificially colored red, then sold to and bought by McDonalds, Taco Bell, Burger King, and schools across America for school lunches. It was then added to their ground beef for school lunches and consumer consumption, which was then sold as "ground beef", and labeled "ground beef", all in the name of greater profit and deception.

Radioactive waste is used to "purify" food, produce, and meat. It's a method of killing bacteria, parasites, etc., and another way to eventually cause cancer in people and animals. Repeated exposure to radiation and radiation waste causes leukemia, cancer, respiratory problems, and lung problems. This was well known before the use of radioactive waste to contaminate food began.

Government subsidies are what has kept American farmers in business for many years. Industrial farming has replaced edible food with genetically modified food that has bad taste and little or no nutritional value. "Liberty Corn", also called "Freedom Corn", is an example. It is resistant to poisons sprayed on it for two plant-specific bugs, so the yield is increased. So profit is greatly increased. This is the corn used for food for cattle, and for sweetener and corn oil for cooking, and for production of bio-fuel. An acre of this corn produces only about a gallon of bio-fuel, the replacement for gasoline. Obviously it's a waste of money as a gasoline replacement. Obviously it's a dangerous thing and the wrong thing to be feeding cattle. Obviously it's hurting humans, because it's in a lot of what they eat. But capitalism and greed justify anything that generates huge profits.

It is not able to be digested by cattle. Instead it accumulates in their bodies causing ulcers, acidosis, and death after about five months. It results in obesity in these corn-fed cows, meaning they sell for more money. Antibiotics are necessary to keep them alive for that five months. The motive behind this is obviously more money, more profit, and greed.

Most prepared food in the grocery store has high fructose corn sweetener in it. Especially soda pop. It has been prepared with this Liberty Corn sweetener, that has absorbed two deadly poisons other corn, normal corn, would be destroyed by. It is possible, then, that this Liberty Corn high fructose corn sweetener, that can't be digested, is connected to the high percentage of obesity, or people just weighing too much in America in the 21st century. This could also be an explanation for the huge increase in acidosis in humans in America. But treating acidosis has become another part of the medical industry in America, and has added another reason to go to an over-priced physician for treatment and help.

Production of Liberty Corn/Freedom Corn is what rainforests are cut down for. Eliminating the production and use of bio-fuel, driving electric cars, and feeding cattle grass, like they've eaten for hundreds of thousands of thousands of years, maybe millions of years, and feeding them what they are supposed to eat, and using only real sugar instead of corn sweetener in all food would eliminate a lot of health problems that have developed and increased immensely in the 21st century. Besides that it would save the precious and not replaceable rainforests with their millions of species of animals, insects, birds, trees, and special herbs and plants, indigenous to rainforests exclusively.

Destroying this to produce more poisonous and deadly genetically modified (GMO) corn that has no nutritional value, all because of greed, all in the name of more money and profit, is representative of the worst in human beings. Besides that, it causes hundreds of millions of people to become obese. These, then, are people who will have more health problems, necessitating more visits to physicians, more hospital visits, more and endless legal drugs, hugely increasing the profits of the medical industry and the pharmaceutical industry, and the insurance industry, the cornerstones of the United States economy. Obviously these problems and suffering are planned.

The United States medical system makes all diabetics victims of the system, and prisoners of the disease that controls their life in a big way. Once someone has diabetes they can't usually lose the excess weight that remains after being stabilized by the medications. Being overweight led to diabetes Type II, and not being able to lose that weight keeps them prisoners of diabetes. But it's mostly only in America that there's no cure or healing for diabetes. The United States medical system and the governments, both state and federal, seem to have collaborated to keep Americans sick and to get them sick. It's a process that most Americans can't avoid.

Cattle are bred for food for humans and for other animals. By feeding them high fructose corn syrup made from Freedom Corn/Liberty Corn, a highly processed food that has no nutritional value, they gain weight much faster than ever before even though they can't digest it. They won't eat the inferior food they are forced to eat, including parts of dead cattle that can't be sold, unless that sugar substitute is mixed with it to hide the awful taste. What happened to grass? They gain weight much faster with the inferior "food" and therefore can be sold for meat much sooner, increasing profits. Like everything else in the United States, especially in the 21st century, profit and monetary gain is most important and the health and well-being of animals and humans doesn't matter.

The high fructose corn syrup made from Liberty Corn/Freedom Corn, a much cheaper corn that is inedible, stays in their stomachs, unable to be digested, so it accumulates there and leads to their death in about six months if they aren't sold and killed before that time for meat for humans and animals. It has become a permanent replacement for sugar, as an additive to most of our food for humans. Why was it named "Freedom Corn"? Freedom for who? Instead it signals a decline in health and gaining a lot of weight for any person or animal that eats a lot of it. Every person or animal has their own limitations, points at which they can tolerate no more physical, mental, spiritual, or physiological abuse, or artificial food abuse. Then health/sickness problems dominate their lives, and can cause eventual premature death from those problems.

Initially, in the early 20th century, Coca Cola had a little cocaine mixed into it. That's why it was named "Coca" Cola. Just enough to cause a little high, a positive reaction to the soda pop, leading to its becoming the most popular soda pop in the World, an empire of profits, of immense wealth, and of international popularity and global dominance in both the 20th and 21st centuries. Of course at some point the cocaine was taken out of the formula, after cocaine became an illegal drug. Since after 2001 all soda pop has been made with high fructose corn syrup in it, instead of sugar, including Coca Cola. Maybe it's the new cocaine equivalent. If you stop drinking pop for a month you should lose weight and belly fat. Like the cows, the cattle, you will gain weight from drinking it and eating it, and like the cows, the cattle, you will not digest it because it is not a food. So, like the cows and the beef cattle, you will gain weight, a lot of weight, especially in the area of your stomach. Try green coffee bean pills to eliminate this excess stomach weight that contributes to the development of diabetes, Type II.

In America both the state governments and the Federal Government encourage dangerous practices of food production, all in the name of profit and capitalism, the free-market, and greed. In fact, the government indirectly sells tons of radio-active wastes to food producers and food produce dealers. It's then a profitable product, instead of having to find a place to bury it. After all, nobody wants it in their backyard, but hey, little do they know they're eating it instead. It's changing poison, toxins, into future business for the medical/sickness industry. It creates business in the future for the medical/sickness industry, a pillar of the United States economy, a necessary part of the United States economy. The masses, after all, are expendable. There is, after all, a method to all government madness. Greed, money, profit, and control are always the motivators.

Since the 1960's hundreds of millions of women in America have taken, have been prescribed, birth control pills and estrogen for post-menopausal problems. The purported benefits, the promise of benefits repeated by millions of physicians for more than 60 years, didn't pan out. Except for the control of pregnancies. It was supposed to reduce heart attacks and strokes, but instead there was a huge increase in heart attacks and strokes. Instead there was a huge increase in breast cancer and other cancers, and in thyroid problems. Maybe Alzheimer's has a connection to birth control pills and estrogen pills for menopause, as it is much more common in women than men.

For more than 50 years, since the 1960's, the estrogen for birth control pills has always been gotten from pregnant mares, millions of pregnant female horses that are forced to stand up for their entire life, for every second of every day, not allowed to lay down ever, so their urine can be accumulated, collected without any chance of losing any horse urine for Premarin birth control pills. "Pre-mar-in" stands for pregnant mare urine. The immense cruelty of this is multiplied by the birth of their colts that are killed after being born so the mare can be impregnated again. Greed and cruelty in the United States has never had any boundaries.

Many legal drugs, as pharmaceuticals, cause heart problems, heart attacks, tuberculosis, kidney failure, cancer, asthma, respiratory problems and failure, skin problems, unconsciousness, difficulty breathing, and endless other health problems. These are delayed effects, delayed reactions. No one knows how many hundreds of millions of people have been victims of these legal drugs. The so-called "race to cure cancer" leads right back to physicians and legal drugs, pharmaceuticals, as the cause, as they are the cause of many other health diseases, chronic or not, and lesser health problems. Maybe that's why hundreds of billions of dollars have been given away to cancer research, mostly to the NIH, the National Institute of Health, for at least 60 years and the causes and cures are found but not officially found, so they are never revealed to the American public. Such a lucrative source of money, millions of dollars of endless money every year, will not be brought to a halt. So the true and actual discoveries for the cure of cancer and other diseases have never been revealed. The medical/sickness industry is a foundation of the United States economy and must be perpetuated as a growth industry.

Legalize illegal drugs and then drug-related corruption, at all levels worldwide, would come to a screeching halt. Policemen, deputies, Sergeants, Sheriffs, Police Chiefs, and everybody else taking bribes, taking pay-offs, in the United States, and in the rest of the world, would end. The very costly and corrupt DEA, the Drug Enforcement Agency, would end, adding billions of dollars to the United States economy and to the yearly budget for legal and ethical purposes, like healthcare and education. But *many* politically powerful and connected people would not allow that to happen. Illegal drugs are here to stay because many millions of people in America are involved in the drug game.

The HPC vaccine is for a virus that causes cancer in teenagers who are sexually active. If a virus causes one cancer then it is only logical that other viruses cause other cancers. The cancer industry is motivated by ego, money, power, and greed, not altruism. All teenaged girls from 13 to 19 are told to get the vaccine whether they are sexually active or not, and the vaccine lasts only four years. It is true that American teenagers reputedly are the most sexually active in the world, and that also explains why the highest teen pregnancy single-mother occurrence is also in the United States. The almost mandatory vaccine for a very unlikely cancer/virus should instead be dealt with at the source, which is the irresponsible, spoiled, and undisciplined teenagers, both male and female everywhere in the United States, some places more than others. Instead of giving them carte blanche for sex, unlimited and irresponsible sex. First and foremost the reason for this problem is, and always has been, the parents. And the media, the irresponsible media, cable TV, movies, and videos in the 21$^{st}$ century.

In 1992 the autism rate was 1 in 10,000 kids. In 2011 and 2012 the autism rate was 1 in 88, more than 100 times worse in only about 20 years. Autism makes kids, then adults, unable to function well in society and socially, and unable to perform intellectually at their normal level. It's just what a closing society needs and wants to be perpetuated. Maybe some drug or some combination of drugs has been given more frequently to pregnant mothers or children before age eight, and that is a cause for increased autism. But it will never be revealed because money, power, profit, and control are more important than the health and welfare of the expendable masses. Increasing health problems requiring necessary drugs and Doctor visits for many years, endlessly, is just what the Doctor ordered. It's just what the medical/sickness industry wants. It's what keeps the United States economy afloat.

The Earth's atmosphere and climate is changing because of pollution, endless tons of poisonous chemicals in the air, and because of other reasons like the changing angles and distances of the Sun. The Earth's atmosphere and light and warmth from the Sun allows life, allows living, to happen on Earth. Oxygen and nitrogen and water from this atmosphere are necessary for human life. The ozone layer that regulates the strength and amount of exposure to sunlight is disappearing. A deficiency of vitamin D from the Sun and a deficiency of oxygen can be factors in development of cancer, and many other health problems. No wonder the Republicans in power are always against regulations to stop environmental damage, or are against enforcing the regulations already in place.

It is possible the Earth is tilting on its axis, changing its angle to the Sun. This would change climates everywhere on Earth. Scientists have said the magnetic field of the Earth is reversing, so the magnetic strength is less. It protects the Earth from radiation. More radiation means more cancer. This natural source of radiation is obviously beyond anyone's control, so the increase in cancer for this reason is also beyond anyone's control. Somehow increasing magnetic exposure for individuals on an individual basis would be the only alternative. But this is a welcome increase in cancer for the medical/sickness industry and the cancer industry. Prevention is not their modus operandi.

One of the three men that developed the PSA test for detection of prostate cancer revealed many years later, before he died, that it was accurate only 3% to 7% of the time. That means 93% to 97% of the men told they had prostate cancer because of that test didn't have it, and always don't have it, and have surgery, radiation, and chemotherapy they don't need. They die, then, from the treatment, not from the cancer that was never really there.

That's the American medical system. Over-priced extremely expensive treatments for the wrong problems, or for unnecessary reasons, and not informing the public, their patients, about what is really going on, about the risks, and never giving options. Full disclosure is rare, and what is disclosed may be in fine print, in tiny little letters, like a business deal, like a business transaction. The medical/sickness industry in the United States is, indeed, a business that serves itself instead of serving the American public. But there is nothing anyone in America can do to change or influence that. Once again, it's all about power, control, money, and profit.

Natural alternatives for health problems are used throughout the World, some with amazing success. If physicians in the United States use these methods they can lose their license to practice medicine or be heavily fined, especially if it concerns cancer, the Holy Grail of diseases in the United States. If anyone else who is not a physician promotes alternatives to cancer treatment, a pillar of the United States economy, they can be imprisoned or heavily fined. They, like physicians, will be stopped by the very powerful, greedy, and apparently paranoid pharmaceutical industry, also a pillar of the United States economy. Legal drugs are always one of the top three most profitable industries in America every year, along with the corrupt oil industry and the corrupt insurance industry. For the past 50 years the American economy depends on sickness for its success.

The cancer industry has always promoted death and suffering from cancer by never finding a cure for cancer. It has been oppression of hundreds of millions of people with cancer and many hundreds of millions of people connected to those victims as friends and family. Financially, the cancer industry has been an astounding success indefinitely for the medical/sickness industry, worth trillions of dollars to the United States economy. In terms of health and actually helping Americans to have a better, healthier life for the rest of their lives it has been a dismal and astounding failure. Sixty years ago about 1 in 1000 people got cancer in America. But now, after 2014, about 1 in 10 people in America gets cancer. This is proof of the gigantic failure of the medical/sickness industry and of the gigantic failure of the cancer industry in America. Cancer should be managed, and not even attempted to be cured and/or eliminated because that often leads quickly, or eventually, to painful misery and suffering and unnecessary death.

But, conversely, diabetes is a multi-trillion dollar sickness industry that keeps Americans sick by managing a problem instead of eliminating it. For hundreds of years, maybe thousands of years, other cultures like in China and India have thought of diabetes as a biological imbalance able to be corrected with herbal combinations and nutrition, not insulin from chemicals or from pigs, or drugs like Metformin and Actos that have side-effects like strokes, heart attacks, heart arrhythmia, heart disease, heart failure, kidney disease and kidney failure, infections, and death. It's another way to add to the sickness arsenal available to American doctors to guarantee their financial success.

Komen For The Cure has had hundreds of millions of dollars donated to it to "end breast cancer". However, their commercials promote the standard diagnosis using x-rays, and cut, burn, and poison (surgery, radiation, chemotherapy) to end breast cancer. It's nothing new to "end breast cancer". It's just the status quo for the past 75 years. It's just the same old thing put into a modern context. Actually, ending breast cancer would be the end of a major part of the cancer industry, with major negative financial repercussions for millions of people who depend on cancer for their livelihood. The United States economy depends on breast cancer treatments and all other cancer treatments.

In the first decades of the 21$^{st}$ century both cancer and diabetes are like epidemics in the United States compared to the first decades of the 20$^{th}$ century. At least a trillion dollars has been spent in an attempt to find a cure for them in those intervening 100 years as Government grants and donations. Do you believe that not even one cure has been found? It's beyond credibility that no cure has been found for either disease. Instead they are managed and became the basis, the foundation for, the hugely profitable medical/sickness industry in the United States. Unlike any other country in the World.

Diabetes is a man-made epidemic involving a much higher percentage of adults and children than ever before. Something happens to tens of millions of people in the United States that raises the sugar level in their blood. Then they gain a lot of weight as a result. High blood-sugar levels is probably the reason for most of the obesity in the United States. Another major reason is thyroid imbalances. It isn't because of eating too much sugar, or too much fat, or too much food. It's _what_ they eat.

It's high fructose corn syrup made from Freedom/Liberty Corn, that's added to almost everything people eat in America that is made in America. It's a sugar substitute because it's cheaper, and it's a flavor enhancer to encourage repeat purchases and greater satisfaction with the food. It's also mildly addictive. High fructose corn syrup has been a product for commercial greed and increased profits since the beginning, having nothing to do with health except the destruction of health. Unlike all other fruits and vegetables grown in the United States it has always been a government-subsidized crop, making it foolproof as a definite huge moneymaker that is here to stay and to be used indefinitely.

It's like the monosodium glutamate flavor enhancer used in Oriental food at restaurants, that encourages repeat purchases and greater satisfaction with their food. Millions of people have had problems after eating it, negative reactions to MSG, mostly because of allergic reactions to it.

About 10% of Americans get Type II diabetes. It usually happens because they weigh too much, especially if they have too much belly fat, which triggers the development of Type II diabetes. Corn syrup made from Freedom Corn is not digested so it sits in the stomach, stays in the stomach, and is a cause of excess belly fat and overweight. Therefore, high fructose corn syrup made from Freedom Corn, and other corn developed to have no nutritional value, causes obesity and Type II diabetes because Freedom Corn, and others like it, have no nutritional value and is not able to be digested. It probably is the biggest reason for the diabetes epidemic and obesity epidemic in America in the 21$^{st}$ century.

Billions of bees are transported in trucks hundreds of thousands of miles throughout America every year in order to guarantee the success of crop pollination of fruit and vegetables and nuts, especially almonds. Upon arrival at their destination they are fed only high fructose corn syrup to sustain them until they can eat enough real and genuinely pure nectar necessary for their nutrition, in order to pollinate the trees and flowers for weeks, 24/7. This is one of the reasons bees have been dying by the billions since after 2001. Even bees are controlled by politics, greed, and money.

The United States medical industry and the governments, both state and federal, have set up a system that makes both cancer and diabetes very profitable industries. Diabetes alone generates more than $200 billion dollars in revenue every year. It controls tens of millions of Americans who are tied to their mandatory medicine and controlled sickness for the rest of their lives. This includes at least four required visits to their physician every year to renew their prescriptions, at a cost of at least $300 for about 10 minutes of the Doctor's time and the simple blood tests to determine prescription dosage, etc. Multiply that times at least 30 million people and it's a real money-maker, adding at least $12 billion dollars to the medical industry revenue and to the United States economy each year. Add the inevitable extremely expensive hospital stays, 10 to 1000 times more expensive than anywhere else in the world, for complications caused by those medications, that mandatory medicine, and then probably eventually dying from those complications, and it's easy to see that diabetes adds more than$200 billion dollars to the medical industry, and to the United States economy, every year.

The most profitable nonprofit organization in the United States is the Red Cross. Their president has long had a salary of more than a million dollars a year. This is excessive for a non-profit organization. Like all non-profits the organization and its employees pay no taxes. For many years, since the 1970's, Red Cross profits from investments like real estate have been at least hundreds of millions of dollars each and every year, also not taxable, and not reported to the expendable masses as income.

The March of Dimes have always said they help babies to be strong and healthy. How do they do this? They don't. For more than 50 years they have advertised they help disabled babies and children, and help babies to not be born prematurely, to prevent premature babies, giving the impression they help both financially and medically if babies are born with disabilities like cerebral palsy. What do they actually do? Nothing. No help whatsoever for parents who have disabled children, therefore no help whatsoever for the child. In 2014 the yearly salary of their President was more than $600,000. No taxes are paid because they are non-profit. What have they done with the hundreds of millions of dollars donated to them each year to help babies and disabled children? They have never even paid their yearly poster kids, or helped their parents financially if they *ask* for help. If you ask them for financial assistance or other help you will get none.

When they began asking for donations to prevent premature births about 60 years ago about one in 1000 babies were born very premature, not just a week or two early. Now, as their advertisements say, about one in eight babies are born prematurely. This is proof-positive that the billions of dollars donated to them, maybe even a trillion dollars, has not been used to prevent babies being born prematurely and to help premature babies. Yet they have never been charged with false advertising, or fraudulent fund-raising, as the company CEOs have become *very* rich for many years and only a few kids, if any, with disabilities have been actually helped by the March of Dimes.

These organizations are really for-profit, not non-profit. The total yearly income of all Catholic Churches in the United States is more than a *billion dollars*. Little if any money is put back into the communities to help the truly poor, the truly needy. Like Government information it is "classified", meaning not accounted for. It's always been a secret, the antithesis of a true charity, of a true church that is really working for the people it is supposed to serve, and claims that it serves. It is obviously not non-profit, but instead is a very profitable for-profit organization. It has always been this way, so why hasn't anyone ever stopped it, changed it? Because Catholic Priests, Bishops, Popes, and administrators are allowed to lie to protect the Catholic Church. It's part of the Church doctrine. Officially, deceit, deception, and lies are acceptable if they are "done to protect the Catholic Church".

Many millions of people think if information is on the TV news, especially on CNN and FOX NEWS, or in newspapers, it must be true. But lies are easily perpetuated and promoted, especially when they are repeated again and again on FOX NEWS and CNN 24/7. It's like propaganda. About 70% of commercials on TV are about sickness, health problems, and diseases, and the pharmaceuticals to take for them, telling you to make an appointment to see your Dr. to get a prescription for the drugs. This advertising hugely increases over-priced Dr. visits, a mandatory part of the drug and Doctor process.

The United States has the largest percentage of unhealthy people in the World. These commercials sell the idea that if you aren't sick now you will be in the future. This perpetuates the control and wealth of the sickness industry in the only democracy in the World, out of 24, that doesn't have free high quality Universal Health care for everyone, at all income levels, and all ages, in their country. Many of these other democracies also provide free health care for foreigners visiting their country, no strings attached. All of this is proof that their medical industries are for altruism and real health, and for actually upholding the Hippocratic Oath.

In 1990 pharmaceutical profits from production and sale of vaccinations was $500 million dollars. Now, more than 25 years later, babies and children are forced to be given two to three times as many mandatory vaccinations, as their yearly profits have doubled to at least a billion dollars a year. Other countries only use the safest methods of vaccine production and the best ingredients in order to protect their children from bad side effects like autism, brain damage, and death. Only the United States does not. As always in America the almighty profit margin is, and always has been, the most important. Profit, greed, and money have always been more important than the welfare and health of children in America. Only in America could this happen. Mandatory vaccinations in America are a big business, and it isn't because of altruism. It's because of the usual greed, power, money, and control.

No one knows how many deaths of babies labeled SIDS, Sudden Infant Death Syndrome, really died from reactions to vaccinations. SIDS is just another medical industry cover-up for their mistakes, deaths caused by the medical industry that has always used the least expensive methods and least expensive ingredients to get vaccines produced. In the process the medical industry has been killing many millions of animals, including chimpanzees that are physiologically 98% the same as human beings, because of endlessly repeated experiments, the same ones year after year, in order to get the same government grant money for those same unnecessary and cruel repeated experiments year after year. Also, animals are killed to get some of the ingredients for the vaccinations.

As an example, this includes killing monkeys for their kidneys, to be used as an ingredient in polio vaccines. Their greed and animal cruelty has always been more important than the welfare of American babies and children. Perhaps the Republican concept and mind-set of "collateral damage" exists in this industry too, not just in the military industry. Creating sickness is big business in America. How many people diagnosed with Alzheimer's disease really have Mad Cow disease, gotten from eating infected cow or cattle meat? Maybe it's more than 50%. No one knows. One reason would be because only about 1 out of 1000 cows or cattle are tested for this disease in the United State before they are slaughtered. For the past 50 years Americans have eaten many *tons* of beef every year, increasingly because of the popularity of fast-food restaurants. But most beef, most hamburgers, taste different than they used to, and don't taste good. Something is happening to the cattle. What are beef suppliers feeding their cattle, what are they doing to the cattle to make the beef so inferior?

The way they force them to live in too confined areas, the way they kill them and what they feed them, has a lot to do with the end-product, the meat. This is also true about the inhumane methods used in the chicken and pork industries in the United States, which are one of the worst in the World, especially compared to the other 23 Democracies in the World. There is a radical need for improvement in all these areas of meat production that is long overdue.

Diabetes, cancer, and high cholesterol make people prisoners of the American medical/sickness industry. That's just what the industry wants. There are no cures, just endless drugs and treatments to manage these problems for the rest of their lives. Drugs that cause more problems that require more too-high medical expenses, and endless too-expensive visits to a Doctor for prescription renewals and more expensive tests, for hundreds of millions of people for the rest of their lives. It is a system designed for control and dependency on usually very expensive drugs and over-priced physicians, 10 to 1000 times more expensive than anywhere else in the World, but not better than anywhere else.

About 1/3 of the United States economy is healthcare. That's about $3 trillion dollars a year. One in eight people work in the healthcare industry. It has replaced manufacturing in the United States economy in the 21st century as one of the top three money-makers. America stopped being the World's industrial leader and became, instead, the World's medical/sickness industry leader and military super-power. Sickness and wars are a necessary part of the American economy. So anyone who pays for vastly over-priced medical services is helping the American economy. Anyone who is an active soldier is helping the American economy and the World image of America as being the military super-power of the World. After all, paramilitary and private military soldiers are infinitely more expensive to use than United States soldiers in their various military capacities.

One in six Americans has an autoimmune disease, meaning their immune system isn't functioning correctly. That's more than 50 million people sick, with a mystery disease that is not really a mystery. It is caused by exposure, internal or external, to chemicals. But the medical/sickness industry and the Government say it's caused by "the environment", which effectively tells people to be anti-environment when the environment had nothing to do with it. This is what the Republicans in power want, when it's really caused by artificial chemicals produced by factories and dumped by the tons, tons of it every day, into the environment, into the air and the water.

Many health problems are also caused by prescription drugs taken by millions of people every day. And caused by drugs, the cocktails of drugs, given before, during, and after surgeries. Then adding drugs appropriate for recovery and maintenance, possibly for years. It is impossible for anyone to avoid medical chemicals, medical poisons, pharmaceuticals, and prescription drugs in the American society of the 21st century, along with the other myriad of chemicals, at least 100,000 of them, that we are all exposed to to some extent every day. Their related sickness and health problems are inescapable and unavoidable. Thus we are all victims.

About 100,000 chemicals are produced in the United States every day. If just ½ of them, about 50,000, or just ¼ of them, 25,000, cause cancer then it is still impossible for anyone to escape exposure or to determine which ones cause cancer. Even if only 1000 pharmaceuticals cause cancer then it is still impossible for most of the 330 million people in the United States to escape exposure. This would be one explanation why 1 out of every 100 people got cancer in America in the 1950's and now, 60 years later, at least 1 in 8 people get cancer. For some kinds of cancer the rate is even 1 in 3 people in the United States, in the second decade of the 21st century. Prevention of cancer will never be a goal. Cancer is absolutely necessary for the American economy, and is a welcomed by-product of the diversified and endless production of poisonous chemicals in the American economy.

Pharmaceuticals have long been one of the top three money-making industries in the United States, a foundation of the economy for many years. The damage it causes to people's health and to the environment, to the water, and to the air have always been ignored, with a let's-look-the-other-way approach to enforcing regulations, like politicians and police and deputies just look the other way, giving preferential treatment and protection to their favorite people. All of this is an American tradition. It is nothing new or unusual.

For about 15 years after World War II the United States Government, the United States Department of Agriculture, sprayed at least *600 million* gallons of DDT every year on farmland vegetables, fruit trees, wheat, and on drinking water for animals and human beings, and directly on people and animals, wild or domesticated, while they were walking or sitting under the clouds of poisonous spray, all done for the purpose of killing bugs, mostly for eradicating mosquitoes. The spray came from trucks and airplanes. Everywhere in America, in cities and towns and on rural land, spraying of DDT happened repeatedly for many years. This DDT killed horses, cows, dogs, cats, millions of birds and wild animals, and all insects, not just the mosquitoes. No one knows exactly what damage it did to the people.

The United States Government knew DDT caused nerve damage and cancer, not just immediate death. If Rachel Carson hadn't researched, written, and published "Silent Spring" the Federal Government wouldn't have stopped using it, spraying it on innocent victims. How many people who were sprayed with DDT poison, including while they sat in their cars watching a drive-in movie, had delayed reactions like Parkinson's disease or cancer years later? It potentially supplied an endless source of people with medical problems for many years in the future. During the writing of her book "Silent Spring" Rachel Carson was diagnosed with cancer. Not long after it was published she died from cancer. Or maybe she died because of the cancer treatments.

The biggest cause of death in the United States is medical drugs, reactions to medical drugs, chemicals, legal drugs. The second and third causes are cancer and heart attacks, which can be caused by reactions to medical drugs, legal drugs, prescription drugs, as long-term or short-term reactions. Hundreds of millions of people have experienced complications and death from medical drugs, and long-term health problems from medical drugs, prescription drugs. Many millions of people have left hospitals after some procedure, after staying in a hospital, with more problems and different problems than they went in with. Americans are powerless to change any of this.

Every person has unique reactions to drugs, to legal medical drugs/chemicals, and to prescription drugs. Every person has their own unique point at which they can tolerate no more chemical stress and exposure, physical stress, mental stress, and emotional stress. There are more than 100,000 chemicals produced in the United States every day. Any of these chemicals alone or in any combination, potentially *many millions* of combinations, could cause problems in any person, or contribute to already existing health problems, both short-term and long-term. Physicians take no responsibility for these bad reactions, taking no responsibility for the prescriptions they prescribe.

They ignore the drug warnings, and the bad side effects easily accessible in their PDR, the Physician's Desk Reference, in all Doctor's offices for the past sixty years for that purpose, but in extremely tiny print, even requiring a magnifying glass to read. Therefore, it seems inaccessible and not user-friendly. But it's easily read on any computer. "Above all, do no harm" doesn't cover bad reactions to drugs, problems from drugs they prescribe. Charging at least $600 dollars an hour, or $150 for 15 minutes, isn't enough for them to take the time to look at this information to protect their patients from the problems designated in this directory, in the PDR. Potential problems could be easily avoided if Doctors took the time to look at their PDR, or at this information on the computer. Most drugs should not be prescribed at all as most are potentially lethal, toxic, poisonous, deadly.

United States scientists and their employees have killed and tortured millions of animals in their experiments for more than 60 years. Animals are not identical physiologically to human beings so scientific results based on animals and their suffering, and their deaths, has always been inaccurate and useless, and often falsified in order to validate getting more grant money. Hundreds of billions of dollars are given every year by the United States Government to the NIH, the National Institute of Health, totaling at least a *trillion dollars* in the past 60 years of torturing and killing animals. Repeating cruel experiments endlessly to get hundreds of millions of dollars in grants, and now *billions of dollars*, from the Government should have ended many years ago. It should never have been begun.

Scientists should have used their billions of dollars of yearly government grant money to do what they've been doing for 60 years, developing synthetic chemical versions of natural substances to be patented as part of the domination by the pharmaceutical industry in the medical/sickness industry.

A chemical version of chimpanzee kidney tissue would have eliminated exposure to SIV for hundreds of millions of children in America. How many Americans given this vaccine developed health problems, or HIV, years later because of that vaccine? No one knows. No one will ever know how many children and adults living in other countries were given polio vaccinations made in America and got health problems, or HIV, years later because of that vaccine. Killing hundreds of thousands of chimpanzees for polio virus ingredients was beyond cruel and should have been substituted by a patented chemical version, the American medical forte', an absolutely essential part of the American medical sickness industry.

Since the 1960's mandatory vaccinations have been given to babies in America for diptheria and pertussis (whooping cough) and tetanus. Within 30 days of being given this some of the babies have always gotten these same diseases in a major way. Like with all vaccinations an unknown number have died or sustained permanent or reoccurring health problems. That's what a live virus vaccine does. It gives the disease to the child in small doses that a percentage of them cannot tolerate. Some of the children will get a full-blown version of the disease, or some other bad reaction. The same is true with animal vaccines, from which a percentage of the animals have always gotten very sick, from which a percentage have always died. The polio vaccine has always been made from monkey kidneys, including chimpanzee kidneys, killing them in the process. No wonder chimpanzees are near extinction, an endangered species.

Chimpanzees are 98% like humans, 98% the same DNA , more like humans than gorillas, or any other animal. Some of those kidneys transferred SIV, the simian version of HIV. HIV was discovered by a scientist in the 1920's, but AIDs didn't show up until the 1960's. Why the 40 year disconnect, the 40 year disparity? It seems to be proof that HIV does *not* cause AIDs. Physicians and scientists have said from the beginning that AIDs wouldn't show up until about 10 years after exposure to it.

All pharmaceuticals, many thousands of them, can have bad side-effects, some as many as thirty problems, including death, added onto the one problem you are taking the drug for. Natural supplements and herbal supplements can have additional benefits, more than what you take them for, sometimes many other benefits, and no bad side-effects. But the benefits aren't immediate like drugs. Instead, their healing actions take days or weeks. Even months. Unlike drugs, they never just cover-up or mask the real problem. Either they will work for you, help you, or get rid of the problem, or they will not. And their costs are much less than drugs, chemicals, pharmaceuticals because they can't be patented. But natural supplements are a billion dollar industry in America, so they're working well for a lot of people who are tired of being manipulated by the always greedy and profit-driven medical industry in America. People are tired of paying excessive over-charges for little or no help.

Government grants, money to the NIH, has been hundreds of billions of dollars spent on torturing millions of helpless animals in scientific experiments repeated year after year since the 1950's. It has been for mostly useless information, as 99% of the time humans have completely different reactions to chemicals, drugs, and pharmaceuticals than the abused and tortured animals. This has included cutting off animal's legs, hands (of monkeys), feet, and heads for awful and unbelievably cruel experiments in the name of science. In Germany the Nazi's had the only other culture that justified and approved such cruelty and demented "scientific" studies and experiments done exclusively on helpless animals and Jewish babies, children, and adults, and on handicapped children, babies, and adults. The German Nazis are, and were, the wrong people to imitate and copy.

For more than 60 years in the United States inhumane and terrible things have been done to caged animals in the name of science, entertainment, and profit. For many years captive wild animals in zoos have lived in inhumane conditions and environments in little cages for their entire lives because most Americans have thought they were superior to all animals, not just superior to other people in other countries. There has been some improvement for animals in the last 20 years, but not nearly enough. People's sense of superiority often translates to cruelty of both helpless animals and helpless people, who are then victims of their cruelty and demented meanness.

Starting in 2014 the United States became the only democracy in the World, out of 24, that forces all of its citizens to buy health/sickness insurance each year from commercial profit-driven insurance companies or be punished and heavily fined. If the insurance costs more than 8% of a person's income they can get financial assistance from the Federal Government to purchase that insurance. This new system was planned to add about 33 million people to the health insurance industry, hugely increasing the profits for the insurance industry, the pharmaceutical industry, and the medical industry, three long-time pillars of the United States economy. All other 23 Democracies have had high-quality free Universal Healthcare for everyone in their country for many years that is systematically being replaced with mandatory United States-style profit-driven privatized healthcare. Otherwise their countries can't receive huge financial loans, billions of dollars, or hundreds of millions of dollars, from the World Bank, etc. to keep their countries and their governments operating.

Mandatory health/sickness insurance has been another freedom taken away from people in America, but this time it will have been taken away by a Democratic President, not a Republican President. The Republicans, both politicians and ordinary people, were against it because it was a Democratic initiative and triumph. Republican politicians were against it because it takes unlimited profits away from the medical industry, specifically physicians, most of who are Republicans.

It's impossible to prevent health problems if the air we breathe and the water we drink are a problem, if they aren't good for us. The air we breathe is 85% nitrogen, 2% carbon dioxide, and only 13% oxygen. A decrease in oxygen and increase in carbon dioxide is found in large population areas of the United States, and in areas near large population centers, including as far away as 100 miles.

Inadequate oxygen causes cancer and other health problems, especially if combined with an increased carbon dioxide level. Add food mostly devoid of naturally occurring nutrition and full of chemical additives and it's a recipe for health problems that cannot be avoided. Add to this the more than 100,000 man-made chemicals with endless bad side-effects that all of us are exposed to every day, causing chronic health problems like heart problems, MD, asthma, cancer, MS, Lupus, and death. We breathe, eat, drink, and digest some of these 100,000 chemicals every day so prevention of sickness is impossible. Or physicians give them intravenously, or by injection, or by prescription for pills. Delay is possible but prevention is not. As an example, almost everybody gets some kind of cancer if they live long enough.

No one knows how many people die every year as a result of chemicals and pharmaceuticals given to them by their physicians. No record has ever been kept because it is impossible to do so. Besides usually not being absolutely sure that was the cause of any death, that, as a cause of death, also involves a huge financial liability, endless lawsuits, and paying too-expensive lawyers for their service, whether they win or lose. It also means insurance companies really would have to pay out million dollar-plus lawsuits instead of lying about it. Physicians and insurance companies are in business to make money, not earn it, not lose it. After 2014 health insurance became mandatory and approximately 33 million more people will be forced to buy it or be fined, increasing the profits of these two industries immensely. The United States is a sickness driven economy.

In 2014 about 1 in 8 men got prostate cancer, at least 10 times more than 30 years ago. About 1 in 10 people are clinically depressed, at least 10 times more than 30 years ago. How much of those increases are caused by reactions to pharmaceuticals? Did the comedian and actor Robin Williams die in 2014 as a result of his reactions to drugs he had been prescribed for his very publicized severe depression? No responsibility is ever taken by pharmaceutical companies, even for famous people.

People often die in hospitals from pneumonia they get while they are in the hospital. Why? They get pneumonia from pharmaceuticals given to them while they are in the hospital. Almost all sicknesses and health problems can be gotten from legal drugs, *caused* by legal drugs, as a result of taking prescribed pharmaceuticals. It's one of the benefits of the medical industry. Sicknesses and health problems caused by pharmaceuticals is a multi-million dollar industry addition to the *multi-trillion dollar* traditional standard medical industry in America, now in the 21st century.

The United States Government, the Supreme Court, and the medical industry legally allow people to die, if they choose to die, only by starvation. Death by starvation in a hospital, overseen by a physician, is the only legal method allowed to not suffer anymore, to stop the suffering caused by health problems and injuries of any kind, and to stop the misery caused by the procedures of physicians. It's the only legal way to choose to die. It's the same method used by the German Nazis to kill many millions of prisoners of war in their prison camps, and by the Japanese in their prison camps during World War II. It is not a humane way to let people die who choose to die, in America. So why is that the only way allowed by the United States Government, the Supreme Court, and the medical industry in America? The Hippocratic Oath "Above all, do no harm" has been violated once again.

There are probably hundreds of legal drugs that will cause death painlessly and quickly. To allow the use of those would be humane. No one knows how many people have died during and immediately after surgeries from the anesthetics, and from the drugs given after surgery. Drugs to put them out, drugs to keep them out, drugs to bring them back, in endless combinations. There has been hundreds of thousands of victims of those legal drugs related to surgeries, maybe even millions of victims in the past 60 years. No records have been kept. So people who choose to die should be allowed to use those potentially lethal drugs as a much better method to die, a much better way to die than the only way that is allowed in the United States, a slow and very painful death by starvation that takes weeks, not minutes.

More than half of the United States population is labeled obese by the insurance industry and by physicians, so it's another industry. Reasons for this all-pervasive problem are blood-sugar problems like an inability to metabolize sugar, or substituting natural and real sugar with harmful high fructose corn sweetener. Or an inability to produce insulin normally, or insulin resistance. Or an inability to metabolize carbohydrates normally. Or thyroid problems causing blood sugar problems. It's not usually because of eating too much food, but instead because of *what* they eat.

And certainly not because of the restaurants people eat at, as black people have falsely claimed in lawsuits against fast-food restaurants. These are backed by their black doctors, their physicians, saying they have been made sick because of food poisoning, or gained excess weight, because of eating at well-known restaurants that don't make other people fat, or sick from food poisoning. The black people suing say things like "It's just a couple thousand dollars for the settlements but it comes in handy, it's nice to have." They feel justified in lying to get their so-called fair share.

Taking financial advantage of other people and businesses is so American, and it's the reason why there are so many lawyers in the United States in proportion to the total population.

In America all vegetables, not just corn, are irradiated with radio-active nuclear wastes after they've been harvested, after having been already heavily sprayed repeatedly with poisons, herbicides, and pesticides as it was growing. Food with less nutritional value than ever before in United States history and more dangerous food than ever before in United States history is what Americans, cows and beef cattle, and pet dogs and cats are forced to eat. It isn't really a "Liberty Corn" or a "Freedom Corn". It's really a "Victim Corn" or "Destruction Corn".

All of this is 21st century nutrition in America. It's mostly overly processed food and unhealthy destructive food. No wonder people in the United States are some of the least healthy people in the world. But unprocessed food like vegetables and fruit now have less nutritional value than ever before in the history of mankind. The only solution is to grow your own food, or buy organic.

For more than 60 years interns and residents at hospitals everywhere in America have worked 24 to 72 hour shifts with no sleep, or with just a few hours of sleep at the hospital. The sleep deprived doctors-to-be make endless mistakes, causing patients to suffer, to have endless problems, or to die unnecessarily. This shows that the medical system is, and has been for way too long, very flawed in the most basic of ways in America. Studies have always shown that only *one* night of sleep deprivation causes anyone, whether they think they are superior to other people or not, to make major and minor mistakes both emotionally and mentally, and to regress both mentally and emotionally.

Two or three nights of lost sleep can be disastrous concerning the mental functioning and physical functioning of an intern or resident who is responsible for the welfare of patients and has to make life and death decisions. Sleep deprivation makes them indifferent to their mistakes and to their patient's needs. Yet this is standard procedure in most United States hospitals, especially teaching hospitals, and has been for more than 60 years. There has never been anything Americans can do to stop or change this very dangerous American tradition. The field of medicine is above the law.

Nobody should be a victim of the American medical system, the medical industry, but being a victim has always been a fact of life, a part of living in America for which Americans are charged 10 to 1000 times more than anywhere else in the World. Lists and records of mistakes and their victims have never been kept. This all contributes, from the beginning, to the attitudes of superiority common to all types of physicians in America. It's a uniquely American phenomenon. In the United States health insurance is an industry that is in the business of finding reasons to *deny* benefits paid to their clients who bought insurance from them. This is also a uniquely American phenomenon.

Lobbyists paid Bush "W" $891,000 to reward him for signing the pharmaceutical bill that forces senior citizens to be part of a Government drug program that forces them to buy the highest priced drugs in the World, even thousands of times more than anywhere else in the World. Bills are supposed to promote national progress and improvements for people. This is another example of how the American Government represents corporations, big business, and the already-rich, not the average person, not the public, not senior citizens. It was because of the same need for more power, more control, more money, and the endless greed that dominates and motivates all Government and corporate decisions. Since the 1960's the American Democracy has been sold to the highest bidder.

An endless array of health problems and deaths are caused by irresponsible prescription writing, giving the wrong drugs or wrong dosage, not listening to or ignoring the patient about their drug reactions or allergies, and not looking up the drug specifications for "don't take if", or not asking the patient if those warnings apply to him or her. Each person, each patient, has their own unique reactions to chemicals, to pharmaceuticals, that cannot be predicted, that can't be categorized.

In the early 1900s Doctors and nurses started washing their hands with soap and water, not just water, before surgery. There was a dramatic decrease in infections and deaths. Today, more than 100 years later, 95% of hospital, clinic, and Doctor's office infections are caused by Doctors and nurses not washing their hands. These infections cause major and minor health problems and deaths, at least 50,000 to 100,000 deaths a year that could have been easily avoided. Not by multi-million dollar grants to the N1H or other researchers, not by multi-million dollar drugs prescribed and sold to the public for a 100% to 10,000% mark-up, but with soap and water.

Billions of female horses have been tortured by drug companies in order to collect their urine for the manufacture of Premarin. Pregnant-mare-urine. The pregnant mares are *forced* to stand for the duration of their pregnancy, and for all of their tortured lives, so that all urine can be collected for production of Premarin. When the babies are born they are killed. If the mares haven't collapsed or died from their inhumane and tortuous treatment they are forced to get pregnant again, and continue in this cycle of torture and suffering until they die from the inhumane treatment. Why hasn't this been stopped, why was it allowed to begin and to continue more than 50 years ago? The answers are money, greed, power, and the inability of the public, or individuals, to change anything important.

There has not been any area of unfulfilled jobs because people are not trained for those jobs since the dot.com boom before 2000. In the same way there are no areas of employment crying out for anyone trained in those areas. There is no void that needs to be filled, especially without experience. Except for nurses. More than 40% of corporate profits after the year 2000 are from financial products. Millions more college graduates is not an answer or solution for non-existent jobs. Fifty percent of the GDP comes from corporations and companies operating in other countries, like GE, employing foreigners for a tiny fraction of the wages paid to people in America for the same thing.

People in the United States are among the least healthy, the most sickly, in the World. Yet, we spend by far the most money to pay for medical costs. This is a sicker generation than their parent's generation. The average lifespan has increased in the United States because the infant death rate is lower, thereby increasing the average age of death and the average lifespan artificially and with statistically manipulated dishonesty. What it appears to be it really isn't.

Man-made chemicals trigger biological mechanisms that shut down, or speed up, hormones that control weight, like cortisol or adrenaline, and that control or prevent cancer and other health problems. Man-made chemicals indirectly cause many health problems because they confuse biological mechanisms and processes, like metabolism. Examples include Lupus, diabetes, MS, Parkinson's, MD, Alzheimer's. Every person has unique physiological reactions to any chemical. What is good for one person can be bad for another.

Of course physicians make mistakes, but they never admit it. This is part of their "God" persona. They have a license to kill because of their mistakes, and to cause pain and suffering. This is also a part of their "God" persona. Only rarely can they be sued. When they are sued other physicians lie for them to facilitate winning, not losing, the lawsuit. It's the brotherhood of physicians supporting each other. After all, God cannot be sued. Their arrogance would radically change if the healthcare industry, the sickness industry, were not-for-profit. For about 40 years the physicians in the United States, other than in trauma centers in hospitals and surgeons, have been pill-pushers and very little else. Extremely well-paid pill-pushers, endlessly supporting and validating the corrupt and extremely rich and powerful pharmaceutical industry.

Residents and interns work 24 to 48 hour shifts in hospital emergency rooms. Their lack of sleep has caused endless mistakes and countless deaths. Because these too-long shifts are dangerous for the patient, even deadly for the patient, why have they long been a part of the system? It's obviously difficult for the resident or intern. It also causes them to violate the Hippocratic oath "Above all, do no harm". The continuance of this dangerous and harmful system should have ended many years ago.

For more than 50 years in the United States at least 70% of the hysterectomies performed have been *unnecessary. Billions of dollars in profits* and *many millions of women* suffering unnecessarily are the result. Women have always been the biggest part of the medical industry's source of profits in America. As a result, women have also been the largest percentage of its victims.

For the past 50 years people who are diagnosed with cancer often feel healthy, look healthy, but decline fast after treatment begins. The treatment has always made them sick, not the cancer. The treatment has often made the cancer spread. Often they haven't died because of the cancer, but have died because of the treatment. Radiation, chemotherapy, surgery, chemicals have killed millions of cancer patients but that has probably never been listed as the cause of death.

Cancer Treatment Centers of America have the highest success rate, of about 85%. They offer non-traditional cancer treatments, without negative side-effects.

Pharmaceuticals for depression can cause, and do cause, people to commit suicide. They can increase depression. Almost all people who have committed mass murders at schools, at malls, at post offices, etc., in the past 20 years have been taking these drugs.

Physician's mistakes and prescribing pharmaceuticals cause hundreds of thousands of deaths a year, or maybe even a million deaths, but no records are kept of this. If they did, lawsuits would have put them out of business many years ago. The Federal Government has a secret data base about disciplinary actions and malpractice suits against physicians. Malpractice information is kept from the public. The priority of medical boards is to protect the physician, not the patient or the public. In the same way the FDA looks out for and protects the profits of the drug companies, not the welfare and health of Americans who are prescribed these drugs by their physicians.

Physicians get paid $1000 a night to be on-call at hospitals at night. Hospital CEO's have salaries of $25 million dollars to $250 million dollars a year. These excessive salaries and excessive costs translate to theft from the American consumer. No wonder hospital costs are out of control and unbelievably high in America in the 21$^{st}$ century, especially compared to the other 23 Democracies in the World. Keeping hospital costs artificially high and dishonestly high is the name of the game.

Statin drugs for cholesterol have been sold and perpetuated by deception. Many studies have shown Zeta and Zocar do not lower cholesterol or lessen arterial placque. Studies have also shown people who die from heart attacks are as likely to have low bad cholesterol as they are likely to have high bad cholesterol. So low bad cholesterol can cause heart attacks as often as high bad cholesterol, meaning cholesterol has nothing to do with heart attacks. One cancels out the other. For many years physicians have been prescribing their patients more than a million prescriptions a month for these drugs. This translates to profits of more than *$25 billion dollars* a year for drug companies for their cholesterol drugs alone.

Most of the people in the United States who are over 50 are overweight, not because they eat too much but because of blood-sugar imbalances and chemicals they are exposed to that change and distort their hormonal balance and metabolism. These hormonal imbalances can cause a lot of health problems, including cancer. Viruses and fungus flourish in external and internal environments that are chemically altered by man-made chemicals. Viruses are the cause of some, or even most, cancers. Whatever is causing the obesity problem can also cause cancer. Man-made chemicals distort, alter, and mimic hormones, thereby disturbing and altering natural hormonal balances, metabolism, and potentially the whole physiological self.

No one knows how many of the people who are told they have cancer really don't have it, because of false positive test results, incorrect reading of tests, mix-ups, mistakes, etc. The PSA test is accurate in diagnosing prostate cancer only 3% to 7% of the time, one of the three developers of the test revealed years after It became a standard testing procedure for diagnosis. The cancer industry both giveth and taketh away, making hundreds of billions of dollars in profits either way every year.

Of the 24 wealthiest countries in the World only one does not have a mandated vacation. The United States. Of these 24 countries the United States has the highest infant death rate, the shortest life-span, the highest percentage of sick people, and, by far, the highest percentage of its population using legal drugs on a regular basis. The cost of healthcare in America is at least 100 times higher than in these other 23 countries.

The United States also has the highest percentage of murders with guns, by far, than any of the other 23 Democracies in the World. This has been true for many years, since the beginning of statistics taken for this poll and for World-wide comparison. Thus, America is a dangerous Democracy to live in, compared to the other 23 Democracies.

Hundreds of millions of people, even a billion, have been prescribed insulin from pigs for diabetes for nearly a hundred years. For centuries other countries have considered diabetes a nutritional problem, a deficiency, not a disease needing insulin from pigs or artificial insulin from synthetic chemicals, as opposed to natural chemicals. Chromium is one of those deficiencies. It increases metabolism. Pig insulin has always caused major and minor health problems for diabetic people that inject it daily. Problems connected to diabetes are caused by the injected insulin and the process of injection itself. The Chinese have used herbs unique to China to control diabetes for centuries with no health problems, and no deaths from complications related to diabetes, as a result of using these herbs. But diabetes in America is an industry, a multi-billion dollar industry, part of what keeps the United States working. It's a kind of sacrifice for the greater good.

Nutritional deficiencies cause many health problems. Supplying those deficiencies can eliminate many health problems, and help many other health problems. In general, everybody needs a daily vitamin and mineral supplement. Beyond that, for all health problems in general, the best supplements available in America are ginseng, flaxseed oil (not processed), calcium with magnesium and D to help make it work, high potency C,E, and A, grape seed, MSM, algae, and B complex.

Many people have iodine deficiencies, which can be the cause, or contributing cause, for many health problems. Many girls and women have iron deficiencies because of their monthly cycles. Taking a multiple vitamin with minerals everyday can solve that deficiency, and help many other health problems. Many women have hormone deficiencies that are helped by saw palmetto, black cohosh, red clover, wild yams, and other supplements and herbs found at health food stores and mail order companies, the best one being Swansons, in North Dakota. Many men also have hormone deficiencies that are helped by taking saw palmetto, zinc, multiple vitamins with minerals, and other supplements to help with individual problems.

Chromium is for blood-sugar problems and blood-pressure problems, the last of which is also helped by calcium and magnesium supplements. Paudarco is an herb used by indigenous tribes for centuries to control or eliminate health problems like cancer. Using unprocessed flaxseed oil for at least a week and then taking paudarco with it every day can yield better results. Eating cottage cheese as a source of protein with flaxseed can control the growth of cancer, and even cure it, eliminate it, as was shown by Dr. Joanna Budwig in the 1960's. She won a Nobel Peace Prize for that discovery to cure cancer more than 50 years ago, but probably no physician in America ever dared to recommend that as a cure for cancer to any of their cancer victims. Altruism and honesty takes second place to not being sued, and second place to not losing your license to be a physician.

More than 3 million Americans have been diagnosed as schizophrenic. Many millions more have other mental health problems. Millions more have yet-to- be diagnosed mental health conditions. This means more than 3 out of every 100 people in America have some kind of diagnosed mental illness. So what's causing this national epidemic? Chemicals and pharmaceuticals, as prescription drugs, and illegal drugs, are to blame for the most part. Heredity for the other part.

In the 1960's the U.S. Government did not regulate the tobacco industry after there was undeniable proof that smoking caused cancer, heart problems, etc. Yet the DEA made using and selling marijuana and Ecstacy a crime, warranting *years* in prison, even though both were used by millions of people with undeniable health benefits for both physical and mental problems, and with no bad side-effects. This was proof that the United States Government does not protect and look out for the welfare of its citizens, its people. Now, in the 20$^{th}$ century, the DEA gets at least *$50 billion dollars* allocated to it every year, even though the anti-drug industry is mostly self-supporting because of about 50,000 drug raids done every year, yielding at least $50 billion dollars in seized drug money. *Where* does all the Government DEA money go, and *who* does all the illegal seized drug money go to?

For years the physician who developed Ecstacy had given it away for free to people he thought would be helped by it. It gave people a feeling of being very happy, thus the name Ecstacy. After those people started selling it the DEA prohibited it, releasing false Government reports and dishonest studies about the supposed dangers of using Ecstacy. It was a threat to physicians, psychologists, and psychiatrists, meaning fewer visits and less money paid to all of them, and also to the entire mental health industry. That very much included the pharmaceutical industry. If happiness was really a part of the American culture then the drug would have been patented and made into a legitimate drug, a legal drug, for consumption by a willing and waiting public. Instead, it was about greed, power and control, and the denial of happiness by the Government, by Big Brother.

Studies have repeatedly shown, for about 30 years, that people are as likely to have a heart attack, or strokes, with low cholesterol as high cholesterol. So low cholesterol causes heart attacks and strokes as often as high cholesterol, and the cholesterol scare is a gimmick to sell trillions of dollars of drugs to lower cholesterol, and to sell expensive Doctor visits to get expensive tests and prescriptions and renewals to be taken for the rest of their lives. Hundreds of millions of Americans are supposed to be a part of the system to make them dependent on drugs for cholesterol for the rest of their lives for the indefinite future, and since the inception of this massive cholesterol drug system designed for money, profit, power, and control.

In the 1990's I told parents of children with ADD and ADHD to give their child natural flaxseed oil, not altered by heating, processing, etc., and a B complex vitamin every day. All of these children became normal, no longer having ADD or ADHD. However, none of the ADD or ADHD support groups in the state, Louisiana, were interested in this revelation. Their purpose was to perpetuate the use and sale of drugs, Ritalin specifically, not to improve the health and behavior of children with that problem. This is an example of how anyone and everyone is most interested in maintaining the status quo, in keeping their jobs and sources of money, in being taken care of by "their" doctor, by a physician, and following and doing what they are told to do by authorities. Most Americans are afraid to follow other health modalities, other than the one sold to them daily by the media, or by their Doctor, or by their children's Doctor, that they want to trust. That they have to trust.

Flouride, a poison, was developed by Nazi scientists in Germany in the 1930's. It was added to the water supply in Nazi concentration camps to cause apathy, docility, and sterility in the millions of wrongfully imprisoned and innocent Jewish men, women, and children imprisoned in the Nazi prison camps. It was a poisonous tranquilizer. Since then, for about 60 years, most of the population of the United States has been drinking water with fluoride in it. Of course that fluoride water is in soda pop, the most popular thing to drink in America. Also, having fluoride treatments by dentists, and using fluoride toothpaste and mouthwash, is mandatory, even though this poison doesn't prevent cavities. Any so-called clinical trials in the United States had to have been falsified, manipulating the data like any so-called scientific study can easily be. Just because it's published in a scientific journal or paper, or book or magazine, doesn't mean it's true, accurate, or right. But fluoride does cause cancer, other health problems, and dental problems, making one wonder why fluoride has been in the American water supply for 60 years. The answer has to be to cause health problems in all Americans.

The purchase of *billions of dollars* of this aluminum industry waste product has benefitted the aluminum industry but it has been the legal drugging, the Governmental drugging, of Americans with this poison since after World War II. The United States Government knew it was a poison used by the Nazis in their plan to dominate and control the World. So it seems to be an attempt to control the American public. If the United States Government just wanted to help the aluminum industry by buying their waste products they could have given them the money, the same billions of dollars in those sixty years, and destroyed the poison or put the fluoride in toxic landfills. Instead, the Government has forced the American people to drink this poison every day for their entire lives.

The HIV virus was identified more than 100 years ago, with a microscope. But AIDS has only been around since the 1960's. AIDS, therefore, is caused by something different than, or more than, HIV. The medical industry comes up with "new" diseases every few years, putting new names on old diseases. Like what happened to syphilis, common prior to the media emergence of AIDs and HIV?

Mandatory vaccinations for animals and children cause untold problems, causing them to get the disease itself, or to go into anaphylactic shock, or cause death, or possibly develop autism or other physical and mental problems. How many of them would have gotten these diseases and health problems if they had not gotten these vaccinations? Probably none of them.

Drug companies and their legal drugs have caused harm or death to perhaps hundreds of millions of people since their inception in the early 1900's. In the process they have made *trillions of dollars* in profit. The same pharmaceuticals, also made in America, are available in other countries for a small fraction of what Americans pay for them. It has been said Americans need to pay more, much more, for these legal drugs to pay for research for new drugs. This, however, is not the truth.

All drug studies can be distorted or false. With the help of the media the American public believes them and buys the legal drugs assuming they are safe, because they are sanctioned by, and given the blessing of, their physicians. When, in fact, drugs called medicine are usually toxic when taken in excess, or for some people when taken as directed.

More than 100,000 chemicals are produced in the United States. The possible combinations are endless. Nothing can undo the damage they have done, or will do. Physical reactions to chemicals can be immediate, or be delayed for months or years. Artificial man-made chemicals are here to stay.

Diabetes is a mega-bucks industry in the United States. People who are pre-diabetic are prescribed Metformin, which blocks metabolism of fatty acids. Hundreds of millions of people in America can be diagnosed as pre-diabetic when their blood sugar level is between 125 and 200. Then, when people are diabetic, they are ordered to give themselves shots of insulin. Diabetes and prediabetes is a big part of the American sickness industry. The perpetuation of it is essential.

In other countries, other cultures, people who are diabetic take herbs to control it or eliminate it. These herbs are mulberry, Siberian ginseng, gymnema sylvestre, prickly pear cactus, banaba leaf, bitter melon. Studies done in the United States in 1996 and 1997 proved that diabetes can be eliminated for some people by taking alpha lipoic acid and chromium every 12 hours for 4 months. Vanadium, vanadyl sulfate, and green coffee bean pills can do the same for other diabetics.

The poison Roundup should be banned because it kills everything it touches, not just weeds. This includes flowers, grass, birds, insects, butterflies, domestic animals like dogs and cats, horses, cows, goats, and wild animals, because it is sprayed on, or near, water they drink, or grass or trees, or anywhere there can be run-off into their drinking water or food supply. Or it causes sickness or autoimmune diseases, or contributes to them, in all human beings. Yet, many billions of gallons of it are used by companies, corporations, farmers, and house and property owners in the United States.

The greed and selfishness of the chemical industry knows no bounds. Hundreds of millions of birds and bees die every year as a result of chemical sprays for agriculture, etc. Chemicals that are outlawed in the United States are then sold to other countries for years, indefinitely. For at least 50 years drug companies have paid physicians, or given them the most expensive cars, international trips, etc. if they agree to push and promote the drugs the drug company wants promoted. It's another kind of kickback, another kind of payoff.

The average American taxpayer pays 10% to 20% of his yearly income to the IRS. President Bush "W" made $20 million dollars in 2006 and paid 1/200 of that to the IRS in 2007. Vice President Cheney made about $100 million dollars in 2006 and paid about 1/200 of that to the IRS in 2007. Their dishonesty didn't end when they became the highest level politicians in the United States.

The IRS needs to end, it needs to be eliminated, as part of the American life. All people in the United States should pay the same percentage of tax on their earnings, with no loop-holes, no deductions, no write-offs, eliminating cheating and not paying taxes at all on the part of wealthy people, companies, the elite, and the corporations and people that rule America. Lobbyists, about 30,000 of them, should be stopped, and their special privileges eliminated from Capitol Hill.

Medical costs, tests, procedures, and equipment, and hospital costs, tests, procedures, and equipment should be lowered at least 50% from the outrageous levels they have become, and allowed to increase only 1.5% a year, like Social Security payments usually increase for many millions of people 1.5% a year. Then costs for insurance premiums should also be lowered at least 50%.

All of these institutions, except Social Security, make life in America difficult for many millions of people. They account for a high percentage of crime, criminal activity, cheating, theft, bankruptcies, and emotional, mental, and physical suffering in America. They *cause* problems and suffering instead of fixing problems and alleviating suffering in America, which is what institutions are supposed to do.

Foreign criminals come to the United States because they can. Other countries are more discriminating about their immigrants. There are hundreds of thousands of unsolved crimes in the United States. Maybe even millions. About one out of every one hundred United States citizens is in prison. About one out of eight black United States citizens is in prison. It has always been true that a percentage of people are unjustly in prison. This needs to change. In the United States there needs to be uniformity of sentencing, not at the discretion of the Judge, depending on the zip code. There needs to be real "justice for all". Despite what is said, the United States does not give equal justice for everyone. This is a justifiable reason to be afraid of law enforcement, Judges, and lawyers.

In United States courts evidence of guilt or innocence can be withheld, resulting in wrong decisions being made by juries and Judges. Resulting in wrongful incarceration and/or excessive and wrongful sentencing. A poor person can steal $1 worth of food because they're hungry and get ten or fifteen years in prison. A CEO can steal millions of dollars from his company and get a year in prison, or just probation, or just community service. And he can keep the millions of dollars he stole. Or his employee can take a roll of toilet paper from the company bathroom and get ten years in prison, as actually happened in 2007. Depending on which state and zip code a murderer is in he or she can get out of prison in three to six years with good behavior, or be in prison for life, or executed.

This is supposed to be a country based on law and order. But laws are distorted like the truth is distorted by people who have the authority to do it. No one in the United States can be sure of a fair hearing before a Judge, or a Magistrate, unless they can afford the most expensive lawyers, and preferably more than one to give the appearance of financial wealth and alleged innocence. Even then the Judge, or Magistrate, has all the power if there is no jury. Thousands of Judges and Magistrates in the United States decide the fate of millions of people in America every year. Only 28 states require that crime scene evidence be protected. As a result, endless mistakes are made in those 32 other states, besides the inevitable mistakes made in the ones that do require it.

There are endless manipulations of the law by lawyers and attorneys. And endless wrong decisions are made in courtrooms, wrong conclusions that negatively effect and change people's lives, sometimes forever. Wrongful convictions and criminals going free are a result of major flaws in the American judicial system. Endless lives have been negatively affected. Probably hundreds of thousands of innocent people, even millions, have been unjustly imprisoned, or even executed, since the beginning of the United States judicial system. Incompetence on the job is common at all levels of society in the United States so there's no reason Judges and Magistrates can't also be incompetent and wrong at crucial times on their jobs. As a result, they can cause endless misery for endless numbers of people who have to count on them to do the right thing.

It's a similar problem with police and deputies everywhere in the United States, some regions more than others. Often they have quotas. This means anyone can get a ticket for doing nothing wrong. This is fraudulent. The city or county makes money from the bogus tickets and their policemen or deputies are forced to be dishonest in order to keep their jobs. In Fort Worth, Texas for many years police have chased cars at high speed in the city, as if it was the Wild West and they were on horses. But it isn't, and they aren't. Their high-speed cars are deadly and have caused endless pain and suffering, injuries and death for innocent people in other cars that get in their way, or are in the path of the pursued vehicle. They usually use no sirens to warn approaching vehicles of the danger. Lawyers in Fort Worth have always protected the police officers in these situations. They have always said "No one can sue the Fort Worth Police Department." They are above the law. Case closed.

Cities like this, counties like this, are dangerous places to live in. Or visit. They should be required by law to have billboards outside their city or county warning people of these law enforcement dangers in their city or county. A "Traveler Beware" sign about high-speed car chases and quota tickets that might get them killed, or just injured and upset if they're lucky.

There are more guns per person in the United States than in any other country in the World. This does not make the United States a safer place to live. It makes it more dangerous. If guns made a place safe to live in the United States would be the safest place to live in the World. Instead, it's one of the most dangerous. One of the safest Democracies to live in has long been Canada, that has more guns per person than does the United States, the most dangerous Democracy to live in in the World.

The polio vaccination was discovered and developed by one man, Dr. Jonas Salk, working alone in his laboratory, not by using millions of dollars of Federal Government grant money. It opened the floodgates for a very lucrative part of the medical industry, research and experimentation, usually done with helpless animals that give results unique to those animals and not able to be applied accurately to humans. After getting about a trillion dollars for research the polio vaccine is still the major accomplishment in that field for more than 60 years. It has been a huge waste of taxpayer's money to give the impression something valuable is being done, and has been done, in the field of medicine, when in fact it is, and has been, just for more profits in the medical sickness industry.

Both prostate cancer surgery for men and hysterectomies for women have been huge money makers for the medical establishment, for the medical industry in America for about 50 years. Millions of men have been told they have cancer based on the PSA test even though the PSA test is accurate, is an accurate indicator for prostate cancer, only 3% to 7% of the time. One of the three developers of that test revealed that astounding fact after it had been used for many years as the primary method of diagnosis. He said in an interview that 93% to as much as 97% of the time the test results were wrong and did not indicate cancer. That means 93% to 97% of the men who have had their prostates removed because of the results of that test have been inaccurately diagnosed. They lost their prostates as a result of unnecessary surgery, chemotherapy, and radiation for many millions of men in America, causing impotence, incontinence, and other health problems.

In the past 50 years millions of American women have had uteruses and fallopian tubes removed unnecessarily. These total, or partial, hysterectomies have often been unnecessary. There were options but they were not informed. Or they didn't get, or couldn't get, second opinions. Doctors in America, after all, are gods whose decisions should not be questioned, and hysterectomies are so common they must be the right thing to do. Besides that getting a second opinion is so expensive it's prohibitive for most people to do.

These are just two of endless examples of how Americans are victims and pawns of the medical system, the medical industry, in America. And nothing, not a thing, can be done to change anything about this huge and massive industry that is a necessary part of the United States economy.

No one knows how many people have died as a result of mistakes made or drugs used as a part of this industry, especially during and after surgical procedures. Having surgery that isn't necessary includes that ever-present danger of mistakes and drugs causing injury or death.

Physicians can cause major health problems because their attempts to fix problems can create other problems that are worse than, or as bad, as the original problem. Legal drugs have caused untold and literally hidden numbers of deaths and injuries and health problems for hundreds of millions of Americans in the past 80 years.

The medical/sickness industry parallels other major industries in the United States, that may or may not also have power over life and death. Some major industries in America just have the power to determine financial failure or success for every person that participates, directly or indirectly.

As an example, in the beginning of the 21$^{st}$ century the Federal Government gave the corrupt and self-serving financial industry gifts of hundreds of billions of dollars to correct their losses, their incompetence, and their theft of billions of dollars from investors, their clients. The Federal Government should have given that money to the American people that needed a better place to live, as money vouchers to buy one of the millions of homes in foreclosure, repossessed by banks and mortgage companies, after they were priced much too high, bought at too high prices and unable to be sold at those prices, or they were unable to be paid for at the ballooning mortgage costs. The banks and mortgage companies would have gotten their money and millions of Americans would have improved their lives and had a home to call their own. Instead, *hundreds of billions of dollars* was given for the continued corruption of the financial industry in America, making the rich even richer and the poor even poorer. The medical/sickness industry has also made the rich richer and the poor poorer, even causing destitution and bankruptcy for too many people.

In order to survive as a politician, especially as a Democratic Senator, you have to play the game right with the Far Right Republicans or you will lose your job with its power, its influence, and its unlimited benefits on the side. Or you may even lose your life. For many years, and especially in the 21$^{st}$ century, politicians, and especially Senators, do not represent the American people unless those people are part of the ruling class, or the elite, or the Shadow Government. The medical/sickness industry also serves the ruling class and the elite better, with more proficiency and higher quality care, than that given to the poor and middle-class in America. It's just a fact of life.

In courtrooms across the country critical information, important information, is often not allowed in courtroom hearings and trials. A poor person can get 15 to 20 years in prison for stealing an apple in a grocery store, and a rich person or politician will get six months to a year in a country club prison for stealing millions of dollars, or even billions of dollars, from their employer or the government, or from taxpayers, or from their own company, and not have to pay it back. Or a poor man will get 15 years or even life in prison for rape and a rich man, or just the upper class, will get six months in prison for rape. It is very possible that evidence was withheld, crucial and critical information, in most cases involving under-represented people, who are then victims of the legal system. In a similar way, people are victims of the medical sickness system because of incorrect and withheld information, and because of physician/specialist/nurse, etc. mistakes.

Since 2012 Asians made up about 3% of the American population and are in movies, commercials, TV shows, and in advertising photos about 1% of the time. Mexicans make up about 18% of the population but are in only about 5% of the movies, commercials, TV shows, and advertising photos in the United States. Black people are about 15% of the population but are about 65% of the appointed Judges and are in about 75% of the commercials, TV shows, movies, and advertising photos. If the President of the United States was Mexican or Asian or Native American Indian it is likely they would also be represented about 65% to 75% of the time in the media. Manipulation is a big part of the American culture, everywhere at all levels.

Proportionately there are more black millionaires and multi-millionaires in the United States than white millionaires and multi-millionaires. How many jobs have they created? Probably none, like the white millionaires and multi-millionaires probably haven't either. The more wealthy a person is the *less* likely they are to create jobs, or better jobs, for the unfortunate masses, the at least 100 million people living near, at, or below poverty level in the United States at the beginning of the 21st century. This is probably true for most cultures throughout the World. It is common for extremely wealthy people to hoard their wealth, or to use it for more investments in the world of finance, in the culture of unlimited possibilities for making more money.

It is a lie that if the upper 10%, or 5%, can keep more of that money by paying even less taxes they will create more jobs for the unfortunate masses with that money, as Republican politicians commonly insist. That political mantra is, and always has been, a way to manipulate people in America. There are more than 1200 billionaires in the United States in the second decade of the 21st century. What good are they to the American economy if they continue to hoard their massive and unbelievable wealth and also pay little or no taxes? A large percentage of the millionaires and multi-millionaires in America are part of the medical/sickness industry, in a multitude of ways.

The richest man in the World is Mexican, living in Mexico, worth $37 billion dollars. That is proof that people who have the most money do not create jobs for the masses. He certainly hasn't. For many years many millions of Mexicans have risked their lives to come to America and get jobs and welfare for women with children born in America. They have paid up to $6000 dollars each for transportation that hides them from border authorities so they can cross the border to the United States so they can get a job. Where do they get that $6000 from? That's a lot of money by itself. For many years there has not been enough jobs in Mexico to support that part of their population.

It's the same way in the United States. The wealthiest people do not create jobs, or better jobs, for people that need that help. In the 21st century they continue to make most of their money from financial investments, supporting the financial industry. Like the United States Government did with gifts of hundreds of billions of dollars to the financial industry, that was really money taken from all people in America. It was money that belonged to them, not to the participants of the massive financial fiasco and thefts done during the first five years of the 21st century. These are the same victims that are forced to support the medical/sickness industry, with its hugely over-priced services, facilities, and procedures.

Many parts of American lives are dominated by science. Without the medical industry, the sickness industry, the United States economy would collapse. Sickness must be perpetuated, as it is a big part of the foundation of the United States economy because the medical/sickness industry is so hugely over-priced, along with the massive and hugely expensive military industrial complex and the hugely inflated costs charged by the oil industry. The pharmaceutical industry, pharmaceutical science, dominates and directs the medical and sickness industries. It is one of the top three most wealthy United States industries every year, along with the oil industry and the health insurance industry. Being sick is a traditional part of the American economy, a necessary contribution to the United States economy. Being sick is part of the American experience, a part of the national culture.

The sickness industry has a stranglehold on the citizens of the United States. It's part of the American psyche. The United States medical industry is one of the worst in the world, at the bottom of the list of the countries regarding success and effectiveness of its medical system. To call it a "health industry" is a distortion of the truth. It's really a sickness industry.

Even though hundreds of billions of dollars have been given to scientists and researchers to find the cure for cancer, MS, muscular dystrophy, AIDs, diabetes, Parkinson's disease, Alzheimer's, Lupus, etc., and on and on, no cure has ever been found for any major disease, for any major sickness. This means bacteria, viruses, fungus, are smarter than the scientists, researchers, physicians that get paid millions to do the research. Apparently these microscopic particles causing death, disease, and sickness mutate faster than the most highly trained professionals can control, change, counteract, stop, or understand. That is, if they are telling the truth.

Allegedly, microscopic cells, with no brains, are smarter than researchers, physicians, and scientists and have been for more than 60 long years. What has been more important, much more important, has been the yearly renewal of multi-million dollar grants, the continuance of the NIH, and the perpetuation of the sickness industry. The perpetuation of sickness and suffering and death has always been just collateral damage. A little Dr./physician humor: What's the difference between God and a physician? God doesn't think He's a physician.

Cures to diseases will not be found, have not been found for more than 60 years and a total of *trillions of dollars* of donations and Government grants, because their perpetuation makes a lot of money for a lot of people. The sickness industry, encompassing all facets including over-priced drugs, over-priced physicians, specialists, medical equipment, medical procedures and tests, salespeople, hospital stays and procedures and administration (especially CEOs), over-priced health insurance (really sickness insurance), over-priced life insurance (really death insurance), and exorbitant funeral costs, is the richest and most profitable industry in the United States. It's the number one industry, the number one source of jobs, usually very well-paying jobs, for millions of American people. There's much more money to be made from sickness than health. Much more money is made from sick people than healthy people, in the United States. That is the American way, what has become the American way in the past 60 years. But it is, and has been, stealing both money and health from all Americans who cannot escape from or change the medical/sickness industry status quo.

United States hospitals, clinics, and physicians charge $100 to $250 for an x-ray and $50 to $150 to read it. Both take 5 to 10 minutes to do. CT scans and MRI's cost at least $2500 and in other countries they cost about $250, only 1/10 of the cost in the United States, while using the same scanners and MRI machines. Hospitals charge up to $150 for a name-brand pill that costs as little as 50 cents to manufacture, and as little as 10 cents in its generic form at pharmacies. In other countries that same name-brand pill will cost about 25 cents to $1 for that pill made in America, including the shipping costs. It costs about $100 for an IV that costs about $1 for the plastic bag and a few cents for the water in it. It costs $300 to $600 for a too small hospital bed with a very thin cotton blanket on it for a 24 hour day, or even half a day, in a too cold room, allegedly to stop growth of germs, for sanitations purposes. This has always been a lie, a hospital industry lie, as temperatures would have to be at freezing level, 32 degrees or less, to destroy any germs. The hidden reason has always been to save money, a lot of money, on heating costs. And to cause pneumonia in too many patients, especially the very young and the very old, creating more profits.

These are more reasons why Medicare takes 40% of the United States GDP every year. When the profit motive is eliminated, when huge financial gain is taken out of the picture, out of the medical care equation, then medical care in the United States would improve and Medicare and Medicaid programs would not drain the national economy. But this will never happen in the United States, and all of these reasons are why the IMF demands that countries with free national healthcare or Universal Healthcare change to privatized healthcare as a condition for getting loans from the IMF. The collapse of their economy, or increasing difficulties in their national economy, are then inevitable when their entire economy has become privatized.

Why do Americans think they have the best medical system in the World? Because that is what they are told. Again and again throughout their lives. And because that is what they want to believe. It's a part of the total package that says America is superior to all other countries in every way.

In 2008 the United States was *last* on a list of 78 countries in the World in terms of length of life. Number 78 in longevity. However, on a list of quality of healthcare the United States was number 38. Yet, the United States population pays 10 to 1000 times more for healthcare than any other country that doesn't have free national healthcare for everyone.

For many years the United States has had the highest infant mortality rate of all the 24 Democracies in the World. Besides that, many millions of American babies experienced birth with forceps that caused brain damage, cerebral palsy, and paralysis. Yet, United States physicians have always denied it, and hospitals have always denied it. So this cruel, harmful, dangerous, and potentially life-changing procedure continued for *many years* after it should have been stopped. No legal liability was accepted until after 2001, too late for the many millions of babies with life-long disabilities created in the previous 75 years.

It has been estimated at least a *billion dollars* of Medicaid and Medicare costs are fraudulent charges by hospitals, physicians, etc., for procedures they never did, for excessive pharmaceutical costs, for over-priced everything. It has been estimated that at least another five billion dollars is charged for fraudulent and over-priced services, equipment, etc.

Varicose veins is now called a disease. Obesity is now called a disease. This means there are now two more diseases researchers and drug companies can get billions of dollars of research money and funding for, indefinitely, for projects that often are unsuccessful, or useless, or redundant, but are repeated ad infinitum with United States Government funding and grants.

The National Institute of Health has gotten hundreds of billions of dollars in the past 60 years for research projects that do not validate initial, or repeated, funding. That's why there are more "diseases" in the United States than ever before in history, and why old sicknesses are reconfigured and given new names. It's one of the reasons there are more "sick" people in America than anywhere else in the World, per capita. These "new" diseases alarm the public and generate new interest that translates into new drugs and Dr. visits, and increases in donations and Government grants to scientists and researchers, etc. And an increase in animals being tortured and killed for these often useless and worthless research projects, many of which were repeated year after year because the Federal Government would give grants to pay for them. This was, and is, taxpayer's money.

For the past 60 years helpless and defenseless animals have been tortured, mutilated, and killed, suffering in the name of science, by United States researchers, often working with the NIH, with the sanction of and financial support of the United States Government. The same cruel and useless tests are performed year after year, most of them with the NIH, even though they are worthless, repetitive, or counter-productive, because it is a source of income for the researchers. For more than

60 years their jobs have been funded by taxpayer's money and taxpayer's misplaced trust.

In the early 1900's mercury was introduced for dental amalgam fillings. Dentists that refused to use mercury amalgam for fillings, because of the inherent danger of mercury to their patient's health, lost their license to be a dentist if they didn't comply.

For about a hundred years physicians have had to follow the lead of the pharmaceutical industry, the legal drug industry, and promote sales of legal drugs to their patients. United States medical protocol has not allowed deviation and use of alternatives. Alternatives that cannot be patented have always been a threat to the profits of the United States medical/sickness industry, to the profits of the United States pharmaceutical industry, and to the scientific research industry. And a threat to the god-like image and status of physicians in America for the past 50 years. But billions of dollars are spent on alternatives by people looking for natural solutions that conventional drugs and medicine, and medical procedures, haven't helped, or have made worse. Alternatives that work as good as, or better than, pharmaceuticals, legal drugs, with no side-effects.

For health-care reform, and immigration reform, the United States needs to copy and learn from more successful and better programs and policies in countries like Sweden, France, Switzerland, Finland, Denmark, and Norway. These Democracies are more truly democracies than the United States, and have succeeded in ways the United States never has and probably never will.

But the policy of the United States Government is to never follow success in other countries, to never copy success in other countries, because that would admit inferiority to those countries. The alleged superiority of the United States has to be maintained at all costs.

# CHAPTER FOUR

## Freedom In America

Now, in the 21st century, rudeness is the new norm, found anywhere in the United States. Disrespect, rudeness, and two-faced behavior are found throughout America, in both sexes, all races, all ages. White male red-neck mentality, once more common in the South, is an obnoxious, mean, unbalanced or excess testosterone problem now found everywhere in the United States, more or less. This is in contrast to the formerly kind-American, the friendly-American, the more balanced American mentality and persona so common in the latter half of the 20th century.

In general, people have regional differences, and regional personalities. The most common shared characteristic of people in America is lying. Whether they were born here or not. It's an acquired dysfunction. Dishonesty, lying, selfishness, and greed knows all colors, all religions, and all financial status, and all levels of intelligence. No one seems to be immune to at least one of these common human short-comings. Americans are no better than people anywhere else in the World. But of course anything can be different than it seems.

As an example, people in the United States are easily fooled by the media. But the media, specifically TV news and newspapers of the paper kind, not on the internet, just gives the public what it wants so people who work in the media can make money and keep their jobs. As usual the problems begin at the top, with the editors, administrators, and owners of newspapers and TV stations, and filters down to everyone else. As always, and as in everything, a little power can be a dangerous thing. And, as usual, a lot of power can be disastrous.

In the United States there are five major institutions in people's lives that directly or indirectly affect everyone. These are science, religion, politics, education, and the media. All are based on traditions, guesses, hypotheses, and lies and distortions, with some facts thrown in. All are connected to advancement of the ego. American politics is like American religion and American science, and the American media and education in America. For each one people can be, and are, manipulated to believe what each institution wants them to believe, based on, perpetuated by, delusion and illusion.

In fact, for the past 70 years, since after World War II, the United States has been run by, has operated on, increasing delusion and illusion. That's what the United States has been perpetuated on. This includes the wide availability of credit and credit cards that give a false sense of wealth and security, that comes before the fall. Lies and greed have been a big part of that delusion and illusion.

Conservative Republican talk shows and Cable TV news shows focus on sensationalism and hatred of the Democratic Party. They're like politically one-sided tabloids would be, at the grocery store checkout. Controlled media freedom in the United States allows this inflammatory approach to living in America that obviously appeals to a large segment of the population. Many millions of viewers, especially the part of the population that carries guns, has guns, or supports carrying guns, is a big part of it. This includes the NRA, thousands of lobbyists, and corporations that give millions of dollars as gifts to the people that run this country. It is impossible that the recipients of these monetary gifts are not influenced in one way or another to support whatever they are paid to support, to support whoever paid them. No one can turn down gifts of a million dollars or more.

It's similar to soldiers in wars, who do what they have to do to survive, to stay alive. It's kill or be killed. In the five major institutions it's go along with the others, be a part of the group of like-minded people, and support each other in a common goal. Rugged individualists who go their own way don't survive in those five major institutions. In general, people do what they have to do to stay alive, to compete, to live their life as best they can.

In the 21st century there are more than 75 million people in the World who are slaves, who are not black, in so far as they work for very inadequate shelter and inadequate food and no wages, or for as little as a dollar or less every day. The United States yearly foreign aid of at least $42 billion dollars has never gotten to them. Instead, it's been hoarded by the rulers, the dictators, and the already wealthy people in those countries, and then using the money designated for required purchases of military equipment, military planes, and weapons from the United States. Of course these 75 million people living in dire poverty get no healthcare, besides living in deplorable shelters often made of just cardboard and having only subsistence food every day.

United States foreign aid should have always gone to these very needy and suffering people but it never has. The hundreds of millions of dollars given to each country every year should have always been conditional, dependent on those extremely rich rulers and dictators helping and taking care of their own people, making sure they have better places to live and better and adequate food to eat. But it hasn't. United States foreign aid has never been to help poor people in other countries.

It has always been, and continues to be, to guarantee sales of military equipment, military planes and weapons, to give more money to the already rich in other countries to buy their co-operation, and to promote and encourage ever-more lethal wars and conflicts with their neighboring countries, carried out with weapons and planes made in the United States. United States Foreign Aid money returns to the United States as mandatory purchases of military planes, equipment, weapons and bombs. Altruism was maybe part of the equation at one time but it got lost many years ago.

All of the at least $42 billion dollars should have been given for specific purposes to improve conditions in those countries. Most Americans have always wanted their foreign aid tax money to go to people who really need it, not to make the already rich richer. They have to trust that their government, both state and Federal, will do what is right because they as individuals have no power to change or do anything. Elections are for show, for theatre, to support America whether it's good or bad. But most importantly elections are for the very wealthy to buy what they want to possess or want to happen by donating unlimited amounts of money to campaigns. These include appointments, positions, policies, favors, or just influence. Everything can be bought, anything is for sale at the right price. Especially since 2001 unlimited amounts of money exchange hands legally and anonymously, making millionaires, multi-millionaires, and billionaires in the process and as a result of the exchange. Everything political, anything political, can be bought and paid for in the 21st century.

It seems that United States Senators, Congressmen and Congresswomen, the ruling class, the elite, and the Shadow Government run the United States, not the President. It seems he's just the spokesperson for them. Since 2001 it seems the United States Government does not advance the interests of the American people. Instead it advances the interests of those people that make up only 1% to 5% of the entire population of America. But these millions of people make up a country of their own, they are like a country of their own, and most of the rest of the American population is not really needed in these people's lives. Why should they care about poverty in America?

A free national healthcare system for everyone would greatly improve the lives of hundreds of millions of people in America, removing sickness, unnecessary death, suffering, and destitution because of huge medical bills, including the excessive cost of hugely over-priced drugs. It would remove stress and worry about the inability to get healthcare or pay for it. This would increase the standard of living in America to better compare with the other 23 Democracies that have *free* national healthcare, or Universal Healthcare, for *everyone* in their countries.

Anywhere in America where there is a Walmart store one or all of the handicapped parking spaces will be occupied by a vehicle that does not have a handicapped license plate. People who are not handicapped are always parking in handicapped parking places at Walmart's. It's part of the Walmart culture. In Baton Rouge, Louisiana, for many years police security in police cars in Walmart's parking lots always ignore them, even when they are parked right in front of them, when they are black women or black men, or black teenagers. It's just part of the Baton Rouge culture, not the culture of the South. It's like how Federal laws that protect people with disabilities from employment and hiring discrimination are useless, and they are easily gotten around, ignored, and are not enforced, everywhere in the United States. It's just a part of the culture of America.

The Life Insurance industry convinces parents if they buy Life Insurance for their child they are "protecting" that child. Life insurance is really death insurance. It gives money to the parents when the child dies. Like adults say, "I'm worth more dead than alive". This has the potential to put a child in a dangerous position, the opposite of protection. The commercials say, the ads say, "Protect your child." Life insurance, really death insurance, protects a child from what? Like many advertisements in the United States it is misleading. It appears to be something it is not. Good parents feel guilty if they don't protect their child, so the ads play upon that guilt. But the truth is it protects the parents, and is for the parents, as financial pay-offs after the death of their child.

In the 1990's health insurance companies raised their rates hugely, beyond reason. Their excuse was allegedly the high cost of medical lawsuits, when, in fact, it was their bad investments and the stock market losses they had had, which they then recovered by charging it to their policy holders as much higher premium costs. They charged the same clients who had given them the money to play the stock market with to begin with, and to lose, billions of dollars in losses.

This same process of massive theft and illegal use of client's money was repeated again in the first decade of the 21$^{st}$ century by the financial market, by the largest banks, by large mortgage companies, by financial investment companies, with losses of billions of dollars of their client's money, with no legal penalties. Theft of huge sums of money, especially by corporations, is protected by the United States Government and by the United States legal system, and the theft of $100, or the possession of an ounce of illegal drugs, results in 5 or 10 years in prison.

People in America don't care what they are charged for medical care, for the past 50 years, because insurance companies or the Government (Medicaid and Medicare) pays for it. This has resulted in outrageously high costs for procedures they did or didn't get, things they did or didn't use, excessive hospital costs, vastly over-priced medical equipment factored in, hidden fees, and pharmaceuticals costing up to a thousand times more than in other countries. Besides that, it has been estimated 30% to 50% of medical procedures done in the United States are unnecessary.

This means health insurance companies can then justify charging much higher premiums to their policy holders. The insurance industry is always one of the top three richest industries in America.

Over-priced insurance premiums support the over-priced medical industry, which supports the over-priced pharmaceutical industry. These were the top three industries in the United States, the top three money-makers, until Exxon oil reported the largest yearly earnings in United States history of $40.6 billion dollars in 2007. These were tax-free earnings for Exxon. The tax-free status of oil companies in the United States needs to end. It is long over-due. The benefits to the United States economy and to all Americans would be profound. More obvious monetary theft from Americans is that every year Exxon also gets hundreds of millions of dollars in tax refunds.

What is the price of freedom? The price of freedom in the United States in the 21$^{st}$ century is the loss of freedoms. Since 2001 there has been a loss of seven freedoms guaranteed in the Constitution and in the Bill of Rights for more than 235 years. How many more freedoms will be lost in the rest of the 21$^{st}$ century? It seems that truth doesn't matter anymore. It seems that what matters more is *hiding* the truth. But the truth belongs to everyone, especially in a democracy.

In 2012 Presidential-hopeful Romney said because of "the sacrifices of United States soldiers" he was "certain the future of America was bright." None of the other 23 Democracies in the World connect the brightness of their futures to the death and suffering of their own people, or of any other people anywhere else in the World. It's an American mindset, mostly because no other country has invaded the United States and conducted a war in the United States, and never will.

America, like all other countries, is a combination of who lives there and who runs the government, and who and what influences the society, the social structure, the most. In the second decade of the 21$^{st}$ century, after existing more than 235 years, America is still moderately free. Unfortunately, most American people, more than 300 million of them, have not had and will not have the ability to keep any of the remaining freedoms and rights formerly guaranteed to them. The continued destruction and distortion of the rights and freedoms guaranteed in The Constitution and The Bill of Rights will continue to be controlled by at least a million people, especially politicians and officials who are elected or not, who do not really represent them, the people of America. Instead they represent themselves and the 1% to 5% elite, and about 30,000 lobbyists, now in the 21$^{st}$ century.

New citizens of the United States have always repeated an oath to "defend and support The Constitution". Since after World War II that has never been the true reason, the real reason, for any American military invasions, attacks, and wars. Instead it's always been about power and control.

From the beginning of the 21$^{st}$ century Americans have not been able to "defend and support" the loss of those seven Constitutional freedoms and rights because it has been the Government itself that has been taking them away, distorting and destroying them forever. Americans cannot change or fight against their own national Government unless they want to be injured, ostracized, lose their jobs, be imprisoned, or be killed in the process. Consequently, it will never happen. Elections since 2000 seem to be just for show, to placate the masses, to involve the expendable masses and make them think they matter in the scheme of things. Elections are to make people think, and feel, they are in control of their national Government and state governments. In 11 states the people really are still in control of their states and of their state governments. Those are the 11 states and the people that passed resolutions against The Patriot Act of 2001, signed into perpetuation by Obama in 2011.

Most people think misery and suffering, chaos and madness, manipulation and meanness, are wrong, and need to be stopped when they happen. But there are always people who like chaos, misery, meanness, madness, suffering, and manipulation. They cause it, they perpetuate it. Then fairness, truth, and order are difficult or impossible to find. Military invasions of other countries and wars are endless chaos and suffering, endless meanness and madness, endless misery and manipulation. But flawed human beings will make sure they continue to happen. Like flawed human beings will make sure crimes, criminal behavior, pain, misery, and suffering are inescapable facts of life.

War-profiteering is always a motive for starting a war, a motivation for starting and continuing wars, in a capitalistic society. Especially during a war or period of invasion any United States citizen can be labeled "a threat to society", or "an enemy of the state", or "a national security risk", and be imprisoned indefinitely without legal representation. This is especially true since The Patriot Act of 2001 and The National Defense Act of 2011, both of which made it unnecessary to be involved in a war or invasion. Any American, anywhere, can be charged with these violations when there is no proof or evidence to prove it, or when evidence is created or manipulated for dishonest purposes.

"The New America in the 21st Century", a plan written and designed by Neo Con Republicans before 2000, became an oppressed America where war-profiteering was done on a much larger scale than ever before. Stealing *trillions of dollars* from Americans from 2003 to 2011 had no legal or political repercussions or legal punishment, and no legal requirement to pay back their massive and unbelievable theft, or to be imprisoned. Of course no one, no company, no corporation, was ever charged with anything, even though *they* were a threat to society, a national security risk, and an enemy of the state. Putting blame where it really belongs doesn't happen in the political arena.

In a real democracy people have the power to change their government, both federal and state, through dissent and elections. If they are kept in the dark, not informed, or given false information or lies, then the public can't do this. False labeling of United States citizens is a very dangerous practice reminiscent of totalitarian, or autocratic, or Communist Governments, and dictatorships. It isn't "a New World order" but instead a repression, a regression away from freedom and liberty which was a big improvement on the old World order.

One reason Guantanamo prison was chosen by the Bush "W"/Cheney/Ashcroft/Rove/Rumsfeld Neo Con crew was because it's in Cuba, where no United States laws would apply. From the beginning in that prison compound there was no rule of law. The United States Government and the United States military did not follow the Geneva Convention laws and rules begun in 1954 to protect prisoners of war, etc., to make sure the terrible treatment of prisoners of war by Japanese and Germans during World I and World War II would never happen again. It was an attempt to make wars more civilized and less cruel. However, the Bush "W" administration and the Obama administration, and the United States military, and all the privatized military and paramilitary employees in Iraq and Cuba, did not follow the Geneva Convention rules and laws at Guantanamo or at prisons in Iraq, starting in 2003 and continuing indefinitely.

Once again, they were and are above the law, both international and national. The so-called "New World Order" designed and carried out by the Neo Cons in power, starting with their takeover of the United States Presidency in 2000 and 2001,placed the United States above international laws and regulations. President Obama said repeatedly, during his unusually long three year campaign before the election in 2008, that he would close Guantanamo if he was elected. Then, as President, starting in 2009, he did not. However, this was nothing new. Presidents rarely keep their campaign promises. It's unusual, and unexpected, if they do.

Since 2011 United States military drones as small as a few inches can be targeted at any Americans in America to kill them, or to kill Americans anywhere else in the World. Or to kill any foreigners anywhere, in any country in the World. This is to be in control, to have the power to destroy and kill on a small, local, and controlled basis.

The upper 5% in the United States has as much yearly income as the other 95%, and pays little or no taxes on their vast wealth, so that 5% won't pay off the Iraqi war debt of at least $11.5 trillion dollars, before the added interest which will at least triple the original debt. Or pay for the billions of dollars paid every year indefinitely to the 100,000 to 200,000 private military, paramilitary, and private contractors left in Iraq after the end of the Iraq war. They will stay there indefinitely, possibly forever, ad infinitum, for their own personal financial gain and for the vastly over-compensated charges by their corporations and companies, not for the welfare and benefit of the Iraqi people or the American people. That is the reality of the planned aftermath of the war in Iraq.

Neo Cons in power from 2003 to 2008 were developers of, and supporters of, cruelty and torture of at least 500,000 innocent Iraqi men in Iraq without justice or rule of law. Obama said repeatedly, during his elongated three year campaign before 2009, that he would stop the war in Iraq. In 2011, after almost three years as President, he had not. This allowed the continuation of a war for eight years that was a radical violation of what America has stood for for more than 235 years. It allowed the continuation of torture, cruelty, and death of at least 500,000 Iraqi men, women, children, and babies, who had done nothing to America, or to Americans, or to American soldiers. How come this did not bother most Americans? What happened to collective and individual conscience and kindness?

Only *1%* of the Iraqi men turned in for money in Iraq, $1000 minimum, were actual insurgents. *None* were ever charged or had legal representation. When they were released, if they were released, many then became insurgents and terrorists because of the terrible things done to them and to their friends and relatives in those prisons and jails by Americans. These were American private civilians, paid by contracts with the newly privatized military, not American soldiers. It was a terrorist-creating and insurgent-creating machine insuring the continuance for America of its presence in Iraq. The continuance of the Iraq war was dependent on creating terrorists and insurgents in Iraq, or created elsewhere and imported into Iraq. Enemies had to be created.

The people in Iraq were never a threat to Americans, to America, or to United States national security, except in the minds of Republicans, especially the Far Right and the Neo Cons. When American soldiers were initially invading Iraq they wore military-issued earphones and players that repeated over and over again "Kill the mother-fuckers", blasting constantly in their ears, as they shot everything that moved, including children, babies, dogs, cats, goats, cattle, not only unarmed Iraqi men and women. They found no resistance. The Iraqi people had no guns, no rifles, no bombs. American soldiers had been taught by their superior officers that people in Iraq were sub-human and didn't value life anyway, so kill them. Without feeling any remorse or guilt, and having no conscience.

But this meant the soldiers who believed and acted on those inhuman and uncivilized premises were also sub-human beings, and the superior officers who bullied and enforced that concept, that belief, were certainly not "superior" officers, but were also sub-human beings. The invasions, occupations, attacks, and the war itself in Iraq were never about protecting Americans, or America. The United States Government allowed no images to be shown on TV of what the United States military and paramilitary, and the privatized military, were really doing in Iraq. No photographs of American soldiers being shot at or killed, or in caskets, could be taken. Since 2003 the United States Government said repeatedly that the United States was in Iraq to "defend America", 6000 miles away. Yet, Iraq had no capabilities to attack the United States *6000* miles away. They had no military planes, no weapons of mass destruction, no weapons of individual destruction.

Joseph Wilson, a former diplomat and Ambassador, wrote an article for the New York Times about his visit to Iraq for inspection of non-existent WMD. Cheney, Rumsfeld, and Rove didn't like it. In retaliation they revealed the identity of his wife, Valerie Plame, as a CIA agent in a newspaper article. This was a Federal crime of treason but nothing happened to them because they were above the law. Democrats in power seem to expect Republicans in power to break laws.

It's just more of the same old thing. So they did nothing about it, as always happens for about the past 50 years. Republicans in power, on the other hand, make mountains out of molehills, exaggerating everything. Like how they try to get legal convictions and legal charges made against the Democrats in power at any given time. For Republican politicians in the 21$^{st}$ century politics is a war, a daily battle to be won by any means. Honesty and the truth have nothing to do with it.

But in the 21$^{st}$ century it seems it doesn't matter whether the President is a Republican or a Democrat, except that Republicans vote against anything that would limit their control and potential for monetary theft. The Neo Con agenda for the 21$^{st}$ century directs either political Party. Campaign promises have meant very little since 2000. They're just words to energize the voting public for the purposes of manipulating them, and to get their votes. Politics, after all, is just a game of winning and losing money, power, and influence. Honesty and truth are just after-thoughts.

In 2001 and 2003 Iraq had no way to fly any weapons of mass destruction to the United States even if they had actually had them. They had been restricted and closely monitored by the United States Government and military for years, leaving them with no capabilities to fly anything 6000 miles as they had no planes. In 2003 Attorney General Powell had said on national TV that Iraq had no weapons of mass destruction. All of these were simple and obvious truths overlooked and ignored by most American people, mostly Republicans, in their mass hysteria to get retribution with anybody for 9/11 in 2001. This is a common Republican trait. They didn't care who was going to be attacked, as they desperately wanted to support their President Bush "W" and his Neo Con crew in their "Plan For A New World Order", begun in the 1970's, in order to control America in the 21$^{st}$ century, and then revised for the new century as "The Project For A New American Century", written and published by the Neo Cons in power before 2000.

But the rest of the World saw through the set-up and resisted. The United States Government spends at least *$500 billion dollars* every year for defense of the United States, protecting the United States from mostly shadow enemies. Nobody can attack the United States, so an attack had to be arranged to manipulate the American public, to unite them like Pearl Harbor had done against Japan after Japanese planes attacked American Navy ships in the harbors of Hawaii on December 7, 1941. Thus, 9/11 was allowed to happen in 2001. According to the Neo Con plans for another Pearl Harbor.

Later, reports by professionals showed proof that bombs had been planted in each of the three buildings to greatly increase the effects and the damage, and to greatly increase the deaths and injuries. It was a massive ugly PR job that killed almost 3000 people, allowing President Bush "W" to say to reporters "They died for a good cause", and then smiling an insipid smile. Only the Neo Cons in power knew what was set-up to happen next. No investigations were ever done to find out who had planted those bombs in those three buildings, or who had set them off. The American public remained blissfully unaware and in the dark about the truth, as has happened repeatedly for 70 years.

Thus began the end of a free Press in America, and the beginning of the end of a TV news media that can be trusted. It opened the floodgates for dishonesty throughout America in all things, in all parts of life, especially the Republican parts, the Republican areas of America. Not surprisingly, people in these areas of America have become increasingly mean, selfish and self-serving. These are some of the major changes in America in the 21st century.

A hallmark of the Bush "W" reign was that he and his Administration made their own laws, revised the Constitution for their own use, and did not follow laws as they were above the law. The Patriot Act was given to Congress between three and four hours before the vote on it was scheduled to take place. It was 345 pages long so no Congressman or Congresswoman read the entire document in those three to four hours. Reading is not their strong point. Neither is work. If they didn't vote "yes" they would be labeled unpatriotic, so they voted "yes" without caring what they were voting for. They didn't need to read it. They obviously weren't concerned about the people they represented. No one wanted to lose the next election because they voted "no" for The Patriot Act. It would have been labeled by the media as an unpatriotic thing for them to do.

Republicans have a reputation for replacing Democrats by making Democrats look bad. That's the Republican m.o. So nobody had to even read The Patriot Act before voting yes. It was a done deal before the Congressional Representatives even saw it. That's how some of the freedoms long guaranteed to the American people, all American people, disappeared on one day in Washington, D.C., in 2001, just days after the tragedies of 9/11 happened.

Starting six months before 9/11, 2001, Cheney's "Energy Task Force" had a suspicious excess of 40 meetings to discuss Iraq's oil fields, Iraq's oil locations, their oil production, and United States Government and United States military acquisitions and theft of the Iraq oil industry and of Iraq's oil reserves. Iraq has the second largest oil reserves in the World.

Years later an official committee to investigate those meetings had Senator Ted Stevens of Alaska as its chairman. After getting $350,000 in gifts from an unknown source, from unknown and hidden oil production sources, he refused to swear in the CEO's of all the oil companies, so they were not under oath to tell the truth. They were free to lie without fear of being charged, and convicted, of lying under oath. But lying under oath happens all the time in United States courts, at all levels, from local to Federal, even the Supreme Court, and nothing ever happens, no charges are ever made anyway, if the liars are connected to large companies, corporations, or are politicians or the very rich, the elite, or the ruling class in the United States. They are usually privileged and protected.

It's about politics and political influence. It's about power. The elite already have power and political influence. Others aspire to gain it. Those who have it will not give it up. Especially the ones who are obsessed with power and everything that comes with it, like the Neo Cons who have become very wealthy after being elected or appointed, and then stealing from and manipulating the American people. The expendable masses have money too. Not much, but it accumulates so that it becomes the rich taking from the poor. This has been a theme throughout the history of civilizations. This has become a theme for America since the Reagan administration in the 1980's.

The manufactured war on terrorism was determined the best way to manipulate public support for attacking Iraq, according to Rumsfeld's comments to the President and to the media. Wolfowitz said the idea of "weapons of mass destruction" was needed to ensure American public support. He was right. They both were right. But the rest of the world wasn't convinced.

One hour before the Columbine High School murders happened in Colorado United States military jets were sent by then-President Clinton to Kosovo. They bombed and completely destroyed a hospital and a primary school, killing all adults and children in those buildings. Those murdered people had done nothing to the United States Government or to any Americans, not even a threat. Nothing could validate those more than a thousand murders in Kosovo on that day by United States military forces in United States military planes. Multiply that times 10,000 tons of bombs dropped *every week* into Iraq for eight years, on innocent and defenseless people in Iraq, to understand the horrors of war perpetuated by the United States without provocation. Lies, yes, but not the truth.

The absence of about 4000 Jewish people from the Twin Towers on that day in September, 2001, was obviously planned and was proof of prior knowledge of what was going to happen. There should have been investigations, demands for explanations, and public disclosure of who, what, when, where, and why that happened. Who had warned them was not privileged information, but public information that was never revealed, or even questioned.

Most murders are never solved, so most murderers go free and are never punished, so this was nothing unusual in the scheme of things. But the scope and dimensions were unprecedented, so the scope and dimensions of who was responsible were probably also unprecedented. Yet, this huge leak was ignored by the media. Maybe because it would have led to the answer, to the solution of who was responsible for 9/11, in 2001.

No matter what they do the Federal Government cannot be sued or have a lawsuit brought against them. The United States Government, the United States President, and the United States military have immunity in lawsuits. They are held accountable for nothing. Americans have little or no control over their Government, unlike other democracies. Elections are a way for making Americans think they *do* have control.

Politics exist to make the rich richer. Politicians are for the rich, for businesses, for wealthy people, and for organizations, etc. who financially contribute the most money to them and support them. Politicians notoriously lie, especially Republicans. It's a part of their job. Voters have come to expect it. It's just part of the game. To get into power Republicans have even paid other Republicans to run as Democrats in elections. Then, either way, a Republican will be elected. Anybody can run as a Democrat when they are really a Republican. Bending rules and laws seems to be a Republican thing. Like arguing about everything just for the sake of arguing is a common Republican thing in the political arena. Corruption doesn't have to be against the law.

How many people have been paid to vote for Republicans running as Republicans? Anybody can buy support for business, for politics, and for personal reasons. That's one of the powers of money when you are a politician, or are aspiring to be a politician. That's one of the powers of being rich, and very rich, in America. Political influence is for sale.

In America the truth can be a dangerous thing. Since The Patriot Act of 2001 Homeland Security preys on people who tell the truth. It's possible that speaking the truth is also dangerous everywhere else in the World that is not a democracy. But the United States is the *only* democracy out of 24 in the World that punishes citizens who speak or write the truth about their national Government, or protest publically or participate in demonstrations about their Government. Most Americans don't want to know about that truth.

Newspapers, magazines, and books have been monitored and regulated since 2001. But Super-Pacs, the brain-child of Karl Rove and of the Republican Far Right to get around campaign finance reform and donation reform, to funnel and channel hundreds of millions of dollars donated to political efforts with no regulation of their so-called investigative newspaper articles, or their published reports, promotions, and negative commercials. Negative and mean ads are their specialty, their reason for being. Corruption, as always, follows the money.

Since 2003 politicians said the war in Iraq was a struggle for freedom in Iraq. Yet, in America if anyone criticizes the President or the Federal Government since 2001 they are labeled "anti-American", or put on lists as possible "terrorists", or "a threat to America", or "a national security risk". Since 2001 it can be a struggle to have freedom of speech and freedom of expression for Americans in America. And protests of anything can be against the law, or made too difficult to actually do. Computer monitoring of *all* Americans leads to possible investigations by Homeland Security, the FBI, local police and deputies, all of which have reputations of not following rules and of corruption. This then can lead to imprisonment indefinitely, with no charges or legal representation. All of it is so un-American. Allowing and encouraging any of this is not what a democracy should do.

Iraq is about *1/50* the size and population of the United States. There had been no threats from Iraq but President Bush "W" just saying they were a threat made it so in the minds of Republicans and some Democrats. However, just saying it was so did not make it so. No 9/11 hijackers were from Iraq. Most of them, nineteen of them, were from Saudi Arabia, a country friendly to the United States Government. There was nothing Americans could do to stop the frenzied and planned Bush "W" and Cheney Neo Con plans to attack and invade Iraq. Millions tried, including about a million people protesting in Washington, D.C., who were stopped by military police, local police, and National Guardsmen. The United States Government was a bully both in America and in Iraq.

Attorney General Ashcroft had decided that Geneva Convention rules did not apply to people taken as prisoners in Iraq so abuse of human rights for millions of Iraqi citizens was acceptable. He had been a former preacher, a Pastor of a church. Although he had been a man of God it was acceptable to him that at least 500,000 Iraqi citizens, including men, women, children, and babies, were brutally murdered. No records were ever kept, so no one knew for sure how many had been murdered. This was in direct contrast to the Viet Nam war, when military records were always kept and eventually totaled more than 6 million Vietnamese people, civilians brutally and cruelly murdered by American soldiers. And in contrast to the war in Korea, where military records indicated more than 4 million Korean civilians had been killed by American soldiers.

No matter what was done by American soldiers it was alright. No records were ever kept of anything regarding numbers, totals, of Iraqi citizens injured and killed. White House Attorney Woo gave his approval and encouraged radical violations of human rights for Iraqi people. Because of Ashcroft, the former church Pastor, and Cheney, Bush "W", and Woo, the people of Iraq had no human rights or civil liberties as long as American soldiers occupied their country. The United States did not bring them freedom and a democracy. Yet there was very little reaction to these lies in America, perpetuated throughout the United States for eight years, and continuing for years later. Was it because of fear of retaliation by their Government? Maybe there is general fear of the United States Government.

Blackwater is a privatized army working for the United States Department of Defense at hugely inflated wages and costs. Their purpose was to destroy Iraqi society and Iraqi life. They assassinated their own employees who co-operated with Federal investigators about excessive money losses, stolen money, billions of dollars disappearing, and questionable disappearances of people, along with unexplained deaths and murders. It's been operating under a web of secrecy, obscurity, and secret ownership of obscure companies, in order to hide crimes and criminal activities. All of this has been funded by the United States Government, Federal money, taxpayer's money. Why doesn't the Federal Government charge and prosecute them? Or even control them? Because they don't want to. Therefore the Federal Government supports all of this corruption in every way. Therefore the American people support this kind of corruption in every way. It has been both a Republican and a Democratic thing, the responsibility of both parties, besides the so-called Shadow Government, the 1% elite, and appointed officials. The people who rule America behind the scenes.

In Iraq Halliburton, Blackhawk, KBR (Kellogg, Brown, and Root), Blackwater, and at least 50 other private companies represented the first privatized war in United States history. As an example, Paul Bremer's private security cost $21 million dollars a year, instead of using military security at no cost except for their military salaries. His employees were paid 5 to 100 times what military personnel would have been paid to do the same jobs. In fact, the military personnel would teach them what to do, how to do their jobs. There were at least 200,000 private contractors as employees in Iraq for eight years. Apparently the war was prolonged for the financial benefit of those private contractors. The continued suffering and deaths of American soldiers and Iraqi citizens apparently didn't matter. It was money and profit that mattered. It was money and profit that perpetuated the war in Iraq.

In Germany in the 1930's, after Hitler was elected by a majority vote in their democratic elections, the Nazi's, as a political party, easily took control of the courts, the law enforcement (police), the radio stations and newspapers. The German people were well-educated, sophisticated, and had a high standard of living. There was no resistance, from the beginning of the slow and gradual takeover. Most Germans probably didn't even know what was happening. There was just apathy, acceptance, and indifference. And general trust of the elected Government. There was a Homeland Security Government agency, supposedly providing security for everyone in Germany. But this was a false belief.

It isn't just a coincidence that the United States has the same Federal Government agency, called the same thing, named after that same German agency of destruction, Homeland Security. In Germany at that time resistance would have resulted in imprisonment, beatings, and death. In America no one knows how many journalists, photojournalists, authors, newspaper editors, and ordinary people who have protested about the United States Government or politicians (in office or not) have been falsely imprisoned indefinitely since 2001, with no legal representation, no charges, and no hope of getting out of prison. And no contact with the outside world indefinitely, especially for those put in solitary confinement. This, after all, was a part of the Neo Con's plan.

In 2012 eleven states had passed resolutions against The Patriot Act for their entire states. This meant these false imprisonments, these wrongful imprisonments, with no legal representation or charges would not have been possible in those states, and all the other destruction of Constitutional freedoms would have been ignored, not enforced. But President Obama signed into law The Defense Act, on December 31, 2011, that reaffirms, that repeats, the restrictions and destructions of The Constitution and The Bill of Rights made into law by The Patriot Act. But the eleven states had asserted themselves and become the last bastions of freedom in the United States. President Obama, a Democrat, took them away again, and for the indefinite future, for perpetuity.

It's all like a big ugly game. Politics in America, politics in the United States. It seems it doesn't much matter who the President is in the 21$^{st}$ century, a Democrat or a Republican. The secretive and controlling Neo Con plans for a new America, in the new century, will be carried out no matter who is the President, no matter what the controlling political party is.

In Iraq between 100,000 and 200,000 Iraqi men, citizens of Iraq, family men, were falsely detained and imprisoned indefinitely, and never charged, by American paramilitary, the pseudo-military that followed no rules, no standards of conduct, no regulations, and were paid much more than regular military would have been paid, that *would* have followed military rules and regulations. The results were hatred of America and American soldiers, the creation of endless insurgents to help fuel the war in Iraq and to validate the War on Terror forever, and the theft of hundreds of billions of dollars every year from the American public that will continue indefinitely, totaling the theft of many *trillions of dollars*. And misery for all the people in America and in Iraq that were connected to, or were families of, both the injured and those people killed in Iraq.

This is the legacy of America that Americans were unable to do anything about, from 2003 to 2011. What will happen to Americans in America as the same paramilitary, located and training in several states, becomes more powerful in America? What will happen when they are in control in America instead of the legitimate military, like what happened in Iraq? And who has been behind all of this? The expendable masses mean nothing to these men, in America or anywhere else. That means that whoever was behind all of this is merciless, and cares nothing about the welfare of all Americans either in America or outside of it. And not for the welfare of people in foreign countries. Unfortunately, the paramilitary are trained to have no conscience or sense of right and wrong, and are very highly paid, in contrast to the military, to the soldiers in the United States military.

If the United States is a country based on laws and justice why is there so much injustice in America? Because of favoritism, selfishness, meanness, and authorities, politicians, and people in power, elected or not, that allow and encourage injustices and breaking of laws. Or they just look the other way, or don't care. It always comes down to money, profit, power, and control.

But anything can lead to imprisonment indefinitely with no charges or legal representation since The Patriot Act of 2001, and since The National Defense Act was signed into law by President Obama on December 31, 2011, after he had signed The Patriot Act into perpetuation in 2011. America has become a potentially dangerous place to live if you are an American citizen and do or say something the Government has designated as being wrong. Since 2001 when anyone talks on a phone anywhere in America they are being computer-monitored by the Government, by Government computers 24/7, for Government-designated red-flag words like "America" and "the President", and an unknown number of additional words, phrases, ideas, and concepts. Since 2001 organizations and their meetings are monitored by the Government, etc., for the same red-flag words designated by the Government, and for other activities, by under-cover Government representatives.

Democratic administrations haven't changed those computerized operations that vicariously watch all Americans and everybody else in America. Cameras can be everywhere in American society since after 2001. Big Brother is watching.

Yet, Obama has publically told other Government leaders in other countries that they should not be monitoring the personal computers and private e-mail accounts of the people living in their countries. It's the common politics of saying one thing and doing another. Let's say we don't, and then do it. This is nothing new.

The United States Constitution says "The people have a right to abolish a destructive government." But in the 21$^{st}$ century in the United States organizing to do that would be impossible and would result in arrest, imprisonment, even death. Even organizing to have a peaceful march can be monitored by Homeland Security, the FBI, and undercover local police or deputies. It isn't worth the risk to protest about anything anymore. And that is just the way it's supposed to be in 21$^{st}$ century America. Apathy and indifference are encouraged and expected in the new century.

In 2012 Republican Presidential wanna-be Romney announced his version of the 2000 and 2001 Neo Con's published reports and their plans for America in the new century. He called it "The Blueprint for a New American Century". So far, in the 21$^{st}$ century, United States Government oppression of United States citizens, denial of their civil liberties and civil rights, lack of integrity and honesty towards its citizens, and lack of conscience in national and international affairs, means it's the American Government *itself* that is anti-American. But it's all legal because the Government is not held accountable for anything. The government, both state and federal, is above the law.

It all starts at the top and trickles down to the American people, modifying their personalities for the worst. It's the collective American consciousness. If Big Brother can do it then so can his little sisters and brothers, of all colors and all ages, everywhere in America, as they copy their Big Brother. The political games are endless, saying one thing and doing another having become so common.

In June 2012 Hilary Clinton was giving a commencement speech at a college about how other countries don't allow protests and freedom of speech. A 71 year old man stood up in the audience and turned his back on Clinton. A policeman and an undercover policeman attacked him, and dragged him away. He was then beaten and imprisoned indefinitely. He had said as he was dragged away "So this is America."

Yet, since after 2001 the United States Government has paid for protests and demonstrations to be done in other countries, paying men from neighboring countries to organize and conduct both violent and peaceful demonstrations and protests about foreign governments, etc. Since after 2001, again and again, people interviewed in those countries have said the protestors are not from their own countries. These foreign men, including criminals and soldiers-of-fortune, are paid *much* more than American soldiers, in order to disrupt foreign countries, their societies and their governments.

Since 2001 if you didn't support the war in Iraq you were labeled "anti-American" by the news media, the TV news, the Press, and Cable TV talk shows, by the Government, by your neighbors, and by your local police. And, of course, not to forget the newly empowered library police at your local library, which include all employees of all libraries everywhere, especially in Republican areas of the country, who can monitor what is typed on their library computers and checked out of their individual library that has red-flag words like "America" in it.

Since 2001 to write anything about America, publishing it or not, or to say that word, or countless other words, ideas, concepts, and phrases on a phone triggers automatic defensive responses, red-flag alerts, suspicious responses, from Government computer networks.

It's a different world out there since The Patriot Act became a law. Freedom and justice has changed in subtle ways and in not so subtle ways, and in obtrusive and unobtrusive ways. Most people are blissfully unaware. The government, state and Federal, has asked for reports of suspicious behavior of American citizens, or of anti-American behavior, according to their guidelines, to inspire patriotism and to manipulate the public to support whatever the United States Government was, or is, going to do. This is to control the American public more than ever before in the history of the United States. Supposedly this promotes national unity, and patriotism, according to the plans of the Neo Cons designed and written before 2000, years before the beginning of the 21st century.

Individuals or groups, authors and journalists, who publically protest anything the Federal Government does, at any level, risk getting death threats, or just harassment, or even what seem to be set-up suicides by people who died mysteriously, who would never commit suicide. In 2012, at a public appearance, a man in the audience told former VP Cheney the United States should never have gone to war with Iraq, and he was then arrested. VP Cheney said that the man had touched him on the shoulder. The man, after being arrested, said he did not touch Cheney. It was the same old thing about the very rich having much more power and influence than the average American. Hopefully someone had a video of it. Otherwise it would be like police and deputies, like law enforcement anywhere in the United States, that can have a standard response "You have no proof unless you have a video recording of it." An impossibility 99% of the time.

All of this happens because of The Patriot Act of 2001, and President Obama signing it into perpetuity in 2011, and then Obama signing The Defensive Act into law in 2012. This essentially repeats The Patriot Act part that says any American citizen can be detained and imprisoned without probable cause or charges indefinitely, and with no legal representation, trial, or hearings. So any man or woman in America is in very real danger of never getting out of prison when they have done nothing wrong. When, in fact, they are completely innocent. Because of these unbelievably awful changes for all Americans, especially the expendable masses, anyone who gets arrested is in very real danger of never getting out of prison. It's a regression back to a time when, or a place where, a person was guilty until proven innocent, like in Europe and Russia in the 1500's,1600's,1700's,and in the 1800's,and probably for centuries before the 1500's. For a long time progression was necessary.

The Neo Con's "New World Order", written just before 2000, are plans to change the United States from a republic to a global empire, for American global domination. Corruption feeds on corruption, and allows the corruption, encourages the corruption, to increase exponentially. It's not imperialism, it's Neo Conism. And, so far, it's only been done on little countries, countries much smaller than the United States. Therefore, it's being a bully, which has endless negative ramifications on whoever is being bullied and harmed, both immediately and for the rest of their lives.

If people write negatively or talk negatively publically about authorities, officials, politicians, especially in Republican cities or Republican areas of the United States, supposedly any action against that person is justified because that word, or those words, may hurt the United States. But the U.S. Government has been a bully of notoriety and reputation spanning at least 60 years, having the most massive, the most expansive, and by far the most expensive military in the World, as the most powerful country in the World. So for the huge and immense United States Government to fear individual people or small groups of people in the U.S. is political insanity and meanness, an undemocratic action in the Democracy of America.

Since 2001 there has been a Government computerized list of more than a million people who are citizens of America who are listed as "possible enemies of the United States". This list has included harmless good people who have visited the United States like the Dalai Lama and Mother Theresa, and good citizens of America like Senator Ted Kennedy, priests, bishops, ministers of churches, harmless but vocal Hollywood actors and actresses, directors, producers, teachers, homemakers, and more than a million harmless men and women who live in America. In 2012 a Homeland Security commercial that aired on national TV said repeatedly to "report any suspicious activity of your neighbors, and strangers you see on the street." This is a kind of Government control of Americans. It turns Americans against Americans. It turns Americans against each other by instilling suspicion and fear. Being suspicious of everyone and everything everywhere 24/7 is an ugly way to live a life. Not remotely like "liberty and the pursuit of happiness" guaranteed in The Constitution. But the United States Government has forced hundreds of millions of people in other countries to do that for more than the past 60 years.

It makes Americans feel important in the so-called war on terrorism. Fear is a necessary part of controlling the masses, the expendable masses, as part of the Neo Con's plan for controlling America in the 21$^{st}$ century. It was part of "The Plan For A New America in The 21$^{st}$ Century", written and published just before 2000 by the Neo Cons in power at that time. Written by the ones who would soon be in power nationally, and in control nationally, for the next eight years, after the corruption, chaos, and fiasco elections of 2000 put what the CIA in Washington, D.C. had years before called "the crazies" into political office, both elected and unelected. It was all a part of the big plan, started in the 1970's, by the newly emerging Neo Cons in power at that time. Nothing was random and chaotic, or by chance. It was all part of a system in place for many years.

Since 2001, since after 9/11, the FBI and the NSA monitors all Americans. Homeland Security and the Federal Government monitor all Americans. Except for the entire state of Oregon, that rejected The Patriot Act entirely for the entire state. Oregon is the last bastion of freedom, for freedom, guaranteed in their entire state for everyone who lives there and who visits there. Except for almost 400 cities that have formally rejected the Patriot Act since 2001.These were cities that stood up for freedom and the retention of freedoms guaranteed in The Constitution and The Bill of Rights, freedoms taken away from them by the Neo Cons and their Patriot Act in 2001, then taken away forever by President Obama resigning The Patriot Act into perpetuity in 2011. Oh what a tangled web we weave when first we conspire to deceive.

In 2012 Attorney General Holder and President Obama were accused of being involved in gun-running operations. Potentially those guns would kill hundreds of thousands of people. Or millions of people. Obama claimed Presidential immunity from any lawsuit or legal proceeding, a law and provision provided by Bush "W", who very much needed that protection. Holder refused to co-operate or respond. If any one of the expendable masses in the United States over the age of 18, more than 300 million people, had done these same things it is certain they would have gone to prison, with or without charges, possibly without legal representation, and imprisoned indefinitely.

For about 200 years many hundreds of millions of school kids, and adults at sporting events, totaling at least a billion people, have recited The Pledge of Allegiance "liberty and justice for all", billions of times. But just saying it doesn't make it so. It's been like a national form of propaganda and subtle mind control for more than 200 years. After the Neo Cons in power began their biggest interventions in 2000 and 2001, and since The Patriot Act in 2001, it's not true anymore. There isn't liberty and justice for all anymore. Since Obama signed the National Defense Act into law, on the last day of 2011, millions of Americans who successfully resisted the ugly changes, who legally stopped those changes in their states, have been circumvented and tricked into submission. Throughout the World Americans are well known for their inventiveness, resourcefulness, innovations, independence. But for now in the 21$^{st}$ century Big Brother has spoken and will not tolerate resistance.

A democracy should promote the public good. A democracy exists to promote the public good. Democratic processes and democracies are supposed to be for the welfare of, and the progress of, all of the people. However, the United States Democracy, the United States Government, especially promotes the progress and welfare of the ruling class, the rich, the wealthy, the elite, Big Business, corporations, politicians, and the industries of oil, medicine, pharmaceuticals, and insurance, the pillars of the American economy, to the exclusion of the expendable masses. Even NATO keeps the rich rich and the poor poor. Even NATO is for the ruling class, the ruling 1% in America, the wealthiest 3 million people. That's a lot of very rich people. If the other upper 9% were included, being the upper 10% then in America, that's about 30 million people. That's like a separate country of *very* rich people who can run the country on their own and provide whatever they need for their privileged selves. No wonder the expendable masses are expendable. They aren't really needed in the scheme of things.

The American Democracy supposedly represents good vs. bad, right vs. wrong. It's the constant struggle that never ends. There are 23 other Democracies to compare the American Democracy with, but arrogance prohibits that from happening. Instead of the ruling class keeping an open mind, as they live in their very privileged surroundings, their special lives, and implementing improvements in America by copying what is superior in other democracies, they rule America and Americans the way they want to, for their own continued benefits and continued control. As always, follow the money and look to see who benefits.

A democracy isn't supposed to have a ruling class, but the United States does. It's a democratic form of a ruling class. The Constitution seems to have been written for them and The Bill of Rights written for the rest of Americans. The ruling class manipulates and controls the American public and their elected politicians, and the Federal and state governments in general. This would be the President, Senators, Governors, and especially Congressmen and Congresswomen, the ones who are supposed to represent the people, the average American, but they do not. So it's a Government for the ruling class and by the ruling class, not by the people and for the people. If the Presidential elections are manipulated and predetermined then it doesn't matter if Presidents, or candidates, have support for their actions from the public or not. Elections have become a way to manipulate the public into thinking they are in control and that their opinion matters.

Representing the people is unnecessary. People in power will do what they want to do. The public, the American people in general, are only necessary to supply them with money. But money can be easily printed legally or illegally by those at the top. Without ethics and integrity and truth it all becomes a game. A deadly game, with the odds against honest and good people, possibly anywhere and everywhere in America. The potential to do harm is always there, just like the potential to do good is also always there. It always comes down to choices, making choices.

There have been more wars in the World in the past century than in any other century in history. The 20th century was a century of wars, killing, and military actions. Why do men go to wars? Their leaders force them to, or they will go to prison if they don't. Or for independence from tyranny, and for freedom. Leaders go to war for triumph over enemies, or to steal land and territory. Or for personal vendettas. Or to get more power. Or to dominate oil production and therefore oil profits in another country. Without oil the American economy would screech to a halt. The United States military couldn't function. Bush "W" said, while he was President, "To improve an economy go to war." In the 20th century American soldiers were told for generations of men that they were going to war and fighting in other countries to bring liberty, democracy, and freedom to the people there. After the Korean War in the 1950's that stopped being true.

As usual, most Americans don't want to know the truth about what's happening in America because of their loyalty to their country. "America, God sheds his grace on thee" is what they want to believe. They want to believe their elected President is doing the right things for them. However, loyalty to anything can be the same thing as delusion. This attitude of God's preferential treatment for Americans has contributed to Americans thinking they are superior to people in other countries, since the beginning of the United States of America.

Since after the assassination of President Kennedy in 1963 the United States has usually been involved in military actions, occupations, invasions, and wars in other countries somewhere in the world. George Orwell warned and predicted in his book "1984" that the American Government would be involved in perpetual foreign wars and control of the American public and of the World. He was right. Thorough official investigation, magazine and newspaper articles, and documentaries, have shown the brutal assassination of President Kennedy was a collaboration between the CIA, the Secret Service, and Army Special Forces military assassination units. And possibly the Mafia in New Orleans and Chicago, who had supposedly arranged with professional assassins to kill both Castro and President Kennedy.

After his brother's murder Bobby Kennedy wrote to someone he knew at the CIA "One of your guys did it." Three days after the murder of President Kennedy there was an official military reversal of Kennedy's order to return all United States soldiers from Viet Nam. So instead of withdrawing soldiers planeloads of more soldiers were sent to Viet Nam. Then, in August of 1964, President Johnson, as the replacement President, announced the Gulf of Tonkin attacks on the USS Maddox justified going to war with North Viet Nam. This was the first major lie about Viet Nam.

It was a complete lie, a story made up by President Johnson and by Bob McNamara, also a Democrat and the Secretary of Defense from 1961 to 1968. There had been no attacks by North Viet Nam on a Navy ship in the Gulf of Tonkin. The Navy Commanders knew it was a lie, and President Johnson and McNamara knew it was a lie. The North Vietnamese leaders knew it was a lie. But no one was held accountable for that. In fact, military planes from Israel had been told to attack the Navy ship until it sank "to the bottom of the sea", as revealed in a taped recording of Johnson talking on the phone shortly after the Israeli planes began the air attacks. The CIA and the United States military needed justification to invade North Vietnam so they planned and created that justification.

As a result, for the next 12 years 4 to 6 million innocent Vietnamese civilians were murdered, often brutally killed at random by American soldiers, a large percentage of whom did not want to be there or killing anyone. They were drafted and had no choice. Millions of people marched against the Vietnam occupation and war but nothing changed. Their protests and marches, their demonstrations by millions of protestors, changed nothing.

Years later McNamara said "We thought it was the Communists we were fighting. But we were wrong. It was just a civil war." That "just" killed four to six million innocent and defenseless Vietnamese civilians, including babies and children, and adults that had no way to defend themselves, or their families or their homes. About 58,000 American soldiers were killed for no reason, for a manufactured enemy, for a created enemy, and for a manufactured war. For, and because of, lies.

Misinformation, disinformation, discrediting, warping and twisting the truth, lies, distorting the truth, distorting information, and manufacturing information is what the American public has had to rely on since then, starting in 1963 with the Democrats in power and especially since 2001, with the Neo Cons in power and the beginning of the destruction of The Constitution and The Bill of Rights. In 2008 Obama was elected on the promises of a more transparent Federal Government, big changes, and ending the war in Iraq. But none of this happened.

After almost eight years none of it had happened except ending the war in Iraq four years after he had promised it. This meant there were many thousands more deaths, especially for Iraqi citizens. Maybe the ending date of using 9/11 again had been planned by the Neo Cons in power before they started the manufactured war. It was done for public relations, a PR date, to connect it to 9/11 in 2001, in order to continue the Neo Con manipulation of the American public, including those people that *wanted* to be manipulated by their Government. Americans can vote for promised changes but they can't do anything about it when they don't happen.

For many years Republican politicians have said that Democrats want too much government and the Republicans want less government, when in fact the most government, by far, happens usually with Republican Presidents, especially Reagan and Bush "W". In 2001 the Republican's Patriot Act increased Federal Government control and Government intervention much more than ever before in United States history. The result was more controlling "government" than ever before in America. The Government abuse of power that was then allowed as a result will continue indefinitely, as will the destruction and elimination of freedoms guaranteed in The Constitution and The Bill of Rights. All of this happened because of Republican sponsored and Neo Con designed control of the Federal Government, the very thing they constantly complain about and accuse Democrats of doing year after year for *many* years. It's been a worn-out lie for many years. It's hypocrisy, plain and simple.

As proof of the long-standing hypocrisy of the Republican Party and the Far Right, $125 million dollars was spent by Republicans over two years to attempt to impeach President Clinton because he was very popular with Americans, in general, and unusually productive as a President. The Republicans had to stop him, they had to destroy his image for all posterity, for all history books, not just for the present voters and citizens of America who gave him majority support and adoration. Most of the public loved having Bill Clinton as President, and the booming economy reflected his positive influence. The Republicans thought it had to be stopped. Henry Hyde was Chairman of the Impeachment Committee, all of whom got paid a lot to just sit in a room for two years and listen to a ridiculous litany of resentment and back-stabbing from those over-paid Republican members of the ridiculous Impeachment Committee. Only in America could something like that happen.

The two-faced hypocritical Hyde had had an affair with a married woman for 5 ½ years, while he was married. Ultimately his marriage ended for that reason. Barr, one of the Republican prosecutors, had also had an extra-marital affair for about 2 ½ years. Kenneth Starr, the main instigator and most important Republican prosecutor at the proceedings, had lied repeatedly in the courtroom for those 2 ½ years. He made up charges about Clinton during those years, and for years before and after.

A former director of counter-terrorism said in an interview on TV that VP Cheney had worked in one of the buildings that were "blown-up on 9/11". Blown up? That's right, not destroyed by a plane flying into it, that was allegedly flown by hijackers from the Middle East. Many experts carefully studied the remains of the three buildings and said one or more bombs, in the basements, blew up each of the three buildings on 9/11. The masses were expendable and had to be manipulated to support wars, attacks, invasions, and occupations done by the United States Government and the United States military for the rest of the 21st century. It was part of the Neo Con's "The Plan For A New America In The 21st Century", published and written and designed by the Neo Cons in power, elected or not, before 2000. The planned control of the masses had officially begun on 9/11, 2001.

Surveillance cameras on top of the building next to the Pentagon building that was blown up clearly showed no plane flew into that Pentagon building before it blew up, before it blew apart. Of course these video tapes were never shown to the American public. Fifteen of the alleged nineteen hijackers were from Saudi Arabia. None were from Iraq. Most of them lived in the United States. And most of them were interviewed months and years later while living in other countries, or in Saudi Arabia.

One of the reasons Bush "W" became President in 2000 was because 1.9 million votes were "lost", according to TV news media and the Press. Where did they all go? Nowhere. They just weren't counted. Investigations showed that the voting machines provided by Diebold Corporation, and other companies, were rigged so that when a person voted for Gore it would go to Bush "W" instead. There never was a Congressional investigation of these federal and state crimes, nor were there any charges made for these crimes. In states like Ohio and Florida 18 million votes in Democratic districts literally were not counted, and extra illegal and illicit votes were added to the state total for Bush "W". In the following years of the Bush "W"/Cheney reign Attorney General Ashcroft, Rumsfeld, Cheney, and Bush "W" had all said they didn't have to follow laws. They were above the law, apparently because of their high status, because they were Neo Cons in their New World Order.

When governments are not responsive to their people, when a government ignores what the public needs and wants, and when that same government thinks they are above the law, then that government is like the Mafia.

The Murdock owned and controlled FOX News and FOX Radio have said for many years every day and every night, over and over again 24/7, that they have "fair and balanced news". Just because they say it doesn't make it true. It doesn't mean it's the truth. But after hearing and seeing it written on the screen hundreds of times, or thousands of times, most people will believe it's true. It's like propaganda and mind-control. Their technique of flashing devisive statements and lies across the screen as people talk is like what Government-controlled TV stations have done in North Korea for many years. It's not something that should be imitated in a democracy, especially in America, allegedly the best Democracy in the World, according to Americans and according to all politicians in America, elected or not, who often repeat that, especially during their election and re-election campaigns and in their acceptance speeches. It's like another form of propaganda, proving they are patriotic and worthy of all voter's confidence.

The expendable masses is a theme running throughout the history of civilizations for at least the last 1000 years. The United States is not the first country, the first Government, to have that attitude. Throughout history there has been immense and horrific cruelties perpetrated upon people in most places in the World at some time or another. It's not that it hasn't been done before. It's that it needs to stop. It's that it should never happen again, especially in America or by the American Government.

Homeland Security in America, after September 11, 2001, was named after the Homeland Security in Hitler's Nazi Germany in the 1930's and 1940's. Of course it was patterned after their techniques too. Control of the masses is part of the total goal, the necessary modus operandi. It's part of the m.o. for the entire 21$^{st}$ century in America. It's the opposite of democracy.

For many years Republican politicians have tried to destroy Government programs that help poor people and middle-income people, on both state and Federal levels. Programs like Medicare, Social Security, Medicaid, Food Stamps. So how do they ever win elections? Why do people vote for them? The answer is corruption and manipulation. Follow the money, especially for the Republican minority in America, in order to defeat the Democratic majority.

After 9/11 happened then-President Bush "W" said "They died for a good cause", in an interview with reporters shown on TV. They died for the Neo Con agendas. Many people, perhaps thousands of people, became millionaires and multi-millionaires because of the war in Iraq. That's why it cost taxpayers *trillions of dollars*, not billions of dollars. It was a business venture for them. Inflated costs and financial theft was the name of the game. Wars always create great wealth for some people. The Iraq war created great wealth, unprecedented wealth, for many more people than any war that came before. Almost none of the trillions of dollars from American taxpayers was used to rebuild Iraq and help the Iraqi people rebuild their homes, their infra-structure, their social structure. Instead it was used to build massive and permanent United States Government buildings for a permanent military occupation by the United States in Iraq, because Iraq has the second largest oil reserves in the World.

The war in Iraq was planned at least seven months before 9/11 happened by the Neo Cons and Far Right conservatives in power, which included President Bush "W", his father former President H.W. Bush, who made daily visits to the White House for daily briefings at that time, and Vice President Cheney, Attorney General Ashcroft (a former preacher of a church), Rumsfeld, Rove, Moro, Gonzalez, Wolfowitz, then-Florida-Governor Jeb Bush, and other unelected Neo Cons and Far Right Conservatives in power at that time. Later Washington lawyer Yoo would join the Bush "W" administration, elected and unelected, in order to legally justify anything they had done or would do.

As a result of the Iraq war Bush "W" and Cheney became multi-millionaires, possibly billionaires, during their eight years in power. But the masses, as always, were expendable.

The planned calamity of 9/11 would give them manufactured justification to control the second largest oil reserves in the world after invading and bombing Iraq. Then they would build fourteen permanent military bases in Iraq, giving the United States a permanent influence, an actual physical presence and control in the Middle East. In 10 years their domination of Iraq would be complete, opening future influence and control in other parts of the Middle East. But this was not something entirely new, as the United States had done similar actions in other countries since after World War II.

TV news media, especially CNN and FOX News, manipulated Americans with lies and half-truths. The war was shown like entertainment news. But the American public expects dishonesty from Republicans because there has been so much of it since 2000. It's the status quo for the 21$^{st}$ century. It's been called "the dumbing of America". The manipulation and viciousness, politicians and speakers demonizing Iraq, had to be continued 24/7 on FOX News and CNN in order to justify the war and to please the Republican audience, the Far Rights and the Neo Cons, throughout America. The media gave them what they wanted. It translated to billions of more dollars for their profit.

None of the 19 hijackers on 9/11 were from Iraq. Fifteen were from Saudi Arabia, that gets *billions of dollars* in foreign aid every year from American taxpayers to give to the Saudi military. However, most of them had been living in the United States. After 9/11 at least a million people had marched in Washington, D.C., and other places in the United States, against attacking Iraq. As usual, they were ignored by their Government and, instead, they were clubbed, shot at, and arrested by law enforcement. As usual, law enforcement was *protecting* no one as the protestors had no guns or weapons of any kind. This has happened throughout the history of the United States, the land of the free, where freedom of speech and freedom to have demonstrations against the Government were supposed to be guaranteed. It was an American tradition that is no more. Times change and the democracy changed, but without the consensus of the people.

For years after 9/11, in 2001, inflammatory statements, including lies, flashed across the TV screen on FOX News as invited speakers and hosts were speaking. It was like propaganda and mind control. Many millions of Republicans liked it. It fortified them and their beliefs, their belief systems. Americans who had authority, who had been sent to Iraq immediately after the first bombings, tried to stop the killing and destruction of property, the tortures, the destruction of the Iraqi society, the theft of money from banks, the illegal imprisonment and torture of Iraqi civilians. But they couldn't stop or change anything. It had a momentum of its own, starting at the top.

Possibly 30 million Iraqi's fled to other countries to escape the American forces, if they had the money to do it. People who stayed to protect their homes, their belongings, their pets, often saw those belongings destroyed or taken from them, and American soldiers killed domestic pets whenever they saw them. Pet cats, dogs, goats, cows, horses, birds, were all shot by American soldiers. The United States Army had drilled soldiers with the belief that Iraqis were not civilized people, so the American soldiers were arrogant about their superiority and killed them, tortured them, at random. Like everything, like always, it started at the top and filtered down to the soldiers at the bottom, in order to control them.

Solitary confinement makes people in prison go crazy, lose their minds. This is understandable, and is expected as part of the process. Just like putting anyone in an insane asylum will make them crazy if they weren't already. The United States Government and military, and especially the para-military and the privatized military that is mostly Blackhawk, employing at least *200,000 people,* knowingly created, purposefully created, men in Iraq that hated Americans and America by torturing Iraqi men that had done nothing wrong. They never had any charges brought against them but were beaten and tortured, and often kept in solitary confinement. This caused resentment and hatred in these innocent men, contributing to the endless supply of "insurgents".

This, then, substantiated the continued presence of America in Iraq. Insurgents were necessary, and they were purposefully created by the United States Government, the United States military, and the paramilitary. Names and words were changed so they could circumvent the rules of the Geneva Convention and NATO. Now, in the 21st century, there were "insurgents", "terrorists", and "enemy combatants" to replace what was formerly known as enemies, soldiers, and prisoners of war. And the prison for them was in a different country, in Cuba, so no previous rules had to be followed.

How did the United States forces get these at least *100,000* innocent Iraqi men as prisoners? It paid $1000 to $5000 dollar pay-outs for each man turned over to the United States military to be tortured and imprisoned indefinitely, without legal representation. Insurgents and terrorists, the enemy in Iraq, could also turn in any man in Iraq to the United States military to be imprisoned and tortured and then be paid the same amount of money, no questions asked. The United States paid out more than a *trillion dollars* for this program of ransom and bounty, leading to torture and imprisonment and death for an unknown number of Iraqi men. Of course no records were ever kept. As in everything, if there's no record of something then it never happened, according to authorities.

Titan and CACI were given $60 million dollars each year, for eight years, to pick up, interrogate, torture, and kill Iraqi men sent to prisons in Iraq and Guantanamo, in Cuba, with no charges or probable cause ever, and no legal representation ever. United States military personnel would be sent to prison or jail if they had done, or did, what these Titan and CACI employees did to Iraqi civilians as part of their jobs every day, 24/7. Rumsfeld said for years that there was no torture or abuse of those prisoners. He always lied. Usually while smiling, his public m.o. for many years.

According to witnesses Rumsfeld ordered and encouraged both private contractors and United States military men, military personnel, to abuse and torture prisoners for five years, until his time as the ruler of the military ended. So he lied repeatedly, often with a smile, his trademark smirk and smile that many Americans thought was proof he was telling the truth, and that he really was a good man. It was like Pat Robertson's and Bush "W"'s trademark smiles to cover lies and dishonesty. It's just the Republican status quo. Smirks and smiles, while they are lying.

For more than eight years, starting in 2003, life was very difficult for millions of civilians in Iraq because of the American occupation of their country. More than 2500 Iraqi civilians were killed at United States military checkpoints. Probably because they could not understand English, the commands and demands spoken to them, shouted at them, in English by the American soldiers. They didn't care if they understood what they told them to do or not because they had been told repeatedly they were sub-humans, and should be killed if there was any doubt. But only about 60 of these murdered Iraqi's were proven to actually be "insurgents". The rest had no guns or weapons and posed no threat to

American soldiers. But the soldiers were just doing what they had been told to do. After all, all people in Iraq were just a part of the expendable masses. They were what Bush "W" and Cheney repeatedly called "collateral damage". But no Iraqis posed a threat to Americans in America ever.

As many innocent Iraqis were murdered at these United States military checkpoints by American soldiers as the people who were murdered at the World Trade Centers in New York City on September 11, 2001 by hijackers from Saudi Arabia, most of whom were living in the United States.

Iraqi social structures and culture were destroyed. Jobs disappeared and banks were robbed of all their money, so there was no money, no income for food and other necessities. After United States forces destroyed the sources of electricity, running water, and plumbing they were never restored completely in those eight years. Millions of Iraqi civilians had those utilities for just a few hours every day for eight years, if they had any at all. United States forces destroyed their infrastructures, after the Iraqis had done nothing to the United States Government or to United States citizens to justify any of it. But, not to forget, Iraq had, and has, the second largest oil reserves in the world.

Bush "W" had said "We will bring them water and food and medical care." They had had all of those for centuries, until American forces took them away and did not restore what they had destroyed, as promised. But American contractors had been given hundreds of billions of dollars to rebuild Iraq. Who stole that money? Where did it go? It was not used to rebuild Iraq. Part of it was used to build permanent United States Government and military complexes, vast structures covering miles of land.

In 2003 about 10,000 Iraqi criminals were released from prisons in Iraq because of the United States invasion. There was no police for protection for Iraqi citizens because they had been disbanded, following orders by American soldiers. So banks were looted, robbed of millions of dollars in deposits, leaving millions of Iraqi people destitute. The American privatized military, the paramilitary, and other contactors followed no rules of conduct, and were free to do whatever they wanted to do to the Iraqi people with no repercussions, being held accountable for nothing. The United States military did not follow the Geneva Convention rules for conduct, etc. in occupied countries. Fear of American men, in and out of uniform, was justified.

American occupation destroyed their cities and towns, their lives as they had been. All this misery was forced on millions of people who had done nothing to America or Americans. They offered no resistance to the American invasion. They had no weapons, no guns to resist the American forces of destruction. Americans in America were powerless to stop any of this, the injustices and pain, the death and suffering in Iraq. They were powerless against the waves of Republican hysteria and hype, the lies, the Government control and Government threats to those who spoke out against anything. America as it had been was no more. The changes and loss of freedoms for most people in America were permanent, or were to become permanent.

American newspaper and magazine reporters who reported what was really happening in Iraq for the American Press were fired, put in prison for indefinite lengths of time with no legal representation because of The Patriot Act, or were murdered, dying mysteriously under strange and unlikely conditions. An example was the newspaper reporter in 2012 who, in the wide open spaces of desolate Syria, died of a so-called allergic attack, a reported allergic reaction to his horse that had never happened before, as he was escaping from Syria with his information, with his articles and reports about what was *really* happening in Syria. He had established for himself a reputation for reporting the truth, for reporting what he really saw in Syria. But in America reporting the truth has become a very dangerous thing since 2001. It isn't, however, worth dying for.

Since the 2000 Presidential election the United States Government infrastructure has represented itself, not the will of the people in America. Except the Republicans, the Far Right, and the Neo Cons, which make up only about 1/3 of the American voting population. Therefore, the United States stopped being a Democracy, a true and genuine Democracy, since the elections of 2000, and especially since 2001. In 2001 Congress signed into law the Patriot Act without any of them even reading it. The rest of America could not have been expected to have read the 365 page document of new laws and plans for a new America in the 21$^{st}$ century because it was not available for the American public to read. That was the job of their elected representatives, who did not do their jobs, who did not do what they had been elected to do and were paid about $150,000 salary every year to do, because they were afraid of being labeled "unpatriotic" in the media, and then not being re-elected. After all, the benefits on the side are up to a millions dollars every year.

Millions of Americans saw documentaries about these problems, and heard coverage about some of these problems on NPR, but no one could change or stop anything. In old Communist Russia people who wanted to reform or change the government, the state, were considered to be insane and needed to be punished and/or imprisoned as political prisoners. Or sent to mental asylums or mental hospitals and heavily medicated with mind-altering drugs until they were unable to function as normal people. Since 2001 and The Patriot Act anyone in America, citizen or not, can be held in prisons indefinitely, forever, without charges and without legal representation and counsel, without a trial. Homeland Security in America was named after and patterned after Homeland Security in Hitler's Nazi Germany, not by coincidence or chance.

America as a nation of equal justice under the law is no more. For more than 200 years this is what set the United States apart from other countries. Because of The Patriot Act of 2001 equal justice under the law disappeared for the majority of Americans, the expendable masses, most of which still don't even know it. The elite, of course, are protected. However, states are not slaves to the Federal Government, so between 300 and 400 cities have passed resolutions against adopting and enforcing The Patriot Act within their boundaries, within their jurisdiction. These are the places in America that are truly democratic, true democracies in a sea of meanness and viciousness that can be found anywhere and everywhere else in America. These are some of the biggest ways that America has changed in the 21$^{st}$ century that were, and are, completely out of the control of 99% of the people in America. Except for the states that refused to endorse and accept The Patriot Act.

Live in these Republican places, and find out for yourself. Republicans, especially the Far Right, the Religious Right, and the Neo Cons, are often mean, controlling, and oddly dangerous people who often will smile at your face and stab you in the back. Apparently they feel they are superior to Democrats, maybe to all other people, for some unknown reason. What used to be a Southern personality type before has spread, permeated, and become the norm for Republicans in the United States, especially Republican and Neo Con politicians, and the Far Right politicians.

Maybe it's the norm for the unelected government and the secret government. Maybe it's what the Shadow Government people have been talking about, and writing about, for almost a hundred years. Just what does this secret government do? Apparently they control the controllers, the elected and unelected politicians of the United States, making *them* the true rulers of America.

When the invading and conquering Spaniards pillaged new lands they tortured and murdered millions of indigenous people in the name of Christianity, for expansion of their empires. Christianity and other religions has been the reason, the excuse, for wars and injustices, abuse of human rights, and torture for more than a thousand years. As an example, in the 1600's Spaniards invaded the Bahamas and tortured and killed all of the three million people, mostly Indians, living on the islands, except for about 300 people. They must have been the elite, the upper class, as Christianity seems to favor the upper class. This is just one of many proofs of the demented viciousness, meanness, and self-righteousness of people, of nations, of governments and of countries who think they are superior to other people, and usually use their religions to justify it.

It has never been just the United States that has been guilty of this, since its beginning, but it has included America since the founding fathers from England began the invasion and colonization of America. The United States has not been better than people in other countries in their quest for dominance, power, and control. But, as a matter of fact, no other country has engaged in wars exclusively in other countries since after World War II, killing and wounding millions of people in the process, except the United States. In America itself there has been constant violations of human rights that were guaranteed in The Constitution and The Bill of Rights for its citizens.

It's not imperialism. It's domination through cruelty since the beginning of America, before it became the United States of America, because of a peculiar and mean sense of superiority to other people that is perpetuated and passed on by one generation after the other, and by the people in power in America at any given time.

In 2012 former Vice President Cheney, 76 years old, got a heart transplant. He jumped ahead of thousands of much younger people who needed a better heart to continue living. It must have been because he was a Neo Con formerly in power, ruling the United States, a Vice President who acted and thought like he was the President, who didn't run for President because he wouldn't have been elected because nobody liked him except the Neo Cons. And who acquiesced to Bush "W" running for President because people liked him a lot better. Cheney always scowled, Bush "W" always smiled.

Or it was because he was a multi-millionaire, actually a billionaire. After all, he was the driving force behind 9/11 happening and the war in Iraq, making more people billionaires in the United States than ever before in American history, including Cheney. In 2011 Democratic Vice President Biden had a yearly income of about $300,000. Odds are if he was on a list for a heart transplant he would not have pushed off thousands of younger people. To prevent rejection of the newly transplanted heart very expensive drugs have to be taken indefinitely. Maybe Cheney got them for free because he was "special", besides having millions, and billions, of dollars to pay for them himself.

A person living in poverty in the United States would not have been able to get a heart transplant because no insurance would cover that. They would have had to pay for excessively high drugs, legal drugs, and excessively high hospital costs because they had no insurance. This would have been an impossibility for hundreds of millions of Americans. Yet, Cheney was special.

He ordered the murder of hundreds of thousands of people in Iraq by the United States military, mostly to be done by about 200,000 privatized military contractors and the paramilitary under Rumsfeld. Cheney had procured no-bid contracts for them, like he did for Halliburton and KBR, which was connected to Halliburton, for which he had been the CEO before becoming Vice President of the United States in 2001.They were paid at least $60 *billion dollars* to do jobs they never actually did. The United States military would have actually done all the same jobs for pennies on the dollar because of their pledged loyalty to God and country, because of their honesty and pride, because they were part of the United States military, the largest military in the World. This, after all, is the reason the United States has been called a super-power, the strongest country in the World.

In 2012 a military man was given a less-than-honorable discharge and his pension was taken away because he had criticized President Obama on Facebook, the social internet site. He said he was exercising his freedom of speech, his freedom of expression. He obviously didn't know The Patriot Act had taken that away from all Americans in 2001,and was signed into perpetuation, perpetuity, by President Obama in 2011, ten years later. It was a two-party coalition from the beginning, in 2001.

Cheney became a billionaire as rewards for his unbelievable selfishness, his ordering of tortures and murders of hundreds of thousands of Iraqi people, and because of his theft from the American people. As an example, Halliburton charged the United States Government $345 to $450 for a six-pack of Coca Cola, produced in Iraq and purchased by the military in Iraq, hundreds of millions of times from 2003 to 2011. Whenever any of this was brought before the Senate it was ignored and dismissed. Obama pressured his white female Senatorial opponent to drop out of the Illinois election in his first run for Senator. Was she paid off? Was it done by the Democrats in power, or by both the Democrats and the Republicans, the Neo Cons, in power at that time? Once she dropped out and was out of the picture he won by default, having no opponent. He couldn't lose. This was part of his progression to be President. But was it legitimate? Being a Senator gave him instant credibility to be the President. It was a necessary part of their total plan. He couldn't lose, just like they/he knew he couldn't, and wouldn't, lose his campaign to be President of the United States.

Perhaps it was a coalition to get the advertised and so-called "the people's President" in power, the first black American President in United States history, in order to counteract the damage, the vast and irreparable damage, done by the Neo Cons President Bush "W" and Cheney as part of the Neo Con's published plans to change America in the 21st century. In his acceptance speech Obama said that his being President was "the people's victory", not just his victory. Nothing that happened in the Bush "W" administration was ever "the people's victory", especially including his being appointed and not elected President in 2000/2001. But maybe Obama as President wasn't really the people's victory either. Maybe it happened because of a collaboration of manipulation of and dishonesty to the American public by both political parties to make sure he became the President. After all, he, and his wife, acted like he had prior confirmation that he would be President after his two-year campaign.

Corruption is part of politics, but that doesn't mean anything should be overlooked because the President is black, as many issues were overlooked repeatedly during his unusually long two year campaign. Many issues and important problems were ignored and avoided for the entire two years. Black people need to have the same standards of behavior and accountability for what they do as the rest of the people, all colors and races, in America. This is so obvious, but it isn't an expectation in America. An arrogant attitude of entitlement to privileged treatment by black people is common. Demand for special money programs and disbursement of money, during crises or not, and special requirements (lower) for anything, are uniquely black in America and not found for any other colors or races in America, or found in any other country in the World.

Lower requirements for jobs, including Federal and state civil service and the private sector, and lower requirements for education, grades, graduation, and college admission are standard. The NAACP has been a powerful force in making sure this is part of American culture, a part of American society. The NAACP is run by, promoted by, influenced by, black men who are racist, so there is a double standard. But double standards are very common in American society, for the private sector and for the public. This includes for male versus female, color, race, and for financial status.

For many years millions of white people have encountered difficulties, hardships, and unfair treatment because of "Affirmative Action". It needs to stop, to be eliminated. It needs to end. It is, and always has been, prejudice against all other races in America that aren't black. An incentive to businesses has long been government supplements for wages if they hire a black person instead of white. This has caused justified resentment of whites, and other colors and races, toward blacks.

Rodney King was being watched by Los Angeles policemen because they knew he usually carried a 357 Magnum. Why hadn't they arrested him for that, as a probation violation? He had killed a man for $11 and gone to prison, but was on probation at the time police stopped him in his SUV and the fiasco ensued. None of that information was allowed in the courtroom during the resulting trial of those policemen. Withholding vital, crucial, necessary information is a procedure repeated every day everywhere in the United States in courtrooms. He sued the city of Los Angeles and won, and was awarded a settlement of $3.2 million dollars. The settlement was outrageous and totally un-called for. Probably at least a thousand other men, white and black and Mexican, and probably Vietnamese and Chinese, had experienced the same police response, the same treatment by Los Angeles policemen and gotten no money for it, no settlement. If a white man had sued for the same circumstances it is unlikely he would have gotten any money at all, let alone $3.2 million dollars, because white people are expected to take responsibility for what they do that is a violation of the law. Unless they are very wealthy, have connections, or are drug dealers, especially in Indiana.

In New Orleans a business called Innovation Emergency Management (IEM) was given a government contract and a grant for $500,000 in 2004 to plan hurricane evacuation, a year before Hurricane Katrina hit New Orleans. Immediately after Hurricane Katrina hit no one was allowed to give help, emergency help, because IEM was supposed to be in charge. Nobody else could do anything. No agency that was private or government, no group of authorities or individual authorities, no rescuers of any type, could do anything until IEM did something because they were supposed to be in charge, according to Louisiana's government authorities. But IEM did nothing, no emergency management, no hurricane evacuation. They were never held accountable for their unbelievable incompetence and indifference. There were no fines and no punishment for the deaths and suffering they had caused, that they had allowed to happen.

A year later IEM was given a Government gift of *one million dollars* to do a study about why they did nothing and, as a result, 1500 people died and half a million people suffered, many for months and years, because of their incompetence and stupidity. IEM should have been sued and put out of business, not rewarded with a million dollar gift from the Government. They must have had the right political connections. One of the many notoriously corrupt Louisiana Senators must have gotten the original contract and grant for them, for someone he knew, and then the renewal of that contract with a million dollar bonus for doing a horrible job, an unbelievably awful job, that meant 1500 people lost their lives as a result. This is a good example of how the wrong people are rewarded in government-related jobs and performances. And it is an example of how the wrong people are hired, and elected, to begin with. Competency and excellence have nothing to do with it.

The Army Corps of Engineers, a Federal agency, had informed Bush "W" that the New Orleans levees had broken, and flooding was inevitable, *24 hours* before Bush "W" had notified New Orleans officials. So people in New Orleans lost 24 hours for evacuation. Because Hurricane Katrina had done little damage, no more than other hurricanes, the worst was not expected. Later, this could have been a reason for impeachment, but because of the cowardice of the Democratic Party nothing happened to President Bush "W" for his incompetence that caused untold damage and suffering and 1500 deaths in New Orleans and the surrounding towns.

Yet, a few years before, the Republican Party spent hundreds of millions of dollars of American taxpayer's money to try to impeach President Clinton because one of his interns gave him oral sex, and Clinton said it wasn't really sex. The Republicans said he was lying. According to them it *was* sex. It didn't matter to them that it was a matter of social and personal definition. This was much worse according to Republicans than the unnecessary deaths of 1500 people, and the suffering of at least a million other people, in a preventable disaster for which Republican politicians and the Republican President were negligent and responsible. This was not what a Government by the people and for the people was supposed to be like. It wasn't what America was supposed to be like.

If the same thing had happened in another country the United States Government would have sent relief supplies, medical help, temporary housing, and millions of dollars of money in monetary assistance within days. But people who experienced major devastation from Hurricane Katrina on the Gulf Coast in Mississippi got nothing from the Federal Government for weeks, or even months, or never. For those people in Louisiana the situation was only a little better. If they had all been in another country they would have gotten a much better reaction from the United States Government. The Louisiana State Government wasn't much better for its own citizens.

Within a few days the Canadian Government offered assistance from Canada, thousands of miles away. The first responses giving help were from church groups as far away as Pennsylvania and North Carolina. They rebuilt and repaired thousands of houses for free, charging nothing, besides giving other help like food and water, especially for victims in Mississippi. Mostly this was done with no news coverage, no media coverage.

Laws can be unequal and unfair. An example is illegal copying of a DVD or video, which is a copyright infringement and violation, validating an investigation by the FBI, a fine up to $250,000, and five years in prison. Murder brings as little as five years in prison, no fine, and getting out in as little as three years because of good behavior or because of prison over-crowding. Or 7 years in prison and out in 5 for possession of a few ounces of illegal drugs. Making a copy of a DVD or video can bring more punishment than committing a murder or having a few ounces of illegal drugs, apparently because it takes money away from someone who has position, wealth, and power, taking money away from someone who is already rich, or from a corporation that is valuable in the scheme of things. Injustices and abuse of civil rights, of human rights, are found throughout American history for all people except the elite, the ruling class, the wealthy, and politicians. The justice system can be, and has been, unjust and unfair for millions of people, who then are victims of the justice system.

There were huge holes in levees in New Orleans before Hurricane Katrina hit in 2005 that had not been repaired because the Army Corps of Engineers was incompetent and corrupt. Not because they didn't have the money to do it. After the resulting loss of lives and property from these avoidable wide spread disasters no charges were ever made, no legal actions were ever taken against the Army Corps of Engineers in Louisiana. They were above the law because they are, and were, a Government agency.

Even though the United States Government gives the Army Corps of Engineers hundreds of millions of dollars *every* year they hadn't used it to repair what needed to be repaired as part of their jobs. Saving lives and protecting the public and their property from disasters hasn't been as important as hoarding that money for themselves. This huge monetary theft from the American people for many years resulted in many levee repairs not being done that the American taxpayer, and especially Louisiana taxpayers, had paid them to do. They were never held accountable for anything wrong that happened because of what they did or didn't do, or for what they had done or hadn't done.

Just like no charges were ever made against the oil companies for the massive and deadly oil spills that covered most of New Orleans after Hurricane Katrina had hit, mixing with the Mississippi River overflowing the broken levees. They were the cause of the death of thousands of people and about 10,000 pet animals. These were deaths that wouldn't have happened if the huge and massive oil containers and the Mississippi River had been properly restrained, and contained, like those industries are paid by thy Louisiana State Government and Federal Government to do. More than eight *million* gallons of oil were released for days into the New Orleans area and into the Mississippi River after the levees failed. Everything that had happened had been preventable if they had done their jobs right, if people had done what they got paid to do, for many years

In 2011 there were still huge holes in levees on the Mississippi River when it flooded again. And again, because of the incompetence and financial theft of the Army Corps of Engineers, thousands of people were left injured or homeless or died, and massive property damage, costing millions of dollars to repair and replace, was the result. Again, there was no punishment, fines, or accountability. It seems that government offices and departments and government agencies cannot be sued or held accountable for anything ever, at both state and federal levels.

# CHAPTER FIVE

## Culture, Politics, and Lies

Part of the American culture is to say "You can be anything you want to be." This is just a fantasy, a theory, a kind of propaganda, because it rarely is true. It rarely is a reality. Instead it's who you know and are you wealthy, from a wealthy and prosperous family background. Or do you know someone who is wealthy and/or connected to politics and politicians in America. Millions of kids at any given time probably think they want to be the President of the United States someday. Maybe one or two of them will. The odds, then, are about a million to one. The odds are better for everything else, for all other occupations, but the reality is still the same. Most people in America cannot be whatever they want to be. The odds are against it. No matter how hard they try.

Albert Einstein didn't make up or invent, or discover, the energy equation E=MC squared. His wife did. They were both in graduate school in Germany, had barely passing grades, and agreed with a professor to accept one passing grade, so both wouldn't fail, by combining the credits both he and his wife had. They had studied together for years and the head of the physics department thought they deserved one degree since they were married. He thought Albert should be the one to pass because he would be the head of the household. Later she wrote a paper about *her* energy theory but put her husband's name on it, Albert Einstein, so it would be published because she didn't have the Ph.D. credentials. He, after all, had been given the Ph.D. as a result of their mutual efforts.

Before he got the Nobel Peace Prize for that paper, that theory, that formula, they agreed he would take credit for it and she would get the prize money of $100,000. After he got the Nobel Prize and the notoriety, the fame, and she got the money she divorced him because of his years of being unfaithful to her, his years of having affairs with other women. She bought a duplex and moved into it with their two sons. He then married his long-time girlfriend.

He never had any break-through ideas, no revolutionary ideas, before that or after that. But in the United States he had national adoration, fame, love, a great career, financial stability, national recognition and respect. To a large extent this was because of the media and the Press promoting him to the American public. He was revered in America because of a lie, a fraud, played out until after he died, that persists more than 50 years after it began. She, however, died in a mental hospital in Europe, never having revealed the truth about her former husband and about E=MC squared, and the truth about the famous paper and very famous formula she had discovered and written about, not Albert Einstein. Apparently she was forced to be in a mental hospital, and to subsequently die, because of covert efforts to make sure the American public and the scientific community would never find out the truth about Albert Einstein and E=MC squared.

In the 21st century a common personality trait of adults in the United States, all colors, all classes, all races, ail cultures, is unfriendliness and suspiciousness. Friendliness is likely to be a means to an end. Truth is often lies. Things often aren't what they seem. People are often dishonest about their honesty, unfriendly about their friendliness, mean about their kindness, lie when they're telling the truth. Corruption and distortion of the truth, at all levels, is part of the American persona. It's the American way, at all levels of society and government, science, religion, politics, and education.

Whatever happens on a national level is often repeated on local levels. It was disinterest on the part of the Baton Rouge Police Department, in evidence given to them from the Breau Bridge Police Department, that enabled a serial killer to continue to kill more women in Louisiana in about 2003. Disinterest in, or indifference to, women who are being harassed or are in danger of escalated danger is too common everywhere in the United States by law enforcement. Preferential treatment of men in general is also very common. Protecting men more than women is common.

The other side of this issue is the unwillingness of Police Departments and Sheriff Departments everywhere in the United States to co-operate with each other, or with the FBI, or with the CIA, etc., or vice versa. This long-standing unwillingness to co-operate has resulted in untold numbers of unsolved crimes, deaths, injuries, suffering, and waste of money and time for many years..

For Attorney General Ashcroft, who had no qualifications to be the United States Attorney General when he was appointed by President Bush "W", it was his disinterest in information repeatedly given to him from the FBI weeks before 9/11, then days before 9/11, that American passenger planes were going to be hi-jacked and then flown into two buildings in New York City by men from Saudi Arabia, that allowed it to happen. That could explain how and why an unbelievable *4000* employees from Israel didn't go to their jobs in the Twin Towers in New York City on 9/11, 2001. It offers proof of a deliberate collaboration between Bush "W", Cheney, Rove, Rumsfeld, Ashcroft, and Wolfowitz to manipulate the American people for what was planned to happen, for what was going to happen, on 9/11, in 2001.

It implies prior knowledge of what was going to happen, which would explain why President Bush "W" did not react after a Secret Service man told him the Twin Towers had been destroyed by alleged terrorists in American planes, as he was sitting in a Florida grade school classroom. Instead, as President of the United States, he sat and said *nothing* to anyone for *seven* minutes. It all seemed to be planned, as a manipulation of the American public, almost 330 million of them, to look like something it wasn't. To provide a cover for everything that was planned to happen after that.

Throughout American history there have been struggles against hostility and violence paid for by and perpetuated by Far Right Republicans and the ruling class, and politicians and organized crime. If America really was the land of the free, the land of justice and freedom for everyone, those struggles for equal and fair treatment for all colors and all races for almost 350 years would not have happened. It's always been who has the best weapons and the most weapons, the biggest and the best guns, and who is backed by the most money and the best political forces.

The struggles of the Native American Indians, the first inhabitants of America, was the longest lasting struggle against vastly superior-armed American soldiers, both white and black. It was a slow and continuing attempt at genocide and annihilation of an entire race by American soldiers who were just doing their jobs, what they were told to do by their superior officers. It was a shameful and unjustified continuing violence and hostility toward the entire race of Indians in America, that continued for more than 250 years. It was a genocide that meant the British colonizers especially, and other nationalities of colonizers of America, were not superior to the native Indians like they thought they were, and that life, liberty, and the pursuit of happiness for all people in America was a lie. In their pursuit of freedom Indians, the original people here, had no freedom and no rights.

Native American Indians that survived were forced to live on Government-run reservations that had inferior land, or even useless land with no access to water for irrigation so they could grow food.

This made them unable to live like they had for centuries, and for even thousands of years. The white man had deliberately killed all the buffalo in order to decimate the tribes. They couldn't escape the destitution and the poverty on the reservations. The United States Government controlled them by controlling their economies, their ability to live and to support themselves, and their supply of money. It destroyed their governments, their cultures, and their way of life.

This was similar to how the United States Government, the IMF, and the World Bank control the economies of other countries in the 21st century, by controlling their money through the International Monetary Fund and the World Bank. Manipulation is a big part of the American culture, nationally and internationally, starting at the top with the ruling elite and filtering down to the expendable masses.

In the 20th century another lesser struggle in America involved millions of working class people against the ruling class, against the owners of industries, politicians, and organized crime that lasted for about thirty years. The methods they used against the Unions of workers, what they did against them, was often illegal, violent, and hostile. But whether something is against the law or not has never meant anything to politicians, to Far Right Republicans, to the ruling class, or to organized crime. Laws have never stood in their way. For them laws are there to be broken. These groups have always been against the formation and continuance of Unions for working class people in America. They have always tried hard to destroy Unions, and have often succeeded.

At one time 39% of working Americans were members of Unions. Now, in the second decade of the 21st century, only 7% of American workers are members of Unions. For many years the Unions have been destroyed by outside forces, with relentless efforts to break them up, with on-going hostilities and violence, including murders of participants and Union officials and leaders, in an attempt to limit their powers and to end their organized and unified power of the many over the more powerful few. It was a noble effort and struggle while it lasted. The concepts and benefits of Unions in America were accomplished, while improving the wages and working conditions for many millions of people in lower-class and middle-class America, despite the efforts of that selfish and rich part of America that was against that happening.

If we are a nation of laws why is there so much injustice? Using fear, bribery, threats, and pay-offs for co-operation and control occurs at all levels of society. Like Democratic Senators were obviously controlled in 2000 so there would be no Senators objecting to the obviously dishonest official declaration of Bush "W" as the winner in Florida in 2000, so he could be appointed the next President of the United States. It was obvious even Vice President Gore had been controlled by the Far Right Republicans as he repeatedly banged the gavel in a rude and disrespectful way to interrupt the Congressmen who, one after the other, tried to stop that illegal process from happening. They were literally standing *for* him, while he was strangely and oddly being against them. But not one Senator would sign the Congressmen's complaints, as was required. It appeared repeatedly that the Neo Cons in power had gotten to them in some way to instill fear of asserting what was right.

In order for the American Government to be by the people and for the people the United States Government would have to stop being corrupt, stop taking bribes and payoffs, stop the manipulating everywhere at all levels, and serve the American public instead of themselves. The vision of United States politicians does not align itself with reality for the American people. It aligns with greed and personal gain and power for politicians, for themselves. Elections bring no relief, no real changes, just *hope* for change, and *promises* for changes that rarely happen. Corruption, fraud, theft, at all levels of

Government, increased more than ever before under the Bush "W" administration.

The good people in America, the honest people in America, don't want this to happen ever again. But this was a part of the New World Order that Neo Con Republicans in power represented and intended to create and continue during the rest of the 21st century. Their plans didn't end when the Bush "W" administration ended.

In the United States in 2010 Democrats were 72 million people, Republicans were 55 million people, and Independents were a surprising 48 million people, mostly voting Democrat. That means a Republican majority is unlikely for a Presidential election. But the Democrats have always been a weak party, unable to change or fight for what needs to be done. Unable to stand up to the Republican troublemakers. Since 2001 Republican politicians argue about everything just for the sake of arguing and polarizing America, because it works.

This includes FOX TV news personalities who spend all day every day trying to polarize Americans, arguing and criticizing endlessly and repeatedly all day every day and night 24/7. Their Republican audience of many millions of people loves it. The manipulative and dishonest Cable TV news personalities give them exactly what they want, and are extremely well paid because of it. Their opinions polarize America. It isn't news, it's just their opinions. Making Democrats look bad is the Republican strategy for the new century to get Republicans voted in and Democrats voted out. And it has worked very well, along with the inevitable corruption thrown in.

For a few hundred years the Republican Party fought against women and black people getting the vote because that would tilt the vote in favor of Democrats, the Party for all Americans, the Party that was by the people and for the people, including everybody, not just the rich. When they were given the vote the Republican Party had to devise ways to overcome the slanted majority numbers and majority sentiments. The Republican powers-that-be developed ways to overcome the constant and consistent Democratic majority. In order to foster the speed of the Neocon Republican plans for "A New World Order In The 21st Century" their systems of corruption stepped in and mostly took over before the 2000 Presidential election of Bush "W".

Then the Republican Supreme Court Judges stepped in and stopped the counting of votes because, despite the massive corruptions of the Republican Party, Gore was still going to win the Presidential election if nothing else could be done. So a criminal act was sanctioned by the Republican Supreme Court Judges to do something that had never been done before in Federal elections. Their cover was a ruling they made that it could never happen again. Subsequently three of the Judges had grown children that were given Federal Government positions with Bush "W" after they appointed him President as a result of their illegal actions, made legal because those laws were temporarily suspended. The "rule of law" did not apply to Supreme Court Judges at that time because Bush "W' desperately needed their help to become President, and they got big benefits in return. It was a corrupt legal and social complicity, probably worse than any other political and judicial complicit dishonesty in the entire history of the United States.

Every United States President since World War I has lied to get the United States into wars, invasions, attacks, and occupations, saying "I oppose war, but war is necessary for peace." Or, "It's being done to bring freedom and peace and democracy to other countries." It has been a political and military complicity, since World War I, that means the United States military kills millions of people in foreign countries, drops bombs on them, shoots at them and injures them, allegedly to bring them freedom from violence and fear of their rulers, to supposedly help them. It's like how American hunters say they have to kill wild animals so they won't die from starvation. It's lies and manipulation.

In both cases it's convoluted and twisted distorted logic and lies to validate and justify their cruelties and unlimited killing, to validate their need for power and control. This has been the price of liberty for people in other countries when the United States brings it to them. Killing people, hurting and injuring people, mass destruction of property and homes, and even destroying entire countries, is an act of kindness and altruism according to United States Presidents, politicians, and to the United States military complex. And, last but not least, according to the American psyche.

Since WW I Presidents of the United States justify military action by the United States military towards little countries, less than 1/10 or even 1/50 the size of the United States, with a tiny fraction of the military size and yearly expenditure for their military compared to the United States. Often, the United States has given hundreds of millions of dollars to that country for weapons to be purchased from the United States. Enthusiasm for these wars is generated by lies, deception, and propaganda, but support *has* to be maintained by the TV news media and the Press. So that necessitates more manipulation of the public. Lies become accepted as truth because of their repetition. The Government controls the media in order to control the public. The media doesn't ask for proof because they are afraid, or are just incompetent. However, there can't be a real democracy without the free-flow of truthful information. History has proven this to be true for all countries.

The TV news media, especially the Republican TV news media, and the press commonly express contempt for anti-war ideas and sentiments, and are vicious and threatening in response. If a person is pro-war then they are being "objective", and if a person is anti-war then they are being "biased", according to these media moguls and their spokespersons, their journalists and writers.

Individuals who have the courage to publically protest anything the Government does, or to reveal anything that politicians do or the Government does that is wrong, risk getting death threats, losing their jobs, damage to their cars or homes, threats to their family members, or actually getting shot at or killed. All of which the police will probably do nothing about. "Protect and serve" is often out of the question. This is America. If you don't believe it talk to people who have experienced it.

For years after one of the Dixie Chicks made a public statement about the Iraqi war, just one short sentence made at one of their concerts, their records were banished from radio stations and radio broadcasts and commercial sales throughout America. Obviously there is not freedom of speech and freedom of expression in the United States unless the Republican side of the altered Democracy gives their approval. Viciousness and meanness in the United States usually comes from Republicans. It's a Republican character trait, and a necessary part of the Neo Con personality in the 21st century.

After 2000 the United States stopped being the model for democracy that it had tried to be since 1776. It stopped being "by the people and for the people". It stopped being "with liberty and justice for all". Democratic politicians didn't stop the Republican corruption in any way, so they were as corrupt in another way. The reputation of the United States suffered greatly under the Bush "W" administration in the estimation of the rest of the world, as they tried to remake the Middle East and spread American power, their power, worldwide.

After the Viet Nam war objective journalism became a thing of the past. National news events have been staged and controlled by the Government, especially since 2000. The American people have been kept in the dark about what's really happening, especially with the military industrial complex. After Viet Nam the American public didn't see human suffering and deaths caused by American bombs, guns, and American soldiers. Just like flag-draped caskets of American soldiers and returning injured soldiers were prohibited from the media since Bush "W"/Cheney were in power. Opposition and dissent and media coverage was destroyed or eliminated when Republicans were in power between 2001 and 2009. Journalists and reporters and photographers who didn't get with the new program were fired, or killed while in foreign countries, like Syria and Iraq and Afghanistan..

Because President Bush "W" was President, and because Cheney was Vice President, United States citizens can be detained, and were detained, in the United States and then arrested and charged as an "enemy combatant". Protesting and marching can be called "terrorism", a crime of course, and "freedom of the Press" was replaced with restriction of the Press because of Federal Government intimidation, Government suppression, and possible arrest. The Bill H.R. 1955 criminalizes free speech and anything against the Government as terrorism.

The owner of Blackwater donated $2.4 million dollars to the Bush "W" campaign and in return got $5 million dollars in "no-bid" contracts in Iraq from the United States Government to rebuild what the United States Government and United States military forces had destroyed in Iraq. So Blackwater more than doubled its investment, which would have been a powerful incentive to invest in the first place. When under investigation the U.S. State Department protected Blackwater by refusing to answer questions and not holding Blackwater accountable for their actions, like murdering and torturing Iraqi citizens in Iraq. But Blackwater, like other U.S. companies in Iraq, did not rebuild Iraq for the Iraqis. Instead, huge permanent buildings were built, vast complexes of buildings covering miles of land, for the United States Government in Iraq, and for the United States military for its permanent occupation of Iraq. After all, Iraq has the second largest reserves of oil in the World.

Because of the Bush "W"/Cheney administration between one and two million United States citizens have been on "The Watch List", a Republican project, as possible terrorists. This Government list included United States citizens that said, or wrote, that the war in Iraq was a war that had no basis. It included benevolent politicians like Democratic Senator Edward Kennedy and even Mother Theresa from India, who was named a Saint by the Catholic Church after she died.

Democratic Senator Carnahan of Missouri and Democratic Senator Wellstone of Minnesota were passionately and fervently against the initiation of the Iraq war and were both killed in small private plane crashes only days or weeks before their pending elections, that also killed everyone else in their planes. Both had majority support and would have won their respective re-elections. Unbelievably, there was no Congressional or Democratic investigation, probably because of the cowardice of the Democratic Party, in general, and of most Democratic politicians.

Republicans call this "collateral damage", like Republicans have called the killing of 100,000 to 500,000 innocent Iraqi men, women, children, and babies by American forces collateral damage. The United States kept no account of these deaths in an attempt to diminish and deny their importance and actuality. It was like the methods of denial and indifference used by deputies and police in America. Namely, if there are no records or reports made then it never happened. Then there is no proof and no evidence. So it never happened, and no one can prove that it really did happen. Or if reports and records are kept they can easily be falsified, or just simply be lies from the beginning.

Distortion of The Constitution started with President Johnson in the 1960's, then continued with President Nixon in the 1970's, then President Bush in the 1980's, then President Bush "W" from 2001 to 2009. It's nothing new, as it continues in the 21st century. It's always been both a Democratic and Republican thing, shared political agendas. But it's mostly a Republican domain. In all free countries Democracies have taken many forms. Democracies both giveth and taketh away.

Congress doesn't represent American voters and the American people, the American public, especially in the 21st century. Instead it represents corporations, lobbyists, military interests, and where the money is. But in a democracy it is the responsibility of the Government to be honest and truthful, and protect its citizens, not attack them, as happened on 9/11, 2001. As was allowed to happen on 9/11, 2001. It's the responsibility of the public, of the American people, to demand it. But not if the United States National Guard or local police force is going to shoot at them. To demand rights given in The Constitution and The Bill of Rights, guaranteed by The Constitution and The Bill of Rights, is a dangerous proposition, especially since 2001.

It has filtered down to local levels, where police and deputy protection and serving the community cannot be counted on, or relied upon ever for any issues. Counting on them to help, in all places in the United States, is a thing of the past. All organized public demonstrations in America since after World War II involving from 10 to 500,000 people, even a million people marching and protesting in Washington, D.C. in the 1960's because of the Viet Nam war, have been ignored by American Presidents and politicians increasingly since the 1960's. For the past 70 years anti-Government demonstrations have never changed anything.

Unlike in other democracies, like France, where demonstrators have always made a difference, making changes where they need to be made as a result of both political reactions and political compromise. In America organized opposition to any government actions, or protests of any kind, have always had the risk of demonstrators, participants, being clubbed, shot at with guns and rifles, sprayed with tear gas, or being killed or injured by the local law enforcement or the National Guard. This has also always happened in regimes, anarchies, dictatorships, and Communist countries, but not in other free countries, not in any of the other 23 Democracies in the World.

What happened to freedom of speech, freedom of expression, freedom of assembly, The Constitution, and The Bill of Rights? Since 9/11 happened in 2001 hundreds of billions of phone calls, even trillions of phone calls, have been monitored 24/7 everywhere in the United States by the Federal Government. Every cell phone and computer in the United States is monitored by vast Government computer spying networks. Targeted words, concepts, ideas set off red-flag responses, and warrant that person being monitored by the Federal Government and Government computers. Since 2001 the predictions of the book "1984", with "Big Brother" watching and monitoring all citizens, had come true. If you didn't support the war in Iraq you were labeled "un-American", "a traitor", or "anti-American", according to official Government records.

After one of the Dixie Chicks, the singing group from Texas, said at a concert that they were "ashamed of President Bush being from Texas", because he started the war in Iraq, the group was blacklisted and sent death threats for years, undoubtedly by Republicans. Their records weren't played by radio stations in Texas, and in other Republican dominated states and cities, or regions of the United States, for about eight years. They received death threats from men, undoubtedly crazy Republican men, for those years.

In general, Republicans think they have a right to threaten, shoot at, and kill anyone who says something they don't want to hear. Just like lunatics and crazy men and women do. But no one, anywhere, does anything to stop it. It's a Republican attitude about America. It's their attitude of "America, right or wrong." But it isn't remotely something that should happen, or be allowed to happen, or just tolerated, in a true democracy. Welfare and safety of *everyone* should be protected.

Helen Thomas had been the leading White House reporter for about 40 years. When she was about 80 years old she said to a sports reporter that Bush "W" was the worst President she had ever covered. The sports reporter reported that, repeating it in a newspaper article. She was never allowed to ask questions at White House Press conferences ever again. She was a threat to the Bush "W" Administration. She lost her long-time job of being a White House reporter for 40 years, as did all other TV and newspaper reporters and editors who criticized Bush "W" or his actions, or asked for proof of anything. The United States Democracy became like a dictatorship for those eight years.

People who are honest rarely survive in American politics. Especially honest Democrats. They are assassinated, die mysteriously or in so-called "accidents", or are voted out by fixed elections. They have to play the game. Like Obama was playing the game since he was elected President. Because of the cowardice of the Democratic Party nothing is done about Republican political crimes, about Republican political criminal behavior, so the Republican Party continues its attitudes of, and practices of, being the bully, twisting and warping the truth, and of being connected to organized crime.

Bush "W" became President because 1.9 million votes were "lost", according to TV news media and the Press. Where did they all go? Nowhere. They just weren't counted. Investigations later showed that the voting machines provided by Diebold Corporation and others were rigged so that when a person voted for Gore it would to Bush "W" instead. There never was a congressional hearing or investigation of these crimes, nor were there any charges in any states or federally. In some states (Florida, Ohio, etc.) votes literally were not counted, and extra false votes were added to the Bush "W" total. The American public complained loudly, but were powerless to change the corruption. In any other election this can happen again. The American people cannot stop it.

In the years of the Bush "W" reign Attorney General Ashcroft, Rumsfeld, Cheney, Rove and Bush "W" all had said they didn't have to follow laws. They were above the law, apparently. Along with Perle, Wolfowitz, Jeb Bush, and Libby, and many others listed on the front of one of their Neo Con 21st century control America reports, they were the Neo Con group that intended to change the United States from a Democracy to an American empire. A new kind of American imperialism was to reign in the 21st century, according to their control America reports published in 1997 and in 2000. The way to do it was through military might and bombing of small countries, telling the American public they were bringing the little countries freedom and peace from their dictatorships. However, since the 1950's the United States has usually installed, put into power, those same dictators. The American public would obey and support them, they were sure, as the American public was easily manipulated.

A "new Pearl Harbor", it says in the reports, would guarantee enough patriotism and coming together of the public to enable them, the Neo Cons, to do whatever they wanted to begin to dominate the world. If not, then threats of made-up alien UFO attacks would come to their rescue, and unite the American public in the future. Plans to reconstruct a bombed Iraq were begun by these men about five months before 9/11 happened, and about eight months before they bombed Iraq. Their plans were written down in their lengthy reports, written years before 2000.

Guantanamo prison was chosen by the Neo Con crew that ruled the United States because it's in Cuba, where no United States laws would apply. In that prison compound there has been no rule of law for the entire duration of the war. The United States military and United States Government also have not followed the Geneva Convention rules, international laws begun in 1954 to protect prisoners of war from terrible treatment used by the Nazis and Japanese during WWII.

Both the senior Bush and the junior Bush had given Saddam Hussein and Osama Bin Laden hundreds of millions of dollars through the Carlyle Group, an investment group of very wealthy people who invested primarily in defense contractors and weapons. They had a lot to gain with the war in Iraq and Afghanistan, that would make them bigger millionaires and even billionaires.

The United States Government has given hundreds of millions of dollars every year as foreign aid to Pakistan since the Bush "W" Administration started in 2001. This supposedly was where Bin Laden was living for years, and it's where terrorist training schools have operated for many years. What was that money used for? Where did it really go? No one really knows. Records are easily falsified. As always, some of it went to people in the United States, and in Pakistan, who then increased their wealth immensely, or became multi-millionaires, while ignoring the suffering and needs of the people in Pakistan. It was just the usual enriching of some at the expense of the many.

Most countries the United States gives money to for foreign aid every year don't need that foreign aid, that money, as much as the United States Government needs that money. In fact, since the Bush "W" Administration, none of these countries have had any yearly national debt, or had a national debt remotely as large as the United States Government debt, that was about $11.5 trillion dollars when Bush "W" left office in January 2009. But most media sources have always reported trillions of dollars less total yearly United States indebtedness, mostly because they are given wrong amounts. Reporters and TV news people only report the news they are given.

Since 2001 the United States Government has given Egypt billions of dollars of United States taxpayer's money. How many taxpayers would have wanted hundreds of billions of dollars of their tax money to go to all these countries? Probably none. Every year since 2001 there has been about 300,000 homeless people in the United States, including about 200,000 homeless veterans each year. Yet for years the United States Government gave a Saudi Arabian radio station $63 million dollars a year. Where did it go? How was it used? No one really knows. It was just another too generous gift from the American Government given to foreign people that did not need it, a gift that took money away from Americans that really did need it, and deserved it. Foreign aid has been a misappropriation of too much money for too many years. And there is nothing the American people can do to stop it.

In the last 70 years the United States Government has given away hundreds of billions of dollars, maybe totaling a trillion dollars of taxpayer's money, to foreign countries and countries that often hate the United States Government and the American people. For about 70 years the way to get financial aid from the United States is to go to war with the United States, or be a leader in a country that hates, or just dislikes, the United States, that then tries to buy their loyalty and affection. How many American taxpayers would have wanted their money to go to these countries and their leaders for at least 50 years? Probably none. Except the elite ruling class, the politicians, and the Shadow Government, who have long been a part of a monolithic and ruthless conspiracy to control the United States, probably since the 1970's. President Kennedy referred to this plan days before he was assassinated. Revealing this plan to Americans was dangerous, and might explain why so many people thought the CIA was involved, or behind, the murder of President Kennedy.

These are some of the millions of people that don't pay any taxes on their immense wealth, thanks to tax loopholes, tax evasion, tax accountants, tax write-offs, and their off-shore tax-free deposits of hundreds of billions of dollars every year, usually on small islands. Thanks to the fact they are citizens of the United States, with a national Government that allows this year after year, while other democracies, 23 other countries, do not allow the same tax evasion by the very rich in their countries. After these multi-millionaires and billionaires accumulate too much money, maybe a trillion dollars, in these tax-free off-shore accounts the Federal Government and the IRS gives them so-called "Tax Holidays" to avoid any semblance of deceit, deception, and theft from the American people, and dishonesty towards the continuance of the whole Democracy of America. But the IRS isn't even a Government agency. No one seems to know why it has so much power and authority.

Because of President Lincoln more than a million soldiers lost their lives in the Civil War, more American soldiers than in any war before or after. President Lincoln caused 450,000 soldiers from the North and 650,000 soldiers from the South to be killed, and at least a million to be injured, permanently or not, so black people could be freed from slavery in the South. Yet, Lincoln is revered as a great President, even "the greatest President" because he kept the union of the North and the South together. However, it seems the black population has never appreciated these sacrifices, the immense loss of life and suffering, the immense destruction and loss of property in the South, and the suffering and sacrifices of at least 100 million white people in the North and in the South.

Black people have expected entitlements endlessly for the slavery that happened in the South starting about 300 years ago and ending about 150 years ago, and special treatment and free money, special government programs and grants, etc. endlessly as compensation for that slavery 150 to 300 years ago. And they get them, because white Americans are easily taken advantage of and white politicians want to get the black vote. This is a different attitude than in all other countries that used black slaves as part of their culture for as much and as long ago as *six thousand years*.

Slavery, selling black people as slaves to the rest of the World, had been a part of the African culture and economy and other black cultures and economies for about *six thousand years*. American use of black people as slaves in the South was just a drop in the bucket compared to the length of time slavery happened in the rest of the civilized world. It's only the United States that has been on a guilt trip since slavery ended for the tiny *1%* of the white population in the South that actually had slaves. And only a small fraction of that 1% actually abused their black slaves. But the truth isn't what the black population in America has wanted for about 70 years. The truth never fitted in their agenda.

For thousands of years, not hundreds, almost every country in the World had bought black slaves, imported from Africa and other countries, as an important part of the African economy. Thousands of years before the United States was even thought of black Africans were captured and sold by other black Africans to other countries as slaves in order to make money. Black slavery export was an important African export industry for *thousands* of years. This is documented World history.

For white Americans to feel guilty about slavery in the South for the wealthiest 1% of that population 150 to 300 years ago is stupid and ridiculous. For about 150 years white Americans have allowed themselves to be pawns in this dishonest, very expensive, and stupid game. It needs to end. The reparations, the entitlements, the special financial programs, the special treatment, etc., should have ended a long time ago.

As an example, Obama would not have been able to go to Harvard, and have his tuition paid for at Harvard, if he had been white. He had had a C grade point average at another college before he was accepted and his tuition paid for at Harvard. No white person would have been accepted into Harvard from another College or University if they had a C average at that other College or University, and also had a C average from high school, like Obama did. That same white person would not, could not, have had their tuition paid for at Harvard. Harvard, along with other Colleges and Universities in America, has been racist for years in favor of admittance of black students and against admittance of even much better qualified white students. More and better is always expected of white people, as higher standards, in most of American life. Except for the white-trash population, millions of Americans in America who have lower standards of behavior, etc., or no standards at all.

Lincoln started and promoted a horrible war. The Union of the States, the United States, was saved at way too great a cost of lives, property, suffering, misery, and money. Maybe it was a tragedy that Lincoln was President of the United States at that time in history. But, as always, history depends on who writes it, and Americans usually believe what they are told and what they are taught to believe. If he was a great President he would have figured out, and implemented, a way to save the Union of the North and the South and free the slaves without a war. Historically, it was and has been the only war conducted in the United States, the only national war in America for hundreds of years.

Martin Luther King said "Negroes should be judged by the content of their character, not by the color of their skin." So be it. That is how they *are* judged. The proof is that almost 40 million white people voted for Obama and made him the President because of his character. That was more than half of the United States white voting population. The Republicans in power must have wanted him to be President, allowing a Democratic candidate to win over a Republican.

Approximately one million white women voted for Obama because Oprah Winfrey told them to. Why? Because of Oprah's character. White women had made her the wealthiest woman in America. They were her largest fan base and group of supporters. Obama won by about half a million votes. So, without Oprah telling her audience and her fan base of white women to vote for Obama he wouldn't have won. This is the power of TV and popular media moguls and celebrities.

In Louisiana, where there's a black majority, 63% of blacks voted for McCain, 37% for Obama. Why? The black majority in Louisiana didn't want a black President who doesn't nurse resentment and anger against whites. He wouldn't play "the victim" card or "the race" card that most Louisiana black people depend on to take advantage of and manipulate white people and "the system". They knew Obama wouldn't give preferential treatment to blacks, or foster the black agenda, as much as a white President would. In Louisiana and in other southern states black people would say "He's not black enough." Or, "It's the worst thing that could happen to us."

Besides that, the NAACP couldn't constantly complain and create problems that didn't exist, or make big problems out of little problems that were of little or no significance if a black man was President. Thus, since Obama became President there has been a lot less complaining from the NAACP in the news about how black people are disenfranchised by white people, how they are mistreated by white people, and about how black people do not have the same opportunities as white people. It would look stupid and it would sound stupid to do that when the President of the United States is black. The fact is, most of those alleged problems have not existed for most black people ever. Enough already. The NAACP is no longer necessary, except in their own minds, and as a kind of intermediary, signifying the power of black people against white people.

Mexicans, including illegals, have long been the majority population in California. The Mexican President in office when Bush "W" was President encouraged Mexicans to migrate to the United States to claim what was rightfully theirs. This was the land of Arizona, Texas, New Mexico, and California that American soldiers, the American military, and the United States Government had taken from Mexico and Mexicans 150 to 250 years ago. There would be no need to learn English in this conquered land and stolen country. Most of the more than 18 million Mexicans in America don't speak English anyway, or speak both English and their native Spanish.

In the same way, black people in America have maintained their separateness, their pride in who they are, and their racial unity by having a dialect and language intonation all their own. Like the Mexicans in America, and all of the other many races in America, they have always wanted to have a separate identity from white people in America. There has never been anything wrong with different races wanting to maintain and encourage separate identities in America, the so-called melting pot of the world. It was the only country that encouraged all races from all countries to be a part of it from its beginning, making it "the great experiment".

But the reality is that if white people talk about the way black people sound different than white people when they speak they can be sued. The reality is that many millions of Native American Indians were murdered and ruthlessly slaughtered in the name of westward expansion and imminent domain. Shamefully, the "melting pot" and "the great experiment" didn't include them, the original people here, the first race of people in this huge country for hundreds and even thousands of years before the invasion and occupation by the white man, specifically the British, who first colonized America in the 1600's in order to have religious freedom. Their right to have religious freedom did not include the right of the native Indians to live and to have their freedoms, to have a right to not be murdered by the English foreigners occupying their native land and burning their settlements.

What unites people in America is the national language of English. Mexicans in the United States maintain their Spanish language, and that unites them. How anyone speaks English in America is a cultural standard, with differences from state to state and region to region. Black ghetto English is a cultural standard in America for most black people, in most states and regions. It is cultivated in America. That is how and why they speak differently than other people in America.

Yet, black people are offended and claim racism and prejudice, or even sue or threaten to sue if white people, especially public figures, say black people can be recognized by the way they speak. The fact is, and has been, that they have always wanted to be recognized by the way they speak, to differentiate themselves from white people and Mexican Americans, both of which black people are usually prejudiced against. To say we are the same and that we speak the same is stupid and ridiculous. And wrong.

People like to be different because of their races, their racial backgrounds, and they are different. Each region, each ethnic group, each race, has their own way of speaking English in America. It's not racism or prejudice to say that. It's just the truth. It's a fact, not racism, like so much of what is called racism is really just facts, things that are true. Black people need to stop manufacturing reasons to complain and be offended so they can sue white people and/or companies in America. They need to stop trying to be given money because of the uniquely white American population trait, and white politician trait, of feeling guilty about things everybody else in the rest of the World would ignore, or think was ridiculous, too far in the past to be of significance or to matter. Or to require guilt and restitution endlessly to appease that unnecessary guilt.

The crude and offensive word "fuck" is the most common slang word in America, especially among white-trash people and black people. It replaces the word "hell", as in "what the..... ". It also replaces "damn", or "God damn". Just what is the meaning of this slang word? It has no meaning and is just a bad language word, an offensive slang word, referring to sex, the sexual act. The characters on the TV show "The Sopranos" used it in every other sentence, especially the men. Thereafter, trashy people everywhere, all colors, all ages, and all income levels, copied this offensive and stupid gangster dialect in their everyday language, that had permeated American movies and TV shows on Cable TV.

It's the word that binds together some Americans of all races, colors, and ethnic backgrounds, and all financial status from rich to poor. It's the tie that binds. It's become a part of the American culture, adding more profanity as part of the cultural identity, and degrading cultural expectations even more. It's indicative of a state of mind. It's often used by people who don't know an actual word to use instead, or they just want attention. For these people the word fuck replaces all adjectives and adverbs. It's indicative of a cultural decline, not an improvement. Especially because it is widely used by all levels of society in America, including the elite and politicians. So it's becoming the new norm in the 21st century.

This stupid and mean word is also commonly used in Britain, especially in English movies. It's certainly not just used in America. It is another example of something small that could be changed in America to make this country a better place to live in a small way. Some of the things that are wrong in American society can be easily fixed. But they haven't been, and they won't be. What's bad according to one person is good according to another. What one person hates another person loves.

If the theory of evolution were true humans would be intellectually and physiologically advanced far beyond what they are today. After about a million years of existence of the human species there are more things wrong with humans than right. There is no proof of improvement. None. Just speculation about the last 500,000 years regarding humans, and also animals and everything else that is alive. That is mostly what science is anyway. Just guesses, speculation, and manufacturing truth where it doesn't exist. But Americans regard the institution of science as the be-all and end-all for humanity. Americans think everything and anything can be fixed with technology and science.

If evolution was right, if it was what really happened to humans and all other species on Earth human beings would now be much healthier and much stronger, much smarter, and more advanced than ever before because of survival of the fittest and natural selection for the past 500,000 to a million years. But in fact people throughout the world, and especially in America, are sicker and have many more health problems than ever before, and, in general, are less healthy than ever before.

They live longer because of drugs, pharmaceuticals, and medical machines designed to keep them alive longer, not because of evolutionary physical and physiological improvement. Usually this is a low quality of life while it keeps people alive, often forcing people to live in very expensive nursing homes and hospices until they die. This is an extension of the very expensive hospitals and hospital care they were released from when nothing more could be done to help them.

It's all a part of the extremely lucrative sickness industry, the extremely lucrative medical industry, the extremely lucrative insurance industry, and, last but not least, the extremely lucrative death industry in America. All of them are inescapable cornerstones of the American economy, as vastly over-priced required commodities. They are the 21st century foundations of America.

There are at least four million living species, invertebrates and vertebrates, insects,plants, trees, etc. on Earth now in the 21st century. It has been estimated as many species as that have lived on Earth before becoming extinct. As an example, there are about 5000 species of ladybugs alive today. This is one example of the types of vast diversity of life on Earth. So religious people think God created these four to eight million living species and the science of evolution people think four to eight million species evolved from single cells in the oceans, and then billions or trillions of cells combining in a logical and necessary order and progression in order to create each vital organ in each living creature.

Producing each complex interactive organ in the right place at the right time in each body for both the original and the first male and female of each and every species of all living things, all happening at the same time, all necessary organs being created and coming together at the same time, during millions of years of Earth history and life on Earth, is preposterous and insane, ridiculous and stupid, and impossible. According to the theory of evolution and its followers this *impossible* process produced *four to eight million* species of living things, including humans, plants, trees, insects, animals, mammals, birds, fish, all of both sexes at the same time as was required to replicate themselves. There must be another answer. Evolution cannot possibly be the right answer, as it is full of flaws, filled with mistakes and impossibilities.

The theory of evolution is a flawed concept, full of absurd ideas, often easily disproven by logic and facts. As an example, a larger brain does not indicate greater intelligence and this is easily disproven. It's full of inaccuracies, guesses, ego-centric scientists, mistakes, exaggerations, alterations of facts, assumptions, distortions, deceptions. As a matter of fact, it's a lot like the United States Government and its political players, whether they are politicians or not, whether they are elected or not, in their manipulation of the American people.

Like for all of science, and for all American institutions, the falsification of records and test results makes the theory of evolution as reliable as politics and religions. Commonly, the falsification of official statistics and official studies for monetary gain, control, or for public information, or for recognition in the scientific community, is easily done for manipulation and financial gain.

Many people think they are superior to animals, and have a right to kill them if they want to because they can pull the trigger of a gun and kill them. Hunters, in general, are low quality human beings, arrogant and selfish, finding exhilaration and satisfaction in pursuing animals like prehistoric cave men did, and in the subsequent suffering and death of other living beings. This applies to the animal slaughter industry also, an industry specializing in the torture, terrorizing, and killing of domestic animals using inhumane and uncivilized and unevolved methods and actions.

The slaughter industry, the meat industry, and the way some people treat animals in general is a shameful example of too little evolution and no progress of human beings. If everybody was required to visit the places where they terrorize and torture and then kill animals for eventual use as meat most decent people would not buy or eat meat again. Most people have a conscience. It seems that nothing is done to improve terrible and unacceptable conditions for all animals killed for meat and human consumption. It seems that there is nothing anyone will do, or has done, to change it. It's not that they can't, it's that they don't.

Millions of tiny three to four ounce doves, completely harmless and defenseless, and fast becoming extinct, are killed each year by cruel men and women in the United States. These beautiful little birds are so evolved that they mate for life. When one of them is killed they do not find another mate. Killing them for the ounce of meat or because of the "fun" of killing them is barbaric and wrong, mean, cruel, selfish, and stupid. It should be stopped. It needs to be against the law. But politicians want their vote, and the financial support and votes from the vastly influential NRA. The National Rifle Association gives hundreds of millions of dollars for election campaigns and lobbyist support.

Hunting continues forever because it builds the sick ego of the hunter. The hunting industry is a multi-billion dollar industry. So the greed of businesses, commercial greed that is so common in America, is part of why it continues. The cost of the hunting is hundreds or even thousands of dollars more than the cost of meat at the grocery store, so it has nothing to do with saving money and putting food on the table. It simply and honestly is the satisfaction and fun of killing other helpless living beings. It's a cruel hobby for millions of hunters in America every year against animals and birds that have no chance of winning, no chance of survival against this technologically advanced game of killing that has no odds in favor of the pursued, of the victim. It's no game at all. It's slaughter.

United States conservation groups and organizations promote protection of habitat so there will be more wild animals to shoot during hunting seasons. However, they promote their image as "protecting animals". They protect them so hunters can shoot them during hunting seasons. Every year American hunting organizations say wild animals have "been harvested", like harvesting corn.

This is an ignorant and manipulative media public relations practice. These animals have personalities, families, intelligence, and suffer when injured by hunters. Plants, like corn and wheat, of course do not. Plants are harvested, not animals. The ignorant and selfish hunter's rationale is "If we don't kill them they will die". This, of course, is stupid and wrong, except in the unlikely situation of starvation. Hunters lie in order to justify the cruel and deadly things they do. Just like politicians do.

International studies done in 2009 determined that the United States was not even in the top 10 best countries to live in the World. The United States was number 13. Sixty years ago it was usually the first, number one, or at least in the top five. Statistics don't lie unless they are distorted and changed, tampered with. Unless they are lied about, which is easily done.

International banks own the Federal Reserve. Therefore, international banks control and regulate the United States money supply. Most people in America don't want to know about this, or even care about it, because there is nothing they can do about it even if they wanted to. That is true with most of what happens in the Democracy and the Government of America, especially in the 21st century. See no evil, hear no evil. Then it doesn't exist, and nothing needs to be done about it. Mostly this is because Americans are lazy about their Democracy and maintaining their rights as Americans. But it's also because Americans, in general, know that there is nothing they can do to change anything, to improve things, to make life better in America regarding the main institutions that are the foundation of America. Voting usually changes nothing.

According to the Bible Adam and Eve appeared about 6000 years ago, in the Garden of Eden. This was in Persia, that is now Iran. Carbon-dating has shown that people have been on Earth for at least 200,000 years, and possibly for as long as seven to eight million years, a huge gap of accuracy and knowledge.  In the original Biblical texts the word that was always translated as "Heaven" really had the true meaning of "the sky". This was a little literary license and a *big* change of meaning, of conveyed idea and concept, for a word that is repeated thousands of times in the English translation of the Bible. This resulted in greater control of the minds of Christian believers, all of whom wanted to go to "Heaven" (really "the sky") and would do whatever had to be done to get to this supposedly perfect and much better place when they died.

The only other Christian option was "Hell", not other future lives, like most of the rest of the World believed, because of reincarnation and karma. The Bible was, from the beginning, an attempt to control Christians by means of distortion, myth, and inaccuracies. The Theory of Evolution was like that, because it filled a need to know and a need to understand where we all came from, because the Biblical explanation was so unlikely, so inaccurate, and can't possibly be true.

Except to the millions of religious Fundamentalists and Evangelicals in the United States who can't tolerate disbelievers. And except to the many millions of Catholics and followers of other religions allowed to practice in America. For them this is the only explanation of the beginning of mankind, of humanity.

The man who wrote what was later called "Revelations" in the Bible, in the New Testament, was left on a remote island purposefully because he was deemed to be crazy. He was insane, and thought to be a danger to other people and society. There on that island, isolated and alone, and insane, he wrote something that many billions of people for about 2000 years think of as "Gospel", written by "a prophet". When, in fact, it was written by a madman who was feared by society, and who had been sentenced to isolation for the rest of his life to protect that society. Yet, many billions of people have been told, and have read in Revelations, that the ideas of this insane man reveal the plans of God for the ultimate end of humanity.

Most Christians don't know where and from who these insane ideas came from. Not by accident but by design was this dire insanity that had been revealed in the writings of a madman, who was a very real and imminent danger to his society, released to humanity pretending to be Gospel in the designed and planned New Testament of the Bible about 300 years after Jesus had died. Christianity was designed to control people and Christians in general, starting about 300 years after Christ died.

In about 325 A.D. Emperor Constantine of Rome and his group of scholarly authorities chose that book, instead of at least 950 other books, to control Christians, an unruly Middle Eastern religious group, and to instill fear. They decided to end the Bible with insane threats from God, which really were the imaginations of a madman, a crazy man, left alone on an island by a society that didn't want him to be a part of that society, that that society was afraid of. He was dangerous to other people, and his writings would instill fear and danger in the minds of all Christians for purposes of controlling them, when it was included in the Bible as revealing and depicting the final hours of the existence of humanity and Earth. An insane man, a crazy man, wrote and unknowingly provided the ending of the Bible, which would be read more than any other book in history. The last chapter was sensationalism instilling fear in a way no sane man could have even imagined. It was a perfect ending for their 30 years of combined efforts to control and create fear in the new religion of Christianity.

Emperor Constantine and his scholarly authorities called the writer "St. John". This of course gave him instant credibility and lasting authority to be a part of the Bible. The Book of Revelations was, and is, fantasy written by a mad man. Not prophetic and accurate revelations never seen or experienced by any other human being before that or after that. This was, and is, the worst kind of manipulation of Christians, who have always accepted all of the Bible as the actual word of God.

Including its crazy and dire ending, written by a madman, about how the World will end. His nightmares became the nightmare gospel of all Christians for the next 2000 years, continuing in the 21st century, depicting how the World and how humanity will ultimately end. It will probably be believed by Christians for another 2000 years, because it's what they want to believe.

However, Muslims and Islamists say they love death, and they say Americans who are Christians love life and are afraid of death. This explains a lot about their history and behavior, and our history and behavior as Americans. In America a higher percentage of the population are church members than in most other countries. Religion, as an institution, is for hope and strength to live life, to overcome the vicissitudes of life, and to control the bad side of human behavior. It's dependent on faith in a fantasy, on something that can't be seen or heard. A Christian church in Houston has about half a million members in its congregation. The church is a football stadium. The leader of the church has a message based on hope. His interpretation of Christianity has made him a multi-millionaire, and has made millions of his followers happy.

Religions give people courage to face death, and eliminate the fear of death, because of the promises of a better after-life after death. These are very useful functions and explain why most old people become religious, guaranteeing them an after-life in Heaven (really "the sky"), supposedly a paradise, if they believe, and if they please God.

In America most charities disperse only 10% to 25% of their donations to the people they exist to serve, who enable them to have a non-profit status. Churches, however, have non-profit status but they actually do disperse a much larger percentage of their donations to those they exist to serve. Except for the Catholic Church, the richest church in the World, despite the fact they falsely declare destitution. There are about 1500 religions in the United States. The United States was begun to give its citizens religious freedom. Separation of church and state is part of The Constitution. All religions give people hope, peace, structure, and feelings of unity. They are a necessary part of life for many people in America, and throughout the World, making the difficulties of life easier to deal with.

As of 2010 there were about 2.2 billion Christians in the World, and about 1.6 billion Muslims, followers of Islam. About 1/10 of these Muslims, about 100 million of these fanatic followers of Islam, are determined to kill all Americans and take over the United States. Their TV and newspaper propaganda and lies tell them constantly 24/7 to do this, to sacrifice their lives for their ultimate goals of dominating the United States and all of Western civilization, specifically killing all Americans.

Many thousands of these radical and fanatic Muslims live in the United States, with the purpose of infiltrating American society to achieve that ultimate end, to destroy America from within. However, most Americans are blissfully unaware of this, as their managed media news hides it.

Catholicism is by far the most popular Christian religion in the World and in the United States, having at least 700 million followers. Then Lutherans and Jews at about 15 to 20 million believers and followers for each religion. As of 2010 there were about 500 million Buddhists, and about one billion Hindus. There are also about 1500 lesser religions throughout the World and in America.

A selling point for Catholicism is the offer of redemption through confession. No wonder there are far more Catholics in the world than any other religion. No matter what you do, how horrible your deeds, God will forgive you, and Heaven awaits. No guilt, no responsibility. It's been a miracle religion for billions of people for about 2000 years, offering them peace of mind and immediate redemption not offered by other religions.

Religion, a massive Worldly institution, has always been an attempt, from the beginning, to control and organize people, like politics does, through fear of God and retribution, pain and suffering. Religion is a spiritual justice system, controlling through fear of God's punishment, like the legal justice system controls through fear of punishment on a judicial, social, and physical level. Instilling fear of the unknown is how the United States Government, politicians, authorities, and people that rule America attempt to control people in America, especially the expendable masses.

Christianity was developed, designed, between 306 A.D. and 337 A.D., as a way to control the unruly and disorganized Christian population. Catholicism became an official religion in 325 A.D. Christianity was designed by picking a few books out of the thousand or so that had been written on the subject over at least 500 years, by a committee of scholars that were chosen by King Constantine and by representatives and scholars chosen from Catholic and Protestant churches in Europe. Christianity, as a religion, was a collaboration of the few in order to control the many.

Higher powers in every religion seem to actually have no powers, except for what is in the imagination of their followers. There has never been any scientific proof or evidence of their real existence, or their alleged powers. Not ever. For more than 500,000 years. Or maybe for just 6000 years. No one really knows. It's all just stories, myths, guesses, and procedures to control followers.

Maybe God is an all-encompassing Universal Consciousness and souls are just individual consciousness, part of God's consciousness, so after death the soul goes home to the Universal Consciousness. It returns to where it came from. The Universal Consciousness, God, controls nothing and changes nothing. It just is. The power God has is what all souls, as parts of It, the "Great I Am", do when they materialize in the Earth experience, a chance to become a being, to materialize and experience the five or six senses. It's a kind of existentialism for God, offering endless opportunities for God to exist through billions of people, besides billions of other living creatures, billions of souls.

This would mean that we are alone in the Earth experience. No higher, or highest, power can do, or does do, anything. This would explain why bad things, terrible things, happen to good people, why good things, even wonderful things, happen to bad people. Why good is not rewarded, why prayers are not answered. Then it's just a coincidence if it seems like prayers are answered. And when a prayer is actually answered it's just luck.

Each life experience is dependent on other people. The God force, the Mohammed force, the Buddha force, the Jesus force, etc., controls nothing. Changes nothing. Each religion is right for the person who believes in it. So there are no wrong religions, except those that encourage or promote causing people pain and suffering. In the name of religion hundreds of millions of people have been tortured and killed in the past few thousand years. Maybe even a billion people have suffered and died in the name of religions since religions began. Yet, because of their religion people still suffer and are killed in the 21st century. As an example, radical Islamists kill other Muslims who disagree with their extremist beliefs about killing all Americans and dominating the United States using terrorism.

Religions have been both the bane of humanity and the blessing of humanity. God, being God, had to know before He arranged the immaculate conception of His son Jesus that His son would be crucified, tortured, and die on a cross. He had to have known that, so He wanted Jesus to die then, to have His "only begotten son" die that way. He gave up nothing, because God wouldn't give up anything He did not want to give up. After all, He can do anything, so He could have stopped it. Since God is all powerful He must have wanted that to happen to his son Jesus. God must have planned it, seen it happening in the future, as what He wanted to happen. And God being God He did not stop it. He wanted Jesus to suffer, be tortured, be crucified, and die. It had to be part of His all-knowing plans.

How can any religion be based on that? God being God He obviously wants all humanity to struggle and suffer. Why is a God like this worshipped? Because of fear, fear of retribution and pain, fear of suffering and death, by the actions of this God. Fear of the retribution of God, of the anger of this God, and of not being allowed into the after-life of "Heaven", supposedly God's perfect domain and the ultimate reward after the struggle and suffering of an Earthly life. In the history of mankind there has never been actual verified scientific proof of any good done by "God". Just stories.

Twenty documents dating back 1500 to 2000 years provide proof that Jesus survived being crucified on a cross, was healed enough in 12 days with aloe and myrhh so that he could escape, and then escaped by traveling to India where he lived the rest of his life. He brought his mother with him so she would avoid persecution. In India he was known as "the all-knowing messenger of God." He had also lived in India when he was 13 to 30 years old, which are the missing years in the Bible. Years later his mother died in India and is buried at a publically recognized location. Jesus died years later in Kashmir, 100 miles away. Both are buried in publically recognized tombs in India, as is Saint Thomas. In India Jesus is a part of their history, in their history books, not a part of their religion.

Without the mythical death and resurrection of Jesus the premise and foundation of Christianity would fall apart. That is proof that the Bible, and the Christian religion that was developed and designed after the Bible, were created and developed to control and manipulate Christians, who were a previously unruly population with a disorganized religion after the alleged death of Jesus.

Religious faith, mostly a belief in fantasies, has been the cause of many wars throughout history. This faith in stories, myths, and allegories, with some actual history thrown in, has resulted in untold torture and murders. There are more than a billion Muslims in the world, a faith and religion based on violence. Fanatical Muslims think all non-Muslims should be killed. No one knows how many they have killed, all over the world, in the name of God, and in the name of their religion.

In 1280 B.C., on December 25th, Horus was born to a virgin mother, after an immaculate conception. He healed the sick, walked on water, was crucified on a cross, died, and then arose from the dead on the third day. Six hundred years before the birth of Jesus Krishna was also born to a virgin mother on December 25th. It was another immaculate conception. He also healed the sick, walked on water, was crucified and died on a cross. Three days later he rose from the dead, like Jesus and Horus did. There's a pattern here, a repetition repeated for the religious leaders of three major religions in the world. Are they all fantasies and stories, or just partial fantasies and stories, or the truth?  No one really knows, although billions of people claim to be sure and to know, and to have faith and believe.

There never has been proof for any of these stories, yet they are the basis of, the foundations of, three major World religions. The Catholic Church is the wealthiest and biggest non-profit business and corporation on Earth, followed, probably, by the Red Cross. In the United States the Catholic Church is legally a "sole corporation", as in "run by one person", the Pope. Thousands of priests apparently don't legally run their respective churches. Most non-profit organizations in America use only about 10% of every dollar donated for what they proclaim they do. They're like politicians. But the Catholic Church has hoarded it's wealth in the basement of the Vatican for hundreds of years. Gold, silver, artwork, statues and paintings by world-famous artists, and so on, besides its massive holdings of real estate owned throughout the World.

Being non-profits they have never paid taxes on their immense wealth in the United States, just as their "CEOs", with million dollar (plus) salaries, also pay no taxes, and never have. The biggest source of their immense wealth is investments in art and real estate, not just donations, for the past 100 years. So they should be taxed like all the people who donate to them are taxed, and like other investors are taxed, and at higher rates than if they were occupying their real estate. Billion dollar pay-outs for lawsuits could not have really bankrupted them in the first years after 2000. The truth needed to be revealed. It's a sin to tell a lie, after all, especially if you're the Catholic Church and tell people what to do, and how to live their lives in order to qualify for a place in Heaven.

For about the last 40 years the United States Government has given citizens of India, and related countries, billions of dollars to buy and operate motels in America, with the understanding that they will keep them in the family, passing ownership and operation to family members only. In exchange for this immense generosity of the American taxpayer, and gift of enduring security, stability, dignity, and a home for life for all of their family indefinitely, the typical motel owner and operator in the United States from India, Pakistan, etc., and his wife and relatives, dislikes the American patrons at their motel, and are disdainful and rude towards them.

This Government money, American taxpayer's money, has always been exclusively for citizens of India, and other related countries. Citizens of the United States are not eligible for this or any related program concerning American motels. As usual, the United States Government does not like to, or want to, provide financial security and physical security and well-being for Americans. Especially white Americans living in America, who are expected to struggle and make it on their own, with very little state or Federal Government assistance because they aren't eligible for it.

Since 2001 the United States gives China billions of dollars to transfer garbage to China from the United States. The United States Government borrowed more than $500 billion dollars from China to keep the United States Government running. The U.S. has long produced surpluses of wheat and wheat by-products. Yet, the United States buys wheat and wheat by-products from China, which are grown with chemicals outlawed in the United States but still manufactured in the United States, and then bought from the United States by China.

A new technology in the United States uses garbage in landfills to turn into a fuel replacing gasoline, costing about a dollar a gallon. The United States Government could save at least a billion dollars a year by *not* shipping this same garbage to China, and instead using the garbage to make this fuel replacement. But the United States Government is not in the business of saving taxpayers money, of using the taxpayer's money to its best advantage, or of saving the environment. America is not lacking in technological innovation to improve things, but it is lacking in responsible actions to use that technology. The power of the oil industry is part of the answer for this and the reason for this. The United States Government supporting the oil industry is another reason, the other part of the answer.

Electric cars didn't use gasoline, or oil, or need tune-ups. They were recalled and disappeared because the U.S. Government ordered them to be destroyed during the Bush "W" Administration. They could not be sold as used cars. They were a small but significant threat to the United States oil agenda of increasing profits, dependency on foreign oil, the Stock Market, and to Wall Street.

It costs about one gallon of gas for a freight train to transport one ton of products, like new cars, about 400 miles. Transporting that same product on trucks would cost about 100 times more. Trains are much safer than trucks, which greatly increase the risks and hazards of driving a car where there are trucks. This increases insurance rates. The number of trucks on the road have increased about 1000% in 10 years. Since there's no logic behind it, something else is behind it. Truck emissions are thousands of times more polluting than cars. Millions of trucks on the road in the United State are the real reason, the biggest reason, along with industrial emissions, that pollution is such a big problem.

They are much more of a problem than private passenger cars. Put the blame where it belongs. Ride behind these trucks any time of day or night in America and you will agree. There are about 12 million car accidents every year in the United States, and about 100,000 deaths from these accidents. This is about 99,000 more deaths per year than American soldier deaths in Iraq were every year. It's more dangerous to drive a car in America than it is to be an American soldier in a warzone. There should be some kind of war against this massacre of innocent men, women, and children in America by other Americans driving their cars, their SUVs and pickup trucks, and by trucks, millions more of them on the roads than ever before. More than half of these car accidents and deaths happen because of alcohol consumption, cell phone conversations while driving, and texting on cell phones while driving.

American corporations and companies pay no taxes on their multi-billion dollar profits when they are located in China, India, and Mexico. This special IRS tax treatment needs to end, and should have ended years ago. The United States economy would greatly improve if it did. It would solve many social, financial, and economic problems in the United States, adding hundreds of billions of dollars, even a trillion dollars, to the American economy every year for the benefit of the American people. That is, if it wasn't stolen first, disappearing somewhere along the line of distribution.

Wages for workers in these countries employed by the relocated American corporations and companies have been only 13 cents an hour up to $1 an hour, but usually about $2 a day up to $20 a week for doing the same work done by workers in America, usually backed by Unions, that used to get $20 *an hour* from these same American corporations and companies. For many years the UAW, the Union of Auto Workers, had made great strides for its members in getting fair treatment on the job and very large increases in hourly wages, yearly salaries, and benefits. But when the auto industry relocated to other countries and they were unemployed they couldn't find work anywhere. There were no jobs paying what they thought they were worth. Thus the failure of Detroit as a thriving city was inevitable.

In about 2012 the GAO reported that *$30 billion* tax dollars are wasted every year by the United States military buying parts and products they don't need, and often are directed to be thrown away, or given away, even before they are received. The Air Force accounts for about $18 billion dollars of this scandalous waste. Hundreds of billions of dollars have been lost or wasted by NASA because of their failed projects, or useless projects. NASA, like other parts of the United States Government, is characterized by misuse of, and waste of, money. Billions of dollars of taxpayer's money.

Without taxpayer's money and financial subsidies national sports teams would lose many millions of dollars every year. Mostly because of outrageous salaries for their players. Therefore it is a lie, a distortion of the truth, to say sports team managers and sports team players are worth these multi-million dollar salaries. Without Government financial support using taxpayer's money they wouldn't exist. They'd go out of business.

A book written by Lieutenant Colonel Corso reveals what he experienced and saw at the Roswell UFO site the day after someone reported it. He said the account was only 10% of what he saw and knew. The rest would be hidden forever because of United States Government rules and secrecy. His knowledge about the Roswell incident would die with him, like it did with everyone else who was there, because of their fear of the United States Government, as a result of Government and military threats to themselves and to their families. It was a justified fear of Government reprisals, a fear of being assassinated, murdered by FBI, CIA, NSA, or military secret service forces.

That is not what a democracy is supposed to be like. Not then, starting in the 1940's, and not now, in the 21st century 70 years later. But there isn't, and never has been, anything Americans can do to change the systems in place, developed beyond the control of the expendable masses from the beginning. As always, money, profit, control, and power are the reasons for this Government and military secrecy and corruption.

He said, in his book, that the spaceship and its occupants had technology that was deciphered and adapted to become our fiber optics, microchips, cell phones, laptop computers, and laser technology. Also, a fiber he said he couldn't cut with a razorblade was copied to become bullet-proof vests. This, then, is part of the reason for the immense and permanent cover-up of the incident. United States authorities and corporations wanted credit for these technological advances.

Under the guise of protecting the American public the United State Government and the United States military has always threatened retaliation and major life-changing repercussions for anyone revealing any information about recovered UFOs. The truth was, and is, that the United States Government and United States military are to be feared, now and in the past. Not the UFOs.

All of the Government men and local residents who saw the remnants of the spaceship at Roswell, New Mexico in 1947, and saw the two dead outer-space people and the two who were still alive standing by the spaceship, without any weapons to protect themselves with, were threatened by United States Government representatives. They were told they would be fined $10,000 and go to prison if they told anyone, even their families, about anything they saw there. They were told to give their word to then-president Truman. Freedom of speech, guaranteed by The Constitution, was violated, as was freedom of information for all Americans. Supposedly the two surviving ETs also had no rights of any sort, and were probably killed, or died unnaturally from scientific and military experiments, after disappearing with their military conquerors to places unknown, never to be seen or written about or talked about again. It was a very undemocratic anti-democracy thing to do for them and for the American people.

Black students graduate from High School, Junior High School, and Elementary School even if they can't read or write, because of the program "No Child Left Behind". Higher education at Colleges and Universities is an industry that is turning out at least a million graduates a year that are over-qualified and not able to fill needs in the United States job market. Or they have learned useless information for four years, in terms of what employers need or want. Like other industries in the United States Colleges and Universities are motivated by greed, not by their common image of altruism or necessity. It is just another business, another industry. It provides something for millions of high school graduates to do.

For many years students at Southern University, in Baton Rouge, Louisiana, have gotten A's and B's in exchange for paying a fee to administrative employees to change their records. Black teachers could get a Master's degree in exchange for a fee, no work required, like the Bachelor's degree students. These teachers, then, got paid higher salaries because they had a pseudo Master's degree.

Even though this had been going on for many years as preferential treatment, bias, prejudice, and cheating for the black students, who have always made-up 99% of the students at that college, these graduates from Southern University would then be hired before white graduates from any normal College or University because of Affirmative Action.

An Administrator at Southern University said, in about 2001, "If someone has enough initiative to come to the SAT (or ACT) testing it doesn't matter if they only have a few answers right. That's good enough to get admitted to our University." That's also all that was necessary to graduate from that University. Students just had to show up for classes, like they did in public schools for the past twenty years in Louisiana, in order to get A's and B's, and sometimes just C's instead of failing, all of which require no work and no tests for black students. If the teacher didn't follow that system their parents would complain in person and threaten to have them fired. Prejudice is a useful concept and a word that covers a lot of bases, and has a lot of uses socially and legally.

During the Government-ordered removal of the Cherokee nation from their homes in North Carolina to Oklahoma some Indians escaped. The United States Government agreed to let them remain in the North Carolina mountains if three of them volunteered themselves to be executed by the United States military. This unbelievably cruel act, a crime by our Government and military on the original citizens of America who had been here for thousands of years, was testimony to the cruel military attitude towards all Indian tribes in this country. It was the worst kind of Government/military prejudice and Government/military domination.

The military had a demented need to kill Indians, murdering innocent and helpless Indians on their own land, in their own villages. As a result of these three brave and courageous Indian men sacrificing their lives more than 1000 Cherokee Indians were allowed to remain in the Great Smoky Mountains, where their descendants still live. Because of the endless brutality of the U.S. Government and U.S. military for about 250 years many millions of Native Americans were murdered and millions more were injured, while protecting their homes and their families, their land, their possessions, and their own lives from the foreign invaders and murderers that were our ancestors. Especially the British, the English from England.

Some of the first English colonists that sailed from Britain in the 1600's slaughtered their first Indian tribe late one night as they slept in their tents, in their homes, shooting hundreds of them as they slept, then burning the entire village of homes with the Indians in them. The entire tribe had only been generous and helpful to these foreign invaders of their community for about a year, sharing their seeds, their food, and leather and furs. These arrogant British men who thought they were superior to the Indians had no integrity or honor. They deceived the Indians, then killed them. They were not superior except in their own minds. The Indians had no guns and couldn't possibly defend themselves. It was the beginning of the manifest destiny and imminent domain mentality of the British in America, followed by other people from other countries in the Old World, coming to the New World for the purpose of invasion, conquest and domination. And freedom of religion.

Throughout history conquered people have been murdered or used as slaves by their conquerors. These were not black people, but people of all colors and many races, used by people in many different countries for many thousands of years. The plight of Native American Indians for about 250 years was unbelievably worse than that of black African slaves in the United States. What white men did to American Indians was worse than inexcusable and cruel, and uncivilized, even though the

Indians were called the uncivilized ones. American Indians have continued to have integrity and dignity, behaving with nobility and intelligence since the beginning. Throughout humanity so-called civilizations have often been uncivilized.

Without the Navajo Code Talkers World War II would have lasted much longer, with many thousands more American soldiers being killed, and with the expenditure and loss of millions of more dollars spent for the war against Japan, after Japanese bombers attacked the American Navy fleet of ships at Pearl Harbor on December 7, 1941. It is also possible that the United States and its allies would not have won World War II against the Japanese, and their allies. Four hundred Navajo men had been forced to join the military and to develop the Code Talker program, for the United States military that had slaughtered many millions of their ancestors.

After the war was won they got no veteran's assistance or benefits. Other veterans got benefits like free college educations and zero down-payment to buy houses, and medical care at Veterans Hospitals. There was no public acknowledgement or recognition for what they had done, while keeping the military program a secret. But the Japanese were always aware of them and what they were doing, never being able to crack the code of the Navajo Code Talkers. Ten of them had been killed in combat even though they never carried any guns. Never having any weapons to protect themselves with meant they sacrificed their lives, again, for the United States military.

The American custom of saying a person is black even if they are only a small proportion black, as little as 1/8 black, is ridiculous. Conversely, if a white person is a small part American Indian they are not said to be an American Indian. After Thomas Jefferson wrote "All men are created equal" he said for years, repeatedly, that he did not mean Negroes. Yet, all men are created equal has been the mantra for, and the impetus for, the black civil rights movement in the United States. It is interesting to note that now, in the 21st century, proportionately there are more black *millionaires and billionaires* in America than white. It pays to be black in America.

Mexico's biggest export to the United States is their poor people, their poverty, and their criminals and crime. For at least 13 years there have been 48 underground tunnels for Mexicans to enter the United States illegally. During the Bush "W" Administration United States engineers tried for eight years to figure out what to do about the tunnels. Apparently they needed a rocket scientist. Filling the tunnels with toxic wastes from nuclear plants, or with garbage otherwise sent to China, would have solved the problem and saved paying China billions of dollars. The real reason nothing was done was that the Republican politicians, elected or not, wanted the Mexicans here. After all, Mexicans living in the United States as citizens usually vote republican. And rich people, usually Republicans, need Mexican migrant workers to work for them to do the kind of work Americans don't want to do. Without Mexican illegal workers many thousands of necessary jobs would go unfilled.

United States law doesn't apply to Mexicans who are not citizens. They get protection from the Mexican Government and when action is taken against them they can sue for millions of dollars, in a law suit, for frivolous things, and win. Mexican immigration to the United States has resulted in adding about $20 billion dollars every year to the Mexican economy. This is money sent by Mexican immigrants to their relatives in Mexico. For years the United States Federal Government has not enforced laws already in place regarding legal and illegal immigrants and immigration. The United States Federal Government has been encouraging and allowing illegal immigration to America.

This drives up the prices of rentals and real estate artificially in the United States for citizens and people who are in the United States legally. Single family houses have become like rooming houses, or hotels, or apartments for 10 to 20 illegal Mexicans, so higher real estate costs are a result. Mortgage brokers speaking only Spanish have long cultivated illegal buyers of real estate in America. Selling false IDs to illegals from Mexico is a very lucrative and easy home-based business, with an easily identifiable market and unlimited potential income. These forged ID's usually cost about $100. Mexico has wealth and financial stability far beyond the United States. There are more millionaires and billionaires in Mexico than in the United States. Mexico has no deficit compared to the United States deficit of trillions of dollars. The media and the Press have avoided informing the public about this.

In order for political candidates to get the Latino vote they have to be pro-illegal Mexicans in the United States. In 2007 Mexicans were about 16% of the population, but about 55% of the babies born in the United States were Mexican. That translates to instant United States citizenship for the babies, and leniency and deferment for the mother. By about 2035 about 50% of the population will probably be Mexican. That doesn't include the Mexicans here illegally, which was about 20 million in 2009. By 2035 there may be 100 million Mexicans living illegally in the United States.

Mexican criminals, many of whom form gangs in the United States, kill about 16,000 people a year in the United States. This would qualify to be an epidemic if it was a disease, as would deaths from car and truck accidents. Eighty percent of criminals in prison are there because of drug-related crimes. Eighty percent of illegal drugs in the United States come from Mexico. The United States is destitute and Mexico is the richest country, the most wealthy country, in the Southern hemisphere. Who made Mexico numero uno?  The United States did.

If these drugs were legal nobody would be getting rich from illegal activity selling them, producing them, distributing them, supplying them. Crime would be a small fraction of what it is. Drug-related crime would disappear. The over-crowded prison population in many states would be a small fraction of what it is, saving millions of dollars. Billions of dollars that go to Mexico, the major supplier, would stay in the United States instead, vastly improving the national economy.

A United States citizen caught with one or two ounces of illegal drugs goes to prison for 2 to 25 years, depending on who the Judge is, where they are in the United States, and who their lawyer is. This, in itself, is a gross injustice and indication of a flawed judicial system. There is supposed to be equal treatment under the law, truth and justice being the American way in all facets of American life. This, however, is not the reality of living in America.

For years Mexicans that smuggle less than 500 pounds of illegal drugs across the United States border have not been stopped by border guards, on either side. Yet, United States citizens would be stopped, arrested, prosecuted, and sent to prison if they had one or two ounces, let alone 500 pounds. This is outrageous. Mexicans, from Mexico, grow millions of dollars worth of marijuana plants in United States National Parks and United States National Forests. They protect their illegal crops with Mexican gunmen. Unbelievably, no United States law enforcement stops them in this on-going process. Yet, if a citizen of the United States grows a square foot of marijuana in their backyard they will be arrested, charged, and go to prison for possibly 10 years, and their plants are destroyed.

The lure of the American West has always been that it symbolized adventure, prosperity, an opportunity to improve your life, and personal growth and freedom. It's always been a place where anything is possible. These are the same things that America has always represented to immigrants from other countries. However, when they got to the United States they were often faced with intolerance, prejudice, loss of position and status, especially if they were physicians, nurses, teachers, or professors in the countries they came from. Usually they then had a lower standard of living in America. They often had to start over again.

Out of necessity they formed their own communities, cities within cities, like Chinatown and Little Italy. Prejudice towards people who were Swedish, Chinese, Irish, etc., was common. The history of prejudice towards white people in America in the 1800s and early 1900s involved white people suffering from bad treatment from other white people. It definitely wasn't just happening to black people. In truth, in reality, America has a history of not accepting a diversity of races when the basic premise of America is to accept, to welcome, all people.

But that's what the Statue of Liberty says, that's the Statue of Liberty idea, and that statue is a gift from France. So maybe it's really just a French concept, what the French would do, or what they thought people in America did. But that was not the American reality at any time since then, or now.

All over America today, in the 21$^{st}$ century, ethnic groups, races, do not like white Americans and other races, other ethnic groups. This is part of their cultures and is, therefore, part of the American culture. All prejudice, justified or not, exists mostly because of the sins and actions of the few.

Texas has a reputation of not overturning guilty verdicts of death row inmates who say they are innocent and then appeal. Even when lawyers prove there were Constitutional violations the Supreme Court Judges have never overturned the conviction, have never changed the sentence to life imprisonment. Instead, they order immediate execution, often within an hour of their verdict. In Texas if you're innocent, appealing a death sentence is punished by Texas Supreme Court Judges with immediate execution. Yes, immediate execution is the punishment for making an appeal.

What unites Americans in the United States Democracy is The Constitution, the rule of laws, basic freedoms, and fairness, and The Bill of Rights. And opportunities to make things right that have turned wrong. Something is very wrong with the Texas judicial system and the power of the Texas Supreme Court Judges that should have been changed many years ago, or never begun in the first place. But people in Texas have been powerless to change any of it.

Because of hidden evidence, lack of evidence, not admissible evidence, lies under oath, distortion of the truth, manipulated evidence and "proof", and biased Judges and Magistrates, probably hundreds of thousands of criminals have gone free in the past 50 years, and as many have been unjustly and mistakenly charged with and convicted of something they didn't do. Black people think this only happens to them but they are totally wrong. All colors, all races, have been victims of this gross lack of justice that has always been happening in America.

Truth and justice can be victims of lies told under the oath to tell the truth in courtrooms all over the United States. Apparently swearing "under God" doesn't mean a lot to a lot of people. If it's true that "everybody lies" then Judges and juries should always take that into consideration before giving a verdict. But what's the truth and what's a lie is, unfortunately, part of the dilemma of life.

Everywhere in America there are leash laws for cats, but cats can't be walked on a leash or kept outside on a leash or rope. This stupid and mean law says cats that are walking, sitting, sleeping, and standing outside need to be killed, need to be destroyed, by very painful and cruel methods. This includes dogs, of course, who are trusting and defenseless to change what they are charged with.

Dogs, of course, may bite, so that justifies a leash law. But the leash law for cats needs to be changed by politicians and authorities, the powers that be. Millions of cats and dogs that have done nothing wrong are killed by animal control departments every year. It is not uncommon for these government employees to get some kind of perverse enjoyment in unjustly capturing and killing these terrified and helpless animals.

Individuals, as voters and citizens, should be given the power to change these cruel and unjust laws and policies but they aren't, they haven't, and they won't be. Cruelty and unbelievable lack of fairness and kindness towards millions of helpless and innocent animals, mostly pets, will continue indefinitely, until American society and the American people become more civilized and advanced, to include kind treatment for all animals. Especially including those millions of animals caught by animal control departments everywhere in the United States every year, animals who are doomed, destined to die cruel and painful deaths.

Politicians don't speak directly anymore. They just "send a signal", "send a message", "urge" or "encourage". They no longer say things directly or say what they really mean. Indirect control or indirect threats is the modus operandi of the Government so far in the 21$^s$ century, and also that of the media reporting them. It is arrogance, and an attitude of superiority, that makes United States politicians and the President think they can meddle and tell leaders of any other countries what they should do. Those foreign leaders don't tell United States leaders what they should do about the United States. Perhaps it all comes back to money. Lots of money as gifts and as foreign aid.

The United States gets no yearly foreign aid from other countries, but many countries get yearly foreign aid from the United States. Hundreds of millions given to each country every year from the United States Government. Maybe that's why the United States Government, and the President, tells those countries what to do in a condescending manner. The United States Government buys influence and control. Money always talks.

Capitalism has been exploitation of people and exploitation of natural resources, for profit and greed. Money, money, money. Privatization of government agencies at all levels of government are an example. Costs can be increased hundreds or even thousands of times. Misappropriation of funds, theft, is easy. They just charge the government agency at the county, state, or federal level whatever they want, no matter how inflated the costs are. Privatization of government projects also leads to theft on many levels. But government regulators, employed by the government at all levels, can also be involved in misappropriation of money by ignoring what shouldn't be happening. Like the misuse of mortgage funds which led to millions of mortgage foreclosures, millions of American homes being repossessed. All of this corruption, theft, and exploitation steals money from Americans but nothing, no legal action, gives it back to them or gives them compensation of any kind.

To make the most of capitalism you have to play the game. Rewards go to the wealthy, to the already rich. Protection is always given to the ones who play the game right, even if the way they play hurts other people, or other living things and the environment. The richer you are, the larger the corporation or bank involved, the more the Federal Government will protect you or it. The goal is always to make more money in any way you can, and the national Government protects and encourages the accomplishment and protection of that goal when it is about millions of dollars. Especially if it's about billions of dollars.

The Bush "W" administration began the privatization of United States wars, invasions, attacks, and occupations in other countries, and tried repeatedly to implement privatization of the Social Security System. Has the privatization of the Iraq war helped the average American or the United States economy in any way? Or eliminated or lessened the United States national indebtedness of trillions of dollars to China? No, of course not. Privatization of Social Security wouldn't either. Instead it would have disastrous consequences. But when there is another Republican President and a Republican majority it probably will be implemented, becoming a part of the Republican drive for increased corporate wealth at the expense of the rest of America. And don't forget the payoffs to the politicians and officials, both elected and unelected.

The United States military complex has had military bases in at least 134 countries, with more than 700 military bases totally. This is a kind of imperialism without being imperialism. The United States wouldn't allow any other countries to have military bases in the United States. Money spent for these bases of power and control, scattered around the world, and money given to countries as foreign aid, even to countries that are independently wealthy from oil production, etc., drains United States taxpayer's money from their Social Security system, deprives them of better schools and a better infrastructure, including safer bridges and replacement and repair of roads, highways, and bridges, and other programs to improve life in America. Is the United States Government borrowing this money, this huge amount of money, to give it away? The answer must be "yes".

John F. Kennedy stood for peace in his Presidential campaign and after he was elected President. He was easily gotten rid of by his enemies that wanted a war in Viet Nam, which included the CIA, the FBI as supporters of the CIA, most of the military complex including Generals and Admirals, and other politicians, mostly Republicans, who notoriously stand for war, death, and destruction. Although he was the President of the United States, the "most powerful man in the world", as Americans are told repeatedly, it was no obstacle of any consequence for the forces working against him, that he was powerless to stop. In America if you are a good politician, wanting to promote peace and love and harmony, you, the politician, won't last long.

They planned and arranged his assassination, and the war in Viet Nam was begun months after he was murdered. No other President in American history had been pressured for the first 1000 days of his Presidency to begin seven different wars. There were unrelenting demands on him from Admirals and Generals and politicians to go to war in Berlin, Cuba, South Viet Nam, and North Viet Nam for those 1000 days, during which he resisted their demands and insisted America would not go to war again. He stood for peace both before and after he was elected President, in what was one of the last honest elections of the people, by the people, and for the people.

The American economy is a war economy, a military industrial complex, since WW II. But the wars will always happen, and have always happened, in other countries. So the process of arranging the assassination of President Kenned was impossible to trace back to any one person because there was no one person. The CIA, the FBI, the NSA, the military industrial complex, especially Admirals and Generals, and politicians like Secretary of State McNamara, all wanted the war in Viet Nam, promoted the war in Viet Nam, supported the war in Viet Nam, and President Kennedy got in the way. He refused to start a war any of the seven times he was pushed by them to go to war in Berlin, Cuba, South Viet Nam, and North Viet Nam. No other President in American history had been faced with as much pressure to start as many wars in just his first 1000 days of office. It didn't matter that the

American people had elected JFK as President because they did not want war with Viet Nam or any other country, and did not want American soldiers to be drafted and sent there against their will. Instead, Americans wanted what President Kennedy stood for. But the powers that be did not let him be President for much more than those first 1000 days. He had told the CIA, the FBI, and the U.S. military leaders what to do.

No one tells the CIA what to do, or the FBI that backed the CIA what to do. They do what they want to do. No one tells the military leaders what to do. They do what they want to do. Oswald said, while he was in jail, that he was a "patsy for the CIA". He was never allowed or given legal counsel or representation, as is guaranteed in the Constitution and the Bill of Rights. After he was assassinated it was proven that he had worked for the CIA in Dallas, Texas, and had been there, at that CIA office, in the days prior to the assassination of JFK.

Before 9/11 President Bush "W" and politicians were repeatedly given opportunities by the military to kill or capture Bin Laden that they turned down. He needed to be alive, or not captured, in order to justify the pending national tragedy of 9/11 by terrorists, 15 of which came from Saudi Arabia, not Iraq, and the planned attack on Iraq, a war with Iraq, to remake the Middle East and spread United States power in that part of the World. Bin Laden was a necessary and vital part of the equation to manipulate the American people. After beginning the war in Iraq it was absolutely necessary that Bin Laden stay alive, be kept alive in obscurity, as long as possible for the continued manipulation of the American public. After spending hundreds of billions of dollars in the quest for Bin laden, and taking the lives of hundreds of thousands of innocent civilians in Afghanistan, Iraq, and Pakistan, the eight year war was allowed to take a turn with the killing of Osama Bin Laden.

The consequences of privatization are destruction of an economy. This has been proven in other countries. The motivation behind privatization is greed, power, and control. Corporate greed. It has caused poverty to double and triple in other countries. Argentina's Government privatized their Social Security system, their utilities, their coal mines, their railroad, and their medical system of Universal Healthcare that was free for everyone in Argentina, because privatization was demanded by the IMF, the International Monetary Fund, as a condition for getting loans from the IMF.

However, the result of privatization was economic collapse, not just a financial crisis, and perpetual indebtedness to the IMF. This scenario has been repeated, and will continue to be repeated, again and again, with the consequences of privatization being destruction of a national economy. That is why it is demanded as a condition of loans, huge loans of hundreds of millions of dollars and even billions of dollars, given by the IMF or the World Bank to any country. Altruism has not been, and is not now, a motivation for financial help from the IMF or the World Bank. The slow destruction of national economies has been, and is, a primary reason, by demanding national privatization, that will lead to economic collapse and economic destruction of that country.

Bush "W" and his Neo Con crew of Wolfowitz, Cheney, Rumsfeld, Rove, Ashcroft, his brother Florida Governor Bush, his father former President Bush, who continued to get daily briefings from the White House for years when his son was President, ignored this proof like they ignored everything else contrary to their plans for eight years, when they pushed hard and repeatedly for privatization of Social Security in America. The fact that privatization doesn't work, and is instead disastrous, clearly is why they promoted it. For power, control, and greed for the few and misery for the many. It's like a broken record, always the same theme, always the same meaning for the past 70 years, and especially since 2000, at the beginning of the 21st century.

In the same manner they ignored authorities and scholars about Iraq and the Middle East who said that chaos and widespread suffering, deprivation, feuds among the many factions resistance to change, and death for the people who lived there would be the result of an invasion of Iraq. His own father had written a book years before saying the Middle East was too complicated, split into too many factions, to attempt any influence and changes there. Meanwhile, Saudi Arabian royalty and rulers had given the elder Bush gifts of hundreds of millions of dollars every year for years, apparently to influence him in some way politically. Bush "W", his son, ignored his father's book, and was more influenced by Cheney and the rest of the Neo Con crew that was planning to reign over America after 2001. Neo Con domination of America was their collective goal for many years.

In the 21st century the Republican Party has had ulterior motives for their financial gain and increased power, and the Democratic Party lets them do whatever they want to do, as if the Democratic politicians didn't represent the people who elected them. It's a disconnect. Once elected, Democratic politicians usually float, not swim. Once elected, Republican politicians swim aggressively with other Republican sharks, and destroy and kill when they think it is necessary to further their agendas and their plans for political domination.

For years the Social Security system had a yearly surplus of $1.5 trillion to $2.8 trillion dollars. That huge surplus of money, payments made by Americans into their Social Security fund, has been disappearing since 2001, starting with the Bush "W" administration. Probably about $20 trillion dollars is owed by the Federal Government to the Social Security fund but it will never be paid back. It probably went into "the Black Project", a secret and hidden part of the DOD that gets at least $1.7 trillion dollars of unallocated money, unaccounted for money, stolen money, each year since about 2000. It's a space-based weapons program and a UFO/ETV reverse-engineering program to protect the United States from alien attacks, to ensure United States global dominance.

This is beyond crazy. So who controls this massive amount of money? No one will say. After all, it's about national security. But it's theft, stealing from the American people, stealing from their Social Security fund that is for their security and retirement as Americans. If it wasn't stealing "they", the Federal Government and the DOD, would be upfront about it. Honesty doesn't hide in "Black Projects", in hidden and secretive projects that have to be dominated and controlled by secrets and lies, by disinformation and misinformation in order to hide it from the American people.

Who will complain when it isn't paid back? No one. No Senator or Congressman. Most Americans don't even know it's been stolen from them, from their social security for their future. It fits into the Republican agenda for ending Social Security as Americans know it, because since then there is a huge Social Security Fund deficit, a false deficit, to manipulate everyone into privatizing it. Since 2001 Republicans have been hell-bent on radically changing or stopping Social Security. Privatizing will allow investors, corporations, etc., to profit from the immense amount of money collected every year from this mandatory payment system for Social Security for all Americans. Republican politicians, Democrats too, will profit from this manipulation of the American public.

So now the Republicans are half-way there. The greed and the lies of power-hungry Republicans never ends. The Democrats have maintained that the Social Security Fund has a surplus and will be secure until about 2035. But that's not enough. They have to be pro-active in stopping the viciousness, greed, lies and selfishness of the Republican Party, of their politicians, who will steal, lie, and manipulate to get what they want. Somebody has to protect the American public from this continuing travesty, from this unbelievably massive and incomprehensible theft, and restore the stolen at least **$20 trillion dollars** to where and to who it rightfully belongs. But that will never happen. But a democracy is not supposed to be like that.

All cruelty in the World begins with demented egos and selfishness. Misery and suffering are always the result. Universal peace and a good life for everyone is not what America is about, so selfishness, lies, arrogance and big egos are very common in America in the 21st century.

In the American Democracy the President is supposed to be the chief administrator for what the public wants, for all the people, for the Republic, for the Democracy. Thus the two Party names Democrats and Republicans. When the public is not given truth and facts but is given lies and deceptions instead they cannot make informed and correct decisions about their Government and what they want the President to do as their Administrator. The manipulated people then have no power. It isn't their Government anymore. The democracy disappears or is broken. When information is controlled and false, starting with the President, the people are pawns in often deadly and harmful political games of power and greed. These political agendas are very common.

Advertising is a business game. Politics is a game of power, control, and greed. Both center their interests on money. So when politicians advertise about themselves they can easily be dishonest and deceptive. The TV news media makes billions of dollars in profits from political advertising, which has replaced objective reporting about politicians in election years. The audience is more easily influenced and manipulated by sound-bites than by newspaper reporting.

When lies are repeated often enough they sound like the truth. If it's what the public wants to hear, or read, it doesn't even have to be repeated. The news media and Press just report what the Government representatives and spokespersons, and politicians, tell them to report. There no longer are investigations into what is the truth, or looking for proof. During the eight year reign of Bush "W" if reporters asked the wrong questions they were fired.

During the 21st century people have come to expect lies and deception from a controlled and biased TV news media and Press in America. It's a status quo. It's become an American tradition.

Democrats are usually good people with good intentions, wanting to help all Americans and promote harmony. But they're weak. They are easily exploited by Republican politicians who are manipulative and mean-spirited, and devisive. Republican politicians take advantage of Democratic politician weakness, like bullies or alpha-male dogs. Or, they just argue about everything. After all, Republicans usually have their own version of the truth.

Politicians can't be trusted to serve the public. For many years actions by the United States Government, by politicians, have caused Americans to not trust their own Government. Most people believe what they are taught in school, by the TV news media, by books, the internet, newspapers. All of these sources can be partly, or completely, wrong but the public usually can't find the truth themselves. Any information can be, and often is, distorted or falsified. It's a free country. A common attitude is that "everybody lies." It's common knowledge that lawyers, keepers of the law, manipulate and lie to get what they want, which is as much money as possible and power. And that Judges, and Magistrates, believe the lies if they want to. Lies, manipulation, deceit, deception, starting with individual Americans, at all social levels, at all income levels, at all levels of government and business, happens every day everywhere in America. Problems and misery are the result.

In 2011 the woman who started the revolution in Libya, with 10 other dissenters, said in an interview "In Libya people can say anything they want. But nothing changes." That's more freedom of speech than in the United States. But the "nothing changes" is the same. And Libya is a dictatorship, supported by the United States Government for many years with yearly gifts of at least hundreds of millions of dollars.

The multi-million dollar United States military defense market, the military airplanes, the weapons, missiles, carriers, guns, ships, etc. produced in the United States, and in other countries by United States companies located there, are bought by other countries with money given to them by the United States Government. Specifically, $28 billion of the $42 billion dollars of yearly United States foreign aid is given for specified military and defense spending to buy from the United States, and $14 billion for economic aid. The United States Government, then, is subsidizing the United States production of defense and military products in order to supply those countries, and in order to subsidize American production, i.e. jobs. It's like welfare for the defense and military industries.

The $28 billion dollars given to these countries by the United States every year comes back to the United States as their mandatory military spending. Lockheed has long been the biggest recipient of that returning money. That same money could be put to better use for Americans in America to make their life better, instead of using it to support and encourage killing, torture, destruction of people and property. Often the weapons, etc., made in America and paid for by Americans, are used against the citizens of that country by their own Government when those citizens demonstrate for jobs, housing, food, and medical care. Or demonstrate for an honest and better Government.

So the United States has, and does, fund killing and torture of people in other countries who are protesting, who are asking for help from their own Government, to get what the United States touts as its own principles for a better life in a better country. El Salvador, Nicaragua, and Egypt are examples of all of this.

An exception to that is that the United States gives Egypt $1.5 billion dollars a year in exchange for use of their vast and expansive desert for military training, and the use of their Suez Canal for economic and military purposes. It has been estimated a total of $70 billion dollars has been given to Egypt by the United States. While the Egyptian President had amassed $70 billion dollars of American money, the exact same amount, for his own personal wealth. Since 1950 foreign rulers have repeatedly used United States foreign aid money, United States tax-payer's money, for themselves.

It's like how the United States Government and politicians supported and paid for the dictator of South Viet Nam in the 1950's and 1960's, supporting his rich and extravagant lifestyle as his people starved and lived in destitution and depravation of the basic human essentials. The United States never demanded that he give that millions of dollars of foreign aid every year to the people that really needed it in his country. Instead, the U.S. eventually killed millions of them.

All major national financial crisis's in the United States since about 1980 happened because of deregulation of the financial services industry, the financial sector of America. In the 1980's Savings and Loans used customer's money, their depositor's money, to make risky investments, etc. that resulted in the loss of that money. Almost 2000 S & L financial executives were prosecuted and imprisoned for theft, fraud, etc. The U.S. Government gave those Savings and Loans $124 billion dollars (some said $170 billion) of tax-payer's money to cover those losses. That was the S & L bail-out by the United States Government.

After the year 2000 deregulation and no enforcement of regulation laws by the SEC or Greenspan, chairman of the Federal Reserve, allowed excessive and illegal profits, salaries, fees, bonuses, for financial executives, brokers, etc., in the mortgage industry, for investment banks, etc. for performance based on lies, dishonesty to their customers, huge financial mistakes, and huge financial losses. No matter what they did, what mistakes they made, they were protected.

After collecting excessive fees for loans they would sell those loans, good or bad, to avoid possible future losses for themselves. After record-setting profits for themselves they had record-setting losses of their client's money, for which the United States Government gave them *$700 billion dollars* of American's money as a bailout, a gift. None of the financial executives behind that national financial crisis were ever prosecuted or imprisoned, or had to return the stolen and lost money to their clients. No matter what theft they engaged in they were protected by the U.S. Government.

Henry Paulson, later appointed Secretary of the Treasury by President Obama, profited at least *$31 million dollars* from that fiasco and theft from the American people. This was never investigated as his own personal theft from the American people, as a result of his illegal activities, making him unfit to be the Secretary of the Treasury. As usual it was ignored, pretending it never happened.

With that huge gift of *$700 billion dollars* from the United States Government those investment banks bought out other banks, like Wachovia and Bank of America, merging with them to create larger banks. The larger the bank the more certain it is the United States will bail-out the bank, so mergers are a safety-net. Also, they then paid their executives much higher salaries, millions more, and much higher bonuses, also millions more dollars, for their continuance of making poor decisions, poor investments, because, among other things, mistakes made the banks billions of dollars richer. Not a paltry millions, but billions.

Since then financial industry lobbyists have been able to spend billions of dollars more to "buy-out" politicians and elections, and to guarantee the continuation of deregulation. And to guarantee regulations and laws will continue to not be enforced, and to ensure there will be no new regulations or new laws for the financial industry in America. Along with some other financial industry insider manipulations, to help them in their endless quest for profits and money at the expense of their customers and the American public.

Any country that has deregulated its financial sector and not enforced existing regulations of that financial industry has experienced disaster and financial devastation of their national economy because of subsequent cheating, fraud, theft, dishonesty. For many years the Security and Exchange Commission and the Federal Reserve have refused to enforce financial industry regulations that were put in place to protect all Americans, not just investors. Especially since the Bush "W" Administration, and always when Greenspan was the chairman of the Fed. But Clinton also supported the deregulation when he was President. In 2010 there were five financial industry lobbyists for each Congressman. No one knows how many millions of dollars were paid to them for their support.

In the United States a financial service executive, or broker, can win with a losing hand by using other people's money. And by betting on the *failure* of whatever financial issue they are also backing. Betting on both the success and the failure of anything guarantees profit on either end.

For 60 years scientists have been given many millions of dollars every year by the United States Government, tax-payer's money, to create cancer in animals, kept for years in tiny cages, tortured and killed. These scientists and lab workers had to create cancer in these animals before they could fulfill their grant requests, to find a cure for the cancer they would create. It is a travesty that these scientists have never, in 60 years, told the American public what they do to cause cancer and demanded elimination of those causes of cancer. Or at least have been required by the Government to tell the public so they could avoid the sources and the causes, like what chemicals were to blame. Or those sources and causes should have been eliminated by the Federal Government. Or, more importantly, the public should have been told about the cures for many types of cancers that they really *have* found. Secrets, lies, and deceptions by the NIH, by researchers, and by scientists, and by the medical sickness industry have meant that one out of two men and one out of three women in America will eventually get cancer in the 21$^{st}$ century.

But that would have meant the loss of their grant money, billions of dollars, for the perpetuation of the cancer industry. That same grant money has always been given repeatedly, year after year, to the same scientists and researchers to repeat the same cruel and inhumane experiments year after year. Profit and money became the primary reason for the existence of the NIH. Not health.

There has never been any end to this huge waste of money, taxpayer's money, by the National Institute of Health, given billions of dollars to make sure they never find the cure for *any* cancer, or any other disastrous deadly diseases. In so doing they are guaranteeing and creating an endless and increasing supply of patients, victims, for the hugely over-priced and manipulative medical sickness industry in America.

For many years these cancer industry scientists have known what the causes of cancer are, and what chemicals should be eliminated, etc. to prevent cancer. Instead, they get millions to torture animals and play the cancer game with the American public every year, often doing the same tests and experiments over and over again, year after year. Why? Because they aren't looking for cures for cancer. And, they've had the answers for a long time. And, so they could qualify for hundreds of billions of dollars of Federal Government grant money for the last 60 years. Most of this money goes to, and through, the NIH, the National Institute of Health. This has been a monstrous waste of tax-payer's money, perpetuating unnecessary sickness, suffering, and death for millions of human beings and for millions of tortured and abused lab animals. The cancer industry is like a cancer, an industry that's out of control but controlled by the Government, that keeps replicating and dividing endlessly, with death the common outcome.

The heads of Fannie Mae and Freddie Mac lost $150 million dollars and manipulated the books, the numbers, for their own benefit. This enabled them to get multi- million dollar salaries and million dollar (plus) bonuses, as rewards for failing to operate these Government agencies the way they should have been run. Then, to add insult to injury, United States tax-payers had to pay lawyers $165 million to defend these corrupt heads of Freddie Mac and Fannie Mae for their crimes against Americans, their theft of tax-payer's money.

Politicians, both Republican and Democrat, and President Obama, ignored the American public, including at least 20,000 e-mails, when they gave $700 billion dollars that belonged to Americans to mega-banks (to hoard) for a fictionalized bailout. This was an action of a plutocracy, a country run by the wealthy for the benefit of the wealthy. Politicians are controlled by mega-banks, as was Bush "W" when he gave banks billions of dollars before he left office. It was mega-money given to mega-banks.

The CEOs of those so-called "failed" mega-banks got multi-million dollar salaries and million dollar (plus) bonuses the following year as rewards for making the banks "fail" and getting $700 billion dollars of free money from tax-payers as gifts for failing to operate banks the way they should be operated. When a Government is run by banks, corporations, oil companies, and the 2% to 5% elite, then it's a plutocracy, not a democracy by the people and for the people.

The original plans for the United States Government had checks and balances, and laws and justice for the average man and woman, but it got lost somewhere along the way. Too often, for too long, justice in America has been a game, and tax-payers have little or no control over how their money is used after it is forcefully taken from them by the IRS with threats of imprisonment, fines, loss of possessions, and loss of jobs. But hey, the IRS isn't supposed to do that in America. Who do they think they are? They are playing the endless dysfunctional IRS game of control, power, profit, secrecy, and ill-gotten money. So what authority is threatening and regulating the IRS because they have gotten out of control, having much more power than was ever intended, doing things they shouldn't be doing? No one. Not anyone ever, anywhere.

The United States national debt was $11.5 trillion in 2010, mostly money owed to China. So why didn't the United States Treasury just print $11.5 trillion dollars and give it to China, like the Treasury does for the United States oil industry, and for the biggest oil companies/corporations? The World's largest banks are the Central Banks that control the International Banking Cartel, which controls the finances and the money supply of most countries. In the United States the Federal Reserve controls United States money. No one knows how much money they are in control of, money that they can do whatever they want to with.

The Fed is not a Government agency or office or department. It is, however, the Central Bank for the United States, manipulating finances, controlling recessions and depressions, and everything in between. The Fed is supposed to protect the nation's money, an unknown amount of money for which it has no audits, no regulations to follow. The Fed answers to no one, and it never has. The members, called Governors, answer to no one. They have uncontrolled access to many trillions of dollars that belongs to the American people.

In 2014 the United States Government, the United States taxpayer, paid them at least $179,000 a year for very little work, and for their devastating mistakes, even though they are not employees of the United States Government. They are appointed by the United States President for fourteen years, and cannot be fired. The Fed Chairman gets at least $199,000 a year, and can stay on the job for as long as he wants. These positions, not really jobs, are like protected and secretive over-paid civil service jobs that very few people in America even know about, even though the people employed by the Fed have access to all money and everything financial in all American's lives.

Every year $42 billion dollars of United States tax dollars are given as foreign aid to foreign countries. Many of these countries don't even like America, or are already very wealthy countries. Like Arabia, that is given hundreds of millions of dollars every year as United States foreign aid that has rarely gotten to the people who really need it living there in Arabia. Does the United States have to borrow that $42 billion dollars to give it away as foreign aid? The answer must be yes, which means the interest on it has to be paid every year besides the principal. When the United States credit rating is no longer A+ or A then the interest rate, and interest amounts, will greatly increase like they do for individual personal credit card accounts. Then, just like for credit card holders, it will eventually become untenable. This has happened to other countries that then have a national financial crisis. They often have to raise taxes to pay for that problem, or borrow more money from the IMF and the World Bank. This increases their risk for eventual destitution of their country.

If that foreign aid was instead kept in the United States to use as domestic aid for the poor and the lower middle-class in America, or to fund a free national healthcare system in America, or instead given as foreign aid directly to the people who really need it in other countries, then it would be a much better use of that money. It would be the Christian thing to do, which Republicans often align themselves with in words but not actions.

Just as the FBI was going to start investigating more white collar crime done by CEO's in the mortgage industry than ever before in United States history, more mortgage fraud than ever before in United States history, 9/11 happened. The FBI then diverted 500 FBI agents to that. Was that a coincidence? Or was it planned? As a result, that mortgage industry fraud was mostly ignored and insufficiently investigated, and ultimately all participants escaped legal actions and retribution, imprisonment and fines. It wasn't of much interest to most of the American public, who were being manipulated by the American Press and the media and the Government and their President to be concerned only with the 9/11 tragedies that had just happened then in 2001. But maybe there are no coincidences. The tragedies of 9/11 in 2001 created public support for declaring a war on Iraq.

Most politicians do not help the people who elected them, unless they are the largest campaign contributors for election or re-election. But they do help themselves. There are about 100 times more lobbyists and members of special interest groups in Washington, D.C. than politicians. They heavily influence how the Federal Government is run, who gets money and how much, and what bills get passed, by giving hundreds of millions of dollars to the politicians in charge of running the United States. These are bribes cloaked as gifts. Politicians are manipulated by money and gifts, and they then manipulate the American public. The $700 billion dollar mega-bank bailout was just one example of this out of thousands.

This is no longer a Government by the people and for the people. The only way to change this bad situation is to not allow special interest groups and lobbyists, or any millionaires or billionaires, to influence politicians with money or gifts. It's like pharmaceuticals pressuring physicians with gifts and money to persuade them to prescribe their drugs, to push their drugs. So, again, they have long been bribes cloaked as gifts. Another example is that the financial services sector, the financial industry, uses hundreds of billions of dollars of their ill-gained profits to influence politicians, mostly to make sure regulations aren't enforced or enacted.

Manipulation of the public is a big part of American politics and government. In a Press conference after invading Iraq President Bush "W" said "I don't know what made you think Iraq had anything to do with 9/11. Saddam Hussein had nothing to do with 9/11." So why did he bomb Iraq and continue military occupation there? So why was the United States military over there in Iraq at all? So why was there a multi-million dollar (allegedly) effort made to find and kill Saddam Hussein? He was shown on Cable TV news as saying the United States was lying, making it all up, to make him the fall guy for what they had done, or were going to do.

What the United States had done, and has done, was mostly kept a secret from the American people. Like how Bush "W" and Cheney knew he had WMDs because the United States had sold WMDs to him years before. Hussein was telling the truth when he had said those WMDs had been destroyed because they couldn't possibly use them anyway because of U.S. restrictions, and destructions of access to oil and planes to fly them anywhere, and certainly not to the United States

6000 miles away. The United States Government had been giving Hussein a total of billions of dollars for many years, after they had put him in power to replace the CIA-assassinated former leader of Iraq, who had been working to establish a democracy, as he was replacing the Iraq dictatorship with a democracy. The United States supports dictatorships and anarchies, usually not democracies.

Oil drives the military machine. Fourteen permanent military bases have been built in Iraq since U.S. occupation began. After Vice-President Cheney gave no-bid contracts in Iraq worth billions of dollars to Halliburton his yearly income on his income tax return form (as public information) increased from about a million dollars to $60 to $70 million dollars a year within five years.

The U.S. knew Saddam Hussein had weapons of mass destruction because the U.S. had sold them to him, not because of satellite photos or spy planes. In the first six months of the Iraqi invasion at least 6000 innocent men, women, children, civilians of Iraq, were murdered by U.S. military "smart" bombs directed at government buildings. So "smart" bombs are in fact stupid bombs. Smart or stupid, bombs kill innocent people. The horrors of war, suffering and death, are not changed.

Halliburton , Vice President Cheney's company, and Bechtel (four congressmen and senators were CEOs, etc. for Bechtel) got multi-billion dollar no-bid contracts to rebuild Iraq after deliberate destruction of Iraq by Bush "W", Rove, Wolfowitz, Cheney, Rumsfeld, and the rest of their Neo Con crew. It was a part of their plans for dominating that part of the oil world, and for building massive military complexes and United States Government buildings to secure and maintain and continue that domination indefinitely. Not to rebuild what the military had destroyed in Iraq, not to help the people in Iraq to recover from the destruction and deaths.

In every case there was a method to their madness. Forcing any country, like Iraq, to be a democracy is undemocratic. Forced elections do not make a country or its citizens a democracy. But it's all a part of the bigger plan for globalization and a global government and a global economy. It's a plan that many thousands of people, maybe a million people, are involved in to make it come true. It has a momentum of its own and nothing, apparently, will stop it. It's the future.

The collapse of the Social Security system in the United States would lead to social collapse and economic collapse in the United States, not just a financial collapse. People with the most money, the elite, do not create more jobs, and would not create more jobs in a situation like that. They invest their endless money into financial investments instead. They certainly have never created jobs for elderly people and disabled people, the people that need to be helped by Social Security the most, the people that depend on it the most. The Social Security Fund, the entire system, must be protected, as it has been since it was begun by President Franklin Roosevelt about 70 years ago, until the theft of *trillions of dollars* every year from the Social Security Fund started in 2001. It's a necessary part of the future for the expendable masses, but the expendable masses are powerless to protect it. There's nothing any one person or group in America can do to get replacement of the stolen at least $11 trillion dollars, to have it put back into the Social Security Fund where it belongs.

In the 1990's the former senior President Bush wrote a book explaining why he didn't invade Iraq when he was President. He wrote about the many factions that disagree, the many problems that foreign occupation would create. He decided it was not an intelligent thing to do. But intelligence never got in his son George's way before, and didn't again when he was President from 2001 to 2009.

In 2007 and 2008 more than 200,000 Presidential e-mails disappeared after they were subpoenaed. The hallmark of the Bush "W" and Cheney administration was deception and dishonesty. When Bush "W" left office in 2009 the United States deficit was more than $11.5 trillion dollars, a historical first of unbelievably awful financial management and theft. But he had inherited a balanced national budget in 2001, and a national budget surplus of hundreds of millions of dollars, from President Clinton. This no deficit with hundreds of millions of dollars in surplus was a political and historical first, a great accomplishment. In contrast, the irresponsibility, theft, dishonesty and incompetency of Bush "W" and Cheney would create endless hardships for generations, for hundreds of millions of people for generations to come. No amount of political rhetoric and lies from the Neo Cons and from the Far Right Republicans, or from just the normal Republicans and the Evangelical Fundamentalists, could make the immense and enormous problems disappear.

For many years the United States Government has given foreign aid to the Saudi Arabian Government, hundreds of millions of dollars every year. It's the wealthiest country in the World, and has no yearly financial deficit. So why has that huge amount of money been given to Saudi Arabia as a gift for many years? After 9/11 happened in 2001 Bush "W" said 9/11 was justification for war with Iraq. That had been the Neo Con plan before he was appointed President in 2000/2001. Yet at least 15 of the 19 hijackers on 9/11 were from Saudi Arabia and none were from Iraq. This is glaring proof about the dishonesty of the Bush "W" and Cheney administration. Why wasn't Saudi Arabia attacked and an occupation and war conducted there instead of Iraq? Because it didn't fit into their plans. And because Saudi Arabia was a long-time friend of the United States Government, and had the World's largest oil reserves. But mostly because that is what the Neo Cons in power had planned months before 9/11 happened in 2001, and had planned years before in their plans for global domination and the Neo Con domination of the United States.

It was like how President Johnson had declared war on Viet Nam and then conducted a brutal occupation and war for years in Viet Nam, later continued for years by President Nixon, all based on lies, all based on manufactured information. Because it fit into his and McNamara's political plans, and the plans of the military leaders, the Generals and the Admirals, and the plans of the elite and the people who rule America, the Shadow Government. Wars make a lot of money for a lot of people, and give powers to politicians, especially the President, that wouldn't happen without the cover of a war.

Bush "W" took no responsibility for his actions, for the disasters he and Cheney had created and left behind. When his term was done he just rode off into the sunset to live in his newly bought multi-million dollar home in Dallas. His job was done. Johnson, on the other hand, felt remorse and expressed remorse for what he had done, for what he had begun, that caused about 25,000 American soldiers to die in Viet Nam during the time he was President. The next President, Nixon, could have stopped it but he didn't, so 28,000 more American soldiers died in Viet Nam before that war ended, along with four to six million citizens of Viet Nam.

Possibly half a million people in Iraq, citizens of Iraq, innocent men, women, children, and babies lost their lives or were permanently crippled because of the actions and words of former President Bush "W" and former Vice President Cheney. "Vice" was an appropriate title for a man who had so many vices and desired to do so much harm to humanity, but not to his fellow Neo Cons. No list was ever kept, and there was no accountability, for Iraqi deaths and injuries done by the United States military and paramilitary, and the very highly paid privatized military that was in Iraq from 2003 to 2011, and is probably still there, secretively. Who paid them their exorbitant salaries? The American Government, i.e. the American people.

Nixon was accused of, and impeached for, abuse of power and obstruction of justice. This is what Bush "W" did repeatedly, for eight long years, but was never charged with doing. Part of the reason this was not stopped was because of the weakness of the Democratic Party, the weakness of the Democratic politicians. Times change, people change, but not for the better.

During the Bush "W" reign whoever criticized him, his policies, or his and Cheney's policies or actions was called "un-American", "un-patriotic", "a terrorist", or "an enemy of the state". How absurd and ridiculous! How stupid and mean and controlling. And yes, how un-American. The perpetrators of this un-American behavior were, of course, Republicans, an inherently mean and increasingly vicious, selfish, and greedy party since 2000. Especially the Far Right, the Neo Cons, and the Religious Right, the Fundamentalists. Finally, and at last, the Neo Cons controlled the United States Government from 2001 to 2009 by stealing the election, the Presidency. Unfortunately those policies and other controlling policies that were un-American were continued by Obama, and signed into perpetuation by him when he signed The National Defense Authorization Act in 2011. It was, as TV anchorman Peter Jenkins had said, "the end of America as we know it."

Bush "W" had said in 2003 that it didn't matter if people were told the truth or not. He said "What does it matter?", and then smiled, in an interview on PBS after invading Iraq, when the host commentator said the American people needed to be told the truth. Corruption, dishonesty, greed, selfishness, and incompetence has been rampant in the United States for many years. Starting with politicians, the very rich, and military personnel at all levels, especially at the top, including every race, except American Indians, an inherently noble and wise race. Low quality character and low quality behavior is found everywhere, not just in the United States. Most of the American public, and probably most of the rest of the World, can be easily manipulated by the media.

In 2004 Pat Tillman, the national football star, was killed in Iraq as he stood on a hill shouting his name at the soldiers from his outfit who were shooting at him from a military vehicle on the road below. "Friendly fire" is what the military calls it. But military leaders and President Bush "W" told the public repeatedly and for years that he was killed by the enemy, the Taliban. His mother and his father knew differently and demanded an official investigation. Finally, in 2007, there was a Congressional hearing of four Generals and Donald Rumsfeld. More than 80 times they said they didn't know anything or remember anything, allowing endless cover-ups. Both Mr. and Mrs. Tillman said they all had lied, under oath, in their testimonies. Mrs. Tillman said her son's death was used as "a tool for political propaganda" and "to promote the war". Mr. Tillman said "Where does it end?"

It doesn't. Lying and corruption have permeated, infiltrated, all of American life. Especially the government, both state and Federal. Those Generals, all at the highest level of military achievement and the epitome of military success and military mentality, had lied repeatedly under oath, a crime done again and again, to protect themselves, their friends, the United States military, and their Government. Rumsfeld, a political servant of the American people and a self-serving politician of high rank, abused his office and responsibilities to all of the American people by lying, by using deceit and deception repeatedly throughout his time in office, or Government affiliation, for many years. Like

Bush 'W", his perpetual out-of place strange smile always accompanied those lies, deception and deceit. It was a signal from both of them that they were being dishonest. It seems that no one or nothing can change the things that are wrong in America because absolute power is absolute. Because absolute power corrupts absolutely.

The people that control America don't want to change the status quo. And the media and the Press are complicit in manipulation of the public by giving them information they want to hear, often not the truth. Often that's what the public wants anyway. If they don't know the truth about anything the public can't do anything about anything anyway. Most people, the American public, operate within the parameters of what they know. They of course can't be responsible for what they don't know, didn't know, or were lied to about. Ignorance, after all, is bliss. Also, it's a way to control people, especially the expendable masses.

In order for anything of consequence to change the leaders of the government and the leaders of corporate America have to change. The structures of government and the structures of corporations, first and foremost the oil industry, would have to change. Of course that will never happen. At least not in the 21st century. And supposedly there won't be any oil left to use in the 22nd century.

Every one of the five major institutions in America are systems that will not change. Most Americans think that is just fine, but the ones who don't put themselves in jeopardy of harm from the part of America that is not free and not democratic. In some parts of America that even includes public libraries since 2001. This would be in the Republican areas of the United States, usually the Far Right Republican areas, where they have readily embraced the loss of Constitutional rights and the loss of any other rights as part of the status quo.

One other free and democratic country also lies to the public and manipulates their public. Before Britain declared war on Germany in the 1930's their rulers decided destroying the Lusitania, the pride of England, would inspire and validate a war with Germany in the minds of the British people. They were right. It did. The Lusitania was sunk by British intelligence forces and British military forces. World War I was therefore justified and declared by Britain after the Lusitania sank and more than a thousand people who had been traveling on it died.

More than 50 years later trains were blown up in Britain by alleged "terrorists" at the same time identical planned war games were diverting and confusing defense reactions and military planes from defending the real attacks. The exact same thing happened in the United States on 9/11, 2001.

On the morning of 9/11 all United States defense mechanisms were engaged in a simulated war game that was a terrorist attack *exactly* like what was happening in New York City and Washington, D.C. on that same day. This is why all responses were delayed or ignored. They thought it was part of the war game they had been ordered to play by the powers that be, by their Government.

No plane fragments or plane engine fragments were ever found at the part of the Pentagon that was destroyed in Washington, D.C. But bodies were found. It is impossible that a metal plane weighing many tons, and its engines weighing tons, completely disappeared but the bodies did not. What happened to all of its millions of gallons of fuel? It disappeared without a trace.

The Twin Towers buildings in New York City had metal frames that had been heated to 4000 degrees by a demolition material before the hijackers crashed the planes into them, causing that metal to buckle and the building to collapse. It was obvious to experts that explosives caused the buildings in both New York City and Washington, D.C. to collapse on 9/11, not the hijacked planes. It was impossible they said for those three planes to have done that much damage. This was according to engineering experts, architects, explosives engineers, materials experts, explosives experts, and construction and metals experts. Besides the input of the men who had designed the buildings to withstand earthquakes and hurricanes.

Yet Americans continued to believe, and continue to believe, that men from Iraq hijacked American planes and caused the massive destruction of those three buildings and the deaths of almost 3000 innocent people on that day in September, 2001. Also despite the fact that the media (wonder of wonders) proved that 15 of the 19 hijackers were from Saudi Arabia, and none were from Iraq. Due to the complicity of the media one could only wonder if, in actuality, all of the hijackers had been from Saudi Arabia. Americans could only be thankful for whatever facts and truth they were given. But who could be believed? What could be believed? The truth was out there but it seemed that no one knew where it could be found. When the truth about a national tragedy is a mystery then the national Government needs to be changed. But it wasn't, and it won't be.

The CIA accessed more than 75,000 pages of transcripts, records, and reports that proved Iraq and Saddam Hussein were innocent of any connection to 9/11. A letter from Italy about Iraq buying uranium from Africa was used by Bush "W", Cheney, Rumsfeld, and Powell to justify bombing Iraq, even though the CIA had said the letter was false, was a fraud. The French version of the CIA investigated it and found it was a fraud. That is why France, the French people, did not support the United States invasion of Iraq. All of the negative Press lasting for months about France and the French people was a distortion of the truth, lies, for political manipulation. Just like almost everything about 9/11 was a manipulation of the people for political reasons, for furthering political agendas.

In 2002, 2003, and 2004 many thousands of people marched in Washington, D.C. and other places against the war in Iraq that followed 9/11. The marches and protests got little or no news or media coverage. The participants were clubbed, shot at with shotguns and pellet guns, sprayed with tear gas, arrested and jailed. This included people on the fringes of the demonstrations who were not participating. Since 2001 it has been very dangerous to exercise your Constitutional rights, especially if they have been taken away by The Patriot Act of 2001,that was signed into permanent perpetuation by Obama in 2011, along with him signing The National Defense Act in 2011. Both of these Acts destroyed a big part of The Constitution and The Bill of Rights without the American public even knowing about it. This wasn't supposed to happen in a democracy.

But the part of America that believes in "America, right or wrong" wouldn't care anyway. And that includes many millions of people, maybe a hundred million people in America at direct odds with the other part of America that *does* care about The Constitution, about maintaining it and following it. This probably also includes at least a hundred million people in America. It appeared the attacks on 9/11 were allowed to happen, to use as propaganda to manipulate the people of the United States, to validate the war in Iraq that had been planned long before 9/11 actually happened, by the Neo Cons in power at that time, elected or not elected, so they could take over the oil fields, the oil production, in Iraq. In 2004, one year after beginning the Iraq war, the invasion, attacks, and occupation of Iraq, the United States had finished building the largest United States military base in the World in Iraq, and the largest United States Embassy in the entire World nearby.

Everything seemed transparent to whoever wanted to see parts of the truth, but those who didn't want the truth refused to see any of it. Being blind to the truth is a common Republican trait, both in the 20<sup>th</sup> and 21<sup>st</sup> centuries, that is also a trait shared by many Democrats. It has become the American way since the elections of 2000, for both politicians and the public.

The Gulf of Tonkin incident never happened, with North Viet Nam being the aggressor and attacker. It was made up and staged with Israeli military planes, bought from America with their yearly United States foreign aid money, in order to legitimize and validate a war with North Viet Nam because it was a Communist dictatorship. North Viet Nam, that is 1/20<sup>th</sup> the size of the United States, would never have been able to dominate and destroy the United States, to make it their own Communist country. There was never any proof of this being their intentions and plans. But it was, of course, written about and talked about endlessly in the American media, on TV programs and in the nightly TV news and in newspapers for years after the Gulf of Tonkin set-up happened in 1964.

Months earlier then-President Kennedy said to the media "There is a monolithic and ruthless conspiracy to control the United States." Too bad he didn't say by whom. A few weeks after he said that to reporters he was assassinated, in what apparently was another national Government and CIA cover-up, another furthering of someone's agenda, involving hundreds, maybe thousands, of people.

Herbert Hoover controlled the FBI for 50 years. He controlled people of influence, people in power, by gathering "the dirt" on them, and threatening to expose that "dirt" to the media, etc. This incriminating info was often gotten by illegal activity like wire-tapping, raids, etc. To control Hoover the Mafia got information and photos about his homosexual activities. So Hoover always maintained there was no Mafia in the United States, to show his appreciation. And to save his job.

After Hoover died, and therefore had to be replaced, the first Mafia boss, the first organized crime boss John Gotti, was arrested, indicted, and sent to prison for life. In the following years 225 Gambino family members were convicted and sent to prison because of mob activity. There was, and long had been, a Mafia in America after all, even though the King of Crime, the King of the FBI, J. Edgar Hoover, always said there was no Mafia. Of course he lied, to protect himself and the Mafia. FBI stands for fidelity, bravery, integrity. But Hoover, for 50 years, lacked all three qualities.

The FBI has a history of throwing incendiary fire bombs into houses or buildings where people are in stand-offs with them. Then, if the people come out to surrender the FBI shoots them, including the children. If they stay inside they'll burn to death, as a result of FBI intervention setting fires. This is FBI cowardice and cruelty, not bravery and integrity.

The father of former President Bush, sr. was Prescott Bush, the director of a New York bank that heavily funded the German Nazis during World War I. It didn't heavily fund the United States, which was fighting against the very aggressive, torturing, and murderous Germany committing genocide of indigenous populations in Europe. The father of President Kennedy became wealthy being involved in illegal production, distribution, and sales of illegal alcohol. It was boot-legging and other illegal activities in the 1930's, maybe also the 1920's and 40's. Both of their goals were to promote their sons in politics. Both of them had become rich through illegal activities and had the necessary connections and money to have one of their sons become the President of the United States. They both succeeded in accomplishing their goals.

In 2002, when Bush "W" was the President, as the grandson of Prescott, the Bush family flew to Iraq to visit with Osama Bin Laden's family. On the morning of 9/11 President Bush "W" was at a secret meeting with Iraqi defense contractors and relatives of Osama Bin Laden, including Osama's brother, who was also an Iraqi defense contractor. Very few people knew about this as it got no news and media coverage. Since the 1960's news coverage has often been actually news cover-up. Since 2001 news cover-ups instead of news coverage has become the norm, the status quo.

Before World War II was declared Australia had told President Roosevelt Japanese warplanes were approaching Hawaii, three days before they attacked Pearl Harbor. Apparently Roosevelt ignored them, or did nothing. Perhaps it was a cover-up for something.

Twelve countries told Bush "W" in 2003 they knew of terrorist plans to hijack United States planes in the United States, and then fly them into New York City buildings. Obviously Bush "W" ignored all of the twelve warnings and did nothing to stop them. In 2001 the FBI and the CIA gave President Bush "W" *55 notices* of Middle Eastern terrorist intentions to hijack United States planes to then fly into Government buildings in New York City and Washington D.C. Obviously Bush did nothing to stop them. It was obviously a cover-up.

Wars allow the United States Government to legally take away citizen's Constitutional rights and liberties, and allow the release of indefinite sums of money to authorities in power to use as they want. Wars are opportunities for unlimited control and power, and huge profits, for authorities, politicians, and people in power at those times, both elected and unelected.

The United States two Party Democracy means about 50% of the people are dissatisfied and unhappy with elected politicians that run the Government at any given time. About 50% of the people that elected them will be dissatisfied with the officials they elected. The United States Democracy, therefore, has a majority of unhappy, dissatisfied people, the citizens who live in it. So a majority of people that are adults usually feel disenfranchised, or not represented, in the United States, no matter who is running the Government, whether they are elected or not.

A possible exception to this was President Franklin Roosevelt, who was elected to an unprecedented three terms because of his immense popularity and extraordinary capability to be the best President. He had a mistress for most of that time, but people and the media thought that was Roosevelt's personal and private business. Unlike how the often mean and devisive Republican Party was with President Clinton, more than 50 years later. His affair with an intern, that only involved oral sex, was a media blitz for more than a year. If the Republican Party, and the media, had had the same despicable obsession with Roosevelt's private life Roosevelt probably wouldn't have been re-elected to a second term, or for his historical third term, and then an unbelievable fourth term. Then the United States probably would have lost World War II, and we would be living in the United States of Japan, or the United States of Germany.

The United States is a democratic republic and is hardly united at all, except by a common language, English. During the Bush "W" administration there was a big push to make Spanish also the official language. When Mexicans are a majority in the United States, in about 2035 or 2050, Spanish probably will be the second official language. In the meantime they should learn English.

Dishonesty, greed, corruption, hypocrisy are everywhere in America, probably just like in every other country. No place in America is immune to negative and harmful human behavior. All of this can be found anywhere at any time, in cities of all sizes, suburbs, rural America, and in small town America. The population of the United States in 2009 was 65% white, 16% Mexican-Latino (citizens, not counting illegals), 14% black, and 5% all others.

During the Bush "W" administration millions of people who bought houses at very inflated prices, with sub-prime loans, knew when they signed the mortgage loan papers that the payments would at least double at the designated times on those forms. Most people bought houses they couldn't afford because of their greed and their deception. Applicants lied about their income and wages, and other important things, in order to buy a house during those times of corruption and leniency. The majority of these were Mexican, Mexican-American, and African-American.

A lot of commercial real estate in large cities in America is owned by people from other countries. Mostly Japan, Saudi Arabia, and China. Rich people from those countries take advantage of real estate opportunities in the United States, but legitimately and with honesty, involving hundreds of billions of dollars in their commercial real estate transactions.

It's almost impossible to get a job in the United States if you're over 45 or 50 years old that is in your field of expertise. But even 70 or 80 year olds can get a job at Walmart. They become valuable commodities to make Walmart much more wealthy. They are much more valuable than sales of merchandise because of the Dead Peasants Insurance that Walmart Corporation takes out on them for millions of dollars per elderly and/or poor health employee they hire. Walmart has been doing this for many years. It has made them the wealthiest corporation in America, and in the World. GE, Westinghouse, and Procter and Gamble have also done this for many years. In 2008 a Walmart store opened in Georgia. There were more than 75,000 applicants for 400 openings.

In 2009 more than 37 million United States citizens lived below the poverty level. During the 10 years before 2013 the salaries of United States Senators and Congressman increased $30,000 to $50,000, to become $125,000 to $175,000 a year. But in the same 10 year period minimum wage stayed the same, about $5 an hour, for hundreds of millions of people. It's the American way. For people living in the other 23 Democracies things are different. Life is different, life is better, the financial gaps aren't so huge, the disparity between rich and poor is significantly less.

The American Government used to be for the middle-class, to help them prosper. Since about 2003 there have been about 11,000 homeless people each year in Los Angeles alone. Too bad they can't get United States foreign aid. The priority of the American Government should be to help all Americans, especially those in need, and those who cannot help themselves, and the expendable masses, to become prosperous. The most prosperous middle-class in history was displaced and unemployed and came to a halt after NAFTA became a reality in the 1990's.

The U.S. Government gave Mugtada Al Sadr, a leader of the terrorists, $30 million dollars, an unbelievable amount of tax-payer's money, during the Bush "W" Administration to work with them, and paid 70,000 Sunis to work with them. That money did not buy their co-operation, but it did buy them a lot of ammunition and guns to use against American soldiers and unarmed, defenseless Iraqi men, women, and children. Meanwhile, in America, there were at least 300,000 homeless people.

Politicians give companies and corporations in America many millions of dollars of taxpayer's money as special earmarks. The company, or corporation, then gives part of that back to the politician. These kick-backs to politicians have been common for at least 100 years, and partly explains why being a politician is much more valuable than the salary they get.

Millions of dollars in farm subsidies go to members of Congress who own farms. Their salaries were about $165,000 in 2010, independent of their often million dollar farm subsidies. In 2014 only 7% of the United States population made more than $165,000 a year. Proof that farm subsidies are not for poor or middle-class farmers. The United States Government is by the wealthy, and for the wealthy, to make them more wealthy. This is like England in the 1800's. In the 21$^{st}$ century small personal farms make up about 4% of the total farms in America. Immense corporate farms make up about 96% of the farms in America. Most of their crops are corn that has no nutritional value, to be made into high fructose corn syrup, and wheat and soybeans. That's where most of the money for farm subsidies from the government goes to. In contrast, fruit and vegetable growers get no subsidies.

Saudi Arabia is a brutal theocracy, with no human rights. Before 9/11 Saudi Arabia supported the Taliban. Osama Bin Laden came from Saudi Arabia. For about thirty years there has been a friendship between the Bush dynasty and the Saudi Arabian dynasty. In 2008 Bush "W" visited these rulers in Saudi Arabia and they gave him about a million dollars worth of precious jewels as a gift. Perhaps it was more than a friendship.

During the first year of his Presidency the Bush "W" Administration emptied the Social Security Fund, the so-called Black Box, the "secret" box, that had trillions of dollars of surplus money in it. No wonder the Social Security Fund was in danger of being depleted, and is still in danger of being depleted. No one knows where this money went. What did the Bush "W" Administration secretly do with these stolen trillions of dollars? No one was ever held accountable, including the President. A hallmark of his Presidency was lack of accountability, and immense waste of taxpayer's money, not just lies and incredible amounts of money stolen from the American people.

For about the last 50 years the Red Cross has made huge profits with its free blood, its donated blood, by breaking it down into factors that sell for two to a hundred times more than whole blood. That's why they never have enough whole blood and have constantly begged for more. Free blood is their mantra. For at least 50 years the Red Cross invested their phenomenal profits into real estate, and has long been the wealthiest non-profit in America. Their CEOs and administrators have multi-million dollar and million dollar salaries. Proof that collecting blood for free has been extremely lucrative for the Red Cross and for the people who run it, for the Administrators and their non-profit but really for-profit style CEOs.

The United States Government gives about $3.6 billion dollars every year as a subsidy to the oil and gas industries, industries that pay no taxes on their immense profits. Why do they need subsidies? They don't. The oil industry is the richest and biggest industry in the United States. Exxon-Mobile, the biggest and richest company/corporation in the United States, has long diverted tens of billions of dollars of its yearly profits to off-shore bank accounts and subsidiaries in foreign countries in order to avoid paying taxes and hide their actual profits. In 2009 and 2010 Exxon-Mobile profits were about $7.5 billion quarterly, and about $30 billion dollars in profits a year, not counting their multi-billion dollar yearly subsidies from the United States Government, i.e. money as gifts from the American people to an industry that is very wasteful, extremely polluting, and always manipulates the American public, it's customers, every day. Thirty million gallons of their crude oil was dumped into the oceans, destroying the ocean's eco-systems, from 2001 to 2014.

They always justify raising gas prices for short-term increase of their profits. The media reports their yearly profits as being in the in the hundreds of millions of dollars, not the actual *billions of dollars*. Yet, Exxon-Mobile continues to get yearly tax refunds from the IRS of about $1.5 million, besides their part of the yearly subsidy of *$3.6 billion* from the Federal Government. The oil industry is a monster out of control, that is used to control the American public and the economy, and the economy of the World. They lie to the public about possible shortages and financial losses, and lie about their true and actual worth and yearly profits. The American public is powerless to do anything about the oil industry anyway, so why the deception? To justify the high prices and endless price increases, their huge profits, and because of their egos, greed, power, and control. It's a game.

Tax-evasion, illegal tax breaks, manipulation of the tax system by lawyers for their clients, is common in the United States. When this involves corporations and companies as wealthy as Exxon-Mobile and thousands of others of lesser value the fraud and theft that is made legal because of lawyers, attorneys, Judges, and Magistrates has illegally, but legally, diminished the quality of life in America for several hundred million people every year.

If this special treatment of the oil industry stopped, if they had to pay taxes on their true earnings from the past 10 years and from now on, if the Federal Government stopped giving them yearly gifts of at least $3.6 billion, and the dishonest $1.5 million from the IRS, then quality of life would improve for everyone in the United States. Money the Republican Party takes away from the American public should be given back, restored, retained by the people that it really belongs to. In reality, all the money that has been stolen by politicians from Americans should be replaced.

There's at least *$15 trillion dollars* of American's money hidden in off-shore bank accounts and subsidiaries to avoid paying taxes by corporations like Exxon-Mobile, by smaller businesses, companies, individuals. Corporations and businesses are taxed about 1/8 of what individuals are. It is obvious the financial burden of running America is on the 75% of the population who honestly pay their taxes, and who are threatened by the IRS with imprisonment and fines if they don't, and who are often struggling to just get by.

Since 2001 the 5% elite have been given legal tax-evasion status, compliments of Bush "W" and Cheney. Republican politicians said it would stimulate the economy, as the tax-free elite would create jobs and new businesses, and business expansion. After 10 years it hadn't happened. There was an unemployment rate of 10% and no new major businesses, creating jobs. But the Republican Party still insisted it would happen because the Republicans are unable to admit they are ever wrong. It's their badge of honor. And the rich would continue getting richer illegally but with the sanction of the United States Government, as the deprivation of the United States economy continued endlessly. In America the rich get richer and the poor get poorer, especially now in the 21$^{st}$ century. It doesn't matter much if it's a Republican President or a Democratic President.

Meanwhile, as the rich were getting richer without having to hide it, the impoverished United States Government and poor and middle-class Americans were getting poorer. Partly because they were deprived of $4 trillion to $11 trillion dollars that was legally theirs in those first 10 years, that would have helped the United States economy be better and improve their lives. Or, be used to pay back a trillion dollars from the debt owed to China, the bank of China, which would have reduced the trillion dollar (plus) yearly interest payment the United States pays to China, thereby lessening the huge drain on the United States economy. Not taxing the 5% elite doesn't stimulate anything, it doesn't create any jobs for anyone, because they have so much surplus money they would create new businesses and new jobs if they wanted to anyway. Their money, millions and billions and trillions of dollars, goes into financial investments, like on Wall Street. So it was another Republican lie, another deception, from the beginning.

If the upper 5% of individuals, the millionaires, the multi-millionaires and billionaires, paid their required taxes like other people in the United States are required to do or be fined and imprisoned, this could yield an additional yearly return to the United States economy of *$400 billion* to possibly a *trillion dollars*. But it's not illegal if you've got a lawyer, an attorney or an accountant, to do it for you, so this will never happen. There are at least a million millionaires, multi-millionaires, and billionaires in the United States since 2003, so the addition of all their required and legitimate taxes paid would have prevented most of the national financial and economic problems since 2003.

Just like it will never happen that the Neo Cons in power will ever admit that the huge structural and financial problems of the United States since 2001, and the $11.5 trillion in national debt created by former President Bush "W" and Vice President Cheney that was left for the next President to deal with in 2009, were all created and planned by them and their Neo Con crew members before 2001. It fit into their planned scenario of a global economy, of a deprived and struggling Middle Class in America, and the global domination by the American elite, the Shadow Government, the people that rule America for their own benefit since the sudden and unexpected death of President Franklin Roosevelt in 1945, and then the end of World War II later in 1945.

The war did not end because of the dropping of the atomic bomb in Japan on Hiroshima. The Japanese were running out of weapons, bombs, money, food, and soldiers so Roosevelt knew they were going to be surrendering soon anyway, without the devastation of the atom bomb. The Republicans and the Shadow Government, the powers-that-be, wanted to establish United States World domination more permanently and more gloriously by dropping the World's most powerful bomb before Germany dropped their atomic bomb, probably on the United States. Roosevelt was not convinced that killing at least a million more innocent Japanese civilians in their largest cities was necessary and the right thing to do. In order to guarantee the newly developed atomic bomb would be used first by the United States Roosevelt had to be gotten out of the way. That seemed to be the reason for his sudden and unexpected death.

Newspaper headlines said "Roosevelt Dies Suddenly". Perhaps he was poisoned at his summer home in Georgia in order to get him out of the way so the ascending powers-that-be could be sure the newly developed atomic bomb would be dropped on Japan Immediately to establish United States World supremacy, giving the United States super-power status for many years to come. And so that Vice President Truman could become President. He was going to be easy to manipulate for the next four years, compared to Roosevelt, who could not be manipulated.

Roosevelt had resisted any of that, and had established himself as the strongest President in U.S. history for the previous 12 years that he had been the President. He was by far the most popular President in history among the expendable masses, but hated by at least a million Republicans, especially by the elite and by Republican politicians. He had a Robin Hood image of taking away from the rich to give to the poor. He was always known as "the people's President". The truth was if the

United States didn't do it first then the German Nazis were able and willing, ready to drop their atom bomb, possibly on the United States. World domination had always been the ultimate goal of the Nazis, and especially of Hitler, and of the rulers of Japan. But after dropping the second atom bomb on Nagasaki the Japanese surrendered three days later.

The population of the United States in 2010 for the census taken every decade was 309 million, 14% of which were living in poverty. At least a hundred million people living in middle-class were barely making it, barely able to maintain that standard of living. Legalized fraud and theft by the very rich have contributed to this unfair situation that continues indefinitely and will never end.

If all of the Federal Government's money was dispensed legally, without deferring it to other places and to its preferred people, it would make life better for all people in America. The American legal system allows this fraud and theft, making what is illegal legal because of manipulation of the laws, of the United States legal system, by keepers of the law, by the lawyers, attorneys, Judges, Magistrates. Good administration of the law is necessary for good and proper administration of a democracy. Without it things start to fall apart, moving away from helping and protecting the expendable masses. That started with the Presidential election in 2000.

This isn't money from new inventions, more exports, increased GNP, taking money from government programs that help people, ending programs that help people, stealing from the Social Security Fund, or money from government programs that promote buying and selling of illegal drugs. Reportedly more than 1000 men, employees of the Federal Government, have been assassinated because they knew too much or didn't co-operate with their supervisors, politicians, officials, authorities, etc. Of course, there would be no proof or evidence to incriminate anyone.

A solution would be to just collect money that is already there, and has always been there for many years. And then getting it to where it needs to go, before it's stolen, before it's illegally "diverted" again. The plight of people stuck in the cycle of poverty and lower middle-class, or even middle-class, would be dramatically improved by collection every year of all money owed to the Federal Government, from the upper 10% and especially the privileged elite, the upper 1%. And then dispersing it in a manner that doesn't replace the old corruption with new corruption.

America has the highest rate of childhood poverty of any of the developed countries in the World. In 2010 about 45 million people lived in poverty in America. About 650,000 of those were homeless. America stopped being "by the people and for the people" a long time ago, but mostly since the elections of 2000, when the Republicans started stealing power and money.

Before about 1960 divorces were shameful. It was a failure to the family and to society. Marriages were necessary to glue the fabric of society together. They were a cultural expectation and legal necessity to make having sex and babies legitimate. Now, in the 21st century, it is common to live together and not be married, and bypass culture, marriage, and divorce. Before about 1960 being a single woman was shameful, and socially unacceptable, and it was better to marry any man than none. Unwed mothers were shameful and socially unacceptable. Illegitimate children were shameful, and a disgrace for their grandparents, a disgrace for the unwed mother's family and friends. There were social, family, and cultural standards and expectations to live up to. But, since about 1970, more than 50% of marriages end in divorce. People no longer felt obligated to stay in a marriage they didn't want to be in, or that didn't work right, for whatever reason.

A much larger percentage of children in the United States were illegitimate in 2010, and for the previous 10 years, than ever before in United States history. Or they were in-vitro fertilizations and, therefore, didn't know who their fathers were. There's been a larger percentage of unwed mothers, at all social levels and income levels, than ever before in United States history. This is a sociological development since about 1985 for white Americans that began after Candace Bergen, as "Murphy Brown", showed females of all ages, every week on the TV sitcom, that it was alright, that it was socially acceptable, to be a white single mom and have a career, too.

In the same way, violence and aggression have been glorified on TV and movies, along with bad and offensive language, and the use of illegal drugs. Social degradation and a moral decline in society follows what happens on TV and in movies, on Cable TV, and in rap music, that is really just angry chanting. They reflect and mirror what happens in a society. This is also true in other countries.

But social expectations had never applied to black American culture, to black American people, who often were unmarried with illegitimate children, and often on welfare. Black American cultural standards and expectations have always been different than those for the white culture in America.

America has by far the highest rate of childhood poverty of all the developed countries in the World. This has been true since about the turn of the century, since about 2000. This is in direct contradiction to the idea that America, the United States, is the best place to live in the World.

For many years at least 20 corporations like Lockheed, Walmart, Procter and Gamble, etc., have taken out "Dead Peasant" Insurance on their employees. When the employee dies the company they work for then gets up to $1.5 million dollar payouts. This translates into immense income, sources of profit, for these companies. A dead employee has been worth a lot more to these companies than when they were a live employee. Their biggest money-making products are their employees when they die. Dead Peasant insurance has been a huge money-maker for at least 20 companies in America.

For almost 30 years an outcome of the national educational program "no child left behind" is that teachers can't discipline students, all colors, unless they want to risk losing their jobs and the wrath of black parents. Students, therefore, can be out of control, completely undisciplined, unbelievably rude and disrespectful, and be failing all classwork, and nothing can be done by the teacher to stop it. This makes it almost impossible for well-behaved students to learn, to study, to prosper, to function normally in a school environment. The emphasis has always been on tolerating behavior that was never tolerated before, in the history of the school systems, so that no child will be left behind, no child will be failing because of their behavior problems in the classrooms or because they are failing in school.

They get a free pass to "Go", graduating no matter what they do or have done that no white student could do and get by with it. It doesn't matter what havoc and chaos that child causes, he or she will pass, often with A's and B's because the parent demands it. These are usually black students, at all grade levels. To say that the national program "no child left behind" is a success, has been a success, is false. It's a lie. Teachers have always spent a lot of time teaching their students the answers to the tests they will have to take as part of the program, to ensure they pass, and to ensure they, the teachers, will have a job for the next school year.

Students, especially black students in the South, pass classes, even getting A's and B's, by default, just for showing up for classes. Or, because their parents demand it. Otherwise, teachers risk losing their jobs. There are schools in the United States that pay black students for going to school, and for taking tests and passing them, giving them a couple hundred dollars for each part of the equation. Yet, white students who have perfect behavior and who work hard to do well in school don't get paid a penny for their effort, and certainly not hundreds of dollars every month. Even if they are very poor, more poor than the black kids. In huge contrast, excelling and getting A's for their true and honest efforts gets white students no financial compensation, because they are not black. This is clearly prejudice against white students in America, and it should have ended many years ago. It should have never been begun.

In general, the payments amount to about $100 to $200 dollars a week, while the rest of the students in the United States get nothing if they're white, or any other color, and go to school every day and are like normal students. This is discrimination and prejudice against whites, and other colors, but nobody, no officials or politicians, ever says anything because of fear of black outrage, black retaliation, and self-righteousness and publicized media complaints from the NAACP. And politicians fear they won't be re-elected. Once again, white people are not unified. All of this adds to, contributes to, the black cultural attitude of entitlement, especially in the South.

The United States Government tripled the size of the United States by stealing land from Mexico and buying land possessed by France. In 1803 France sold about 500 million acres to the United States for about three cents an acre, as the Louisiana Purchase. The Mexican Government didn't want to sell any of its land to the United States, so, in the 1800's, the U.S. military invaded northern Mexico to take land from Mexico. From that land New Mexico, Arizona, Texas, and California were created. To say it was annexed from Mexico, like American history books say, is not the truth. The United States stole the land from Mexico in the 1800's, and killed thousands of Mexicans in the process.

In 2011 there were about 18 million Mexicans living in America legally, and an unknown number living in America illegally. Most of them lived in states that had been land that belonged to Mexico for hundreds of years. For this reason Mexican Presidents have told their people, citizens of Mexico, that they have a right to be in America, and should claim what is rightfully theirs. Former President Bush "W" wanted Spanish to be an official language of the United States, as part of his push for globalization. If Mexicans want to live in America they should be required to learn English, to speak English, like the rest of the approximately 320 million people who live in the United States. It's ridiculous to say Americans should be required to learn to speak Spanish.

Most ethnic groups in America have always preferred segregation in terms of where they live, their neighborhoods, and maintaining their culture. But with each generation their cultures diminish because of the influence of living in the United States. An exception to this has been the city of Miami, in Florida, that has become a majority of Cubans instead of a minority. They don't have to segregate in the same way because Miami has become a Cuban-American city, maintaining and retaining everything Cuban.

The wealthiest man in the World is from Mexico, worth about *$14 trillion dollars*. The next two wealthiest people in the World are from the United States, specifically Buffet and Gates. China had 115 billionaires, and Russia had 101 billionaires, as of 2014.

It's no wonder extra-terrestrial beings have avoided face to face contact with officials and the military in the United States as it is a very violent and selfish country, run by very selfish, unevolved, controlling and violent people. Certain death and destruction and violence for the ET's would have to be the result, and has been the result. For many years the United States military mantra has seemed to be "If you don't know what it is kill it, shoot it." Or "if you can't control it, kill it."

This has also been the mantra, but in a less aggressive way, for top-secret groups in the United States like the FBI, the CIA, the NSI, the Secret Service, the NSA, and the top-secret military groups for the Army, the Navy, the Air Force, the Marine Corps, and, last but not least, private secret control groups including the paramilitary and the privatized military. This includes JSOC, a paramilitary group for the President. And, on a local level, thousands of police and deputies, etc., and maybe millions of individual American men of the aggressive and violent sort. This kind of personality is the American way in much of America. No wonder ET's do not choose to be seen by people in America, do not choose to interact with aggressive Americans in any way. Americans are, and can be, very dangerous.

No one in America, the American public, really knows what has happened in other countries in terms of actual ET contact. It's not surprising this information would be kept secret from the American public. But paintings from more than a thousand years ago have depicted UFOs in the sky, in the background of other painted subjects. In the United States, since 1946, if anyone has reported seeing a UFO, ETV, or ET, or knows anything about the remnants of a crashed UFO or ETV, they have been threatened with loss of their life, loss of their job, loss of their family because of assassinations or disappearing, false imprisonment for indefinite periods of time, fines of at least $10,000, or loss of their pensions. Or, they become victims of forced so-called "suicides". Or, if they're a prominent person then just victims of ridicule and personal harassment from Government-related sources, if they are lucky.

If a person doesn't co-operate, or gets in their way, or speaks out about it publically, or just knows too much, they have been, and are, assassinated. Possibly hundreds or thousands have been murdered or threatened, including President John F. Kennedy, Bobby Kennedy, Marilyn Monroe, President Eisenhower, scientists, Senators, Congressmen, and both military and commercial pilots who have been told since about 1945 that their careers will end, etc., if they talk about their UFO and ETV encounters in the sky to anyone. This also has included law enforcement people, military personnel, and average people who "know too much". The UFO, ETV, and ET secrecy agenda got out of control many years ago because of excessive secrecy and need for control, and because of arrogance, selfishness, meanness, the need to dominate, and the endless desire for power. But mostly because of the need for greater powers, secrecy, and control of the expendable masses, by the Military Industrial Complex, a testosterone-driven entity with a life all its own.

These are the same reasons all institutions get out of control, including the government on a national and state level. This is the explanation for why these institutions will not change, as many millions of people are involved and do not want anything to change. They like things just the way they are. No one wants the status quo to change, unless it's changed in their favor.

FDR died at his summer home in Georgia, at the beginning of his fourth historically unprecedented term. Was FDR murdered, poisoned, eliminated so his UFO policy and attitude of opportunity and potential good for all Americans would never happen? If so, there has been a cover-up for seventy years by the military and Government about his death. Subsequently there has been assassinations, secrecy, disappearances, and threats because of UFOs, ETVs, and ETs. Control, power, money, greed, arrogance, and selfishness justifies everything. It's the need to control and destroy and dominate. Endless power-trips and egomaniacal behavior are like the Italian Mafia in the United States, not just in Italy, and like the ruthless German Nazis in Germany.

Not long after FDR died and Truman was his replacement, after World War II had ended high-ranking Nazis were relocated by the United States Government to the United States and given *asylum*. This was morally reprehensible and unbelievable. More than 1000 high-ranking Nazi scientists, Nazi military officials, and Nazi government officials escaped punishment for the parts they had played in the torture and murder of at least *38 million* innocent men, women, children, and babies. Instead, they were protected by the United States Government and by the United States military and asked to be an influence at the highest levels in the United States indefinitely. Not being held accountable for one's actions has been the norm, the status quo, the usual m.o. for "special" people, for the privileged people.

The industrialized world has been dependent on oil production for many of its advances in the past 125 years. Forms of energy are dependent on each other for the complete and total production of that energy. This includes natural gas, coal, and gasoline for cars, trucks, etc., wind energy and solar energy, and electricity. When there is no more oil, possibly in 50 years, or when the price of oil is cost-prohibitive for most of the industrialized World because of the greed of the corporations that produce the oil and refine it, or because of the increasing scarcity of it, natural gas, coal, wind power, solar power, and electricity will not take up the slack. Oil is used in many of the processes for the production and delivery of these other energy sources, including production and delivery of natural gas and coal. To prolong the supply of oil these alternatives should have been used in conjunction with oil many years ago. They never could have completely replaced the need for oil anyway, just supplemented it in a very efficient and cost-effective way.

In order to save civilizations and to save the immense advancements made in the past 125 years free energy like anti-gravity propulsion reverse-engineered from UFO's and ETV's will have to be revealed, instead of being kept a secret by the United States Government, scientists, the military, and the Shadow Government. All United States taxpayers have paid for that information for more than 70 years, so it belongs to all Americans. Free energy would drastically improve the United States economy and the World economy in general. That is why it hasn't been revealed and shared, and used and promoted, with the people in America, with the American public.

The anti-gravity propulsion and electricity created by plutonium reactors used in these recovered UFO's would revolutionize the American economy, replacing oil, eliminating the need for oil production and the use of gasoline and oil, and natural gas. This would devastate the enormous wealth, control, and power of the oil industry, as energy for propulsion and electrical power would be free. This would drastically alter the economy of the United States, and of the rest of the world, improving living conditions for everyone who is not financially wealthy and changing the power structure, the power-elite, ending poverty and starvation. The powers-that-be have not allowed this to happen, and will not allow this to happen, because they will not give up their positions as World powers, as controllers of the United States and of the rest of the World, because of money, control, power, greed, and ego. So the rest of the World, the population of each country, will continue to struggle and suffer indefinitely. It's a tradition, it's the status quo.

Organized demonstrations, protesting, opposition to United States Government policies and actions in Washington, D.C. or anywhere else, even by 225,000 to half a million people at one time, has always been ignored by both Republican and Democratic Presidents, and by the Federal Government in general. Letter writing is futile unless it supports the politician's agenda. Elections can be, and have been, fixed. So the individual in the American Democracy is of little or no importance or significance. Unless they are very wealthy, because money talks in the American Democracy. Or unless they are part of the ruling-class elite or the Shadow Government, with unlimited power and influence, and unlimited money. And unless they are Republican, Neo Con, or Far Right.

In America the only way to change things, maybe, is to bring the matter before the public in a magazine or newspaper, or on the radio or TV. Letters to politicians, officials, or authorities do no good, and demonstrations of up to a million people rarely change anything. Instead, use the media to implicate and expose the powers that be so that they could lose their sources of power and money, their wealth, or be embarrassed. However, the problem is that the media is corporate-controlled. Since after 2001 the mass media in America is corporate-controlled by five corporations. Information is, therefore, slanted, biased, diluted, ignored, eliminated, and controlled by the heads of these corporations. Freedom of information and freedom of the Press is conditional. But "we don't print anything that will upset the public" has been a journalistic and editorial mantra for at least 40 years.

This control of available information for Americans supposedly prevents unrest, protests, rebellions, revolutions, and dissention in general. Knowledge and awareness is power and strength, and lack of knowledge and awareness about what is happening is weakness. Corporate-controlled media means there is no freedom of important information, just freedom of unimportant information.

Other democracies exist to make life better for all of their citizens, for all the people who live there, to help them live as good lives as possible. This includes Sweden, Denmark, France, Switzerland, Australia, New Zealand, England, Norway, Canada, etc. Free healthcare for everyone has long been a  basic right of living in these Democracies. The United States is the only Democracy in the World, out of 24 countries, that doesn't have free health care for everyone, free universal or national health care for everyone living in America. Even Cuba, a Communist country, has exceptional free universal health care for everyone living in, or visiting, Cuba.

The American Government is supposed to be by the people and for the people, but it's by the Government and for the Government, by and for politicians who do not represent the American people after they are elected, and by and for political insiders. It's by and for lobbyists and special interest groups who vastly outnumber elected politicians in Washington, D.C. It's by and for the ruling elite, the rich, by and for corporations and big business, by and for the oil industry, by and for corruption. Especially since the national elections in 2000 things have changed for the worse.

Why would there be a ruling class, the ruling elite, in a democracy, in the United States? Power, control, money, greed. A game of power, control, and greed, and arrogance and ego, with the losers being the American people, the expendable masses. This ruling class and Shadow Government controls and manipulates the American Democracy by controlling the media, the Press, banks, finances, money, commerce, legal drugs, pharmaceuticals, illegal drugs, the insurance industry, politics, and the military industrial complex. That's why United States Presidents are puppets, and why writing letters, having public protests, elections, and public demonstrations change nothing.

President John F. Kennedy said there was a "ruthless ruling class in America" that wanted to control America. He asked for all UFO records to be released by the DOD, the CIA, the FBI, etc. Ten days later he was assassinated. Fifty years later those UFO records are still a secret kept from the American people. In all ways, and always, it has looked like a conspiracy of both Democratic politicians and Republican politicians, officials, military authorities, and on and on.

Before 100 B.C. Roman coins had UFO's, flying saucers, shown on them. Renaissance paintings showed UFO's in the background with, or without, people and animals standing looking up at them in the sky. Ancient Mayan civilizations left carvings in stone depicting UFO's, spaceships, and the hieroglyphics used by ET's. Throughout the World there have been about 25 different types of aliens seen, some looking like human beings. In 2009 and 2010 the Governments of Denmark, France, Germany, Russia, released to the public thousands of pages of information about alien contacts and UFO sightings happening throughout their histories. The United States has always been secretive and militant about UFO information because of control, power, arrogance, and greed, so such an action and sharing of information has never happened, and will never happen, in the United States.

The United States has always maintained aliens and UFO's were a threat to United States national security. If UFO's and aliens were a threat they would have done something hostile in the past 250 years of United States history, or in the *thousands* of years of history for other countries. After the camera was invented in the 1800's UFO's began being photographed in the background of photos. Since then UFO's have been photographed all over the World. Often the UFO wasn't even noticed, or visible, until the film was developed. Nothing is more advanced than UFO's and what is inside of them. Reverse engineering, beginning with recovered UFO's in the 1940's, resulted in technological advances like the microwave, cell phones, laptop computers, flat-screen TV's, the Stealth Bomber, the Drone, bullet-proof vests, etc. In order to remain numero uno the United States must be the most technologically advanced nation, and alien technology, once deciphered, has allowed that to happen since the 1940's or 1950's.

In 1945 President Roosevelt was informed by the military about a UFO that had crashed and been recovered. He said first the war had to be won and then he would talk to the American people about it. He regarded it as an opportunity, not a security threat. After all, there had been historical evidence of UFO's for more than a thousand years and they had never been a threat to any other country. Not long after that he died suddenly and unexpectedly while at his summer home, in 1945.

His replacement, Vice President Truman, had a conference months later in 1946 with high-ranking officials about UFO's. As a result the NSA was formed with a policy to deny the existence of UFO's to the American public. This policy of denial would involve misinformation, disinformation, ridicule, lies to the public, and threats to whoever reported having seen UFO's or anything connected to UFO's. Instead of promoting the good for all people, as President Roosevelt had planned, there were self-interests and greed to reverse-engineer the UFO technology for personal profits and power and control over the American people and the World.

Obviously the UFO technology was highly advanced and beyond anything the United States could even hope to have. The powers-that-be wanted Roosevelt out of the way so they could make sure Roosevelt would not talk to the American people about it, as he had said he was planning to do. Truman was able to be managed by the powers- that-be, Roosevelt was not. Everything about UFO's was kept secret then and for the indefinite future, except from the military, for the Military Industrial Complex, that has gained, developed and demanded immense power and control since 1945.

Since the Roswell, New Mexico UFO incident in 1947 the United States military became fanatical and militant about UFO information. Since then UFO's have been reported and documented going 3000 to 20,000 miles per hour in at least 20 other countries. There has been 70 years of secrecy and stealing at least *$20 trillion dollars* from the American people, money mostly going to "the Black Project", the hidden and secret projects at the DOD to reverse-engineer UFO's, ETV's, and ET robots, and then to translate and use information from actual captured ET's. All of this will continue to be kept as secrets indefinitely.

Copying of ETV technology secretly advanced American technology at least 500 years in only 60 years. Now, when anyone sees a UFO it might be made in the United States on Nevada, Arizona, or New Mexico military bases. These are top-secret military bases, heavily guarded, where even politicians have been met with threats of being shot if they try to enter. For many years if civilians have gotten anywhere near these bases they are confronted with security forces and threats, with guns and rifles. Maybe so-called chem-trails in the sky 24/7 are a product of this.

Since the 1940's ETVs and UFO's have gotten their signals scrambled from Earth-bound radar signals and crashed. Radar was a new technology in the early 1940's during World War II. Or, they have been shot down by the United States military, notoriously a very territorial, paranoid, controlling, and excess-testosterone-driven system, that loves to shoot at things and kill them.

It's dangerous to rock the boat, to be a whistle-blower, to reveal things the way they really are. Those negative repercussions and reactions are a result, at no matter what level, what status you are. This is the Military Industrial Complex and secret government that President Eisenhower warned the American people about in the 1950's before he left office. He couldn't elaborate about it because of the usual assassination threats, etc. for both him and his family. This explains why Americans are still in the dark about UFO's, ETV's, and ET's (and everything else) after 70 years of this deadly game-playing by the United States Government, the military, the elite, the Shadow Government, and the people who rule America. Ten years later President Kennedy would talk about the same thing.

In 1977 the so-called Shadow Government, the Neo Cons, and representatives from other more civilized and advanced countries met at Fairfield Industries in New Jersey. They created plans to dominate the World by gradual steps so there would be no revolts and revolutions against the process for a globalized World economy. Their topic of discussion was an eventual and inevitable global government. A war was to happen in the 1990's in Iraq with Saddam Hussein, who the United States would be putting into power in Iraq years before. Or there would be a war with Khadafi, who would be put into power in Libya. After that, national fear would be created about terrorism, terrorists, and threats of terrorism. Then, international fear of terrorism and terrorists would be created. These were some of their long-term plans for eventually controlling the World.

September 11, 2001 was an outcome of that plan in 1977. When then-President Bush "W" said "They died for a good cause" it is likely that is part of what he was referring to. The next part of their master plans was to instill fear about asteroids hitting the Earth, and then UFO's and ETV's and aliens attacking the United States and other countries. Then space-based weapons would have to be used to defend the United States, to allegedly destroy them, to destroy the so-called enemy from outer-space, the imaginary enemy from outer-space. Bush "W" and his Neo Con crew repeatedly pushed for building those space-based weapons when he was President.

At that time and place in 1977 they had decided attacks from outer-space would justify a World Government, a globalized government dominated by the United States, in the government-manipulated minds of all Americans. And that the public would be grateful for the space-based weapons which have been being developed as a result of reverse-engineering UFO and ETV technology for many years, using many trillions of dollars during that time, taxpayer's money secretly taken and trillions of dollars stolen from the Social Security Fund, for the benefit of the few at the expense of the many for years.

This is where some of the yearly hundreds of billions of dollars, totaling *trillions of dollars,* that have disappeared from the Social Security Fund for all Americans has gone to, disappearing, being stolen from to also falsely justify and validate the repeated Republican political demand for privatization of Social Security. This would be a *proven* disaster that those politicians have always ignored and vehemently denied. They want the United States economy to fail, to struggle, to fall apart in a way that benefits them, and to bring immense hardship to the expendable masses. Along with their other ulterior, secret, and hidden motives, many decided upon in plans made in the 1970's.

Russia has documented at least 50 styles and types of recorded UFO's and ETV's in their country. At least 30 types and styles of ETV's and UFO's have been documented in other countries that encourage their citizens to report any UFO and ETV and ET contact information, without negative repercussions and punishment from their Government and/or military. This includes all countries in the World except the United States, the so-called "land of the free". For more than 70 years UFOs and ETVs have been tracked and documented, and identified on radar, all over the World, and they have been taken to secret United States military places when they are shot down. This is one explanation for why the United States has more than 700 military bases in 134 countries.

In the 1970's when inter-ballistic missiles, IBM's, were sent to the Moon to explode on the Moon they were intercepted and vaporized by laser beams sent from documented ETV's and UFO's. This was apparently done to protect and defend their civilization on the Moon, or something else they wanted to protect on the Moon. Why would the United States military, on Earth, justify the cost and stupidity of sending very costly IBM's to the Moon to explode unless they were aiming at a target? And what was that target? Obviously "it" was nothing that had ever harmed the United States in any way and did not justify what had been done, the extremely aggressive, violent, very expensive, and potentially mean actions of the United States to secretly explode IBM's on the Moon.

Lies and deceptions have been the United States military way, their modus operandi, both to the American people and to the rest of the World, in order to maintain their super-power status since after World War II. So of course there never was a truthful explanation to the public. Keeping the public in the dark is what the United States Government, the United States military, and most state governments have been striving to do for more than the past 70 years, and they have succeeded. Keeping the public in the dark is what they will always try to do, and they will succeed. Perhaps breaking any secrecy is too dangerous. It's not worth it to be honest.

Since 2000 at least $1.7 trillion dollars of United States taxpayer's money disappeared into the Department of Defense every year, money not allocated as part of the yearly United States budget, that Is used for undocumented purposes and unknown reasons. It's money that is not accounted for that goes to "the Black Project" at the DOD, the secret and hidden projects. This is in addition to the yearly $700 billion dollars that goes to the DOD each year as part of the yearly allocated budget that is accounted for, usually in *very* wasteful and vastly over-priced expenditures and projects. No one knows how many blank checks are given to the United States military complex for their production of space-based weapons and vehicles, designed from the secret and super-secret ETV and UFO technology that has been reverse-engineered for many years, since after FDR died in 1945, and after World War II ended months later in 1945.

Apparently domination of the Universe, or of just the World, of the Earth, is the reason behind all of this happening with the Federal Government and on secret military bases in the United States, and on about 700 United States military bases in 143 countries in the World. Other countries have records of UFO's visiting their countries and their civilizations for more than a thousand years. Obviously the UFO's have always been peaceful throughout recorded World history. Obviously they could have destroyed the United States any time they wanted to. So the United States military reaction of fear and needing to provide security for all Americans is either paranoid or calculating for supremacy, power, control, and greed. This has been the military attitude for more than 70 years, since after World War II, so it's not surprising. The status quo and military and Government tradition is hard to change. Systems don't want to change.

A value of the internet is that it allows and encourages a free flow of information that a democracy requires, but has mostly disappeared from American TV news media and the no-longer-free Press. It allows and encourages a free exchange of information and freedom of expression. The corporate-controlled media will try to change that, if they haven't already. Most of the information in this book was found on the internet, but most likely it isn't there anymore. Systems exist to control.

The book "Disclosure", by Steven Greer, M.D., has testimonials from 69 high-ranking military and Government officials about their UFO experiences. His internet site "Disclosure Project" had testimonials from 400 high-ranking Government and military officials posted on it about their UFO experiences. If people choose not to believe in the face of so much credible evidence that is their business, but criticizing or harassing other people for believing in UFOs is narrow-minded. But it has been an American reality for many years, as promoted by the media and the Government.

Free-energy methods deciphered from UFOs, now called ETVs because they are no longer "unidentified", is the biggest secret kept from the American people. This includes hydrodynamic waves, zero-point energy (which is vacuum energy), anti-gravity energy and propulsion, and other methods of free energy found from reverse-engineering of UFO's and ETV's, and from information from the ET's captured and held hostage because their spaceships had been destroyed by the United States military. Consequently they had no way to return to where they came from. High ranking but retired government and journalism officials have referred to earlier meetings between them and ETs in long white robes, worn so as to make them appear more like humans in their high level and secret, super-secret, meetings in undisclosed places.

All of this extremely advanced information would dramatically change the United States economy, and the economy of every country in the World. The manipulative and dishonest oil industry would collapse. Oil and gas monopolies would go out of business. But oil is always one of the top three richest industries controlling Americans so that, of course, will never happen. No more pollution, actually saving the wildlife and saving the environment, and ending World-wide poverty, would be other benefits the powers-that-be will not allow to happen.

Nobody of prominence dares to end the silence, the secrecy, the lies in Britain or the United States because the risk is too great. Assassinations, denials, ridicule, discrediting, and disinformation will continue to be the way this is hidden from the public. People that rule America, that rule the world, don't want these major changes. They like things the way they are. They want to be in control, having power and greed forever.

Is this why NASA is shutting down, retiring its rockets in 2014? The whole antiquated program is out of date and a huge waste of Federal Government money in comparison to ETV technology, reverse-engineered for more than 60 years. But NASA has been a good cover for the Black Project, etc. Maybe NASA is merging with the DOD Black Project, the Department of Defense secret project. The American public has a right to know where the money goes, where their money goes.

Supposedly, it was learned from captured ETs that were in crashed UFOs that Mars has a civilization many thousands of years old that started a civilization on Earth about 4500 B.C. Supposedly NASA also knows that the other side of the Moon has a civilization that United States landings and satellites have "discovered" and revealed. Astronauts have always been prohibited from talking about what they see on their space missions, like military pilots and commercial pilots have been prohibited and always sworn to secrecy about UFOs they see while flying above the Earth.

In a similar policy American soldiers have always been sworn to secrecy, to silence, about their military experiences. That's why soldiers don't talk about war experiences and attacks, and invasion and occupation experiences, about their personal experiences in any conflicts, to their wives and husbands, or to their friends and relatives, after they are discharged. It's fear, fear of the United States Government and United States military retaliation. It's probably pretty much the same in other countries. It's not that the United States military is worse or better than other countries.

The United States military complex is the biggest user of oil and gasoline in the World. By far, there's absolutely no comparison. It uses more oil every year than most other entire countries. The only way the United States can remain the World's super-power is to continue to be an industrial military complex, continuing the business of production of war products. These are usually out-sourced internationally to increase profits from lower wages, etc. The yearly profits are usually 25%.

The New World Order that Hitler talked about in the 1930's and 1940's, then talked about by the first President Bush in the 1980's, then by the second President Bush "W" after 2001, is dependent on privatization and globalization. Globalization is dependent on privatization. The United States, however, can't compete globally with production of anything. There's equal or better quality but at a *much* higher cost. When former President Clinton signed NAFTA, the North American Fair Trade Agreement, into law 250,000 American jobs moved to Mexico, where employees were paid 1/100 to 1/2 of what their counterparts in the United States had been paid. And the prices for those products in the United States remained the same. So, as usual, the rich got richer and the poor got poorer in America, because of NAFTA. Capitalism is motivated by and dependent on profit, the bigger the better of course, so NAFTA was a goldmine for corporations that relocated to other countries.

For more than 80 years the United States has usually been engaged in wars, invasions, attacks, occupations, and conflicts somewhere in the World. This costs United States taxpayers $70 billion dollars to $2 trillion dollars every year to conduct these aggressive actions that include destruction of foreign property, the death and suffering of innocent people in foreign countries, the death and suffering of American soldiers in those foreign countries, and the misery of their families and friends in this country and in almost all other countries in the World. This is the legacy of the United States since the end of World War II. Is this how Americans want their money spent? Democrats say no and Republicans say yes.

Republicans don't compromise. It's always "It's our way or no way." They are like adult bullies in a schoolyard. The majority of Americans don't want their country run by people like that, don't want their money spent by people like that, so there are millions more Democrats than Republicans. Still they win elections. Why? Because of corruption and money, dishonesty, lies, and manipulation.

Most prepared food in the grocery store has corn sweetener in it, not sugar. It's not sugar that has been making people fat, it's high fructose corn sweetener. It has replaced sugar. Especially in soda pop, that has been prepared with sweetener made from Liberty Corn, also called Freedom Corn, that has absorbed two deadly poisons other corn, normal corn, would be destroyed by. These deadly poisons then cause unknown health problems for anyone who eats them, in the future, if not immediately. Liberty Corn, Freedom Corn, cannot be digested by animals or by humans. That's one of the immediate health problems. The high percentage of obesity or just weighing too much in the United States is caused by, or is connected to, the Liberty/Freedom Corn sweetener that can't be digested, that causes obesity in beef cattle in order to increase what they sell for on the open market for meat.

Because of the bad health effects of the Freedom/Liberty corn sweetener the cattle live only three or four years anyway. This is also an explanation for the huge increase in acid indigestion for Americans and other related health problems. It's the usual "Oh what a tangled web we weave when first we conspire to deceive." This deception is a multibillion dollar profit center for agri-business that is hugely subsidized by the United States Government. Fruit crops, in contrast, get no government subsidies.

Government subsidies are what has kept American farmers in business for many years. But since the 1970's industrial farming has replaced family farms, producing mostly corn, wheat, and soybeans with genetically modified seed. The food produced has bad taste and little or no nutritional value. Liberty Corn, or Freedom Corn, are grown from GMO seeds. It is resistant to poisons sprayed on it for two plant-specific bugs, so yield is greatly increased. So profit is greatly increased. This is the corn used for food for cattle, and for sweetener and corn oil for cooking, and for production of bio-fuel. It's used as a sweetener, after being converted to high fructose corn syrup, to cover the bad taste of other ingredients in food for cows and beef cattle. This includes parts of other dead cattle and cows that can't be sold for human consumption that cows and cattle are forced to eat. This includes the brains of other cattle that they are forced to eat, which is what causes Mad Cow disease, not a virus or bacteria like the public has been told.

Foods grown with GMO seed, for corn and wheat and soybeans, are also used in food for pet dogs and cats in the United States and could easily be the explanation for the common obesity and overweight problems for both of them, hundreds of millions of them, in the United States. This would contribute to the cycle of increased health problems in pets in America as they age, like it contributes to the increased health problems of hundreds of millions of American people as they age. It could be a reason for the huge increase in childhood diabetes, and in adult Type 2 diabetes. One in eight people got diabetes Type 2 by 2010, and it has been projected that one in three Americans will eventually get diabetes Type 2 in the 21st century. Most diabetes Type 2 is really insulin resistance, and high fructose corn syrup is likely to be one of the hidden causes of this. It's a secret way to make most Americans unhealthy gradually, requiring repeated medical care for many years, and never getting truly healthy again. Sick Americans, debilitated Americans, are very valuable to the American economy. Sickness is a foundation, a cornerstone, of the American economy in the 21st century.

All of this contributes then to increasing the visits to over-priced veterinarians for hundreds of millions of pets, and to pet dogs and cats getting diabetes in record numbers. For humans it means hugely increased visits to over-priced physicians for prescriptions for over-priced drugs, and over-priced medical procedures, and to a life-long dependence on the medical system that has profits, immense profits, as its main goals.

If a person, or cat or dog, has insulin resistance why would they want to put more insulin, artificial insulin or insulin from pigs, into their body? They wouldn't. This isn't logical and is obviously not a safe procedure prescribed and ordered to be done by hundreds of millions of people of all ages in America.

Endless health problems can easily be the result. When cells resist the intake of insulin injecting more insulin into the body cannot be the best solution that scientists have discovered and developed after being paid *trillions of dollars* for their research about diabetes in the past 60 years. It's a secret industry, like cancer is a secret industry, for making huge and immense profits from sickness, from suffering, and from death in America.

At least 80% of cancer patients die from the cancer treatments, and at least 80% of diabetes patients die from problems connected to their diabetes and its treatments. There has been little improvement in these statistics and realities in more than 60 years. In fact, incidence of cancer and diabetes has hugely increased in America in those 60 years.

An acre of GMO corn produces about a gallon of bio-fuel, the replacement for gasoline. Obviously it's a huge waste of money as a gasoline replacement. Obviously it's a dangerous thing, the wrong thing to be feeding cattle used for milk production and for meat. Obviously it's hurting humans because it's in a lot of what they eat. Obviously it's hurting pet dogs and cats because it is in their food. But capitalism and greed justify anything that generates huge profits, especially in the United States. It's part of what separates us from the other 23 Democracies in the World.

It is not able to be digested by cattle, but accumulates in their bodies causing ulcers, acidosis, and death after about five or six months. It results in obesity in these GMO corn-fed cows, meaning they sell for more money and faster. Antibiotics are necessary to keep them alive for those five or six months. The motive behind this is obviously more money, more profit, and greed.

Production of Liberty Corn, Freedom Corn, is what rainforests are cut down for. Millions of animals indigenous to rainforests have been killed, or then have no place to live, no food to eat, no water to drink, and no shelter. Cattle should be fed grass. This is what they are supposed to eat and what is safe. Using corn sweetener made from Liberty Corn, Freedom Corn, needs to be stopped. This would also save the rainforests that are not replaceable, with their millions of species of animals, insects, birds, frogs and other amphibians, and special herbs, trees, and plants indigenous to rainforests exclusively. But destroying this to produce more poisonous and deadly GMO corn that has no nutritional value increases the profits of the cornerstones of the American economy.

Pharmaceuticals have killed an unknown number of people in the United States. When people die during surgery often that happens because of reactions to individual drugs or the combination of drugs used for the surgical procedure. It's the so-called drug "cocktail", to make it sound as innocuous as a leisurely drink. But these drugs can be, and have been, deadly for as many as a million people every year undergoing surgery in hospitals and clinics.

Millions of American babies, children, adults have been forced to live with the debilitating problems, including cerebral palsy, which is brain damage, that were caused by using forceps during the birth process, especially if the baby was premature. The birth was forced by forceps being clamped around the baby's head and pulling the baby out, with damage to the brain, skull, and face. These medical problems, these devastating and life-changing physical, mental, and spiritual problems, could have been easily avoided by the attending physicians, or residents, or interns by refusing to follow the system and using forceps. But the Hippocratic Oath, "Above all, do no harm", was ignored, and has been ignored hundreds of millions of times for about 60 years.

Physicians, nurses, medical professionals, and hospital administrators didn't stop this horrible procedure, this wrong procedure, because that would mean admitting guilt for all the damage, often devastating damage, that had been done to babies for about 60 years. Money, greed, and arrogance are the primary forces behind the American medical industry for at least the last 60 years. The victims of this arrogance and irresponsibility, the babies and children, the adults, have suffered for their entire lives in ways unimaginable to anyone who has not been a victim. And the medical system and the medical people that caused these problems obviously never cared enough to stop it, doing immense harm in the process.

Under the cover of being medical procedures and medical products untold damage has happened in America to many millions of people in the past 60 years, under the guise of modern medicine. In the same way, under the cover of religion atrocities have been committed throughout history in most civilizations. Civilizations often haven't been civilized.

After 2001, under the cover of the United States Government, something that was very wrong and illegal destroyed the financial lives of at least a million Americans, causing loss of life savings, pension funds, huge investments, etc. But, as always happens in America, the United States Government made it all right for the perpetrators, for the ones that had become dishonestly richer, millions of dollars and hundreds of millions of dollars richer. They were protected and rewarded with a gift, a bail-out, of $700 billion dollars. As always happens, the U.S. Government did nothing for the victims of this heist.

The $700 billion dollars was the American people's money. The stolen money should have been required to have been given back to the ones who had been scammed by the financial industry. If you're big enough the United States Government will bail you out from financial loss, mistakes, fraud, and public scams. The United States Government has a pattern of financially rewarding the companies and the corporations who cause the biggest problems, who have the biggest losses, and then turning it back onto the American people to cope with it after they are the victims of fraud, theft, lies, and suffer financial devastation, or lesser problems, as a result.

At the same time as the $700 billion dollar bank bail-out was happening the *$13 trillion dollar* yearly tax-cuts for the wealthy had begun. In the United States the wealthier you are the more you will be protected by the Federal Government and by state governments.

Derivatives had been the final straw in the financial system. Derivatives were the final downfall of the financial services industry. Under the cover of what seemed legal billions of dollars, maybe *trillions of dollars*, were stolen from American investors and never returned. It's the American way. It's an American tradition.

In about 10 years the heads of Fannie Mae and Freddie Mac "lost" about $10 billion dollars. During this time they gave themselves yearly bonuses totaling $52 million dollars. The United States Government never required that any of it be returned to the American people, or to the Federal Government. This is a hallmark of the United States Government. Finders keepers, losers weepers. If you can steal millions of it you can keep it. We'll pay for it, we'll compensate for it, say the politicians, by cutting programs for the poor, denying people their civil rights, and eliminating any programs, etc. that improve life for anyone but the already rich. The Bill of Rights guarantees security and liberty for all Americans but most politicians, especially the Republicans, and corporate heads, etc., are most interested in the preservation and increase of their rights and their wealth.

The United States Government began to be stopped being by the people and for the people about 50 years ago, and increasingly more so with each decade after that.

Corporations pushed out smaller private farms, replacing them with corporate farming. Corporate banks will continue to push out, buy out, smaller banks. Corporations will eventually run America, if they don't already. Corporate farming produces very inferior vegetables and fruit, but they look alright. They just taste awful and have no nutritional value of any consequence, permanently altering and destroying the health of America in favor of the pursuit of the almighty dollar. Money. In the same way greed and money will be the mantra for America when corporations run the United States for their benefit, not the benefit of the American people. Corporate take-overs always lessen the quality of whatever it is they are taking over. Eventually corporations will lessen the quality of American life even more than they already have.

In 2014 there were about seven billion people in the World, two billion of which were starving or didn't get enough to eat. So who in the United States is behind the stupidity and inhumanity of growing a ton of corn to be converted into a gallon of gasoline, i.e. ethanol, for cars, etc., or to be converted into dangerous high fructose corn syrup with no nutritional value, instead of growing nutritional and normal corn to give to those people who desperately need it to survive? In capitalism profit is always more important than the health and well-being of the expendable masses.

The United States Government spends $1.2 billion dollars a year to recruit soldiers. War is a business, an industry. The drafting of soldiers of soldiers caused too much dissention (the Government hates dissention) and disruption from the public. The public is supposed to be obedient and apathetic so the Government can control the public, especially about wars that should never have been begun.

The majority of homeless men in America for the past 60 years have been former soldiers. The majority of handicapped men in the United States are crippled because of having been a soldier for America. Wars are declared, and continued, for financial profit and political profit and control. Men, mostly young men, then risk their lives and their psychological, mental, physical, and spiritual health, their well-being, to fight those wars, attacks, or interventions and invasions for those political and financial agendas.

But men like wars, especially the male politicians and their wealthy supporters, who never fight those wars, etc. They make sure their sons, or grandsons, don't fight in those wars, invasions, attacks, and occupations either. It's all a game of war, a war game.

What has the immense suffering and death of millions of military soldiers and personnel been for since the end of World War II, for the past 70 years? Like all wars, it's been for financial profit and political power, for personal profit and personal power. For money, profit, power, and control. The American public, in general, is easily manipulated with lies by politicians and by the media. Republicans say "You have to break some eggs to make an omelet." Is this what 9/11 was, is that an explanation of why it was allowed to happen?

During the Bush "W" administration dissent and criticism of the United States by United States citizens was regarded as espionage and treason by the United States Government. Freedom of speech disappeared because of the Neo Cons who were in control of America from 2001 to 2009. An example of this was in 2008 at the Republican convention in St. Paul, Minnesota. About 600 peaceful protestors, with or without signs and many just sitting on the grass in a nearby park, were arrested. Minnesota, especially in Minneapolis and St. Paul, used to be bastions of freedom and what it meant to be a good American, the best of what America had to offer. It was another example of Neo Con Republicanism and The Patriot Act showing their ugly faces, flexing their undemocratic muscles.

In contrast, in France, which is also a democracy, people protest freely, demonstrating and holding signs, and are never arrested. In France citizens of France do not have to fear their Government, as their Government represents *them*. In America citizens of America have to fear their Government as it does not represent them since 2001. Yet freedom of speech is the first Amendment to The United States Constitution and has been guaranteed for more than 250 years, along with the guaranteed freedoms to organize and to protest about the government, both national and state.

With the simple Congressional "yes" votes of 2001, and with no involvement of about 300 million adult citizens of America, The Patriot Act was passed and seven freedoms immediately disappeared then in 2001. Most Americans, hundreds of millions of them, didn't even know what had happened. The protestors that were arrested in St. Paul in 2008 learned about some of it the hard way. When nothing else can be done, when people can't do anything to stop what is wrong, when they can't change things for the better, then they give up. When faced with futility people give up.

This isn't supposed to happen in a democracy, especially in the allegedly superior American Democracy that has a centuries old tradition of superior leaders and visionary people with high moral character, who work hard to realize the American Dream. Not always of course, but usually. Since 2001 the United States Government has been in the business of "sending messages", and keeping secrets and telling lies, instead of just being up-front and telling the truth. Instead of just saying what it needs to say to the American people, most of which are expecting they can trust their Government to do what is right for them. But endless experiences have shown that this is not true.

In the movie "North Country" a lawyer in a court scene said "What do you do when the people who have all the power are hurting the people who have none? You stand up. You stand up and tell the truth. Even if you are the only one." California Senator Sonny Bono was going to do just that, expose politicians, corporations, etc., for illegally dealing multi-million dollar weapons and illegal drugs transactions. A few days before the Senate reconvened from a vacation, when Senator Bono was going to blow their cover, news coverage said he had died as a result of skiing into a tree on a ski slope in Nevada. This was exceedingly unlikely. The autopsy clearly showed he had been beaten to death from behind, with blunt force trauma to the back of his head, not the front as was reported on the news, with extensive bleeding and injury on his back. But the truth was not revealed to the American public.

No Congressional investigation, or any other investigation, was conducted by anyone, including his wife, who then became a California Senator as his replacement. At his funeral his former wife Cher was crying but his current wife looked pleased, triumphant, and not even sad. People who saw the autopsy said he had fought back valiantly before dying. This information is available on the internet for anyone to see. You just have to look for it.

It's like most everything else in life. You have to look for it, for the lies, for the corruption, and for the dishonesty amongst the truth. It's much easier to be informed than ever before in history because of the vast and comprehensive information on the internet.

Good people in America who fight for truth, justice, and freedoms formerly guaranteed to them are punished by their national Government, especially since 2001. This is what happens in dictatorships, anarchies, tyrannical governments, and Communist countries like North Korea. Americans are powerless to stop any of this, to change any of this. So Americans can easily become victims of their own national Government, victims of the injustices of their own Government. Like with all major businesses, people who know too much about what is supposed to be hidden, who know information about secrets, can be eliminated.

An exception to this has always been the injustices committed by Priests in the Catholic Church in America. Since at least the fourth century A.D. in Italy at least 10% of ordained Priests have been getting by with raping and sexually abusing and molesting their women parishioners and the teenagers, children, and babies of women parishioners. For almost 1000 years it has been a well-guarded secret throughout the World, and then also hidden from the people in the newest country of America, the United States, for the next 400 years, as the Catholic Church attempted to dominate it religiously, usually killing the indigenous people who refused to convert. Often giving them only minutes or hours to make that decision, to accept Christ as their savior, or be killed. Probably many millions of children, both male and female, in America have been raped, sexually abused and molested, by those 10% of ordained Catholic Priests since the Catholic Church began to be located in America, with no accountability and no punishment by the Church or legally.

Historically, ordinary men have been hung, shot and killed, or sent to prison for years or for life for committing rape, life-changing crimes against children and women. The Catholic Church, as a system, has always protected their Priests, lying for them, using deceit, deception, dishonesty, and lies to shield them from any responsibility for their devastating and destructive crimes. It is, and always has been, dirty politics in the Catholic Church. This ugly fact has made the Catholic Church like the Mafia, both in Italy and in America. Or like drug systems and drug bosses and their drug dealers in America, getting away with drug crimes because the establishment and law enforcement lets them, looks the other way, making it a secret but done out in the open. All of them are, and have been, like organized crime, but hiding behind normal institutions and social expectations and responsibilities.

Throughout history victims and their parents who come forward with the sordid ugly truth have always been made to look like enemies of the Catholic Church. The truth historically has been twisted and distorted, and lies are told to protect their property and their Priests. This is like how the United States Government makes innocent individuals, groups, and entire countries look guilty, sound guilty, to look like they are enemies of the United States, by lying and twisting and distorting the truth. This is like how deputies, Sergeants, police, Sheriffs, and Police Chiefs lie and twist and distort the truth to make themselves look innocent, to make guilty drug bosses and guilty drug dealers look innocent, to make the innocent people who dare to report them look they are the ones who are guilty of doing something wrong. Oh what a tangled web they weave when all of them conspire to deceive.

# CHAPTER SIX

# American Wars, Invasions, Occupations and Attacks

Especially since 1963 the United States Government has operated on the principle the American people don't need to know what's going on politically, they don't need to know what their national Government is really doing in the United States, and in the rest of the World. Secrecy by the Federal Government became the status quo, increasingly accepted as the norm as the years passed by. The people who rule America and elected and unelected politicians think the American people don't need to know the truth about their Government.

During World War I and World War II, and until the Viet Nam War, America stood for what was good and right, and for liberty and the pursuit of happiness. After the war in Viet Nam, after occupying a country the United States military and CIA had no business being in because it was "just a civil war", as Secretary of State McNamara said years later, and after American military forces tortured and killed four to six million civilians in Viet Nam and an unknown number of North Vietnamese soldiers, destroying millions of homes and villages, and after North Vietnamese soldiers tortured and killed 57,000 American soldiers in Viet Nam, after all of that America standing for what was good and right, and for liberty and the pursuit of happiness, seemed to be a lie. The United States had changed, permanently, and in the wrong direction for most Americans. Especially for the millions of Americans who took risks to protest about what they knew was going on, about what their national Government was really doing in Viet Nam, Laos, and Cambodia. Especially for Americans who had a conscience and felt a responsibility for the suffering of other human beings.

Of course, as in all wars and occupations, some people got very rich. They made a lot of money because of the misery and sufferings of war, as happens in all American wars and occupations, but it still was miniscule compared to the war profits, the war-profiteering, in Iraq that was yet to come. Both President Johnson, a Democrat, and President Nixon, a Republican, lied repeatedly to Americans and could have ended the war any time, as the majority of Americans wanted it to be ended. Both parties, therefore, did not represent the majority of American people but instead represented only a small minority of war-profiteers and the people that rule America, besides the ever elusive but always present behind the scenes Shadow Government.

It isn't the rich, the elite, or politicians, or the ruling class, that have ever made America great. It has always been the expendable masses, the common man and woman, that has made America great and made sure it was a democracy. By fighting and dying in United States wars, invasions, attacks, and occupations, and by demanding truth and equality, by voting in elections, and by struggling for freedoms and justices. The greatest President the United States has ever had was President Franklin Roosevelt, who truly rescued America and kept it from failing, from falling apart, without killing millions of Americans in the process like President Lincoln did. Because of his many great accomplishments, his brilliance, his love for the American people, his love for the common man in America, and because of his incomparable competence and abilities Roosevelt was re-elected to an unprecedented third and fourth terms. This was never to happen again, not before or after that crucial time in American history.

After World War II the United States was known throughout the World as the defender of liberty, and Americans were justly proud of their country. During the Viet Nam War, 1964 to 1975, World opinion about the United States changed and many Americans were no longer proud of their country any more. Except the Republicans, the Far Right, who always believe "my country, right or wrong", an attitude that has continued for at least 50 years and into the 21$^{st}$ century. It has contributed to, or caused, the death and suffering of many millions of people both inside of and outside of America.

Elections have not been the answer to straightening out inequalities and problems, or stopping wars, attacks, invasions and occupations of other countries. Keeping America a democracy is difficult as elections are easily fixed and manipulated. Especially since 2000 and 2001.It's now become more expected and more common, just a part of the total game of politics, even though it certainly isn't right in a democracy. But elections are really won and lost because of electoral votes, an outdated and antiquated system that should have been abolished a long time ago. Politicians are rarely elected because of getting the most popular votes. Despite what the American public has been told.

People need hope and inspiration, and that's what Obama gave Americans with his words and his speeches. But not with his actions and his mostly non-existent fulfillment of promises made during his two year unusually long campaign. His eight years in office had few accomplishments, no outstanding actions, and fulfillment of only a few of his promises.

Elections are supposedly to put people in power as politicians who will promote and work for national or state growth and prosperity, legitimately, not dishonestly. For all Americans, not just for the already rich and for themselves. Since 2001 that mostly has not happened.

The Republican Party pays professionals and non-professionals for its election-year jobs that the Democratic Party relies on volunteers for. It's like a war fought with paid soldiers, professionals, etc. versus a war fought with volunteers that never get paid and have no training. Usually the side with the most money wins, like in the Civil War, when the Union side won because they had more money and could continue the struggle longer. Politics, in America, is a kind of war that never ends. The Republican Party always has the most money. Republican ideas about how a democracy should be run are different than that of the Democrats. The cowardice of the Democratic Party allows problems to happen. But like the Confederates, the South in the Civil War, they have more people behind them.

In America people who hear voices are diagnosed as being crazy, mentally ill. Other countries are different about this, being more lenient about behavior problems and peculiarities. Former President Bush "W" said, several times to the media, that God talked to him and told him what to do regarding being the President. He was "the chosen one", so to speak. Actually, he had been chosen to eventually be a President by the Neo Cons in power in the 1970's, as a part of their plans to take over America, to change America to be the way they wanted it to be in the coming new century, and then to take over the World. Or at least most of it, for "the new World order".

According to Republicans the junior Bush was "blessed by God", not crazy because of his conversations with God. Republican politicians always align themselves with God and religion because the proximity, the association, pays off in voter support and support from religious organizations like the Evangelists, the Fundamentalists, the Religious Right, and their subsequent campaign contributions of many millions of dollars. They seem to think the closest thing to putting God into office as President, or any other political position, is to make sure a Republican wins the election.

Also, for Republicans, it is proof they really do stand for God and country, besides war, weapons, and guns, and money and greed. Without Evangelical support, and support from the Religious Right and the Fundamentalists, Bush "W" probably would not have become President. However, the Superior Court Judges appointing him President trumped any power of those religious groups.

Bush "W" said "The best way to revitalize an economy is to have a war," then smiling. The Iraq War, Bush's war, drained the United States economy, and nearly destroyed the United States economy and the Social Security Fund in the process, having cost more than $300 billion a year (nobody really knows the actual yearly costs) since 2003, mostly because of the money paid to the privatized military, to the paramilitary, and to the private contractors in Iraq. This included KBR (Kellogg, Brown, and Root), Halliburton, Blackwater, and many other contractors employing at least 250,000 people at very high wages. Compared to the United States military that would have done the same jobs for pennies on the dollar, and not stolen *trillions of dollars* from the American people in the process of war-profiteering, as the first privatized war in the history of the United States did.

The national debt left by Bush "W" and his Neo Con administration in 2009 was at least $11.5 trillion dollars. This was a big part of the bad legacy left by Bush "W" and Cheney, that America and Americans will be struggling with for generations to repay, to compensate for. The business of war, the racket of war, gives many people the power to manipulate and to control the American economy.

Between 400,000 and 600,000 Iraqi civilians, including babies, children, men and women, and elderly people, were murdered by American forces in Iraq. No counts were ever kept of actual deaths of Iraqi civilians. No one knows how many Iraqi men have been tortured by American forces, mostly by privatized military forces located in prisons, but the estimate is between 300,000 and 500,000.

Before the year 2000 former President Bush, Governor of Texas Bush "W", and Governor of Florida Jeb Bush, Wolfowitz, Ashcroft, Rumsfeld, Rove, and other high level Neo Cons created "The Project For A New American Century". It included suppression and elimination of freedoms and rights that had been guaranteed in The Constitution and The Bill of Rights for about 235 years. It included the need for "a new Pearl Harbor" to unite Americans toward a common cause, to increase patriotism, to control Americans and America in an endless cycle of wars in other countries in the 21st century. It was the Neo Con's plan for an American transformation by the same men who were called "the crazies" in the 1980's by people in Washington, D.C., by journalists, by editors, by newspaper reporters, and by the CIA. Intelligent and knowledgeable people saw them for what they really were. Crazy. With a mission to control America, then control the World, in the 21st century.

The American people think their politicians, their Congressional Representatives and Senators, will do the right things, will watch out for them. In fact, all but one Representative voted "yes" to pass The Patriot Act in 2001, that officially eliminated and destroyed American rights and freedoms, as was planned by the Neo Cons before 2000 in "The Project For A New American Century". Oddly, for other acts and resolutions to be passed there usually are only about 30% of Representatives and/or Senators actually showing up instead of being officially absent, and therefore not voting at all.

That's the norm, meaning they rarely do their jobs, they rarely do what they get paid to do, i.e. represent the American people, who pay them their inflated salaries for doing little or nothing, except promoting themselves. As an example Obama, as the Illinois Senator, rarely voted. In fact, he was rarely there at any time. Being a Senator was the means to an end, to being the President.

Twice as many American voters are classified as Independents than before 2000. Twice as many American voters don't want to be associated with either the Democratic Party or the Republican Party since 2000, and are voicing their dissatisfaction in that way, the only way they can.

A war with Iraq, and a war with Afghanistan, and a war with Khadafi or assassinating him, after putting him into power and keeping him there, were all planned in the late 1970's by the Neo Cons in power at that time, in their plans to dominate America and then to dominate the World in the 21$^{st}$ century. Also, they had planned to make Bush "W" the President after 2000. It was a done deal about 20 years before it actually happened. It was part of their "Plan For A New World Order" written and published in the1970's, for the Neo Cons to share amongst themselves. Of course it wasn't written or published for the public to see. It was all a secret agenda. Oppression, secretiveness, arrogance, and selfishness have always been the modus operandi of the Neo Cons as a group and as individuals. It must be one of the requirements of being a member of that group, of being a member of that part of the Republican Party.

For years the Saudi's gave Bush, sr. an unbelievable $1.4 billion dollars every year. Why? When his son Bush "W" was President he continued to receive daily Presidential briefings for him to read the entire eight years. He was still a part of that current Presidency, his son's Presidency. Two Bushes were President at the same time, the elder one in the shadows and the younger one in the forefront for the public to see. This was how it was planned in their secret publications and secret meetings starting in the 1970's. The younger Bush "W" would be the United States President no matter what happened, no matter what had to be done to get him there, as the first Neo Con leader of the free World. It was a very well planned set-up for the Neo Con group members to eventually control America and then the World, like their publications of thousands of pages planned and revealed.

After "The Plan for A New World Order" was written and published for them all to read and follow they decided a revolution was necessary, as progress since their meetings and plans starting in 1977 had been too slow. The Neo Cons old plan was replaced with "The Project For A New American Century". It said it was necessary to speed it up with "a new Pearl Harbor". This was intended to intensify and manufacture patriotism and support for Bush "W", for America itself, and for the American Government and for the American military. They thought it would bring Americans together, united against "the enemy", just like Pearl Harbor had done in December of 1943. But this time it would be a set-up to instill patriotism and allow control of Americans and America.

A national catastrophe would provide justification for a manipulated war with Iraq, and the American people would be easy to manipulate with the usual standby of using fear for that manipulation. Exactly 12 months later "the new Pearl Harbor" happened on a day no one could forget, 9/11, because it was the emergency phone number for all Americans to call anywhere in the United States. There would already be social conditioning, acceptance, and familiarity for all ages for all Americans that those numbers, 911, meant calling for help and that it was an emergency. Nobody would ever forget that date, like so many people forgot the date of the beginning of World War II, and all other wars. The stage had been set. The set-up was begun.

The war in Iraq had been planned at least eight months before the attacks and bombings, the invasion and occupation, began. The reasons behind it were political power and control, and greed, money, and oil production in Iraq. The plan was to remake the Middle East. All done under the nretense of spreading democracy by forcing democracy on Iraqi's, in Iraq, whether they wanted it or not. This had been part of The Plan For A New World Order" developed as a result of the Neo Cons secret meetings in 1977, and a part of the newer "Project For A New American Century" written and published before 2000 specifically for the Neo Cons in power at that time. In general, people in America believe what the Press tells them, what the TV and radio news tells them, especially CNN and FOX News. So the Neo Cons were to rely heavily on those as purveyors of their messages, as providers of "proof" that the so-called "enemies" from Iraq were indeed enemies, at least in the minds of Republicans in America.

On 9/11 15 of the 19 hijackers were from Saudi Arabia, not Iraq or Iran. Their visa applications to stay in the United States, to live in America, had mistakes and omissions and lies written on them. But, oddly, these were all ignored or missed by the employees at the State Department, the FBI, the Immigration Department, *and* the NSI. If they had been doing their jobs right the visa applications of 15 hijackers from Arabia, not Iraq, and three hijackers from Egypt and one from Kuwait, would have been rejected because of their mistakes, lies, and omissions. So that means 9/11 wouldn't have happened, couldn't have happened. The incompetence of United States Government employees is rampant, is well-known. They are usually underworked and over-paid and incompetent. But they always think they are overworked and underpaid, especially the privileged black segment of civil service employees, throughout the United States. So these visa applications were accepted no matter what was, or wasn't, written on them. The end result was a catastrophe that could have easily been avoided, again and again, but was allowed to happen.

After 9/11 happened the United States intelligence network told Bush "W" and Cheney it was Al Qaeda in Afghanistan, not the Taliban in Iraq, that had done it. But Bush "W" and Cheney ignored them. Their specific plans had already been made about eight months before, and the general plans had been begun many years before that. The conspiracy and corruption had a momentum of its own. The conspiracy and corruption had a life of its own.

After 9/11 happened, after almost 3000 innocent people had been killed in horrendous tragedies and unbelievable nightmare conditions, Bush "W" said, in an interview with reporters, "They died for a good cause", as he smiled a smile of confirmation. The Neo Cons and 9/11 had caused hundreds of millions of people to suffer emotionally and psychologically and physically for months and years in their quest for control of America and Americans, in their quest for control and power to rule America and eventually the World. The expendable masses were something to use and to manipulate. Like pawns in a game of chess.

For more than a month before 9/11 happened, in 2001, the FBI tried to give information they had about pending plane crashes into buildings in New York City by people from other countries to Attorney General Ashcroft. He told them he didn't want to get any more information from them about it, and refused to talk about it. Apparently he was protecting his biggest campaign contributors, his fellow politicians, and his fellow Neo Con crew members.

On 9/11, in 2001, all Israeli employees, about 4000 Jewish people, were absent from their offices in the Twin Towers in New York City. This had to be an orchestrated and planned absence of 4000 people that was indicative of prior knowledge of what was going to happen on that day. It's very good that 4000 people were spared the tragedies of that day at that location, but it deserved an explanation. It should not have been ignored by the media and by the Press. Why were *they* warned, but all the other people in those buildings were not warned? Filtering, censorship, deception are the status quo for what was once the free Press and freedom of information for all people in America. Fear breeds repression and oppression. Apparently the people who run America have been afraid of the truth, or are afraid to convey the truth to the American people. Or they are just secretive and deceptive, as a result of their need to control. As usual, everything comes down to power and control, and greed and profit. As usual, follow the money.

The Jewish word for God means "someone with a womb". Is God, therefore, half man and half woman, or only a woman? Maybe the Jewish people have inside information because Jesus was Jewish. So why has this not been revealed to other Christians, or at least been a topic for discussion and common knowledge for centuries, or for even 2000 years? Perhaps it has just been another form of repression of women, not just repression of the truth, for thousands of years.

A paranoid or totalitarian government reacts to protests with imprisonment or murder. Is that what the United States is moving towards, repression and oppression? To prevent anyone entering the United States illegally on the Pacific Northwest Coast of Oregon, since 9/11, Homeland Security has positioned *one* security man. He is the *only* Homeland Security man for hundreds of miles, for the entire coast of Oregon, to patrol and protect that easily accessible part of the United States. It is obvious that Homeland Security and the United States Government knows there is no real danger.

Manufactured threats and exaggerated threats to United States national security have been the justification for United States military attacks for many years, since after World War II. The reason is always to protect Americans and America from the perceived but not justified threats of foreign enemy forces, as they are living thousands of miles away in other very small countries, with military and defense forces a tiny fraction the size of what the United States has.

An example was Iraq. In the 1980's Saddam Hussein was hired by the United States Government to assassinate the leader of Iraq because that leader wouldn't do what the United States Government told him to do. Hussein failed to assassinate him, to murder him, so the United States military was sent into Iraq under the pretense of a threat to United States national security 6000 miles away. This has usually been the same pretense, the same excuse, for attacks, invasions, occupations, and bombing of all other countries since after World War II. It doesn't matter if it's a Republican administration or a Democratic administration. Either way, Congress has to provide the funding for any conflict or war, or attacks, invasions and occupations. Congress is the war monger.

After United States forces assassinated the leader of Iraq, Hussein was put into power as the new leader of Iraq by the United States Government, by the powers-that-be. However, years later Hussein wouldn't co-operate with the United States Government, the powers-that-be. He wouldn't do what the United States Government told him to do, so he had to be eliminated, he had to be assassinated. The same pattern has been repeated again and again since the 1950's.

However, the United States military Special Forces Division weren't able to complete the mission. He could not be assassinated, so the United States Government sent in the entire military in 2003 under the pretense of alleged threats to United States national security, 6000 miles away. The false threat of weapons of mass destruction was added on to get support from the American people. The United States knew he had had weapons of mass destruction because the United States had sold them to Hussein years before. And the U.S. Government knew he had destroyed them when the U.S.

Government required it years before. But nothing works better than instilling fear in Americans so their Government can control them. Government control of the media and of the press ensures control of information known by the public. Creating fear, fictional and imaginary fear, is the best way to control the public, the expendable masses, and to control the events and so-called realities surrounding the issues and reasons for that control.

After 9/11 happened physics experts, architectural experts, and engineering specialists all said it was structurally impossible for the World Trade Center Buildings to collapse in the free-fall manner that they collapsed in if only a plane had hit them. When the North Tower exploded it was already so hot steel was literally flowing in and out of the building within minutes. *Tons* of melted steel were literally *flowing* and iron was melted, and steel beams were actually *ejected* even though there were *80,000 tons* of built-in structural steel resistance from when it was constructed and built.

There was no possible way to heat the steel to so high a temperature with normal fires resulting from the crashing of the two hijacked planes into the two buildings, that would make the steel melt and flow instantly, with great force,  that continued for as long as six weeks. It *had* to be thermites used to demolish the Twin Towers and the Pentagon, commonly used in demolitions of large buildings and used for the obviously controlled demolitions of the Twin Towers and Pentagon on 9/11 in 2001. Further investigations determined they were special thermites designed for excessive heat and explosions, beyond the normal reactions and capabilities of the usual thermites used for normal demolitions.  This was proof, according to scientific forensic evidence, that both Towers were blown-up by explosives placed in the basements, etc., besides each being hit by a plane.

 The entire North Tower exploded and fell in a free-fall manner only done by explosives in demolitions of tall buildings, so obviously that happened because of explosives, not a hijacked plane. Only thermites can heat to such a high temperature necessary to melt steel, steel beams, and iron, so that it literally flows for days. Explosives would also account for the black and grey extremely heavy and thick, and toxic, smoke that hung in the air for many hours, and even days. There was no Congressional investigation, no official Federal Government investigation, not from the CIA or the FBI or the NSI, or any of the military intelligence agencies, about all of these expert's findings. All of this proof still needs to be officially and truthfully revealed and explained to all Americans. But it won't be, not now, not in the past or in the future, not ever, because then the truth about why 9/11 happened in 2001 would be known.

 A hallmark of the Bush "W"/Cheney Neo Con administration was that they ignored expert opinions, information, and advice because they thought they were smarter than everyone, and because they had plans to follow that were designed before, and after, they got in office. They allowed no intrusions on their Neo Con revisionist plans. Representing the American people never had anything to do with whatever they did for their eight years in power, and also for the years leading up to and including the election campaign fiascos in 2000. The people were just an afterthought, pawns and puppets to manipulate and control.

 To increase Federal power and control, to increase their power and control, the Bush "W" administration, the Neo Cons, created The Patriot Act months before 9/11 happened. The Patriot Act took away American's civil rights guaranteed by The Bill of Rights and The Constitution. It was the destruction of seven Constitutional amendments, including number one, four, five, eight, and fourteen. These were freedom of speech, freedom of assembly, the right to protest, the right to privacy, and the guarantee of no unlawful imprisonment without legal counsel and legal representation. These guaranteed rights, as amendments, disappeared by an undemocratic process, by a kind of theft and fraud committed by elected members of Congress. It was an unprecedented abuse of power. Now, since 2001, anyone in the United States, citizen or not, can be imprisoned without legal counsel or representation even if it's based on hearsay, i.e. "without probable cause".

Nobody read the Patriot Act before signing it into law, before voting "yes". It was a done deal. No one in Congress wanted to be labeled a traitor or unpatriotic by the media and the press, or by the Neo Cons in power, or not be re-elected at election time. That's how seven of the freedoms and rights that had been guaranteed to Americans for 235 years disappeared.

After The Patriot Act became law in 2001 between 300 and 400 cities passed resolutions against The Patriot Act being enforced in their cities in order to protect their residents from this federal takeover, and the destruction of The Bill of Rights and The Constitution. The Federal Government is supposed to recognize the sovereignty of each state. Perhaps in the future a Republican administration will also take that away.

This was one of the worst disloyalties to the American people, to the expendable masses, but nothing happened to any of the guilty elected politicians and officials as a consequence. They had done nothing to protect their constituents from this permanent abuse of their civil rights in America. Ten years later, in 2011, President Obama, a Democrat, signed The Patriot Act into perpetuation permanently. The restrictions and loss of freedoms and rights became a permanent part of America.

In order for the President to have unlimited power a war has to be declared. The Iraq war served that purpose. Government surveillance of citizens began. A Government paramilitary force was built, with bases in several states like Ohio, Illinois, and Idaho. Black Hawk is the largest. A private intelligence agency had been begun because the CIA would not support the plans of Bush "W", Cheney, Ashcroft, Wolfowitz, Rove, and Rumsfeld to attack Iraq. These were the same people called "the Crazies" by the CIA, and by others in Washington, D.C. in the 1980's,and now they were the Neo Cons in power, just as they had planned in the 1970's. Their plan was based on lies, on fiction, on manipulation and control of the American people and of America in the new 21$^{st}$ century.

Thus began the "George W. Bush Center For Intelligence". His father, former President George H.W. Bush, had been the Director of the CIA at one time. Now, Bush "W" was the self-appointed director of his own brand of CIA, the CFI. Cheney distrusted the CIA, the CIA distrusted Cheney. So the Neo Cons created their own version of the CIA that manufactured its own "intelligence" to justify bombing Iraq. The American people accepted fiction as fact. Questioning it became like an act of treason. The Neo Cons had more control of America and Americans than ever before in United States history. Truth became lies and lies became truth.

It was a total package including the tragedies of 9/11 in 2001,The Patriot Act of 2001, Homeland Security, the private Bush "W" intelligence agency to replace the CIA, and the war in Iraq and Afghanistan. But this was not just a Neo Con control thing as President Obama, a Democrat, signed the Patriot Act into perpetuity in 2011, allowing all of this to have happened without legal recourse, without any charges, or legal responsibility, and allowing it to happen again anytime, forever in the future history of America. The Patriot Act of 2001 permanently took away control of a big part of the

American Democracy from the American people, in an undemocratic un-American way.

In 2003 the Iraqi Ambassador to the United States said "The Iraqi people were just cannon-fodder" to the Neo Cons in power, to the United States military, to America in general. For the next eight years Republican politicians would refer to Iraqi civilian deaths as "collateral damage". No records were ever kept by the United States military as to the total of Iraqi civilian deaths, estimated between 400,000 and 600,000 innocent and unarmed men, women, children, and babies in those eight years. There were no Iraqi soldiers to defend their innocent civilians. There was no way Iraqi people could hurt America or Americans in America. No Americans had *ever* been hurt by Iraqis.

No wonder photographs of the war, images and coverage for newspapers and videos, and filming and reporting for TV production and TV news, showing what was really happening in Iraq, were all prohibited from the beginning in 2003. Since after the Viet Nam war, starting in 1964 and ending about 11 years later, and increasingly so since the 1980's and President Reagan, the United States Government operates on the principle that the people in the United States don't need to know the truth. That they shouldn't know the truth. Out of sight out of mind would make a more compliant and accepting population, a significant improvement on the problems created for the American Government, for its politicians, and for the military during the Viet Nam war by Americans who knew the truth, and who knew too much to be accepting and compliant.

It has been well known for many years that American embassies in foreign countries since World War II have been the source of conspiracies against those governments, and cause coups. When leaders of the indigenous people emerge, and are supported by the people, the United States brings in the CIA and the military to destroy those leaders and their supporters. The United States paramilitary, the CIA, and the privatized military stage foreign coups, revolutions, protests, and demonstrations. So-called "rebels", paid for by the United States, lead and carry out foreign military coups and revolutions against foreign governments in order to install right wing dictators who will do what the United States wants them to do, who will co-operate. When they stop co-operating they are assassinated. Or at least attempts are then made to assassinate them.

Sometimes they are so well protected that is impossible to eliminate them, to assassinate them. Like it was for Castro in Cuba, who was both very well-protected and well-loved by the people in his country, making it impossible to assassinate him for many years. And like Hugo Chavez. So Chavez was given cancer by the CIA, also given to leaders of other countries, all at about the same time. Hugo Chavez died from that cancer, and from the standard Western medical procedures of poison, cut, and burn, i.e. chemotherapy, surgery, and radiation. There's no law anywhere against murdering leaders of countries by giving them cancer so lethal they can't survive it.

In 2011 revolutions and demonstrations swept over the Middle East, one after the other in quick succession. So-called "rebels", usually Shiites, were recruited and paid for by the United States Government to begin and carry out the demonstrations, the "revolutions", in each country. Weapons, bullets, and military-type uniforms and clothes were supplied by the United States free of charge. In the past this was something a Republican President would do, but this time a Democratic President, Obama, was responsible. However, a lot of the people living in each of the countries were not fooled.

In June 2011 the BBC reported that one group of these so-called "rebels" had told the United States Government they needed another $3 million dollars to continue their demonstrations and to pay the demonstrators and protesters in the Middle East. So that explains what Obama called "the wave of discontent in the Middle East" in the spring of 2011, and the United States military involvement in Libya to oust Khadafi. Months later the United States wanted to recognize the "rebels" in each country as the "new government", as paid for by the United States, but there was no cooperation from the paid-for "rebels" themselves. Time would tell what kind of influence the United States Government would actually have. After that Khadafi was killed by some of those "rebels". That Neo Con mission planned back in the 1970's was finally accomplished.

The United States has a reputation of starting wars on false pretenses. Protests, coups, demonstrations, and uprisings are much cheaper to sponsor, to organize, to supply than a full-blown all-out war. But a problem is that the so-called "rebels" are difficult to control, and cause a lot of killings, rapes, torturing and injuring of the civilians of all ages, ransacking of property, killing their pets and livestock, shooting at everything just because they can, and because they are the lowest of low-quality human beings. They are the scum of the Earth, who are often criminals in their own countries of origin, or criminals recently out of prison and jail who can't find employment. They are always recruited from other countries, not the same country of the staged procedures.

Much of this awful behavior is reminiscent of things that happened in Viet Nam perpetrated by United States soldiers, the United States military, against Vietnamese civilians. And also similar to what British soldiers have long had a reputation of doing, for centuries, to people in countries that Britain invades, conquers, takes over, and controls. United States news reporters can't report things like this. They can't report what has been really happening in the Middle East, especially in Iraq and Afghanistan, because of the United States interfering with foreign governments and hiring "rebels" from other countries to carry out the planned procedures of revolutions, etc., at much higher salaries than American soldiers would get. Because of The Patriot Act, in 2001, if they do news reporters will be threatened, lose their jobs, be imprisoned, or put into solitary confinement, or murdered, possibly in set-up "suicides". Or at least never be able to pursue news reporting again.

This is one of the checks and balances that has disappeared in America. News reporters in World War II reported that torture and cruelty causes people to give false information in order to stop the torture. This is logical and common sense, but was completely disregarded and ignored by the United States military and the Government in its mistreatment of 100,000 to 200,000 Iraqi men, civilians who were imprisoned as a result of their neighbors and members of Al Qaeda, the sworn enemy of America, reporting them to the Americans in exchange for a minimum of $1000. The United States was in bed with the enemy. Oh what a tangled web they weave when they conspire to deceive.

This unbelievably cruel hoax against the Iraqi people was allowed and encouraged by the United States military and the United States Government for about eight years, as part of the American privatized war in Iraq. News reporters from the United States could not report any of this as it was happening, for more than eight years. This was just one of many seismic changes, of massive proportions and consequence for millions of people outside of America and inside of America, affecting the past, the present, and the future in ways that are very undemocratic. The democracy in America was disappearing in secretive, shameful, frightening, and dishonorable ways.

The United States military didn't care who reported them, 99% of them innocent men, as none were ever charged with anything, but all were beaten and tortured. Unbelievably, no screening of whoever turned them in was ever done before giving them their reward money of $1000 to $3000.

There was a huge problem for those who were turned in to be interrogated by men who didn't speak their language, or speak it well enough to understand everything they said. Not understanding the language meant disaster for them. Tortures and killings of these innocent men were the result.

None of these 100,000 to 200,000 detained Iraqi men were ever charged with anything. All of this un-American behavior is part of the legacy of the United States in Iraq. Vicious and brutal treatment of Iraqi men, women, children, and babies who could not understand English was like what had happened before in Viet Nam. But it had been more of a catastrophe in Viet Nam and Cambodia in the 1960's and 1970's because of the brutality, viciousness, and killing of about six million Vietnamese and four million Cambodians by the United States military, by the CIA, and by the American Government. It was, of course, a shared responsibility.

None of the more than 300 million Americans, as part of the expendable masses, could have done anything to stop or change any of what happened in Iraq and Afghanistan, just like millions of dissenters and protestors in America were never able to stop or change any part of the war and invasions of Viet Nam. It has been estimated that 10 to 12 million people have died throughout the World as a result of CIA interventions and interferences, and CIA and United States Government instigations and manipulations of so-called foreign uprisings, military coups, protests, foreign revolutions, and demonstrations.

Since after World War II the CIA and the United States Government has recruited, funded, supplied, financed, and armed so-called "rebels" from foreign countries to lead and carryout these actions against targeted foreign governments in many different countries, always very small countries, in order to install right-wing dictators who will do what the United States wants them to do. Over-throwing leaders who are working to make their country a democracy has happened repeatedly as a result of United States Government and CIA intervention. It's always been the opposite of the image of what America supposedly stands for.

Usually these manufactured" revolutions" are against leaders that represent a democratic social structure, a democracy in the making, leaders the majority of people in their countries want to lead them, to lead their country in a better direction. They have a majority of popular support from their people, but no support from the United States. Violence and widespread human rights abuses follow the installations of the right-wing dictators, done secretly by the United States, or follow the victory of the so-called "rebels", who are also supported and funded by the United States.

The CIA School of the Americas in Fort Benning, Georgia, originally in Panama, teaches foreign men, especially from Latin America, to conduct coups, etc. with the hiring of so-called "rebels" in the respective country, and interrogation of the civilians, and torture and murder. They teach violence to these foreign men. As an example, the CIA funded 1500 Jihadists from Afghanistan to begin the so-called Libyan "rebellion". The British Broadcasting Corporation, the BBC, interviewed Libyans there on the street in the beginning, who all said the same thing, that the "rebels" weren't from Libya. They were saying "They don't dress like us. They don't look like us." And, "They don't sound like us when they talk". These "rebels" were imported from Afghanistan, hired, financed, funded and armed by the United States Government and the CIA.

These policies and actions are not a secret. They have been happening since the 1950's. This same pattern, this same modus operand, has been happening for about sixty years. When uprisings happen anywhere CIA covert operations are likely to be behind it. It isn't a secret.

In 2012 the new leader of Egypt, a woman, said on BBC radio that the United States gave $1.5 million to pro-democracy groups in Egypt that have been fronts for United States espionage and intelligence. The Egyptian public, people on the street, said the pro-democracy groups from the United States were in Egypt to create chaos, paying so-called "rebels" to create chaos, uprisings, demonstrations, and revolutions, like in other Middle Eastern countries in 2011 and 2012. It was President Obama's so-called "wave of unrest" that was sweeping across the Middle East because of United States Government intervention and plans.

But controlling the "rebels" was impossible. These were the imported and over-paid "rebels", who were, as usual, raping native women, rampaging the towns and cities, killing innocent civilians, behaving violently, and killing animals, pets, just for the sake of killing. These men were often out of control in their paid and hired violence of causing death and suffering. As always, they were uncivilized invaders of other countries who create havoc that the United States Government is secretly responsible for, but takes no responsibility for. No matter what the goal is the result is more destitution, suffering, poverty, chaos, death, pain, and corruption. That has been the legacy, and continues to be the legacy, of the United States Government and the CIA operating in other countries. It isn't a secret. It is a well-known and accepted fact.

The image United States politicians and the population has always had of itself is that it is the only country chosen by God to do whatever it does. America has always thought of itself as exceptional and better, a force for good and virtue. Supposedly, America is God's chosen nation, God's chosen people. This has always been the idea behind the United States Democracy, since the beginning of America. It isn't a secret, and it's nothing new.

The CIA admitted to eight attempts to assassinate Castro. Yet, after Hurricane Katrina Castro was the first leader of any country to offer help to the victims in America. He was turned down by Bush "W", who had done *nothing* to help the victims by then, four days after Hurricane Katrina had hit Louisiana and Mississippi. Castro's offer was a Christian thing to do, an act of loving and helping your neighbors, except Castro had always been labeled a Communist by the United States Government, portrayed as an evil man and someone to be afraid of. In this case the ones to be afraid of were, had been, and would be Bush "W" and his Neo Con Administration. Even though Bush "W" had often referred to, during his election campaign and after, his being a Christian, an Evangelical Fundamentalist, and that he had been chosen by God to be President, and was in fact guided by his contacts from God.

Thousands of people would die and hundreds of thousands more would suffer after Hurricane Katrina because there was no help from the President, Bush "W", or from the Federal Government. And because of incompetence from the Mayor of New Orleans, and incompetence from the Governors of both Louisiana and Mississippi. But, as always since 2001, if any authorities or officials, or politicians, criticized President Bush "W" they would be labeled "anti-American", or even lose their jobs. "My country, right or wrong" has been the Republican attitude since 2001, and especially since 2003. Corruption, lies, suffering, disinformation, and misinformation doesn't matter to them if Republicans are the perpetrators.

After the 1950's being a Communist was a terrible thing. The United States Government had been teaching Americans this. After all, the implication was that Communists were going to take over the United States after attacking it and destroying our democracy. Supposedly, theoretically. So in the 1950's air-raid drills were mandatory in public schools across the nation to prepare for these future attacks. After that, starting in the 1960's and continuing for 50 more years and indefinitely, the United States Government and the U.S. military did exactly that to one tiny country after another. Attacking countries and destroying governments in foreign countries became the American status quo, with no end in sight. After NAFTA the United States was no longer the industrial leader of the World, but easily maintained its World super-power position as the most expensive and strongest military in the World.

The United States Government has tried to develop and generate fear of other countries much smaller than the United States, like Cuba, Iraq, Libya, North Korea, North Viet Nam, Bosnia, and Kosovo in order to justify attacking them, bombing them, invading and occupying them. The rationale seemed to be if little Germany could start World War I, and if little Japan could start World War II by attacking the American Naval fleet in Hawaii, why wouldn't other little countries do the same thing in the future? After World War II the United States invested hundreds of times more, even a thousand times more, than any other country into its defense, into the Department of Defense, the DOD. Never again would the United States be caught off guard in an inferior position of military strength.

Thus, the United States became the World's super-power and has maintained that position for about 70 years, since World War II, and has had national justification for bombing, for attacking and invading, little countries much smaller than the United States that couldn't possibly win in any direct confrontation with the United States. But often they have won, triumphed, over the Invasions and attacks by the World's super-power, the United States military. When the United States military occupies their country indefinitely what it controls is their oil production, not possession of the country.

Bush "W", as President, told the President of Argentina "To revitalize an economy go to war". In the month before 9/11 happened in 2001 Bush "W" had a month-long vacation at his Texas so-called ranch. (How could it be a real ranch anyway if it had no animals?) It appeared to be a political set-up. The pending planned war with Iraq would do the work for him. After 9/11 happened he said "They died for a good cause", then he smiled, and his approval rating soared. No news reporters, no articles or broadcasts, questioned him as to what "good cause" they had died for. But it seemed like the rest of the World was suspicious and saw through the fog of American politics, as was evidenced in their foreign news media and their commentaries on their radio and TV, and in their newspapers.

Anyone who criticizes the United States Government can be put on a government-watch-list of "possible terrorists". No one knows how many of them have been imprisoned, or charged, since the Patriot Act was signed into law by all of Congress in 2001. Except not by Congresswoman Barbara Lee, who wasn't afraid to stand up for what was right, or wrong. There's another Government list of American citizens that can be shot, and killed, with no probable cause, in the United States or in any other country in the World. Apparently that's a side-benefit of being the World's super-power.

If elected government representatives, and their private employees, that develop and drive United States policies and actions, like Carl Rove did for Bush "W", like the privatized United States Government and the privatized national military has done since 2001, if they are not for all Americans, for everybody in America, then there is nothing Americans can do to influence their own government, at all levels.

Congress is supposed to represent all Americans, but they definitely do not. America, then, is no longer a democracy. And that is what America has been in the 21st century. A new kind of controlled democracy, with a shadow-government that has really been there for more than 40 years.

The French man who designed the Statue of Liberty paid for the production of it with donations from more than 100,000 French citizens, as a gift to America. He said the statue represented "Liberty enlightening the World." At that time someone commented that it was "for Americans that had too much freedom, from the French who didn't have enough freedom." More than 100 years later the situation is reversed. It's the Americans that don't have enough freedom and liberty, or at least as much as they think they do. Americans buy into a system that is different than what they think it is. But ignorance is bliss. Maybe.

Will there be more suppression and elimination of freedoms and rights guaranteed by The Constitution and The Bill of Rights? The rights and freedoms Americans have had for more than 235 years can be easily taken away when the people in power want to do it again. The ruling class and the government-elite manipulate and control the American public, as they have always done, and so it will continue indefinitely. The American public is powerless to do anything about it, before or after it happens. There is no reason to keep it secret, as no one can do anything to stop it anyway.

During the Iraq war 99% of the deaths and injuries were suffered by Iraqi civilians. This is proof the American war in Iraq was a war against Iraqi civilians, including helpless and defenseless babies and children, not just helpless and defenseless women and men who lived there, adults who had nothing to defend themselves with against the invading American soldiers. As an American citizen did you support this carnage, these murders and tortures? If you did not, as you should not have, there was no way to stop it anyway, as Congress was essentially the only ones who could stop it as they controlled the flow of money into that war, and every other war. Again, Congress is supposed to represent all Americans but they definitely do not. Instead, they represent themselves, other politicians, and the 30,000 lobbyists.

Millions of American people protested publically against the Viet Nam war for years and nothing changed. Thousands of these protestors were beaten, clubbed, and shot at, and some killed, but nothing changed. Nothing happened, nothing was stopped, no lives were saved in Viet Nam. The American public was powerless and couldn't do anything about it. In the same way the American public was powerless to do anything about the war in Iraq. The powers-that-be, the people in power in America, do what they want to do regardless of what the public wants. If the public can be manipulated to support them that's nice, but if they can't, well, that doesn't matter. Power corrupts absolutely. Nobody tells them what to do. Nobody tells absolute power what to do. Certainly not the American people. But this isn't like a democracy is supposed to be. Especially the American Democracy, supposedly the best democracy in the World, according to United States politicians and Presidents.

Since World War II invasions, occupations, wars, and attacks have been based on deception and begun on deception. Presidents then say, at some point, that "withdrawal is an unacceptable option" as it will lead to World War III, etc. However, there never would have been World-wide support for another World war. It can't be a World war if no other countries participate. So it has always been a scare tactic, an exaggeration, to manipulate the public. Instilling fear in the public has long been the national Government modus operandi to control the public. And it always works. Why mess with success.

In America people who criticize the American Federal Government are labeled "anti-American" or "enemies of America", or "threats to national security", or "traitors", by their national Government and by the national media, and even by their local library employees as self-appointed library police, or by their local law enforcement. This is also inaccurately called "espionage", a Federal crime. Leaking information has long been done and is done often and easily by politicians, but if journalists and the expendable masses engage somehow in this they are called traitors, guilty of treason, and guilty of espionage, all justifying imprisonment, confinement, charges, assassinations by the CIA and military hit-men, or just harassment and threats. Politicians, however, are and always have been protected from all of these legal actions and life-changing charges and repercussions. It pays in many ways to be a politician in the United States.

All of this is insanity and ridiculous. In fact, people who criticize the American Government are so pro-America they are willing to risk stupid and mean reactions and ridicule from other Americans, from the legal system, from politically supported secret investigative agencies, both Government and private, mostly from Republicans, and possible imprisonment indefinitely, even in isolation, with no charges. They are even risking assassinations, as staged "suicides" and so-called "accidents".

Certainly these are risks not worth taking. No legal representation, no lawyer, no trial, and no media coverage to inform people about problems that need to be fixed add to the potential problems. Knowledge is power. Usually. For 235 years they were expressing rights, freedom of speech and freedom of expression, that disappeared with The Patriot Act of 2001, that was signed into law weeks after 9/11 happened in 2001. It had been written before 9/11 by the Neo Cons in power but had been initially rejected by Congress before 9/11 happened.  After 9/11 it was a different story. Congress then embraced it with open arms, fearing they would be called traitors, un-American, and unpatriotic, during the hyper-sensitive, Neo Con and Republican aggressive, and retaliatory attitudes of heightened patriotism created by the tragedies, the horrors, and deaths on 9/11, in 2001. There very definitely were methods to their madness. It was a massive scheme and set-up. And it worked.

John Adams, a signer of The Constitution, said in 1775 "Liberty, once lost, is lost forever." All of the 24 Democracies in the World have true and real freedom of speech and freedom of expression except in the United States. That Constitutional right in the United States was taken away by the Neo Cons in power in 2001 with the passing of The Patriot Act, after 9/11 happened. After that there has been more suppression of Americans and suppression of information than ever before in all of United States history. The United States has become a different kind of democracy since after September 11, 2001. In the 21$^{st}$ century it's a controlled and limited democracy, which really isn't a democracy.

Since World War II the United States Government and the ruling elite have created illusions in order to control the masses, but increasingly more so after September 11, 2001.The illusions have always been a form of propaganda. The day 9/11 was a form of propaganda because 911 was the national number to call for emergencies. The day of 9/11 had built-in public relations value. It was a number no one anywhere would forget, and there would be subconscious, or conscious, connections every time the national emergency number of 911 was seen or heard, ad infinitum. The actual date would never be forgotten, like the date the Japanese bombed American ships in Pearl Harbor has, in general, been forgotten by most Americans for many years. A  just and free society has free access to *all* information and ideas, not just filtered and limited or distorted information and ideas, and controlling manipulative lies, like Americans get since after 9/11 in 2001. When information is controlled then the population is controlled.

Suppression of civil rights, suppression of justice and of important and truthful information, and suppression of criticism of the government and of government policies, has been a fact of life since September 11, in 2001. It didn't just happen. It was planned by a system beyond the control and knowledge of most Americans, by the people that rule America.

The right to publically assemble and to protest publically has been taken away since 2001. But so what? It doesn't matter anyway. A misinformed and uninformed public can't protest anyway. Public protests and public assembly have done no good, have accomplished nothing, and have changed nothing in America for more than 50 years anyway. So to take away that freedom only means no more innocent civilians will be shot at or killed, or clubbed, or sprayed with tear gas by law enforcement or the National Guard. Or arrested with false charges.

Just what national thing has the National Guard been protecting for more than 40 years when they shoot, club, spray, or kill marchers who are expressing their Constitutional rights, and who never have any weapons, no guns, nothing that's going to hurt anyone? The National Guard is always "just doing their jobs", protecting the powers-that-be from nothing but loss of control of the masses. They themselves have never been charged with any pain and suffering and death or murders that they have caused. It's always been government-sanctioned. They are just doing their jobs.

Rumsfeld promoted abuse and torture of Iraqi citizens and lied repeatedly to the world for five years, with no legal repercussions or charges. There were none for Bush "W" either. He signed into law legal protection for himself as President and for all Presidents to follow. Halliburton charged United States taxpayers, the United States Government, $45 dollars for each six-pack of Coca Cola that was produced in Iraq (not imported) and bought by military personnel. Halliburton charged $100 for each bag of laundry from soldiers, who had a mandatory requirement to not wash it anywhere else or they would be punished by the military. Halliburton charged $80,000 to $200,000 for each new semi-truck that Halliburton employees were told to blow up when they had a flat tire or needed oil, so that loss would be charged back to the United States Government, to increase Halliburton's huge financial war-profits.

Halliburton charged the United States Government $40,000 to $60,000 for new equipment they would purposefully destroy every week. Halliburton charged the United States Government $250,000 dollars a year for each new Humvee, etc., that they leased, not bought. Halliburton, KBR, and Blackhawk employees lived in the most expensive hotels in Iraq, drove the most expensive leased SUVs, trucks, Humvees, and cars, and ate the best and most expensive food at those hotels where they lived every day for eight years. All of these excessive expenditures were charged to, and paid for, by United States taxpayers in the form of national debt, that was at least $11.5 trillion dollars at the end of 2008, the last year of the Bush "W" and Cheney Neo Con Administration. Both Bush "W" and Cheney were at least multi-millionaires, or billionaires, when they left office.

This is an example of what the free-market system, uncontrolled capitalism in a free-market system, can result in. The result was uncontrolled and massive theft from the American people, the expendable masses, with no accountability or responsibility for the theft from Halliburton, etc.

American soldiers, meanwhile, lived in tents, slept on cots, wore heavy uniforms in unbearable heat, and got low wages for their time and effort. For their military meals, provided by private contractors at very elevated prices, they would have to stand in line outside for up to an hour in 125 degree heat, with heavy military uniforms on. Besides risking their lives every day, including while standing in line to get meals, their salaries were 1/100 to 1/1000 of what the privatized military and the paramilitary got for doing the same jobs. Often the soldiers were the ones who trained these hugely over-paid men from the private sector what to do.

It was a falsely begun war, perpetuated on false information gotten from falsely imprisoned and tortured Iraqi male civilians, who were never charged with anything after they had been turned in by anyone, including their neighbors and real and actual enemy terrorists or insurgents, in exchange for payoffs, rewards, of $1000 to $5000 paid by the United States Government.

It has been well established since World War II that confessions gotten as a result of torture are what the victim thinks the torturer wants to hear so they will stop the torture. This is both logical and obvious. But the United States privatized military and paramilitary of the 21st century ignored that truth, and freely used cruelty and torture as a means of usually unnecessary interrogation, that sometimes resulted in death for the Iraqi prisoners, all of whom were innocent civilians, who were *never* charged with anything. No one was ever held responsible for these tragic and cruel deaths.

The Press has always been the only check against Government abuse at all levels and Republican lies and viciousness. After The Patriot Act, in 2001, threats to reporters or imprisonment because of charges of treason, terrorism, and espionage meant investigative reporting was no more. It's not worth going to prison for. Or being shot at, or killed. Starting in 2012 drones are flying in the air in the United States, like they fly in the air and are sent to targets in Iran, Iraq, and anywhere else in the World. No one wants to be the target of a drone. No job is worth that.

President Obama said repeatedly during his unprecedented campaign of two years that he would welcome and encourage criticism. However, under Obama there has been more imprisonment for these actions than ever before in United States history. He didn't close Guantanamo prison, or end the Iraq war for almost three years, which is what the Republicans, the Neo Cons, had planned to do anyway before 2001. He didn't fix healthcare/sickness-care or fix the national debt. All of these things he said he would fix. He said one thing and did another, a time-honored American tradition, a political custom for a few centuries for most American Presidents and politicians.

In a real democracy the people have the power to change their Government through public dissent and elections. But a public that is given false information and misinformation, disinformation and lies, can't do that. Political agendas that are contrary to the good of the people are impossible for the public to stop. But a democratic government is supposed to pay attention to the people, listen to the people, and change in the ways that the people want the Government to change.

When they are elected, not appointed, many politicians, like most Senators, Congressmen and Congresswomen, Governors, Mayors, and Police Chiefs and Sheriffs, have represented themselves, not their constituents, along with the political agendas of their Party. The national Government is usually divided and divisive, not productive. But it's productive for individual politicians, as most of them become very wealthy, often even millionaires and multi-millionaires, as benefits for them on the side. It seems a lot of politicians are in business to create prosperity for themselves, not for other Americans, not for their constituents, not for the voters who put them in office. Perhaps that's because it's not the voters that put them in office. Perhaps it has long been a grand illusion.

Congress fuels any wars by providing the funding for that war. Ending the funding ends the war. So it was Congress that continued the Iraq war and the Viet Nam war, for 8 years and 10 years. This is proof that Congress hasn't represented the American people since 1964, when President Johnson began the invasion of and the war in Viet Nam based on false information, based on lies to the American people. Millions of people protested and marched against it on and off for about 10 years but no politician, no President, paid attention for those 10 years. Nothing changed, nothing was stopped. Maybe because the President did not control the funding, or make the big decisions, about that war.

Under Hoover the FBI was a political police force used to stop dissent and kill leaders of dissent, including in other countries. People like Hoover, Nixon, and Bush "W" represented death, killing, wars, and the military industrial complex. People like Lennon, Martin Luther King, and President John Kennedy represented life, love, peace, and were a threat to the death-mongers, the war-mongers, a threat that had to be closely monitored and stopped. The FBI, the CIA, the Secret Service, and other secret agencies in the United States, and the military industrial complex, perceived them as threats.

The CIA and the United States military powers-that-be wanted to have a war in Viet Nam. These three good men stood against a Secret Service back-up that couldn't be trusted, in the case of President Kennedy, that was instrumental in getting him killed, assassinated, and against the military men that run the United States Government that wanted to kill men, women and children in foreign countries because of falsely constructed political agendas. Since after 1960 wars have been created and maintained on lies, with lies to the American public to justify any actions of war, invasions, attacks, occupations. Since then, Government-sponsored intelligence agencies have worked against people who publically promote justice, freedom, and democracy.

Writing books for the sake of making money that are completely, or mostly, lacking in truth is always possible. In 2011 and 2012 Republicans were still writing books and newspaper articles, and magazine articles, saying the Bush "W"/Cheney/Rumsfeld/Rove, etc. invasion and bombing of Iraq starting in 2003 was "for humanitarian reasons". No records were ever kept of the number of Iraq civilians killed but estimates of the carnage has been 400,000 to 600,000 innocent and defenseless men, women, children, and babies murdered by United States soldiers and weapons. For 8 years millions of Iraqi civilians lost their homes because they were destroyed, or they were forced to leave their homes, and their cities and towns were destroyed. At least 10,000 of their pets and domestic animals were killed by American soldiers because American soldiers liked to kill anything that moved or looked at them. Like for the Viet Nam war, American military superiors had taught their soldiers "Kill or be killed", as their daily mantra. In order to control soldiers, fear must be instilled.

The Iraqi social structure was destroyed, besides their entire electrical and plumbing systems, and their normal sources and supplies of water. They lost their jobs and their sources of money, including their money kept in their banks that was stolen. All of this happened under the U.S. Government pretense of "helping them", for "humanitarian reasons". All of this was combined with the insanity of living with daily bombings, and U.S. soldiers breaking into their homes, for 8 years.

Only the Far Right, the Neo Cons, the Republicans in general, would believe the obvious lies that supported their mean actions. Wars are always ugly, mean, selfish, cruel, and the United States Government has chosen to sanitize them with lies and control of information for Americans in the 21st century. During Obama's first campaign Michelle Obama had said people in America were "mean". Unfortunately she spoke the truth about most Americans. Politicians writing and publishing lies can sell millions of books, and help politicians in their endless quest to make more money and to take money from the American people. After all, lying is just another way to make money in a capitalistic society. The truth is dangerous, and most Americans want to believe the lies, they want to hear the lies.

Soldiers have said they live each day as if it is their last. Each day they stare death in the face, and usually cheat death. Maybe the closer they are to death the more alive they feel. Maybe that has been one of the appeals of wars and conflicts for soldiers, the appeal of serving in the military.

In 1900 there were 65 million people in America. The majority were immigrants, often making difficult transitions from other countries because of social intolerance in America, and because of financial difficulties. There were no Government programs then to help immigrants, as there have been for about the last 50 years in the United States. A century later, in 2000, there were 320 million people in America, with about 65 million of them immigrants. Freedom is the basic right of all people, of all of mankind, but only in democracies has this been guaranteed. But everyone everywhere has the right to pursue the truth, the eternal quest for the truth.

From the late 1700's to about 1900 the American West, the Old West, attracted people who were looking for more freedom, or for another chance to succeed, in a place of unlimited possibilities and unlimited freedom and hope. But it quickly became a place of intolerance, inequality, and brutality, dominated by bullies with guns and rifles. Cowboys were unique to the Old West. They were actually riding and working with cattle on trails to markets for only about 20 years, because of the new railroad eventually and amazingly covering 100,000 miles, eventually transporting cattle to market instead of cowboys and their horses.

The Old West was mostly a society without laws and rules for conduct, with little or no law and order enforced, often ruled by white men who were mean, selfish, dishonest, and without boundaries or rules. When rules and laws did exist they were easily broken and ignored. Instead of the Old West being a better place to live, where people could change and improve their lives for themselves and their children, a place where they could start over, it was often dangerous. Even the weather could be brutal, with extremes of hot and cold, with blizzards and tornadoes.

It was dominated by low-quality dangerous white men with no conscience. Native American Indians who had been badly mistreated, with *millions* of them murdered for a few centuries by the U.S. Government and the U.S. military, were a danger to settlers because of their mistreatment by U.S. soldiers, by the U.S. military, and by low-quality selfish white men, and bad cowboys. But it was a chance to live a life they couldn't live in other places in America, or anywhere else in the World. It was always a land of unlimited opportunity and freedom, and unlimited possibilities.

The crimes of politics and the politics of crime permeated the Old West, even more than in the more civilized parts of America. Treating each other right, living in peace with each other, with people of all ethnicities and colors, often did not happen in the Old West, in the seemingly endless spaces of the Old West, until possibly after 1900.

Silence is a multitude of sounds. Wherever you go, there you are. Wherever you are, the past is always with you. People have a need and a desire to talk about themselves to someone who will listen. So that explains the popularity of psychology and psychiatry in the past 70 years in America. But things have changed. No more talking it out, discovering how your past is the reason you are miserable, and how other people are the reasons your life is a mess. Or that your parents are to blame for everything wrong in your life, or not. Or finding out about resentments that are right or wrong. Psychology and psychiatry in America today is about mini-sessions, 15 minutes to get your psycho-prescription renewed for the excessive charge of at least $200 for that visit. For legal drugs that cause suicides, mass murders.

# CHAPTER SEVEN

## Capitalism in America

Capitalism dominates the World. But capitalism is a miserable failure for the vast majority of people in the World, more than a *billion people*, who live in poverty because of capitalism, who live in deprivation, destitution, and financial hardship because of the free-market system of capitalism. But several *million* people throughout the World have become millionaires and multi-millionaires, even billionaires, as a result of capitalism. Capitalism promotes huge inequality. There needs to be the development of a superior system of greater equality as no other system tried throughout the history of mankind has been better, and many have been worse. But, of course, capitalism is here to stay.

If the at least $11.5 trillion dollars of United States money that is hidden in off-shore accounts by the millionaires, multi-millionaires, billionaires, was instead taxed at 20% to 30% in the United States it could eliminate all poverty in the United States, and pay for a free Universal Healthcare System for everyone, if it wasn't then diverted, hidden in another tax-free place, like the Cayman Islands, and other islands. Trickle-down economics doesn't happen except in the minds of Republicans and economists who get paid very well for doing nothing of value, and who are usually wrong about their forecasts, etc. But trickle-down dishonesty and hypocrisy does happen.

The United States Government controls other countries by controlling their economies and policies through the IMF and the World Bank. The result is an exploitation of the poor. This is called "predatory capitalism". The World Bank and the International Monetary Fund have destroyed economies of other countries by demanding privatization of railroads, utilities, airlines, hospitals, communications, and TV and radio stations, as conditions for giving the loans. They demand that their Universal Healthcare systems be eliminated and replaced by privatized Western-style healthcare/ sickness care instead. Each of these countries is then destined for destitution of their economies.

As an example, Portugal got a loan from the IMF and the World Bank and had to destroy its free healthcare system for all its citizens because of the requirements of the loan. As a result, because people couldn't afford the new very high privatized medical costs, the death rate increased by at least 20% in 2011. They were the expendable masses, according to the philosophy of the IMF and the World Bank. Ultimately, as a result, a large percentage of the population lose their jobs and their sources of income. Or this eliminates their chances of escaping poverty because cost of living prices double or triple, or increase as much as 10 times. Privatization of any country results in widespread destitution. This has been proven repeatedly.

The spreading of global capitalism by the United States Government happens by forcing it on countries by giving them high interest loans from the IMF. Conditions for the loan must be met that include privatization of most, or all, of the countries infrastructures which causes loss of jobs and increased widespread poverty. The IMF does not allow early repayment of loans. They want indebtedness and control. If the country cannot repay its high interest loans they will be indebted to the IMF and/or the World Bank indefinitely. This makes them like loan-sharks.

So predatory capitalism destroys foreign economies and the people living in those countries by forcing them into poverty and destitution from which they are unable to escape. It follows a pattern, like a criminal does. For years United States foreign policies have forced instability and problems in foreign countries, in foreign economies. The United States Government destabilizes their economy, and interferes with their economy and government by regulating and controlling their currencies through the IMF and the World Bank. The IMF is located in Washington, D.C. Then the IMF controls their economic policies and their political leaders. The end result is called predatory capitalism.

After United States soldiers left Iraq at least 15,000 highly paid private United States contractors stayed in Iraq, mostly on 14 permanent United States military bases built during the 8 years of occupation and war. They replaced military personnel who had done the same jobs, the same work, for pennies on the dollar in comparison, so they will be a permanent drain on the United States economy. Obama didn't fix this republican Neo Con corruption strategy, just like he didn't fix the Iraq war by ending it immediately as he promised repeatedly during his unusually long two year campaign before 2009, mostly funded by the people of Illinois because he had been elected to be a Senator of Illinois. He mostly followed the previous Neo Con plans in both cases.

The Neo Con plan in 2003 was to end the war in Iraq on September 11, 2011, apparently for public relations impact, to manipulate public support, a date designed to look good in the press and in the media and in history books. The 911 war began on 9/11 in 2001 and was planned to end exactly 10 years later on the same day, 9/11 in 2011. It was part of the war game. But Obama ended it two months after the Neo Con's had planned, in November, 2011. No one knows how many more thousands of Iraqi civilian deaths happened in those extra two months, or how much excessive debt was accumulated. Hundreds of billions of dollars were overcharged to the United States Government by the private companies Bechtel and Halliburton in those 8 years of occupation and war, with the help of the United States Government and politicians. Perhaps that was why the war was prolonged.

After campaign funding reform began in 2011 Carl Rove was the instigator of new campaign funding methods called "Citizens for Unity". It was formed to receive unlimited and unanimous contributions for the Republican Party and for future elections. That's campaign funding reform according to Republicans, after campaign contributions were officially and legally limited because of legislative efforts. True to form, the Neo Con Carl Rove manipulated legislation for his benefit, and for the enduring and endless benefit of all other Republican candidates in future elections.

In the first decade of the 21$^{st}$ century Freddie Mac, which is taxpayer owned, was given billions of dollars by the United States Government for a bailout because of their theft and mismanagement of taxpayer's money. They were paid for their so-called losses and didn't repay their customers for their actual losses. After that, Freddie Mac hedged their bets against mortgages they had previously given financial support for by making financial wagers against these same home owners being able to refinance their home loans at lower interest rates. So Freddie Mac didn't allow millions of people, many of them with perfect payment histories and good credit, to refinance at lower interest rates. As a result some of the Freddie Mac administrators, especially the head of Freddie Mac, stole multi-millions of dollars with no fines, no penalties, no charges, no imprisonment. The head of Freddie Mac didn't even lose his job, or have to pay back what he had stolen. Perhaps it helped that he was black.

It was like how the head of the Red Cross in Mississippi did not have to pay back the millions of dollars donated after Hurricane Katrina that she kept for herself. She legally and socially got away with not paying back the millions of dollars she stole from these donations to the Red Cross by just saying "I gave it away to my friends." Case closed, money not accounted for, apparently because she was a privileged black person, a black woman with special treatment and hierarchy, like the black man who was the head of Freddie Mac. It always pays to have high political connections, for both black and white people. Connections in high places are valuable for all colors of people everywhere for everything.

An example of this is the Boeing Corporation. Boeing is a multi-billion dollar company that pays no taxes because of using tax loopholes, tax-breaks, tax subsidies, tax evasion, tax write-offs, besides the most expensive tax lawyers that money can afford. All businesses can, and do, do the same thing and pay little or no taxes. The 35% tax rate for businesses doesn't mean anything. It's easily gotten around. It's easily avoided. If Congress was, in fact, serving the American people they would have stopped this gross injustice many years ago. Instead, the IRS and Congress look the other way.

In a capitalistic society like America for-profit prisons make at least one million to two million dollars profit operating each prison every year. In the land of the free, in America, more than one out of every 100 people are in prison. Many more than any other country in the World, much more than any of the other 23 Democracies in the World. The profit per prisoner has a lot to do with it. More crime and more criminals means much more money, much more profits, for the owners and administrators of prisons. Crime, after all, is a business for everyone  involved, both coming and going.

Crime is an industry employing many millions of people in America. Building and operating prisons has become a very profitable industry in the 21st century. It's a big business in the United States economy. That's why a higher percentage of the United States population is in prison than ever before, a higher percentage than any other country in the world. It costs about $50,000 to $80,000 a year per prisoner in America. To whom and where does all that money go? Is it for the great food and rehab therapy sessions with psychiatrists and vocational training so they can get a job when they get out? No, no, no, and no. None of that is a part of being in prison in the United States. At those costs, for those charges, prisoners should be better able to function productively in society when they get out into society again, instead of destructively. But most prisoners end up back in prison again because they are dumped back into society in worse condition than when they went in. Often they can't get jobs or a place to live, or they end up homeless, alone, and starving.

Private prisons are a multi-million dollar industry for the financial benefit and profit of whoever operates them. The average profit for privately run prisons, not government-run prisons, is at least $200,000 to $300,000 dollars a year per prison. This doesn't include the so-called country club prisons where preferential treatment for the rich is found even in prisons.

It's been said that if illegal drugs were legalized half of the people in prisons in America would be set free. So this is another reason illegal drugs will never be legalized, or stop being allowed to be imported from South America, Mexico, etc. America is the biggest importer and user of illegal drugs in the World. Illegal drugs, and all the problems they cause, are a multi-billion dollar industry in America.

The DEA has been a dismal failure for many years, for at least 30 years, and a huge drain on the United States economy, with hundreds of billions of dollars spent and lost for very little value or improvement. There are too many people making too much money so it continues, and will continue endlessly. United States customs officials take bribes, like politicians do, like police and deputies do, like police chiefs and sheriffs do, and like FBI agents and CIA agents do. It's part of the culture. Customs officials inspect just 1% of the containers coming and going, so it's easy to get cocaine, heroin, and all other illegal drugs, in and out of the countries. Canada exports about $10 billion dollars in cocaine and heroin to the United States every year. Mexico exports much more, maybe $50 billion dollars, maybe more, to its biggest market, the United States. If these drugs were legalized all this would end. But rich and powerful people in the United States, in Canada, and in Mexico make sure this won't happen.

Stopping the illegal drug trade would be easy to do. Just stop the flow of illegal drugs from Canada and Mexico by enforcing laws in place for many years. Trucks with 500 to 1000 pounds of illegal drugs cross borders easily every day of the year. Eliminate the sources crossing at the borders and the supply would end. Eliminate the supply to stop the drug trading, the illegal drug industry in America. Drug dealers are rarely stopped in America, even though they would be easy to stop, charge, arrest, and put in prison. The law just doesn't see them, or hear them. Deputies, Sergeants, and police officers ignore them. They look the other way. Drug dealers make pay-offs to the law to be allowed to continue their nefarious and disgusting drug trade. The demand for illegal drugs is greater in America than anywhere else in the World. The illegal drug industry is here to stay.

Since Nixon started "the war on drugs" in 1971 at least 40 million to 45 million people have been imprisoned for drug-related crimes. The cost has been immense in innocent lives lost. Billions of dollars have been wasted as millions of people have been imprisoned for years for possession of an ounce or less of drugs, while people found with pounds or hundreds of pounds of it are not even charged at the official Mexican border crossings. For years Mexican drug dealers have been allowed to bring hundreds of pounds, even thousands of pounds, into the United States. Legalizing alcohol in the 1930's ended the alcohol-related violence, and the government corruption and public corruption. Legalizing drugs would do the same. But rich and powerful people in the United States, in Canada, and in Mexico make sure that doesn't happen, and make sure it will never happen.

In the United States race horses are given excessive use of pain medications, etc., to enable them to race. Other countries do not allow this. They prevent the further injury of the horses by not allowing them to race until their injuries are healed. Young adolescent horses, two and three years old, are commonly used as race horses in America. This is equivalent to being an eight to twelve year old child. Obviously those horses are not done growing, are not fully developed physiologically, and do not have the strength of a grown horse. All race horses in America, any age, are commonly given drugs, chemicals, to mask their health problems and bone, muscle, and ligament problems, like tendonitis, that result from physical stress and strain during races and training.

In the United States at least 20 race horses die every day during or after a race. Nowhere else in the World has nearly as many deaths, or allows these practices, or allows heavy medication of horses and other abuses that should not be happening at all. In America horses are raced in public races that should not be in those races at all. In the United States protecting the horses is not as important as the profit motive and the possible financial gain. This is the main motive and incentive for almost everything in America. It is American capitalism.

Since the Viet Nam war, since the 1960's, at least a million veterans, of all colors, from all United States wars, attacks, occupations, and invasions since then, have been homeless. There seems to have been a system to *not* help veterans that had post-traumatic stress, or debilitating injuries that were physical, mental, and emotional because of combat experiences, making them unable to take care of themselves in a normal way, unable to get a job, unable to get help anywhere, unable to get or keep a place to live. Government support of veterans has always mostly ended after their discharge from military service. Then their own personal battles begin.

Why hasn't the "best country in the World" ever fixed this problem once and for all, instead of a Band Aid approach? No other democracy has done the same, which is nothing, to end the problem and actually help the men, and women, the former soldiers who are desperately in need of help. This includes millions of veterans in the past 70 years, since after World War II. The U.S. Government and military are interested in creating killing machines who are of no use to the system when they are discharged. For soldiers to give their life psychologically or physically has been of no interest to the military system, not ever in the history of the United States. It's just a continuation of the status quo.

Since the 1980's there have been United States Special Forces military men trained as killing machines. In the 21st century, especially since 2003, the Neo Cons in charge of this secretive JSOC use these heavily armed and deadly trained men to conduct raids, usually at night, by kicking open doors of private houses, forcing entrance with rifles aimed to kill, and then killing the occupants of those houses, including the women, the elderly, and children. JSOC considers them just as dangerous as men in order to justify killing them. Since 2003 in Iraq and Afghanistan *1000 to 2000* of these Special Forces JSOC raids, killing thousands of innocent civilians in their homes, have been conducted every *month.* No charges are ever made, no arrests, just forced entry and shooting and killing of the people living in the houses, apartments, tents, and tribal communities throughout the World. This has been happening in almost every country of the World since 2003, including in America. This is not something from a democracy, but rather something awful and beyond belief like in Nazi Germany, or a totalitarian or fascist government, or something in a dictatorship.

Drones are directed to hit anyone that the United States military and the President have targeted. This is a lethal killing machine that can be aimed at anyone anywhere in the World, that has been used to kill an unknown number of people throughout the World and Americans in other countries. As an example, a 12 year old son of a naturalized American man, who had moved his family back to his former country of residence to be near his parents, was killed by a drone aimed at him while he was playing outside after school with his friends. An unknown number of those friends were also killed by that drone. His father had been killed by an American drone weeks earlier, after an order by President Obama. Neither the father nor his son had done anything wrong or harmful to any Americans in or out of America. Both of them had never broken any laws or been charged or arrested because of breaking even one law. The father was regarded by the United States as suspicious, and his son was guilty of being his father's oldest son. Proximity and influence were the apparent reasons for President Obama and the United States military to kill them both with American drones in other countries. But, of course, they didn't have to have a reason. They were accountable to no one.

The JSOC killed Bin Laden in his home in Pakistan, and vaporized all contents of their crashed United States military helicopter. JSOC is designed, the system is designed, to kill and leave no traces. Whether the victims are guilty is of no concern and no consequence. It means nothing to these trained killers who are employed to only kill. There is nothing people in the United States can do to stop this new way of conducting wars, as President Obama referred to it in 2014. Guilt and innocence has nothing to do with it. Many thousands of innocent people have been killed in the process.

The United States seems to have set up a system to keep poor white people poor. That's right. Not poor black people, who have endless special opportunities, special programs and grants, special government help, and special social and financial help on a community level to get out of poverty.

This has always been help that white people don't have and never have had. It's a long-standing government prejudice against poor white people.

In general, the most racist people in America are black people. Racism has been perpetuated endlessly by millions of black people, not just tens of thousands of white extremists who are disgusting, stupid, mean, and awful people who do not represent the average white American and never have. Black culture has perpetuated it, involving many millions of black people. But the average white American, many hundreds of millions of them for about a hundred years, has had to pay for it, socially and financially, with endless compensation and special treatment for black people because of the harmful and wrong actions of the much smaller prejudiced white extremist minority in the United States. The blame for perpetuating it needs to be placed where it has always belonged.

The NAACP behaves itself when there has been a black President of the United States because that forced them to grow up and to stop behaving like a spoiled child, having tantrums and expecting special treatment, and even repeatedly demanding it for many years. The NAACP has been <u>much</u> less in the news as constant complainers since Obama's election in 2009. Since the U.S. President is black, and many appointed high offices in the Federal Government are filled by black people, continued constant complaining would be ignorant and stupid. They're like Republicans, like Republican politicians, who are always complaining about whatever Democratic politicians do. White people vote for the best candidate more often than for the Party, and black people vote for the person who is black regardless of the party. But without a majority of *white* votes Obama would not have been elected President in 2008, and would not have been re-elected in 2012.

For about 100 years real estate values in the United States have increased an average of 6% a year except for market and price surges that are artificial and manipulated, like the stock market and commodities markets are artificial and manipulated by the part of the upper 1%, or 5%, that controls America because of their positions and financial wealth. Those markets are manipulated and do not reflect real and actual value when there are sudden and large, even huge, cost increases. Market collapses happen after temporary market price and value surges. Regardless, most personal wealth in America has been a result of home ownership and owning commercial and rental real estate. Often that personal wealth, that financial prosperity, has been inherited.

Home ownership is usually necessary for individual prosperity in a democracy and is a big part of inherited wealth, of ongoing prosperity for all generations, and for a personal sense of peace and security. But America has always had the lowest percentage of home ownership of all 24 democracies in the World. This is even more true since the national real estate fiasco that began in the first decade of the 21$^{st}$ century. Artificially high values and inflated costs made a lot of money for a lot of people, and made a lot of people losers of a lot of money, losers of artificial real estate value and loss of temporary personal financial worth after the collapse of value and prices in those artificial markets.

In 2012 about 47 million Americans lived near, at, or below poverty level. That's about one out of six Americans who can't qualify for a home mortgage because of their income. But at least 50% of Americans can't qualify anyway to buy a house because of their credit record, a record that is often inaccurate with mistakes that credit bureaus usually refuse to correct. This can have negative influences, often for the rest of their lives, for at least 50% of the people in America. Their enemy is the incompetent, error-ridden, and mistake-laden credit bureaus, drunk with their own importance and refusing to change, to improve the error of their ways. Credit Bureaus, the three credit agencies, are an institution cheating most Americans since about the 1990's.

Governments, especially democracies, have a moral responsibility, a moral obligation, to help people who need help in their country. Instead, the United States has given hundreds of billions of dollars for many years to leaders of foreign countries, and to their militaries specifically. These are always countries that are much better off financially than the United States has been in terms of national debt. United States yearly foreign aid, using American taxpayer's money, hasn't ever helped people in those countries living in dire poverty, for at least the last 50 years.

Most of this foreign aid comes back to the United States as mandatory purchases for military weapons and equipment, planes, jets, guns, bullets, tanks, etc., made in America or out-sourced from America, and as partial payment for loans given at high interest rates to these countries from the IMF and from the World Bank. It's like the United States Government gave everybody with a student loan or a house loan in America enough money to pay back that loan every year. This would then be a financial gift every year from the United States Government that people would then be giving back to the United States Government, with taxes added on, in a win-win situation.

The United States could eliminate poverty in the entire World for $20 billion dollars a year if that foreign aid went directly to all impoverished people in the World. The United States spends at least $500 billion dollars a year on its own military and defense, by far the most money of any country in the World. It isn't that poverty in the United States can't be eliminated, or even World-wide poverty eliminated. It's that the people in power that run the World, and the people in power that run America, don't want it to end. They, in fact, have done whatever they can do to vastly increase poverty to at least 400 million people in the World living at or below poverty level in the first part of the 21$^{st}$ century. In many other countries that means living in dire destitution.

There is world-wide domination by the IMF and by the World Bank, by large corporations like Bechtel, KBR, Halliburton and many others, most of which became billionaires because of the privatized war in Iraq by overcharging and cheating American taxpayers by means of the United States Government, and killing about 500,000 innocent and unarmed Iraqi civilians. Forcing countries to become privatized, to privatize their institutions, utilities, and medical systems as a condition for getting loans from the IMF and from the World Bank, has happened repeatedly. All of this has forced extreme poverty on indigenous people throughout the World since the beginning of the 21$^{st}$ century. It's always for the same reasons of greed, power, control, selfishness, profit, and money. As always, follow the money to find the answers.

There have been no attacks from other countries on the United States since World War II was declared because of Japan's air attack on American military ships in Pearl Harbor, in Hawaii, December 7, 1941.The hijacking of American planes on 9/11 were by men mostly from Saudi Arabia, that had been living in the United States. Nobody from Iraq, flying a plane from Iraq, could possibly have ever attacked the United States. Since then the 911 Commission has rated the Homeland Security Department with D's and F's in national security, and in most everything else. This honesty was unexpected. National security and a free and safe democracy has not been a result of the Homeland Security Department in America, except in the minds of Republicans. Closing down a free society *has* become a result of Homeland Security in America, like it played a part in closing down

Hitler's Nazi Germany many years ago. Germany's Homeland Security was a cruel and controlling Government agency used to dominate people in Germany in the 1930's and 1940's, to close down their democracy and free society.

Almost a trillion dollars has been paid by the American Government to Iraqi men in Iraq, including to insurgents and terrorists and anybody else, in exchange for turning in Iraqi men for $1000 to $5000 pay-offs per man. Like bounty hunting, except any man anywhere in Iraq was fair game. There have never been any charges made against these more than 200,000 Iraqi civilians who were then imprisoned indefinitely, tortured, beaten, and some killed, with no probable-cause or legal help, or legal representation. This is the America you thought you knew. This is the privatized army and the paramilitary that American taxpayer's have been funding since 2003 with too high salaries, with billions and trillions of dollars wasted, and with money used for torture, killing, and imprisonment of innocent people. Only 1% of these Iraqi prisoners were actual enemies throughout the entire United States occupation, the longest war in American history, since 2003.

The massive United States indebtedness in 2009 for at least $13.5 trillion dollars was because of the war in Iraq that allowed, that encouraged, that had planned, massive price-gouging and massive overcharges by a paramilitary, by a privatized army, and by private companies like Kellogg, Brown, and Root (KBR) for at least $20 billion a year, and by Halliburton (Cheney's company) for at least $20 billion dollars a year, by Lockheed and Blackhawk for at least $20 billion a year, and by at least 20 other private United States companies in Iraq. This accounts for trillions of dollars stolen from the American people for at least 10 years, most of which cannot be accounted for. It was stolen by individual Americans and by groups connected with these corporations, with no charges ever made.

The United States Government has been the Big Daddy of all credit cards for politicians to use for whatever they want to buy for at least the past 50 years, thereby giving their constituents endless public indebtedness. The interest payments alone for these Big Daddy Government credit cards will take all the money the United States can pay every year, ad infinitum, without ever paying down any of the principle. It's like the hundred million Americans with their credit card debts they can't get out of, that they can't ever pay off.

Yet the United States Government has continued to borrow at least a billion dollars every year to give as gifts to foreign countries as foreign aid. No other country in the World gives financial aid, or has given financial aid for about 50 years, to foreign countries, except the United States. It must be a "super-power" thing. Borrow money to give it away, hundreds of millions of dollars a year starting with President Reagan and then borrowing at least a billion dollars a year, mostly from China, to give as foreign aid in the 21st century, which then deprives the American people because *they* are indebted to pay it back. The Federal Government is just an impersonal entity, requiring the uninformed public to support it financially and politically, and to bail it out when necessary. Deceit, deception, secrets, and lies are the glue that keeps it all together in the 21st century.

The Federal Reserve and the Federal Bank and Federal Taxes are not Federal Government entities. They are not Government-related. They are privately-controlled. Federal taxes are un-Constitutional, and were *never* approved in about 25 states. Federal tax money paid pays off the yearly national debt interest payments of at least $1 trillion dollars on the yearly national debt of at least $12 trillion dollars, now in the 21st century.

The Government of a country should be for improving and bettering the life of its citizens, looking out for the welfare of all of its people. That's what 23 other Democracies do. But the United States is a different kind of democracy. The money to do that has been there, and is there now to do that, but because of massive corruption and theft vast sums of American's money, trillions of dollars of their Federal Government's money, disappears, is stolen every year , especially since 2001. It's become an American tradition in the 21$^{st}$ century.

Since 2001 the Pentagon cannot account for 25% of the money it has spent, about $3 trillion dollars every year since then. It's always been "classified", meaning "not needing to be accounted for". Who stole it? Where did it go? Probably to the DOD, or to Black Projects, meaning "secret projects", and to politicians and other people on the side. This massive monetary theft and corruption has never been prosecuted, will never be prosecuted, with no charges ever made, because rich people and politicians are privileged in America. It's an American tradition.

The United States does not have equal justice under the law. Dishonesty and corruption are rampant. Dishonesty and corruption are a big part of the reason why the United States actual national debt in 2011 was still at least $12 trillion dollars, and why a larger percentage of the United States population is struggling financially than since the Great Depression of 1929 and the early 1930's. It's a big part of the explanation why inequality is everywhere and why a much higher percentage of the American population lives at poverty, near poverty, or below poverty than ever before in United States history.

More college graduates, and increasing the number of college graduates every year, would not improve the United States economy. There are not jobs going unfilled because of a lack of college graduates to fill them, except in nursing and engineering, as has been true since the 1960's. For at least the last 50 years the largest percentage of college graduates, hundreds of millions of them, have not found work in their fields of study. About 1/3 of all Americans have a two year or four year college degree. For many millions of Americans a four year college degree has been useless, or nearly useless. It's just a four year long diversion from the workforce and from the reality of what life is really like in America for adults. It's a kind of vacation from reality.

But it creates jobs every year for millions of people who work in the college and university industry of education. That is why more students are always needed, an increasing yearly enrollment, to pay the over-priced tuition, often more than 100 times higher than 50 years ago, in order to pay the salary increases for the personnel and for the huge profit increases for the colleges and universities, in general. Colleges and universities used to be beacons of altruism, but for a long time they've just been another capitalistic industry. The graduates aren't usually necessary to the economy as college graduates, but they *are* necessary as students financially contributing to the higher education economy for as many years as possible.

The hugely over-priced educational institutions generate hundreds of billions of dollars in revenues for the American economy every year. The educational industry includes financial companies and banks that give tuition loans to students that require 10 to 30 year paybacks with high interest payments, with increased interest payments if they are not paid back on time, and with Government guarantees if they are not repaid. Students are valuable to the United States economy because of the money generated by their attendance, by their Government grants, guaranteed student loans, tuition payments, and by supporting the people that work in all those related areas, thereby supporting many millions of people working in higher education-related jobs. Not because of the jobs they fill when they graduate.

In 2012 the Presidents of 36 colleges and universities got yearly salaries of at least $600,000. Many of these yearly salaries were a million dollars or more. That is one of the reasons why tuitions have increased so much since 2001. Higher education is an industry, whether it's a non-profit college or university or not. Of course no taxes are paid on their huge profits when they are classified as "a non-profit" college or university. Loopholes are an American tradition.

Most four year college courses teach no skills. The ones that do are often of no real value in the real world. If four year colleges teach skills at all they demand four years to teach what could be taught in one year. Except engineering, nursing, and medical school. Medical students, nursing students, and engineering students don't need four years of undergraduate school. Why not one year as an undergraduate and then on to medical school? Then new (and old) physicians couldn't justify, in their minds, the outrageous fees they charge for what they do, which is mostly to write prescriptions and order tests to be done by other specialists, to make sure they can't be sued for oversight, etc.

Four year colleges and universities are clearly an industry based on profit and greed, just like all other industries and businesses in a capitalistic society, even if they are called "non-profit". As a result of being overly educated in nothing of any value, and having no marketable skills of any value to anyone, hundreds of millions of college graduates can't find jobs of any value in the real World. Or they think they are under-employed. Colleges are just vacations from the real World, and from the realities of living in that World as an adult. As a result four year colleges create problems in America. But for many Americans the best time in their lives was when they were going to college, or a university, especially if they lived on campus. For that reason alone it's a worthwhile institution.

The United States ranks #11 in the World in quality of college educations. Yet, costs for college education have increased 10 to 100 times per college from when the United States ranked near the top 50 years ago. This is proof that cost does not equate with quality. The same proof applies to public schools. Black leaders, for many years, have said the quality of education everywhere is inferior for black students, that they are singled out for inferior education. But the quality of education everywhere can only be as good as the quality of the students in any classroom or school.

Money spent is secondary and is another excuse for poor academic performance. The real problems are caused by lack of discipline, both public and private. Lack of discipline is rampant in schools in many places in America, especially from black students who cannot and will not be disciplined, especially if their teacher is white. Threats of losing their job, not getting hired anywhere else, and/or being sued by the black student and their parents is ever lurking in the background.

In the past 25 years modern innovations to improve and change public education have failed. Those methods in place for more than 100 years were more successful. Kids are more sophisticated and worldly because of exposure to TV news media, to the internet, to Cable TV, and to movies that are violent and adult in content. But that doesn't mean they are more intelligent. It just means they are more worldly and knowledgeable about the ways of the world. And that, in turn, doesn't mean they can be rude, undisciplined, and disrespectful to adults, to their parents, and to their teachers. Respect for adults is still a necessary part of American culture, and should still be taught and expected by parents. But it usually isn't.

Poor school behavior and performance, inappropriate behavior in schools, is not the fault of teachers or because the books aren't new, or because the student doesn't have a personal computer, or because the school building is old. It's the parent's fault. Lack of discipline in schools happens because teachers, principals, administrators fear being sued by parents and students, especially by black students and their black parents, who apparently do not discipline their kids at home and obviously do not expect them to be disciplined at school. Or, they fear losing their jobs.

This varies from region to region in the United States, like most everything else. The learning capabilities of all students are affected by the selfish behavior of rude undisciplined students. Many more students than ever before drop out of school, don't finish high school. A higher percentage than ever before can't read, write, or do simple math when they graduate, because of "No Child Left Behind". This stupid program, this very harmful program, should have been stopped, should have been left behind, a long time ago. Discipline and expectations of good behavior and good performance in school need to be restored both at home and in school. Improved school performance will be the result. Improved social behavior everywhere will be the result.

Students who are black are socially conditioned to believe that they should get special treatment in American society and in education. They get paid to go to school, they get paid to take tests at school. Like $100 for each test they take, no matter what grade they get on that test. They get extra points on tests because of what color they are. Hundreds of thousands of them have gotten free lap-top computers, when white students do not, have not. No matter how poorly they do in school they will pass and go to the next grade, or be graduated from high school, because of "No Child Left Behind". They are also a bigger part of the disciplinary problems at schools.

More than 50% of actors in commercials are black, but they comprise only 15% of the population. Being black must be special, it sells, and black people apparently have a larger percentage of the advertising market in the United States. Apparently that's where the real money is.

For many years black people have had special qualifications (leniency) for standard programs and special programs just for them for rental assistance, childcare programs, financial aid and grants for educational programs, payment for school attendance and taking tests ($200 to $400 a month), special purchase programs for houses, etc. "No Child Left Behind" was a free pass through grades one through twelve, the only requirement being some school attendance, no participation required, and misbehavior and disruption of classrooms has always been allowed. That extremely lenient policy didn't lift any black kids, or white kids, out of poverty, but it did give millions of black kids, teenagers, even more disdain and dislike of white people and the system they were able to abuse and take advantage of endlessly. As a part of their culture they are taught to take advantage of and abuse the white cultural system in any way they can for their own advantage.

Dislike of white people is a part of their culture. It's something that is taught and passed on from generation to generation, mostly from mother to child, as the father is rarely there at all, and rarely is he ever married to the mother. For more than 100 years this has been a black cultural thing that white teenagers and white women have stupidly copied, as the percentage of unwed white mothers has dramatically increased in the past twenty-five years. This seems to have been since the "Murphy Brown" TV character made it fashionable and the right thing to do, to have a career and a baby but no husband, in the 1980's.However, most unwed black mothers and white mothers don't have that kind of high-level career. They just have a tedious job and/or welfare for both mother and child to exist on.

A study of America has to include sex. It's a part of everyone's life in some way. Good or bad it's a big part of TV and movies and books and magazines, and in songs, in music, especially in rap noise and lyrics. But white men and white women are different than black people. One big difference is sex. Black men have a laissez-faire attitude about sex. Any woman, anywhere, any color, any shape or size (fat is fine), any age, homely or not, is fair game and is sexually desirable to most black men. It's their culture, their tradition. Come one, come all! They will gladly impregnate *any* female, donating their sperm at random. Black women also have sex at random with any man, while retaining an attitude of condescension and superiority. They seem to be saying "Don't forget that I'm better than you are because you're a man, and don't forget that we're better than all the other women that aren't black."

However, it's only fair to include white-trash men and white-trash women as having basically the same no-standards and no-limitations approach to sex. Thus these black people and these white people have been responsible for the vast majority of illegitimate kids, hundreds of millions of them in America, especially since the 1980's. The 1960's was a new time of "free love" for all people who were in their late teens and twenties, because of the new birth control pills, and because of the Viet Nam era of discontent and rebellion against the establishment and authorities.

Since the 1960's Republican politicians in America always spend much more money than the Democrats, leaving the biggest national debts. Yet, they always preach the opposite. Yet, they always chant their party mantra about the Democratic politicians spending the most and wanting bigger government, more spending. It has never mattered that the facts and figures don't support Republican claims. Democrat politicians don't stand up against any onslaughts and lies. Usually they just smile and look like it's just more of the same old lies, the same old distortions, dishonesty, and manipulations by the Republicans in power. Democratic politicians have a reputation for tolerating Republicans.

At some point it became useless to point this out to Republicans, to Neo Cons, and to the Far Right in power, and most everybody just gave up and let them be what they are. Bullies, mean Republican and Neo Con and Far Right bullies. Since the 1960's Republican politicians have been the bullies on the playground, and Democratic politicians just smile or ignore it, walking away from the endless lies and inaccuracies, their twisting and distorting of the truth. But hundreds of millions of people have believed the Republican lies and inaccuracies. It's like business advertising. Both politics and business advertising don't have to be truthful. People expect dishonesty in both. Let the buyer beware.

In the 1980's Republican President Reagan left a record high debt of *$4 trillion dollars*. He was the first President to take the Social Security Fund yearly surplus for his own use. All Republicans and most Democrats thought he was a great President. So corporate America was easily able to use Reagan to start deregulation on a national basis and to not increase regulations already in place. It was the beginning of the triumph of the American culture of corporate corruption. Reagan allowed it.

Later, Democratic President Clinton straightened out Reagan's financial mess. Clinton did a remarkably good job, but his fellow Democratic politicians gave him little public recognition for turning it into an amazing *$20 billion dollar surplus* to give to Bush "W"/Cheney, and their Neo Con crew, who used it for their own secretive purposes, as the $20 billion dollar surplus literally disappeared within a year after Bush "W"/Cheney took office dishonestly, by stealing the Presidency from Gore. This monstrous theft of $20 billion dollars from the American people was ignored by Democrat politicians, not just the Republican politicians. Hear no evil, see no evil, and out of sight, out of mind. They just pretended it never happened. They looked the other way. They ignored it and allowed it.

Using the vast reserves of gas in the United States to replace oil for electricity production would cut costs in half, and greatly lessen damage to the environment, including global warming. In 2012 the cost of gas was 1/3 of what it had cost in 2008, 40 cents per BTU vs. $1.20, but gas companies like Vectren did not lower its gas cost for customers by 1/3 in 2012. This is an example of how conspiracy and theft keeps utility costs unreasonably high and of how the customer is powerless to change any overcharges. Utility companies like Vectren had been charging their customers for the *same* gas and electricity again and again, month after month. For years if you brought it to their attention, demanding refunds, you would get non-compliance, arguments, and no restitution, no refunds, or just partial refunds. If you complained to your state's Attorney General he would do nothing to correct the overcharge, the theft. Multiply this times more than a million customers, most of which do not watch their monthly bill to see if they have been charged twice, or three times, for the same gas and/or electricity, and you have the reason for the record profits every year of a utility company like Vectren for millions of dollars, or multi-millions of dollars, every year.

Oil has a stranglehold on the United States economy because the oil industry makes too much money for too many people to change to other energy sources. That's why gas and other alternatives have not, and never will, replace oil. Helping Americans have the best life possible, helping and saving the environment, have nothing to do with it. Greed, power, money, profit, control, and selfishness are supreme in the United States. Oil is the King of America.

Oil originating from the United States is highly refined oil, superior oil, that is then sold to other countries, not sold to Americans. Oil that originates in Alaska, or in Canada, comes to the United States as very crude and thick oil. When demand for oil is high then the supply goes down, with prices increased. It's all regulated and manipulated for the most profit, not for the benefit of consumers.

Average annual returns on hedge fund investments are 2%. The rest, 98%, goes to management for fees, etc. Wealthy people give millions to account managers because they hope they have magical ability and understanding of hedge funds to manipulate it into huge profits for them. The profit, however, 98% of the time is for the managers. The same scenario is true for mutual funds, where the average annual return for investors is -2%., a 2% loss. Putting money into a bank is 100% secure, with at least a 2% interest paid on it. But wealthy people can afford to lose after taking a big chance for the tiny possibility they will win. The financial industry is just another form of gambling, like in a casino.

The Social Security Fund has had a yearly excess of $2 to $4 trillion dollars a year since about 2000. This is the Social Security Fund yearly surplus that is money paid by the American people. It's their money, for their security, to be used to pay for Social Security payments now and in the future. Since Bush "W"/ Cheney and their fellow Neo Cons started their rule of America in 2001 Republican officials, authorities, and politicians have been chanting their mantra of lies that Social Security is depleted, or deficient and nearly bankrupt, and needs to be "privatized", invested in stocks, bonds, mutual funds, commodities, and hedge-funds.

This is to guarantee the bankruptcy and/or failure of the Social Security Fund after making hundreds of thousands of investors and financial operatives, mostly Republicans, even more rich than they were before. The destruction and failure of the Social Security Fund, of the Social Security system in place since President FDR created it for the benefit and security of all Americans, would destroy the middle-class and ensure poverty and below poverty was the reality of life for the majority of Americans. Chaos, insecurity, and destitution would be the cultural and social norm in America, with the elite and the very rich living the other end of the spectrum, making inequality vastly greater than ever before.

The Neo Cons in charge want greater discrepancy between the rich and the poor, and elimination of all levels of the American middle-class. Destruction of the Social Security Fund, of the very necessary and very successful Social Security system, would guarantee that.

Since 2001 at least $2 to $4 trillion dollars has been stolen from the Social Security Fund surplus every year by the Neo Cons, by the Republicans in power each year, and by the United States Government. The Democrats in power must know about it, but as usual are apathetic and weak and do not protect the people that voted for them, or their constituents. It's classified as "official" information, meaning secret information. No one will ever have to reveal where *$20 to $40 trillion dollars* of Social Security Fund money has disappeared to, or who stole it, or for what purpose. If the Social Security Fund is being bankrupted, if it is inadequate, it's because the United States Government, including people who are elected or not elected, have stolen it from Americans, trillions of dollars since 2001.

Reagan was the first President to take the Social Security Fund yearly surplus. At that time it was billions, not trillions, of dollars. It belongs to all Americans, not to the political thieves. No one will ever be held accountable for the yearly theft of this financial security for all Americans that has continued unabated. The American people have been powerless to change, or to stop, any of this. A true democracy would not make its citizens victims of this massive, gigantic, political theft, especially not continuously, year after year, indefinitely.

When teacher's pension funds became privatized in the 1990's they lost billions of dollars as a result. As a result of investing in stocks, bonds, mutual funds, hedge-funds, annuities, etc. their pension money was lost In the same way that privatization of the Social Security Fund would destroy the Social Security Fund. That is obviously what the Neo Cons and Republicans in power want to happen. Since before 2000 they have wanted more destitution, more discrepancy between the rich and the poor and the middle-class, more poverty, and more control and oppression of the expendable masses. Including a gradual destruction and disappearance of the middle-class. In terms of debt, in the 21$^{st}$ century the United States is the poorest country in the World. All of this is about money and power. It's not about doing the right thing for people in America. Most of this began to be true starting in the 1960's.

Since Reagan was President in the 1980's the United States Government supports capitalism, not democracy, in America and in other countries. Since before Reagan the United States Government, the FBI, and the CIA have given millions of dollars to assassins to assassinate leaders of other countries that the United States labels "tyrants" and "dictators", even if they were fervently supported and loved by the majority of people in their own countries, and even when they were changing their countries to democracies. The replacement leaders have been men who are easily manipulated by United States powers, who, in turn, may eventually be deemed a problem by United States powers and are then assassinated, murdered, by United States military, CIA, or Special Forces.

United States Presidents, Governors, Mayors, Senators, Congressmen, politicians and officials, elected or not, have a long reputation of saying one thing and doing another, of doing one thing and saying another. This, then, pleases both sides of a perpetually divided America. It's hypocrisy.

The United States Government has a long history of it, beginning most notably with cheating, lying to, and killing millions of Native American Indians, killing entire tribes, for about 250 years, in order to steal their ancestral land that they had lived on for centuries, possibly even for thousands of years, in order to control and dominate the Indians. It was a super-power thing starting from the beginning, being bullies and being mean to the helpless and innocent unarmed Indians in America, the original inhabitants of America. Apparently it has always been an inherently white man thing, especially an English and German thing, both in America and in England and Germany historically.

This is where the United States reputation of imperialism began. The Indians, millions of them, were eventually forced to move onto reservations on very inferior land, even useless land, making them unable to live off the land as they had for thousands of years, by migrating according to the seasons. But for about 200 years before this at least 5 million to 10 million Native American Indians of all ages were murdered, killed, assassinated even as they slept for the night in their homes, their teepees being their only refuge from the invading white men, eventually under the auspices of American soldiers.

The Lakota Sioux are an ancient tribe. Their word for death means "going home". Perhaps they had inside information about what happens after death. Maybe that's what happens to everybody, to all colors of people, when they die. "Heaven", the after-life , is home for everybody because that is where they came from, where their souls came from originally. For perhaps thousands of years the Lakota Sioux passed this knowledge down from generation to generation. American Indians, after all, historically are more inherently noble and spiritually enlightened than white people in America.

While the Indians in America have always been forced to live in dire poverty and destitution since they have been dominated by the white man and the United States Government, in huge contrast, since after World War II, the United States Government gives billions of dollars every year to other countries, some of which are run by unelected officials from their own military, not by their politicians. Some of which are run by dictators and tyranny. Most of these financial gifts called "foreign aid" are given to countries much better off financially than the United States, with its true national financial debt after Bush "W" of at least $13.5 trillion dollars. However, that fluctuates from year to year in the 21$^{st}$ century, to include huge yearly interest of at least a trillion dollars paid on that immense and monstrous out-of-control national debt. The United States foreign aid goes directly to their leaders and to their military, which is then often used against their own people who rise up against their cruel and/or unfair government and military, tyranny and dictatorships. The American people have paid for that cruelty and for those dictatorships and cruelty for more than 60 years.

To maintain global super-power status the United States Government has spent 100 to 1000 times more every year than all other countries do on weapons and on defense, for the Department of Defense and for the military. Since after World War II the CIA has been instrumental in assassinating leaders of countries that do not co-operate with the United States Government, even when those leaders have total support from the majority of people in their country. Even when their governments are democracies. Often the replacement leaders are put into power with assistance from the United States Government, the CIA, the FBI, the United States military. Often those replacement leaders are dictators and tyrants that do not represent the people in their country. But they do represent United States political and military interests. Allegedly for United States national security the United States military has military bases in at least 140 countries, in countries that have no capability to attack the United

States. Like Iraq had no capability to attack the United States when the United States military attacked and invaded Iraq in 2003, occupying it then for 11 years and then perpetually, indefinitely, making it the longest United States war in American history. But the war on terror will probably never end.

American freedom and democracy cannot be taken away by foreign military forces, by foreign countries, since after the Japanese attack on Pearl Harbor more than 70 years ago. Freedom and democracy can only be taken away by forces in this country, by elected and unelected officials, authorities, and politicians that manipulate the United States Government and the American people.

Thousands of people rule America from banks, from the Federal Reserve, from the IMF, and from the IRS, that is not a Government agency even though people think it is. The IRs is not governed by laws, it's governed by codes, by tax codes. It enforces tax codes, not United States laws.

Also ruling the United States are at least 30,000 people as members of special interest groups and lobbyists that influence with hundreds of millions of dollars as gifts to about 500 politicians to make them do what they want them to do. Also ruling the United States are the ever-present Neo Cons, known in Washington, D.C. as "the crazies" before they dominated the United States power structure starting with the Presidential elections in 2000.

Corporations, the 1% elite, probably the 5% elite, and the medical/sickness industry, the pharmaceutical industry, the insurance industry, the oil industry, and the financial industry also control and rule the United States. The President of the United States is their spokesman. In the 21st century this is more true than ever before, but it all started mostly in the 1980's, with President Reagan. Oh what a tangled web they weave when they conspire to deceive. It is always about power, control, profit, selfishness, deceit, deception and lies, and money, money, money.

Since 2001 FOX NEWS and CNN demonized foreign leaders day and night 24/7, saying they "are enemies of the United States", flashing negative messages across the screen as people are talking, for purposes of propaganda and manipulation of the masses, the expendable masses. This has happened for many years, but especially since 2001, when foreign leaders are not co-operating with the United States Government, or if they disagree with United States leaders or the United States Government, or if they won't do what the United States Government tells them to do. This is more proof that the United States Government is not really a democracy. Just saying it is a democracy does not make it so.

Republicans, the Far Right, and the Neo Cons then react with viciousness and meanness on FOX NEWS and Democrats, as always, are apathetic. As always since after World War II, the foreign leaders are then eventually replaced with United States funded and United States supported leaders. Or they are assassinated, or foreign coups are arranged, designed, and conducted by the United States, by the CIA, with foreign "rebels" paid and supplied by the United States Government to do their jobs. It's the 21st century version of "soldiers of fortune".

The wealthiest people in the newly capitalistic Communist China and in the democracy of England, one of the oldest capitalistic countries in the World, share the traits of hoarding wealth and being very conservative in the process. There are two basic kinds of capitalism in the 21st century. These are Communist China capitalism and the 24 capitalistic Democracies.

The United States shares one characteristic, one social rule, with Communist China. If an average American publically expresses a negative opinion about the United States President or the military, especially if it's published or on the news, they can go to prison, go to jail, for saying that, possibly with no charges and no legal representation, with no due process as guaranteed in the American Constitution. This is just like in Communist China. Only other politicians can publically and openly criticize the United States President and the military in the 21st century. That is not a democracy. Especially vulnerable have been teachers, professors, writers, journalists, reporters, authors.

The upper 1% in America has more money than 99% of the rest. Yet, that 1% has usually paid 1% or nothing as taxes on their income. If the lower 75% didn't pay taxes on their income they would go to prison and be fined, besides having to pay the taxes due. This is more proof that America is not a real democracy in the 21st century, and that Congress does not serve the people of America in the 21st century.

In the 21st century capitalism in Communist China has made it the richest neo-capitalist country in the World. Most of the United States debt of at least $13.5 trillion is financed by and paid with loans from China to the United States. Therefore, Communist China is no longer vilified as evil and dangerous by United States politicians. If the former Soviet Union had loaned billions or trillions of dollars to the United States Government then maybe their status, their image with the United States Government, would have been changed to benefactor. The fact is China now owns a lot of the United States, owning real estate, businesses, corporations, and parts of the financial market, and is very much a part of the American economy. It's all a part of the free-market of capitalism. Attitudes are changed by money and profit. Follow the money to find the answers, as always.

For many years the Communist country of North Korea has been brutally vicious and cruel and manipulative to its own people and to their foreign enemies. It's been a cruel Government to be feared for more than 70 years. It doesn't remotely have a capitalistic type of economy.

People need to have good things they can count on in their lives, to help them when they need it, that will be what is good and right with consistency. Family can be this for most people. But people need to be able to count on their government to be what it stands for and to give them help when they need it. People need to be able to trust that their government is doing what is good and right for everyone, for all the people in the United States and outside of it, not just in their own states. Not for just a few hundred thousand people, or a few million people, who are the elite and the rulers, elected and unelected, of the American population and of the Federal Government. People in America need to know they really do live in a democracy, that their country really is the democracy they think it is. But most Americans just don't care. Apathy and indifference are so easy. It's much easier.

Since The Patriot Act of 2001, and since the national domination by self-serving self-indulgent Neo Cons during and after the elections of 2000, people in America cannot ever be sure what their Federal Government is really doing. This is one way America is different in the 21st century. But most people in America are blissfully unaware of it, of the controls, of the changes that have been spreading in America since 2000 and the passing of The Patriot Act in 2001. Complicity and approval of authorities at the highest levels allows, and has allowed, these negative changes at all levels of American culture, potentially everywhere and anywhere in American society.

All of this is just the tip of the iceberg. It's just a piece of the puzzle. Dishonesty and fraud, meanness, selfishness, and lies are everywhere, some places more than others. Most people don't want to hear it or see it, so they don't. They won't. They refuse to see or hear things as they really are, to look or think beyond the facade. Their reality is lies. This is mostly a Republican characteristic, a Republican personality trait involving about 58 million Americans. As they say, everybody lies in Hollywood, and everybody lies in Washington, D.C. That's just an unpleasant reality of life.

People informed with the truth have elevated consciousness. People informed with lies do not. Throughout history people like that have caused a lot of problems. That's the truth. That's life.

What can Americans do about changing something they don't like in their government, or in their country in general? Usually nothing. Not a thing. Voting gives a false sense of importance, of being important, for voters who have voted for whoever wins in an election, and for whatever passes or is adopted. It's a smokescreen, a mirage in the desert of politics.

The Dead Sea Scrolls, written about 100 B.C., said people thought life was a struggle between good and evil. More than 2000 years later life is still that way. It probably always has been, and it probably always will be. Living in America is the same. America is no different today, in the 21$^{st}$ century.

Illegal drugs, drug cultures, and drug systems, anywhere in America in the 21$^{st}$ century are obviously negative influences that cause declines in social standards and personal standards, in general, affecting all Americans indirectly and directly. Tens of thousands of ego-maniacal mean drug dealers, with no conscience, are at the center of this reality, of social and personal degradation and decline.

In 2016 I drove by an old sign flashing on a liquor store in Evansville that said "Make your ideas a reality." What that had to do with liquor I didn't know. A car turned into the lane in front of me. It was in wretched shape, an old junkie car. A large new colorful sign was taped with duct tape across the back of his car, covering the trunk and the sides. It said "Trump--Make America Great Again." The driver of the car was obviously a member of the expendable masses, who was going to vote Republican, out of desperation, to replace the Democrat Obama, who had had empty promises of "Hope" and "Change" eight years to ten years earlier. Hope for what? Change what? The poor driver of that car was trying to make his ideas a reality, with his impossible-not-to-see huge sign covering the back of his car, hoping to make his life great, and everybody else's in America.

Unfortunately hope is just a word, an emotion, having no utilitarian value. In the end only memories remain. When it's over, it's over. But it isn't over until it's done. Whatever that means. But like someone said on the TV show Saturday Night Live, "Hope is what we cling to when reality leaves us nothing else." That's just another reality of life.

About 50 years ago in India Mahatma Gandhi was asked what he thought about Western civilization. He said "It would be nice if it was." After more than five years of concentrated searching and researching, and after living in 15 different states and in 45 different cities and towns in those states, after traveling at least 10,000 miles with the purpose of investigating America after 2003, I had found America, in all its tainted glory, flaws and foibles, after the beginning of the 21$^{st}$ century, in the first and second decades of the 21$^{st}$ century. In a way my journey, looking for America, had ended. In another way, it would never end.

It seems there is no ending to any of this. It just goes on and on forever, repeated endlessly, with maybe some improvements along the way. But, in general, life just is what it is and people just are what they are. As a result, most things happen for better or worse beyond the control of individuals, or beyond the control of the expendable masses. That's life. And that, for better or worse, is..................

THE END.

www.ingramcontent.com/pod-product-compliance
Lightning Source LLC
Chambersburg PA
CBHW081344280526
45788CB00009B/2767